GENDER AND
POPULISM
IN
LATIN AMERICA

GENDER AND POPULISM IN LATIN AMERICA

PASSIONATE POLITICS

EDITED BY **KAREN KAMPWIRTH**

FOREWORD BY **KURT WEYLAND**

THE PENNSYLVANIA STATE UNIVERSITY PRESS

UNIVERSITY PARK, PENNSYLVANIA

Library of Congress Cataloging-in-Publication Data

Gender and populism in Latin America : passionate politics /
edited by Karen Kampwirth ; foreword by Kurt Weyland.
p.   cm.
Includes bibliographical references and index.
ISBN 978-0-271-03709-7 (cloth : alk. paper)
ISBN 978-0-271-03710-3 (pbk. : alk. paper)
1. Populism—Latin America.
2. Women in politics—Latin America.
3. Latin America—Politics and government—1980– .
I. Kampwirth, Karen, 1964– .

JL966.G46 2010
320.5—dc22
2010008197

The Pennsylvania State University Press is a member
of the Association of American University Presses.

It is the policy of
The Pennsylvania State University Press
to use acid-free paper. Publications on uncoated
stock satisfy the minimum requirements of American
National Standard for Information
Sciences—Permanence of Paper for Printed
Library Material, ANSI Z39.48–1992.

Contents

Foreword   vii
Kurt Weyland

ACKNOWLEDGMENTS   xiii

Introduction   1
Karen Kampwirth

1
The Politics of Opportunity:
Mexican Populism Under Lázaro Cárdenas and Luis Echeverría   25
Jocelyn Olcott

2
Changing Images of Male and Female in Ecuador:
José María Velasco Ibarra and Abdalá Bucaram   47
Ximena Sosa-Buchholz

3
Gender, Clientelistic Populism, and Memory:
Somocista and Neo-Somocista Women's Narratives in Liberal Nicaragua   67
Victoria González-Rivera

4
From Working Mothers to Housewives:
Gender and Brazilian Populism from Getúlio Vargas to Juscelino Kubitschek   91
Joel Wolfe

5
Women and Populism in Brazil   110
Michael Conniff

6
Populist Continuities in "Revolutionary" Peronism?
A Comparative Analysis of the Gender Discourses of the
First Peronism (1946–1955) and the Montoneros   122
Karin Grammático

7
Populism from Above, Populism from Below:
Gender Politics Under Alberto Fujimori and Evo Morales   140
Stéphanie Rousseau

8
Populism and the Feminist Challenge in Nicaragua:
The Return of Daniel Ortega   162
Karen Kampwirth

9
Waking Women Up? Hugo Chávez, Populism,
and Venezuela's "Popular" Women   180
Gioconda Espina and Cathy A. Rakowski

10
Gender, Popular Participation, and the State in Chávez's Venezuela   202
Sujatha Fernandes

A Few Concluding Thoughts   222
Karen Kampwirth

NOTES ON CONTRIBUTORS   229

INDEX   233

Foreword

Kurt Weyland

A quarter-century ago, Paul Drake wondered whether the time had come to write "a requiem for populism." After the populist leaders of the 1930s to 1950s, especially Juan Perón in Argentina, Getúlio Vargas in Brazil, and Lázaro Cárdenas in Mexico, had brought momentous changes to their countries and put them on new development trajectories, populism seemed to have exhausted itself by the 1970s and 1980s. Tighter socioeconomic constraints seemed to make the economically nationalist and socially distributive policies pursued by populist leaders unsustainable; and the wave of military governments from the 1960s to 1980s had forcefully sought to dismantle populism by attacking its social basis, for instance, trade unions. For both reasons, any effort to revive populism seemed destined to fail, as the spectacular crisis caused by neopopulist Alan García in Peru (1985–90) appeared to confirm.

Just as the obituaries were being drafted, however, Latin American populism experienced a stunning revival. While one version had run its course, new variants unexpectedly emerged. In the 1990s, a number of neoliberal populists arose: They combined a populist political strategy and style, characterized by personalistic leadership and a noninstitutionalized, unmediated relationship to an ample mass following, with economic policies that were diametrically opposed to those implemented by classical populists. Indeed, the political heirs of Perón and Cárdenas, Carlos Menem in Argentina and Carlos Salinas de Gortari in Mexico, as well as newcomers Fernando Collor de Mello in Brazil and Alberto Fujimori in Peru, dismantled the state interventionism and protectionism instituted by the earlier wave of populist leaders. In this way, populism gave political sustenance to market reform during the 1990s.

The years since 1998 have seen another surprising twist in the story of Latin American populism. In the past decade, a revived radical populism exemplified by Hugo Chávez in Venezuela and the new ethnopopulism forged by Evo Morales in Bolivia have set out to stop and reverse neoliberal change. These leaders have sought to push their countries toward a new, amorphous, ill-defined, that is, typically populist version of "socialism" or—in the eyes of critics—back to the nationalist state interventionism that prevailed before the debt crisis of the 1980s. Born in adversity and facing multiple crises, this new variant of populism has again demonstrated a surprising degree of political skillfulness and sustainability.

Owing to the political creativity that gave rise to all these twists and turns,

Latin American populism has been alive and well during the twenty-five years since Paul Drake issued its provisional death certificate. Given the significance of populist leadership in contemporary Latin America, there has been an outpouring of scholarship on this topic. Even the notorious difficulty of defining and delimiting this slippery concept has not deterred academics and other observers from taking up their nets and trying to capture this winding eel. In fact, conceptual controversies have fueled the proliferation of studies about populism. There have also been many analyses of populist discourse and style and of the policies designed by populist leaders, especially their differential relationship to the wave of market reforms.

In all this burgeoning literature, however, the gender aspects of populism have received very little and clearly insufficient attention. This omission is surprising, given the gendered nature of populism. Populist leaders deliberately project a very masculine image; indeed, the neopopulists who have emerged in Latin America's media-saturated mass societies during the past two decades and who appeal to the population's "low" instincts (in Pierre Ostiguy's terms) are even more macho than their classical populist models. Whereas Getúlio Vargas ran for president in 1950 as the jovial "father of the poor," Carlos Menem liked to be photographed with red sports cars and blond supermodels, and Ecuador's Abdalá Bucaram was notorious for his gross invocations of (allegedly) "typically male" fantasies. No wonder that many neopopulists had serious problems with their wives! Both Menem and Alberto Fujimori, for instance, went through noisy and embarrassing separations and divorces.

Despite their masculine antics, however, neopopulist leaders paradoxically broke new ground in promoting women to positions of political power. Menem blazed the trail in the area of institutional change by passing a quota law that ensured female politicians greater chances of election; this innovation helped to trigger imitation by many other Latin American countries. Collor was the first Brazilian president to appoint a woman to the powerful position of finance minister, and Fujimori named several women to important executive posts or drafted them for Congress.

Thus populism clearly has important gender dimensions, which—typically of such a multifaceted and ever-changing political strategy—are quite contradictory. Fascinating questions therefore arise: Does thoroughly masculine populism open up space for the advancement of feminine issues, that is, questions related to the traditional role models of women as wives and mothers? Can it even accommodate feminist demands, which challenge these traditional role models? Does it promote female leadership, or does it treat women as subordinate beneficiaries and followers of male leaders?

This volume offers the first focused and systematic analysis of these important questions. It covers an impressive variety of populist experiences that range from classical populism to neopopulism and that assess the latter phenomenon in both its neoliberal and its revived radical variant. The book brings together scholars from various disciplines and opens up a productive dialogue between long-standing analysts of populism and specialists on gender issues. Based on two panels held at the 2007 congress of the Latin American Studies Association in Montreal, it constitutes a model of the interdisciplinary scholarship that area studies produce.

To stimulate this dialogue, it may be useful to derive some general reflections from the literature on populism. In particular, how much space does populism open up for pursuing gender issues? The assumption underlying these thoughts is that gender politics is essentially issue-based, whereas populism is not defined by any commitment to specific issues. Women activists demand greater rights and benefits for their female colleagues; these substantive concerns are what drive their demands and actions. But if anything has emerged from all the analyses of the twists and turns in Latin American populism, it is the opportunistic, unsteady nature of populist leadership, which is not anchored by any particular stances on issues. Therefore, whoever seeks to advance specific issues by linking them to populism makes—if this is not too strong a way to put it—a pact with the devil. Populism offers significant opportunities for opening up space for change, but it also imposes constraints and sets traps. In my view, the downsides may outweigh the opportunities.

There are three main reasons for this mixed and, overall, skeptical outlook. The first "contradiction" arises from the one definitional trait (among several) that most students of populism agree on, namely, the outstanding role of personalistic leadership in populism. Populist interest representation differs from programmatic representation, which advances a set of goals, maxims, and principles. In populism, by contrast, the followers delegate interest representation to a person who has a large degree of discretion in defining, framing, and pursuing popular interests. The populist leader literally "speaks for" the people; only the leader can embody the unitary "will of the people," and he is hard for groups of constituents, who appear as mere "factions," to challenge. Moreover, because of the personalistic and top-down nature of populism, institutional mechanisms of accountability are weak. In fact, populist leaders seek to enhance their autonomy and power; once they are elected president, they try to weaken the checks and balances arising from other institutions, such as Congress and the courts. Personalistic leadership does not want to be confined by institutional constraints but seeks to bend or even break those limitations.

The personalistic nature of populism is a double-edged sword. On the one hand, it generates an impulse for change. Populist leadership has a transgressive character; it is more transformative than transactional, in the terminology of James MacGregor Burns. Unwilling to accept established institutional and policy arrangements, populist leaders seek to effect reform. They accept risks and do not shy away from taking on the defenders of the status quo. Sectors that advocate change, such as increased rights and benefits for women, can thus use populist leaders as rams that batter holes through ossified structures and create openings for improvement.

On the other hand, the personalistic nature of populism prevents the followers from controlling their leaders. Accountability inside populist movements is deficient. The followers trust the leader to advance their interests but cannot ensure this outcome. Relying on a populist leader is therefore a gamble: He may advance followers' interests, but he may also renege on his promises and do whatever he sees fit. Carlos Menem exemplifies this danger with his appeal, "Follow me! I will not defraud you." Despite his pledge, he soon diverged from popular interests, going so far as to siphon off public funds into private bank accounts. But his followers and Argentine citizens in general faced great difficulties in controlling these abuses. Thus populism constitutes a risky bet.

The second contradiction emerges from the populist effort to bring about majoritarian inclusion. On the one hand, populism seeks to incorporate social sectors that feel excluded. By appealing to underprivileged groups and mobilizing them for political action (most significantly, voting), populism offers opportunities for these disadvantaged sectors to advance their issues and interests. Demands that had previously been neglected can thus enter the political arena.

On the other hand, populism is a majoritarian movement that appeals to the will of "the people," understood as a fairly homogeneous unit. It therefore tends to advance issues that are in line with the interests and sentiments of the majority. Populist leaders are reluctant to push for demands that are "unpopular." A very progressive program that is "far ahead of its time" cannot expect to find strong support from populists. Thus populism is selective; it pursues some interests but not others. The majoritarian nature of populism creates limitations as popular sentiments and resentments serve as filters for the kinds of issues that populist leaders press.

The third limitation, which applies specifically to gender issues, emerges from the masculinity embodied in populist leadership. In fact, this macho nature has become ever more pronounced in recent decades, as mass politics have fully taken hold in Latin America, for instance, with the enfranchisement of illiterates and the spread of mass media. As leaders such as Menem and Collor make very masculine appeals to the public, they would be hard-pressed to embrace postmodern feminist demands, such as lesbian liberation. The masculine nature of populism thus reinforces the selectivity of interest representation just discussed. Specifically, feminine issues seem to fit in with the populist project much better than feminist issues do. Feminine demands seek specific, practical improvements for women while taking their basic insertion in society and family as given. Feminist demands, by contrast, seek to transform this insertion through strategic reforms designed to guarantee women autonomy and equality. Obviously, macho men are more at ease with femininity than with feminism. Accordingly, populist leaders often seek to facilitate and ease women's fulfillment of their current roles but are much more reluctant to push for a thorough restructuring of these roles and an attack on what are depicted as male privileges.

In other areas, however, populist leaders may indeed advance women's rights and offer women significant benefits. Given the majoritarian nature of populism, which seeks to mobilize large numbers of followers and channel their political participation, one could hypothesize that classical populists played a special role in instituting female suffrage. The prototypical case is of course Juan and Evita Perón, who took this important step in 1947. Even on this issue, the contributions of populism are less clear than expected. Despite all his power, Lázaro Cárdenas, for instance, never tried very hard to give women the vote; they had to wait until 1953. Brazil's Getúlio Vargas did pass female suffrage, but in 1932, before he had morphed into a populist. And Ecuador's Velasco Ibarra rose to prominence after Ecuador—surprisingly, the first Latin American country to do so—had conceded women the vote in 1929. Thus the picture is mixed.

Did the neopopulists of the past two decades do more than their predecessors to extend women's political rights? I mentioned Menem's introduction of a quota law, and it would be interesting to examine the role of other populist leaders in the rapid spread of this innovation in Latin America. Also, was Collor's and Fujimori's promotion of women to positions of power part of a broader trend? For instance, Colombia's neoliberal populist president Alvaro Uribe guaranteed gender parity in his first cabinet, and Bolivia's Evo Morales had his "Movement to Socialism" elect an indigenous woman as president of the constituent assembly that elaborated a new charter.

The role of women in populist movements is another fascinating subject discussed in the present volume. Latin American populism seems to confine women mostly to subordinate roles; they rise as wives, daughters, or nieces, not as leaders in their own right. And they have so far not managed to acquire the prominence and sustained political influence that women populists in other regions, such as South Asia, have attained, where leaders such as Indira Gandhi or Benazir Bhutto for many years played a central role in national politics. Despite the precedent of "Evita" Perón, there has never been a female populist of that caliber and significance in Latin America. Even Cristina Fernández de Kirchner in Argentina rose on her husband's coattails, and a number of the problems plaguing her government have arisen from Néstor Kirchner's insistence on remaining the power behind the throne and dominating economic policy, in particular. The limited role of female leaders in Latin American populism is a fascinating topic for future research to analyze and explain.

As these reflections suggest, it is high time to analyze the opportunities and constraints that Latin American populism creates for gender issues, especially feminine versus feminist demands. In examining this long-neglected area, this volume makes a decisive contribution. It sheds new light on gender politics in the region and offers a deeper understanding of populism, this multifaceted, chameleonlike but seemingly irrepressible phenomenon. For students of populism, who have so long pursued this shifty eel in vain, it is gratifying to get help from scholars of different backgrounds who are placing their intellectual fishing rods in promising spots. Maybe together we can successfully grasp a phenomenon that refuses to disappear from the Latin American political scene.

Acknowledgments

First of all, thanks to the very smart and hardworking people who agreed to write chapters for this volume: Mike Conniff, Gioconda Espina, Karin Grammático, Victoria González-Rivera, Sujatha Fernandes, Jolie Olcott, Ximena Sosa-Buchholz, Cathy Rakowski, Stéphanie Rousseau, Kurt Weyland, and Joel Wolfe. Originally Victoria González-Rivera was to be co-editor of this book, but then her busy life made it impossible for her to continue as my editing partner. Although she did not continue with the editing part of the project, many of her clever ideas continue to inform this book. Plus, she is a wonderful friend. For all those reasons she deserves special thanks.

Sujatha Fernandes's chapter is a significantly revised version of an article that was published as "Barrio Women and Popular Politics in Chávez's Venezuela" in *Latin American Politics and Society* 49, no. 3 (2007). Thanks to Wiley-Blackwell for permission to use this material.

I am particularly grateful to the Latin American Studies Association (LASA) for providing the opportunity for us to get together and present early versions of these essays in a double panel at the 2007 conference in Montreal. Another group of people, without whom this book would not exist, are the many Latin Americans who made critical contributions to all of the chapters: granting us interviews, helping us navigate archives, sharing their homes and their stories. I wish I could name them all here.

As always, I am grateful to Knox College, both for providing the grants that made my trips to Managua, Caracas, Buenos Aires, and Montreal possible and for supporting me whenever I feel like teaching a new course, no matter how unusual the topic. The students who took Class, Gender, and Populism in Latin America in the spring of 2008 were a lovely group. I am grateful to all of them for spending a term thinking through, and sometimes joking about, the many facets of Latin American populism. Because of them the introduction and conclusion to this book are far better than they would have been otherwise. Thanks to Keren Bhujel, Shanna Collins, Katie Fronczak, Dee Goebel, Jennifer Hoben, Angharad Hollingworth, Heather Kopec, Ana Márquez, Samantha McDavid, Ashley Olson, Loli Povoas, Kathryn Sweet, and Daisy Venegas.

Finally, I could not have edited this book without Duane Oldfield. As a friend once observed, "he knows everything." He generously offers to take care of our girls for weeks on end whenever Latin America calls, and always has suggestions that improve my drafts. In short, he is a great husband and daddy. Sophie and Vanessa Oldfield—also known as "the fabulous girls"—deserve special thanks for sharing their interesting views of the world.

INTRODUCTION

Karen Kampwirth

How can you—they would say to me—direct a feminist movement if you are fanatically in
love with the cause of a man? Isn't that a way of recognizing the total superiority
of a man over a woman? Isn't that contradictory?
No, it is not. I "felt" it. Now I know it.
The true, the logical, the reasonable point is that feminism comes out of the very nature of
women. And what is natural for a woman is to give of herself, to give herself up for love,
that in this giving up is found her glory, her salvation, her eternity. . . . I believe that
Perón and his cause are sufficiently great and dignified as to receive all that the
feminist movement offers to my Fatherland.
—*Eva Perón (1951/2004, 34)*

Every day the whole women's movement takes on a form that is clearer, stronger, more
committed and more beautiful, of course, for everything that a woman touches and sees
becomes beautiful, that is true, it is even true for us, the ugly ones, they even see us as
handsome. . . . An infinite kiss for all Venezuelan women! And my heart and soul,
recognition, affection, and strength so that you continue carrying out the historic
work of re-seeding, of reconstructing, the great woman who is Venezuela.
—*Hugo Chávez (2004, 6, 12)*

Populist politics has always been about passion. It has been passionate in the
romantic sense, as is clear in the words of Evita Perón and Hugo Chávez. It has
been passionate in the sense of strongly emotional, the politics of personal charisma rather than the politics of abstract policy. And it has been passionate in
generating strong feelings of love for the people, and hatred for those who are
defined as outsiders. As populist politics is the politics of personality, it has always
been about gender, about particular models of masculinity and femininity.[1]

---

1. To argue that populism—which always involves a relationship between a charismatic leader
and devoted followers—is passionate or emotional is not to imply that emotions are inherently
irrational. But emotions are something in addition to the rational, or beyond the rational. Along

The new wave of populist politics in Latin America has led to a flurry of analysis of the latest populists as well as a renewed interest in the populists of the classic period.[2] But this work has rarely consciously analyzed populism from a gender perspective.[3] Such analysis is long overdue.

My goal in introducing this book is not to offer a new definition of populism. Many insightful definitions of Latin American populism have already been written; that wheel does not need reinventing. A comprehensive definition was offered by Kenneth Roberts, who argues that populist movements are characterized by "five core properties":

1. a personalistic and paternalistic, though not necessarily charismatic, pattern of political leadership
2. a heterogeneous, multiclass political coalition concentrated in subaltern sectors of society
3. top-down process of political mobilization that either bypasses institutionalized forms of mediation or subordinates them to more direct linkages between the leader and the masses
4. an amorphous or eclectic ideology, characterized by a discourse that exalts subaltern sectors or is antielitist and/or antiestablishment
5. an economic project that uses widespread redistributive or clientelistic methods to create a material foundation for popular-sector support. (Roberts 1995, 88)

Although it does not explicitly refer to the highly gendered nature of populism, Roberts's definition can certainly be read that way, considering its attention to personalistic and paternalistic leadership and to the subaltern nature of populist coalitions. In this introduction, I consider what has already been written

---

with scholars like Jean-Pierre Reed (2004), I think it is important to treat these emotional components of political activism seriously. Nor do I mean to imply that emotions are inherently female. Indeed, most of the leaders analyzed in this volume are men, men who have often described their feelings for "the people" in very emotional terms, declaring their love for them and their righteous anger against the people's enemies.

2. Recent works on Latin American populism include Burbano de Lara 1998; Conniff 1999; de la Torre 2000; Green 2003; Knight 1998; Leaman 2004; MacKinnon and Petrone 1999; Plotkin 2003; Roberts 1995, 2007; Weyland 1999, 2001. All translations are my own unless otherwise indicated.

3. The following works analyze gender and populism: Auyero 2000; Becker 1994; Centurión 2007; Conniff 1999; Crespo 2005; Fisher 2000; Grammático 2007; Green 2003; Kampwirth 2003; Lind 2005; Lobato, Damilakou, and Tornay 2005; Luna 2000; Milanesio 2006; Navarro 2005; Plotkin 2003; Rousseau 2006; Schmidt 2006; Taylor 1979; Wolfe 1994; Zabaleta 1997; Zink and Di Liscia 2007. But the only in-depth works on the relationship between gender and populism analyze Peronism; the others are articles or books in which gender and populism is a minor theme.

on the complicated role that gender plays in Latin American populism and present the five themes that inform the chapters in this book. The idea is to provide an overview of the populist experience in twentieth- and twenty-first-century Latin America, and a context in which to understand the chapters that follow.

First Theme: Gender and the Waves of Populism

In the literature on populism in Latin America, a distinction is generally made between two waves: classic populism (roughly from the 1930s to the 1960s) and neopopulism (roughly from the 1980s to the present). In the early twentieth century, political movements that became known as classic populist movements emerged in a number of Latin American countries, including those led by Arnulfo Arias in Panama, Lázaro Cárdenas in Mexico, José Figueres in Costa Rica, Jorge Gaitán in Colombia, Victor Raúl Haya de la Torre and Luis Sánchez Cerro in Peru, Juan and Eva Perón in Argentina, Anastasio Somoza García in Nicaragua, Getúlio Vargas in Brazil, and José María Velasco Ibarra in Ecuador. These movements responded to a series of socioeconomic changes.

Urbanization, driven by immigration from the countryside or from other countries, created new groups of unaffiliated people who were available for political mobilization. Organization was easier in the city, both because people lived and worked closer together and because poor urban dwellers did not tend to be under the political control of local economic elites, as was the case for poor people in the countryside.[4] While earlier politicians had to generate followers through political parties and networks of local strongmen, the politicians of the populist era used newly available technologies like radio and television to create direct personal ties between leaders and their followers. At the same time, industrialization and the opening of new markets gave clever politicians the resources to provide those new groups with services (Conniff 1999, 7–10). "That these expanded government services also opened many jobs for the middle classes was a happy bonus to populist leaders. . . . Millions were made beholden to those who dispensed the benefits from the top down" (Wirth 1982, x–xi).

In many cases, the people who provided expanded governmental services were women. This was certainly true for services in areas that extended traditional female roles, such as education, health care, and the provision of food

---

4. There are exceptions to the tendency for classic populist movements to be urban: both Lázaro Cárdenas of Mexico and Anastasio Somoza García of Nicaragua made significant efforts to mobilize rural dwellers.

(Milanesio 2006; Navarro 2005; Plotkin 2003). And these new government jobs often went to women, who were not able to get private-sector employment because of discrimination and who were grateful to the populist leader for these opportunities (González 2001).

In addition to the new, expanded services that were provided to, and often by, women, the most direct way that many populists incorporated women into the body politic was through the vote. Many of the classic populists—Arnulfo Arias, José Figueres, Juan and Eva Perón, Anastasio Somoza García, Getúlio Vargas—gave women the right to vote (or at least took credit for it). Many others, like Lázaro Cárdenas and Jorge Gaitán, actively campaigned for women's suffrage.

Lola Luna argues that these two ways in which the classic populists interacted with women—expanding their political rights and providing them with new social services—were intimately linked. Women's suffrage and other forms of political participation were justified in terms of the social exclusion of maternalism, an ideology in which women are politicized around traditional female roles (Luna 2000, 200; see also French and James 1997, 15; Molyneux 2001, 170–71).

The classic populists were not gender radicals. As they extended political rights and opened new educational and employment opportunities to women, they took care to justify these rights in terms of an essentialist notion of women's roles as mothers and even, at least in the case of Peronism, beauty queens (Crespo 2005; Lobato et al. 2005; Plotkin 2003, 70, 73–74, 79). Through their new public roles, women would make the public sphere more moral and more beautiful.

Though the populists were often successful in building strong political movements and incorporating previously excluded groups, many thought that the age of populism had reached its end by about the midpoint of the twentieth century. "Certainly, by the late 1950s, [populism] was losing the capacity to deliver more goods and services to more people. . . . Expanding the social benefits could only be sustained by rapid economic growth, which slowed. . . . Concurrently, swelling electorates rendered the Latin American state less able to insulate itself from populist pressures for redistribution. Control of the masses, always fundamental to the success of populist politics, was now in doubt" (Wirth 1982, xi).

With the triumph of the Cuban Revolution in 1959, Latin American politics entered a new, more radical phase. Although this new phase had many causes, one of them was that left-wing political activists believed that the populists had mobilized too little and provided too little social justice. Radical leftists responded with a series of guerrilla movements in most Latin American countries, although the only ones to seize power were the Sandinistas of Nicaragua. Right-wing activists, by contrast, feared that populists and leftists had mobilized the masses too successfully and had promised too much social justice. They responded with a series of brutal military dictatorships.

In the 1980s and 1990s most of the region returned to democracy, and most of the guerrilla movements were defeated or transformed into political parties. Populism also returned, but this time it was dramatically different from the populism of the classic era. The neopopulists, as they were called, no longer had the resources generated by inward-looking industrial growth, a strategy known as import-substitution industrialization (or ISI), that their classic counterparts had used to cobble together coalitions. Quite the opposite: Following the 1982 debt crisis, the dominant economic strategy of the late twentieth century—known as neoliberalism—required that politicians slash spending on basic social services and open markets to the outside world so as to be able to pay off their international debt. The antiunion politics of neoliberalism undermined one of the groups that had formed the base of many a classic populist coalition.

These did not seem to be promising times for populism. And yet populism is a form of politics that tends to respond to crises, and the crisis of neoliberalism provided an opportunity for politicians who presented themselves as personalistic, antielite, antiestablishment outsiders. The great irony is that these neopopulists—leaders such as Arnoldo Alemán of Nicaragua, Abdalá Bucaram of Ecuador, Fernando de Collor of Brazil, Alberto Fujimori of Peru, Carlos Menem of Argentina, and Carlos Salinas de Gortari of Mexico—responded to the crises generated by neoliberalism by promoting neoliberal policies, although they did target some services to the poorest of the poor (de la Torre 2000, 81–82; Knight 1998, 223; Roberts 2007, 4–5; Weyland 1999).

The gender politics of the neopopulists tended to be more complicated than those of the classic populists because the world had changed. Classic populists acted during the first wave of feminism, which emphasized expanding women's access to education and legal rights (especially the vote). And so it was relatively easy for them to meet feminist demands by opening schools and changing laws.

In contrast, the neopopulists confronted the second wave of feminism, a movement that retained the commitment to legal and public rights but embraced a more complicated view of gender equality, addressing a range of "personal" political issues, among them domestic violence, sexuality, and reproductive rights. In this they shared much in common with second-wave feminists in the North. And yet the greater poverty and inequality in Latin America, compared to the United States and Europe, and the legacy of women's (sometimes armed) mobilizing against the state gave a particular character to Latin American feminism.

Neopopulists often found themselves confronting a highly organized and combative movement that was not as easily co-opted as the first wave had been (González and Kampwirth 2001, 11–21; Molyneux 2001).

Some neopopulists addressed the challenges of second-wave feminism by attacking feminist leaders. Arnoldo Alemán, for example, portrayed feminists within the nongovernmental organizations as elites who were not truly Nicaraguan, and blamed them for failing to eliminate Nicaragua's poverty (Kampwirth 2003). Others, like Alberto Fujimori, sought to incorporate second-wave feminists through a variety of means, including electoral gender quotas, the appointment of women to cabinet positions, expanded access to contraception, and state services for victims of domestic violence. Although he addressed many of the second-wave feminists' historic demands, Fujimori failed to incorporate Peruvian feminists into his coalition. The problem was that the feminist movement was strongly committed to national democracy and respect for movement autonomy, both areas in which the Fujimori government had problems, to say the least (Schmidt 2006; Rousseau 2006).

Another factor that shaped the gender policies of the classic and neopopulist periods was the change in the nature of the region's political economy. Thanks to revenues generated through import-substitution industrialization, the classic populists had some resources to offer their followers, including women. Neopopulists, in an era of crushing debt and neoliberal policies, have found it harder to incorporate women into their coalitions through jobs and other material resources. While the politics of personality complemented the politics of patronage for the classic populists, in the neoliberal age personality politics increasingly is offered as a substitute for patronage politics. Of course, such a substitute may work only temporarily. Witness the neopopulist Abdalá Bucaram, who was thrown out of office a mere six months after his election. "Serial populism" (Roberts 2007, 12) has become the norm in many countries, as voters seek the salvation of new personalities, who almost inevitably disappoint, as they lack the resources to fulfill their promises.

From the perspective of the early twenty-first century, it is clear that the age of classic populism is over, but is the age of neopopulism also over? Certainly the latest populists differ in significant ways from those who governed in the 1980s and 1990s. The neopopulists have all implemented neoliberal policies (though some of them campaigned on anti-neoliberal platforms). In contrast, the latest wave of populists—including Hugo Chávez of Venezuela, Rafael Correa of Ecuador, Fernando Lugo of Paraguay, Evo Morales of Bolivia, and Daniel Ortega of Nicaragua—reject neoliberalism.

So what do we call them? One obvious term for the stage after neopopulism, neo-neopopulism, is aesthetically displeasing. All of these anti-neoliberal populists are considered part of the pink tide in Latin America, so perhaps that makes them pink populists? Or should we consider returning to the language of populism without adjectives when thinking about them? But that may just cause more confusion. Certainly, contemporary populists are not the same as their classic predecessors: They face different challenges and therefore must govern differently.

In our chapters on Hugo Chávez and Daniel Ortega, respectively, Sujatha Fernandes and I suggest that this brand of populism might be thought of as revolutionary populism, though we both use that term with caution. Arguably, revolution (a concept that is both collective and transformative) and populism (a concept that is individualistic—focused on one leader—and typically reformist) are inherently incompatible. Or, if they are not incompatible, at least they must exist in tension. Moreover, the term "revolutionary populism" does not travel well across the region. In fact, Ortega is the only member of the third wave who originally came to power through a revolution (as one of the leaders of the guerrilla movement that overthrew the dictatorship of Anastasio Somoza Debayle in 1979), and even Ortega has long since given up his guerrilla ways for electoral politics.

In his foreword, Kurt Weyland refers to this third wave of populism as radical populism. Hugo Chávez himself has referred to his style of politics as "radical populism," as Gioconda Espina and Cathy Rakowski note in their contribution to this volume. Though Chávez did not explain why he called his movement "radical populism," Espina and Rakowski argue that Chavismo needs to be understood as something distinct from both classic populism and neopopulism. While no term is perfect, "radical populism" is probably the best choice for labeling this third wave of Latin American populism. On the one hand, it seems that radical populists would like to return to the redistributive days of the classic era (though, with the exception of Chávez, they lack the resources to do so). On the other hand, they face far larger electorates, and more powerful international institutions, than the classic populists faced. So, both domestically and internationally, they must address louder demands, and those demands are often mutually exclusive.

Will the radical populists find the funds to buck the neoliberal trend, providing new services to the citizens of their countries, or at least to their own followers? To the extent that they can do so, they may succeed in incorporating more women, including poor women, and maybe even including feminists. Or will they yield to populist temptation, governing by skirting the rule of law and concentrating power in their own hands? They could thus empower certain women, at the same time that they exclude others and polarize their citizenries. What sort of models of masculinity help these politicians meet the challenges of governing in the twenty-first century? And what are the benefits and costs of those choices for themselves and their societies? The chapters in this volume on radical populism in Bolivia, Nicaragua, and Venezuela suggest some answers to these questions (see the essays by Espina and Rakowski, Fernandes, Kampwirth, and Rousseau).

Second Theme: Masculinity, Femininity, and Populist Leadership

The populist movement that has been most analyzed in terms of gender is Peronism, no doubt because it is the only national-level populist movement in which a woman played such a prominent role. Though she never held elected office—and did not even have the right to vote until shortly before her death at the age of thirty-three—Evita Perón was one of the most powerful women in Latin American history. Her husband, Juan Domingo Perón, built an extremely successful populist movement in Argentina in the 1940s and 1950s on the foundation of male-dominated union support. "He also recognized that women, still without the vote and making up a substantial section of the labor force, were an untapped political resource" (Fisher 2000, 323).

Marysa Navarro has argued that without Eva, Juan Perón's charismatic authority would have become routinized and less effective after he was elected president in 1946. By delegating responsibility for the Ministry of Labor to his wife (who eventually also oversaw the Partido Peronista Femenino and the Eva Perón Foundation), "he gave her the legitimacy she needed to be accepted by the descamisados,[5] transferred to her part of his leadership, and in so doing prevented its 'routinization'" (1982, 55). Evita turned out to be very effective in cutting through red tape and providing new services; for example, from the offices of the Eva Perón Foundation, "she subsidized vacations of descamisados, gave them funds for their union headquarters, and built luxurious hospitals, modern clinics, low cost housing projects, and elegant hotels for them" (57). As a result, she became a powerful leader in her own right, although, as Perón's wife,

---

5. Typically translated as "shirtless ones," descamisados really means something more like "jacketless ones," or "open-shirted ones," and refers to working-class men who did not wear a coat and tie. In fact, they always wore shirts of some sort.

she presented no threat to his leadership. Just in case, she always emphasized in her speeches that she was nothing and he, everything.

> Using a language that was extracted from the soap operas, she transformed politics into dramas dominated by relentless invocations of love . . . the love that united Perón, Evita, and the *descamisados* was the cause of the oligarchy's hatred towards them. Her scenarios never changed and her characters were stereotyped by the same adjectives: Perón was always "glorious," the people "marvelous," the oligarchy *egoista y vendepatria* (selfish and corrupt), and she was a "humble" or "weak" woman, "burning her life for them" so that social justice could be achieved, *cueste lo que cueste y caiga quien caiga* (at whatever cost and regardless of the consequences). (Navarro 1982, 59)

Ordinary Argentines reacted strongly to Evita's words and deeds. During her lifetime she was portrayed both as the "Lady of Hope," a saintly figure akin to the Virgin Mary, and as the woman of the "Black Myth," a woman who could do no good. Decades after her death, a third myth emerged, that of Evita the revolutionary. Without much evidence, the Montonero guerrillas of the 1970s proclaimed, "Si Evita viviera, sería montonera" (If Evita were alive, she would be a Montonera, i.e., an armed revolutionary), and insisted that they were the truest heirs to the Peronist tradition (Taylor 1979).

Evita is a critical figure. In fact, the joint leadership of Juan and Eva Perón is often considered the paradigmatic example of populism in the region. But Evita is not the only populist leader who may usefully be analyzed in gendered terms or the only populist to passionately declare love for the people. Her husband explained, "I want to tell the Argentine people that I do not wish to govern based on any other bond . . . than the union that is born from our hearts. I do not wish to rule over men, but over their hearts, because mine beats together with that of each *descamisado,* whom I understand and love above all things" (quoted in Plotkin 2003, 64). Luis Sánchez Cerro also spoke of his strong feelings for the people: "I love the masses with gratitude and conviction" (quoted in Stein 1980, 107). Abdalá Bucaram "always spoke about love: he loved *el pueblo,* he loved the poor, he loved Ecuador. The only ones he did not love were the oligarchy, who were excluded from the 'real' Ecuador, personified by Abdalá Bucaram" (de la Torre 2000, 95).

By projecting a variety of masculine images, the populists seem to suggest that larger-than-life figures like themselves are uniquely suited to attacking elites, to uniting the true people against outsiders, to embodying the nation. These masculine images have included populists as ladies' men, often surrounded with scantily dressed dancers (Abdalá Bucaram, Hugo Chávez, Alberto Fujimori, Carlos Menem, Daniel Ortega). That model of masculinity sometimes shades into the populist as vulgar man. For example, at a rally celebrating the anniversary of the end of the Pérez Jiménez dictatorship, Hugo Chávez commented on U.S. Secretary of State Condoleezza Rice's criticisms of his government.

> First, a few days ago, she said she was very bothered by Chávez, the tyrant Chávez, the strongman who is a threat to the people of the world and of America. Later, the next day, she brought it up again; it seems that she dreams about me. . . . Look, even though as the secretary of state of that imperialist government, Dr. Alí Rodríguez would be the one to meet with her, I am willing to invite her to a meeting to see, what is the thing you have for me? Let's see if we can arrange something. [Applause.] Do you want me to invite her? I will do whatever you tell me. A little while ago somebody suggested, "Look, why don't you ask her to marry you?" [Audience: Nooooo!] That lady has very bad luck. You said no. (Chávez 2005)

Periodically throughout the speech, Chávez returned to the theme: "That's why I say that I can't marry Condolencia;[6] because I have a lot of work to do, she'll have to look elsewhere, to try to forget about me a little. [Pointing to others on the stage] Alí Rodríguez, he could do it, Cristóbal Jiménez is right there, he's available, Juan Barreto is single; let someone else make this sacrifice for the fatherland" (11).

Abdalá Bucaram was also known for his vulgarity, as when he praised Ecuador-born Lorena Bobbitt, famous for cutting off the penis of her American husband, John Wayne Bobbitt. Bucaram invited Lorena Bobbitt, who had been acquitted of her crime on the grounds that she acted in self-defense, to the Congress, where he declared her a national hero for having "cut off neocolonial relations" (quoted in Lind 2005, 113). As with Chávez's comments about Condoleezza Rice, vulgar jokes became a way of symbolically defending Latin American countries against the much more powerful United States.

Other models of masculinity that populists have drawn upon include the athlete (Abdalá Bucaram, Fernando de Collor), the military man (Lázaro Cárdenas, Hugo Chávez, Daniel Ortega, Juan Perón), and, perhaps most commonly

---

6. Throughout his speech, Chávez referred to the secretary of state as "Condolencia" (condolences).

- vulgar man -father
- athlete
-military
-priest

in a region that is predominantly Catholic, the priest or even Jesus Christ himself. In one speech, Luis Sánchez Cerro told the crowds, "there is no effort, no sacrifice of which I am not capable. . . . Every morning when I awaken, I renew my vows, before the altar of the fatherland, to carry on my duties as ruler with the purity of the priesthood" (quoted in Stein 1980, 107).

The APRA movement, founded by Sánchez Cerro's competitor, Victor Raúl Haya de la Torre, drew on similar traditions. "The repression of the original student-worker front induced the likening of the movement to a persecuted sect with an evolution akin to that of early Christianity" (Stein 1980, 176–77). "Numerous party tracts [were] filled with comparisons of Christ's suffering with that of Haya de la Torre" (265n42). Like many of the populists, Victor Raúl Haya de la Torre suffered long periods in prison or in exile, only to rise from the political dead. "With his exile in 1923 the legend of the eternally persecuted Haya was born. . . . Terms like *apostle, mission, crusade,* and *faith* proliferated in public references to Haya during his exile and later set the tone for much of Apra's 1931 campaign rhetoric" (145–46).

Haya de la Torre = Jesus Christo

Loyalty Day celebrated the founding myth of Peronism, Juan Domingo Perón's release from imprisonment on Martin García Island on October 17, 1945, in response to pressure from his supporters, many of whom had gathered in Buenos Aires's Plaza de Mayo. Over time, the Peronist government framed this event in increasingly religious terms. "Peronism needed 'apostles' to 'preach' its doctrine. . . . [The Peronist newspaper] *Democracia* characterized the Seventeenth of October as a 'lay Mass' and kept repeating that 'God is a Peronist'" (Plotkin 2003, 79).

Perón

In another variation on the theme of the leader suffering for his people, one newspaper wrote of José María Velasco Ibarra's political death and later return: "President elected by the popular Ecuadorian vote drowned in the blood of the martyrs of 12 January 1940, and resurrected in the blood of the martyrs of 29 May 1944" (quoted in de la Torre 2000, 53). By late in the twentieth century, Protestantism had become a major religious movement in Ecuador and many other Latin American countries, and so Abdalá Bucaram "used religious elements of popular culture, especially of the Protestant sects, to present himself as a new Christ, the new messiah who would redeem the people from their suffering" (109).

Ibarra

Redemption and images of the populist as savior were not always restricted to religious populists. For Lázaro Cárdenas, carrying out the agenda of the Mexican Revolution required wresting political power from the hands of the Catholic Church and turning Mexico into a secular republic. Yet many saw him in almost

Cárdenas

religious terms. "In this myth, Cárdenas is styled as something of a latter-day Jesus, a redeemer who traveled from village to village performing wonders. . . . Most spectacularly, while Cárdenas multiplied no loaves or fishes, he divided large estates into peasant plots. In response *campesinos* crowded around to pay homage to him and his government" (Becker 1994, 248).

But of the various masculine models that the populists have drawn upon, the most frequently invoked is that of the father. According to Michael Conniff, "virtually all populists assumed roles as paternal figures to their followers" (1999, 199). Similarly, Steve Stein notes that these movements "derived their real cement from the presence of a strong leader with whom people could identify above all in emotional terms. . . . He was perceived as a generous father figure who could capably direct the political affairs of his less sophisticated children" (1980, 11).

Haya de la Torre was known for patting and hugging his supporters, and his "predilection for physical expression became an integral part of his paternalistic style" (Stein 1980, 181). Juan Perón's calm, "fatherly" tone has been contrasted with his wife's "passion and fury" (Navarro 1982, 58). Getúlio Vargas called himself the "father of the poor," though some have noted that he was really more grand-fatherly (Conniff 1999, 49; Wolfe 1994, 81). Lázaro Cárdenas was called "'Tata Lázaro,' or Father Lázaro" by indigenous people in the Mexican state of Micho-acán (Basurto 1999, 76). And the supporters of Jorge Gaitán were known to chant, "'Guste o no le guste, cuadre o no le cuadre, Gaitán será su padre' (like it or not, agree or not, Gaitán shall be your father)" (quoted in de la Torre 2000, 20).

Third Theme: Gender, Populism, and Democracy

Populists have had an uneasy relationship with democracy, and the father meta-phor is at the root of some of those difficulties. In some ways, the politician as father is a compelling metaphor. Stereotypically, to be a father is to be wise, brave, strong, responsible, protective. These are certainly characteristics most people seek in a leader. And yet fatherhood entails other characteristics as well.

Most disturbingly for democratic politics, the father metaphor turns citi-zens into children. It turns the politician into someone who understands the interests of the citizens—even when they do not—and who may punish way-ward children who fail to recognize his wisdom. Of course, fathers are fathers for life and cannot be voted out of office. Many of the populists seem to have seen their own jobs as lifetime commitments: rewriting constitutions, shutting down other branches of government or packing the courts, seeking military backing so as to continue their good works. A father's work is never done.

Yet in speaking to the previously excluded, who often include women, especially poor women, populism may be profoundly democratic. After all, if they fail to incorporate all sectors of society, democratic procedures result in a very thin democracy. At the same time, however, incorporation of the excluded can happen in the absence of democratic procedures. Populists have sometimes used the democratic process to concentrate power in their own hands. Indeed, in some cases, populism has developed in the context of authoritarianism.

Opponents of particular populist leaders often blame the populist movements themselves for the weakness of democracy in their countries. This is sometimes the case: "popular activation occurs through movements that acritically identify with charismatic leaders, who are often authoritarian. Moreover, the Manichaean populist discourse that divides society into two antagonistic fields does not permit the recognition of the opposition" (de la Torre 2000, 26–27). Yet one could just as reasonably argue that populism is a symptom of the weakness of democracy in Latin America, not its cause. "The poor whose rights are specified in constitutions and laws, do not have the power to exercise those laws," writes de la Torre. "They have to rely on protectors who can help them to take advantage of their rights and who can defend them from the arbitrariness of the police and the powerful. Politicians who have become such guardians have organized clientelist networks that have allowed their followers limited access to goods and services, not as rights but as concessions to interest groups" (xi–xii).

These clientelistic political traditions are a response to inequality, and Latin America is the most unequal region in the world. In a reciprocal fashion, populist movements, which emerge in response to limited citizenship rights, also contribute to the weakness of democracy. For all these reasons it is likely that Latin America will remain the region that is most characterized by populist politics (Conniff 1982, 22–23; Drake 1982, 224–26, 241; Roberts 2007, 9–11; Wolfe 1994, 87).

Fourth Theme: Populism and Feminism

Populists have not always enjoyed good relations with organized feminists, sometimes not even when they have promoted feminist issues. Lola Luna (2000) notes that while Colombian feminists supported Jorge Gaitán because he promoted women's suffrage, Argentine feminists disliked Juan Perón because he stole the issue they had worked on for decades—women's right to vote—and took credit for it (or, more precisely, Evita took credit for it). Clearly, the way in which each politician supported the feminist demand for women's suffrage mattered as much as suffrage itself.

As I noted above, relations between populist leaders and organized feminists have only become more difficult over time. In some cases, as in the movements led by Arnoldo Alemán, Daniel Ortega, and Alberto Fujimori, feminists were almost entirely opposed to populist figures. In Hugo Chávez's Venezuela, organized feminists are about evenly divided between strongly pro-Chávez and strongly anti-Chávez activists (Gioconda Espina, personal communication, January 2005; see also Rakowski and Espina 2006, 320–25).

In some ways, the frequency with which populists have clashed with feminists is surprising. Populism is potentially a deeply feminist movement, in that women are typically the most excluded of the excluded. But populism is a style of politics that tends to scapegoat elites or constructed elites. All too often feminists are portrayed as overly educated intellectuals who fail to fit into the mainstream of real women, in short, as elites. And even if they are not scapegoated, feminists may have reason to worry about the cult of (male) personality that has been inherent in populist movements since Evita. Whether they find populist movements to be full of opportunity or full of threat depends to a large extent on the nature of the feminists' demands. Within Latin America, as elsewhere, there are many versions of feminism, and some are more compatible with populism than others.

Fifth Theme: Women as Populist Followers

An important but understudied theme in the literature on populism is the nature of populist followership. This issue has been neglected in part because it is easier to focus on a single leader than to study followers who may number in the millions. And evaluating the relationship between followers and leader is tricky. "The main challenge in the study of populism lies in explaining the appeal of leaders for their followers, without reducing the latter's behavior to either manipulation or irrational and anomic action or to a utilitarian rationalism, which supposedly explains everything" (de la Torre 2000, 1).

Keeping our eyes open to what de la Torre calls "the complexities of populist seductions" (ix) complicates our job as students of populism, though it also makes it more interesting. Many, perhaps all, of the Latin American populists reached out to women directly. Certainly they did this because they wanted women's votes, and sometimes that strategy worked very well. Juan Perón was reelected in 1951 with "a much higher percentage of votes from women than from men" (Horowitz 1999, 36). The same was true of Getúlio Vargas: "Vargas enjoyed a substantial lead in preferences among women" (Conniff 1999, 49). Similarly, opinion polls in 2000 showed that Alberto Fujimori enjoyed much more support from women than from men (Schmidt 2006, 164). But there are no systematic studies comparing the gender breakdown of votes for populist leaders. So it is not clear that women were generally more supportive of populist politicians than men were, or whether men were sometimes more supportive. In a survey leading up to the referendum to recall Hugo Chávez, men were somewhat more likely to oppose the recall than were women; the majority of women supported Chávez, just not proportionally as strongly as men did (Hellinger 2005, 21).

In addition to seeking votes, populists had other reasons to reach out to women. They often sought to mobilize female followers because, owing to their position in the gendered division of labor, they could do certain things that men could not. Mariano Ben Plotkin notes that the Peronist "government not only tried to gain the support of women as voters but also as potential 'missionaries' who would spread the Peronist word in the privacy of their homes. . . . Women and children would serve as a link between the Peronist state and the family" (2003, xii, also 178). Missionaries are outsiders, in this case outsiders to the world of politics. Their outsider status makes them uniquely qualified to spread the good news of a transformed world. And long after Juan and Eva Perón were dead, their female followers continued to embrace the role of missionary.

In his analysis of contemporary grassroots Peronism, Javier Auyero follows Peronist brokers who oversee soup kitchens, monthly food distribution, free haircuts, and a long list of other benefits that help explain why the Peronist party is still the most powerful political party in Argentina. But their relationship with Peronism is not limited to distributing goods. Auyero argues that with their bleached blond hair, their familiar manner with the recipients of their largesse, even their Evita wristwatches, they "perform Evita" (2000, 140). This performance is not just for outside consumption. Just as important, they perform Evita for themselves, for in asking themselves *What would Evita do?* and then acting on that answer, they make sense of their lives. Auyero summarizes the stories these followers of Evita tell.

> Their work is more to them than just a job; it is a vocation, a mission fueled by a compassion for the poor that was recognized early in life. Their birth

coincided with Peronism, and their political careers are closely tied to that of the mayor [a Peronist]. They have a special relationship with the poor—in terms of mutual obligations, in terms of the love they feel for them—that keeps at bay bureaucratic indifference. Their work is motivated by a "passion for the people." They are willing to sacrifice all and work themselves to exhaustion on behalf of the poor. . . . Their work is not a job but something that comes naturally to them, because they are self-sacrificing and hardworking, they are the mothers of the poor. (127)

The language with which these women discuss their work echoes the discourse of contemporary party leaders as well as Evita's words from decades earlier.

But this does not necessarily mean that they are manipulated. Joel Wolfe notes that the relationship between leader and follower is a complicated one. "Scholars often assume that workers . . . entered into a 'populist coalition' with Vargas. But, when these workers considered Vargas and other politicians, they did so skeptically. . . . Urban workers and rural proletarians have not necessarily been coopted by populism" (1994, 82). Many workers wrote Vargas directly to try to negotiate solutions to their personal problems, problems they often framed in gender terms.

One man noted that an industrial accident kept him from heavy work, and he asked Vargas for permission to sell popcorn on the street, explaining, "I am a man and I am ashamed of not working" (quoted in Wolfe 1994, 98). Another man complained that he felt "humiliated" by the way he was treated at General Motors do Brasil (95). One woman complained to Vargas that her boss made "improper proposals [that were] inconceivable for a poor girl, who is in fact honorable and moral" (96). When she refused his propositions, he cut her pay, a fact that she documented in her letter to Vargas. At least some of these direct appeals to Vargas got results: Vargas ordered an investigation of the allegation of sexual harassment, though the woman eventually lost the case. In response to other complaints, "Vargas eliminated the discount in the minimum wage paid to women" (96).

Women provided Lázaro Cárdenas with unique political resources as well, despite the fact that Mexican women did not yet have the right to vote when Cárdenas was in office. "[The Cardenistas'] plan was to reconstruct the countryside through a combination of land redistribution and cultural transformation. . . . In addition, the revolutionaries planned to recast peasant culture, the peasants' way of seeing the world. . . . Rural teachers and agricultural agents who identified with Cardenismo would sport varying faces of liberalism" (Becker 1994, 257). This was an ambitious plan, to say the least.

Land reform is always difficult, as few big landowners willingly accept it. But the greater threat came from the Catholic Church, which organized armed resistance to the government (known as the Cristero Rebellion), told parishioners that beneficiaries of land reform would go to hell, and threatened to excommunicate those who sent their children to the Cardenista schools (Becker 1994, 257). Mobilizing women behind Cárdenas's plan was critical, as women were seen as closer to the church than men. So the Cardenistas "established women's leagues, in which women learned that Cárdenas championed their husbands' (and by implication, their families') rights to governmental land. In the leagues revolutionaries also discussed the evils of alcoholism" (258). But by far the most remarkable incident in which women were mobilized to support Cárdenas took place at a church in Michoacán.

Entering the church at night, male followers of Cárdenas stole the icons, including that of the Virgin. The next morning they burned the icons in the central square and "appropriated the church. They hired a band and issued invitations to their wives, daughters, and girlfriends. When the women entered the church it would have looked very different. The priest was gone. The image of the Virgin was missing. The band was playing popular contemporary music. And suddenly the women, too, were not quite the same. Their Catholic training, their lessons in humility began to recede, and the women, suddenly transformed, began to dance before the altar" (Becker 1994, 259–60). Needless to say, the burning of the Virgin and the women's dance in the church shook the town. For in doing so they attacked the old hierarchies of daily life, and indeed their opponents responded with the most traditional gender slur—accusing the dancers of being prostitutes.

If populist followers are not always people out of place, the undermining of hierarchy and tradition is certainly a recurring theme. Poor Mexican women's dancing at the altar echoed the Argentine working class's seizing of the Plaza de Mayo to demand the return of their beloved Perón. Supposedly dressed improperly for a downtown gathering, some even waded in fountains. Many of the female workers who wrote Brazil's Vargas also clearly felt out of place, for they had to defend their new roles as factory workers, roles that they insisted should not diminish their status as honorable women. In some sense populist followers are always out of place, as they are the previously excluded, the people who for reasons of class or gender or ethnicity were not legitimate participants in national politics until the populist came along.

Hugo Chávez speaks to his followers in just these terms, asserting that those who used to be out of place—the poor and dark-skinned—are the true

Venezuelans and dismissing the old elites as the *escúalidos,* the squalid ones. Though these distinctions are oversimplifications, they speak to underlying truths about exclusion and inclusion, as the old elites did tend to be more middle-class and light-skinned than the average Venezuelan. It is equally true that under his administration thousands of previously excluded women, especially poor women, have become politically active.

Yet mobilizing is sometimes akin to joining a movie star's fan club. Hugo Chávez encourages such movie star adoration, proclaiming in the epigraph to this introduction, "An infinite kiss for all Venezuelan women!" His followers often comment on how handsome he is and frequently adorn their workplaces and homes with his images, especially romantic images, such as the photo of Chávez holding a red rose.[7] This does not mean that his female followers are simply manipulated, or that they are unconcerned with the material benefits to be had by supporting his movement. But it does mean that we cannot fully understand populism without paying attention to the emotional, and even passionate, nature of the relationship between leader and follower.

Overview of the Book

The five themes I have just outlined inform all the chapters in this book, although the weight granted to each theme varies from chapter to chapter. Many of the chapters analyze two or three themes in depth and touch on the others. The salience of the various themes shifted over time and from country to country, although remarkable similarities sometimes emerged between populists over the course of the century or so considered in this volume. The chapters follow chronological order, starting at the beginning of the particular populist's career (or the first populist's career, in the case of comparative chapters).

In chapter 1, Jocelyn Olcott analyzes populism in Mexico under Lázaro Cárdenas (1934–40) and Luis Echeverría (1970–76). Both administrations paid careful attention to women's roles and gendered images. Analyzing Cárdenas's various efforts to incorporate women into Mexican political life and Echeverría's hosting of the UN's 1975 International Women's Year conference, Olcott argues that

---

7. A conversation I had in the poor Caracas neighborhood of Petare in January 2005 was telling. Following a meeting of a women's organization (Movimiento de Mujeres Manuelita Saenz, held in the offices of Patria para Todos, a group allied with Chávez), some women in their early twenties crowded around me, asking what I thought of Chávez. I tried to answer in a neutral way, saying that he was interesting but that since Venezuela was not my native country, I shouldn't take political positions. "No," they said, "what do you think of his *physical* appearance [que piensa en lo *físico*]?"

both men addressed issues of masculinity and femininity, as debates over women's status fueled "anxieties about changes in the most intimate realms of daily life, particularly in such areas as sexuality, household labor, and family relations." But followers or potential followers did not respond passively to their leader's policies; in both cases ordinary people sought to take advantage of the opportunities provided by Cárdenas and Echeverría.

In chapter 2, Ximena Sosa-Buchholz compares José María Velasco Ibarra, who served as Ecuador's president five times between the 1930s and the 1970s, with the short-lived presidency of neopopulist Abdalá Bucaram (1996–97). Both appealed to "the people," as populist leaders typically do, but they constructed "the people" very differently. Velasco Ibarra's beloved *chusma,* or rabble, was composed of artisans, small merchants, small farmers, private and state employees, teachers, bus drivers, and factory workers, but excluded indigenous people, who were largely illiterate and therefore ineligible to vote. Bucaram's concept of the people was more inclusive, as illiterates had gained the right to vote by the time he ran for president. Perhaps because they reached out to different sectors, the models of masculinity they projected differed significantly: Velasco Ibarra was a distinguished and mild-mannered Catholic, whereas Bucaram was a flamboyant and sometimes vulgar man of the people. Furthermore, Sosa-Buchholz argues, although both men were elected democratically, they also threatened democracy in various ways: Velasco Ibarra declared himself dictator three times (for the good of the people, of course), while Bucaram's various attempts to skirt the law eventually provoked a mass movement that drove him from power.

Victoria González-Rivera argues in chapter 3 that although the Somóza family, which ruled Nicaragua from 1936 until 1979, was violent and corrupt, it was also heir to the liberal tradition that had advocated women's rights since the mid-nineteenth century. She shows that many women were deeply involved in helping to shape the Somocista movement and working especially hard to win over other women through populist rhetoric and clientelistic promises. González-Rivera examines the roles women played as followers of this right-wing populist movement and considers the ways in which modern-day neo-Somocistas remember the legacy of the Somoza years.

In chapter 4, Joel Wolfe considers Getúlio Vargas's first period of rule in Brazil (1930–45), focusing on his attempts to govern as a populist in the early 1940s as the "father of the poor" who would personally guarantee social justice for the majority of Brazilians. He compares Vargas's rule with that of Juscelino Kubitschek (1956–61), who oversaw the creation of the national automobile industry and the building of a new capital, Brasília. Gender shaped Kubitschek's policies as they had Vargas's, but rather than position himself as the father of Brazil's poor, he promoted a middle-class ethos for all Brazilians based on the ideal of a wage-earning father and a stay-at-home mother. Citizenship was not to mean the same thing for men and women.

Michael Conniff also analyzes gender and Brazilian populism, but from a rather different perspective from Wolfe's. Instead of considering the gendered policies of male politicians, Conniff looks in chapter 5 at the often hidden roles of women. Analyzing the roles of two of Getúlio Vargas's female relatives (his daughter, Alzira, and his great-niece Ivete), Conniff finds that women often played important roles in populist campaigns, but behind the scenes. He also looks at Heloísa Helena, a radical populist senator from the state of Alagoas. Thus Conniff suggests interesting strategies for studying women in political history: by looking behind the scenes and at local and regional politics, he finds that Brazilian populism is less masculine than it seems from a national perspective.

In chapter 6, Karin Grammático compares the images of women and the gender policies promoted by the first government of Argentina's Juan Domingo Perón (1946–55) with the gendered ideals promoted by the Montonero guerrillas of the 1970s, an organization that claimed to be both socialist and Peronist. Although the Montonero women's front, known as the Agrupación Evita (Evita Group), reinforced a gendered division of labor and embraced the classic populist discourse of self-sacrifice for the people, it also eventually opened doors to rethinking relations between men and women in politics and daily life.

Stéphanie Rousseau, in chapter 7, analyzes the gendered policies of Alberto Fujimori in Peru (1990–2000) and Evo Morales in Bolivia (2005–present). Rousseau finds that "they pursued different political agendas in relation to distinct female constituencies, and their discourse on gender differs." In spite of vast differences in their political styles and economic policies—Fujimori is a neopopulist who pursued a neoliberal agenda, while Morales is a radical populist, or an "ethnopopulist," who rejects neoliberalism—their gender policies have much in common, Rousseau argues. Both have had significant problems with organized feminists and both have gone out of their way to promote women to positions of leadership.

I argue in chapter 8 that Nicaragua's Daniel Ortega (1984–1990 and 2007–present) acted within the populist tradition in the years leading up to his reelection, a major change from his origins as a guerrilla and revolutionary. The story of this transformation from revolutionary to populist was highly gendered at key moments, culminating, in the 2006 campaign, with his turning his party's long-standing commitment to a moderate form of women's emancipation on its head by seeing that abortion was banned under all circumstances, even to save the life of the pregnant woman. Daniel Ortega can tell us a great deal about the relationship between gender, feminism, populism, and revolution. The case of Nicaragua suggests that it is very likely that the linking of a revolutionary agenda, an agenda of social change and social justice, to one individual (normally one man) will undermine feminist gains within a revolution.

In chapter 9, Gioconda Espina and Cathy Rakowski evaluate the gendered policy and discourse of Hugo Chávez (1999–present) of Venezuela. Through both words and deeds—including the creation of a national women's institute, a women's development bank, and a series of "missions" that provide education and other social services to the women (and men) who join them—Chávez has generated a passionate following. Chavista populist discourse resonates with many poor women for reasons of class but also because Chávez has reached out directly to women. Espina and Rakowski argue that the language used by Chávez and his followers reinforces "an image of Chávez as the liberator of women, a leader who has a special place in his heart for popular women, who understands and appreciates their sacrifices and struggles to care for their families and communities." While the Chavista women's institute claims to promote "popular feminism," Espina and Rakowski note that in official discourse, women's rights are attributed to socialism and, more specifically, to Chávez.

Sujatha Fernandes also looks at politics in Chávez's Venezuela, but from a grassroots perspective, that of the poor women who have become politically active as a result of Chávez's appeal to them as caregivers and mothers. She argues in chapter 10 that this relationship is complicated, for at the same time that they are followers of Chávez, they are also critics. Despite male leadership and authority, the growing presence of women in local committees, assemblies, and communal kitchens has created forms of democratic participation that challenge gender roles, collectivize private tasks, and create alternatives to male-centric politics. Women's experiences of shared struggle in past decades, along with their use of democratic methods of popular control such as local assemblies, help to prevent the state's appropriation of women's labor for its own ends. But these spaces of popular participation exist in dynamic tension with more vertical, populist notions of politics that are characteristic of official sectors of Chavismo.

This book concludes with some thoughts on the findings of the chapters, identifying a series of new questions raised by the authors of those chapters.

References

Auyero, Javier. 2000. *Poor People's Politics: Peronist Survival Networks and the Legacy of Evita.* Durham: Duke University Press.

Basurto, Jorge. 1999. "Populism in Mexico: From Cárdenas to Cuauhtémoc." In *Populism in Latin America,* ed. Michael Conniff, 75–96. Tuscaloosa: University of Alabama Press.

Becker, Marjorie. 1994. "Torching La Purísima, Dancing at the Altar: The Construction of Revolutionary Hegemony in Michoacán, 1934–1940." In *Everyday Forms of State Formation: Revolution and the Negotiation of Rule in Modern Mexico,* ed. Gilbert Joseph and Daniel Nugent, 247–64. Durham: Duke University Press.

Burbano de Lara, Felipe, ed. 1998. *El fantasma del populismo: Aproximación a un tema [siempre] actual.* Caracas: Editorial Nueva Sociedad.

Centurión, Ana Josefina. 2007. "Las mujeres en la resistencia peronista: Sentidos y representaciones." In *Historias de luchas, resistencias y representaciones: Mujeres en la Argentina, siglos XIX y XX,* ed. María Celia Bravo, Fernanda Gil Lozano, and Valeria Pita, 233–65. San Miguel de Tucumán: Editorial de la Universidad de Tucumán.

Chávez, Hugo. 2004. "Día internacional de la mujer." Speech given March 8, Caracas. http://www.gobiernoenlinea.gob.ve (accessed February 15, 2005).

———. 2005. "Cadena nacional, marcha defensa de la soberanía: Concentración frente al palacio de miraflores." Speech given January 23, Caracas. http://www.mci.gov .ve/alocucion.asp?numn=251 (accessed March 8, 2005).

Conniff, Michael. 1982. "Introduction: Toward a Comparative Definition of Populism." In *Latin American Populism in Comparative Perspective,* ed. Michael Conniff, 3–30. Albuquerque: University of New Mexico Press.

———. 1999. "Epilogue: New Research Directions." In *Populism in Latin America,* ed. Michael Conniff, 191–203. Tuscaloosa: University of Alabama Press.

Crespo, Edda Lía. 2005. "Madres, esposas, reinas . . . Petróleo, mujeres y nacionalismo en comodoro rivadavia durante los años del primer peronismo." In *Cuando las mujeres reinaban: Belleza, virtud, y poder en la Argentina del siglo XX,* ed. Mirta Zaida Lobato, 143–74. Buenos Aires: Editorial Biblos.

de la Torre, Carlos. 2000. *Populist Seduction in Latin America: The Ecuadorian Experience.* Athens: Ohio University Press.

Drake, Paul W. 1982. "Conclusion: Requiem for Populism?" In *Latin American Populism in Comparative Perspective,* ed. Michael Conniff, 217–45. Albuquerque: University of New Mexico Press.

Fisher, Jo. 2000. "Gender and the State in Argentina: The Case of the Sindicato de Amas de Casa." In *Hidden Histories of Gender and the State in Latin America,* ed. Elizabeth Dore and Maxine Molyneux, 322–45. Durham: Duke University Press.

French, John D., and Daniel James. 1997. "Squaring the Circle: Women's Factory Labor, Gender Ideology, and Necessity." In *The Gendered Worlds of Latin American Women Workers: From Household and Factory to the Union Hall and Ballot Box,* ed. John D. French and Daniel James, 1–30. Durham: Duke University Press.

González, Victoria. 2001. "Somocista Women, Right-Wing Politics, and Feminism in Nicaragua, 1936–79." In *Radical Women in Latin America: Left and Right,* ed. Victoria González and Karen Kampwirth, 41–78. University Park: Pennsylvania State University Press.

González, Victoria, and Karen Kampwirth, eds. 2001. *Radical Women in Latin America: Left and Right.* University Park: Pennsylvania State University Press.

Grammático, Karin. 2007. "La Agrupación Evita: Apuntes de una experiencia política de mujeres." In *Historias de luchas, resistencias y representaciones: Mujeres en la Argentina, siglos XIX y XX,* ed. María Cecilia Bravo, Fernanda Gil Lozano, and Valeria Pita, 267–82. San Miguel de Tucumán: Editorial de la Universidad de Tucumán.

Green, W. John. 2003. *Gaitanismo, Left Liberalism, and Popular Mobilization in Colombia.* Gainesville: University Press of Florida.

Hellinger, Daniel. 2005. "When 'No' Means 'Yes' to Revolution: Electoral Politics in Bolivarian Venezuela." *Latin American Perspectives* 42 (3): 8–32.

Horowitz, Joel. 1999. "Populism and Its Legacies in Argentina." In *Populism in Latin America,* ed. Michael Conniff, 22–42. Tuscaloosa: University of Alabama Press.

Kampwirth, Karen. 2003. "Arnoldo Alemán Takes on the NGOs: Antifeminism and the New Populism in Nicaragua." *Latin American Politics and Society* 45 (2): 133–58.

Knight, Alan. 1998. "Populism and Neo-Populism in Latin America, Especially Mexico." *Journal of Latin American Studies* 30 (2): 223–48.

Leaman, David. 2004. "Changing Faces of Populism in Latin America: Masks, Makeovers, and Enduring Features." *Latin American Research Review* 39 (3): 312–26.

Lind, Amy. 2005. *Gendered Paradoxes: Women's Movements, State Restructuring, and Global Development in Ecuador.* University Park: Pennsylvania State University Press.

Lobato, Mirta Zaida, María Damilakou, and Lizel Tornay. 2005. "Las reinas del trabajo bajo el peronismo." In *Cuando las mujeres reinaban: Belleza, virtud y poder en la Argentina del siglo XX,* ed. Mirta Zaida Lobato, 77–120. Buenos Aires: Editorial Biblos.

Luna, Lola. 2000. "Populismo, nacionalismo y maternalismo: Casos peronista y gaitanista." *Boletín Americanista* 50 (1): 189–200.

MacKinnon, María Moira, and Mario Alberto Petrone, eds. 1999. *Populismo y neopopulismo en américa latina: El problema de la cenicienta.* Buenos Aires: Editorial Eudeba.

Milanesio, Natalia. 2006. "'The Guardian Angels of the Domestic Economy': Housewives' Responsible Consumption in Peronist Argentina." *Journal of Women's History* 18 (3): 91–117.

Molyneux, Maxine. 2001. *Women's Movements in Comparative Perspective: Latin America and Beyond.* London: Palgrave.

Navarro, Marysa. 1982. "Evita's Charismatic Leadership." In *Latin American Populism in Comparative Perspective,* ed. Michael Conniff, 47–66. Albuquerque: University of New Mexico Press.

———. 2005. *Evita.* Buenos Aires: Editorial Edhasa.

Perón, Eva. 1951/2004. *La razón de mi vida.* Buenos Aires: Buro Editor.

Plotkin, Mariano Ben. 2003. *Mañana es San Perón: A Cultural History of Perón's Argentina.* Wilmington, Del.: Scholarly Resources.

Rakowski, Cathy, and Gioconda Espina. 2006. In *De lo privado a lo público: Treinta años de lucha ciudadana de las mujeres en América Latina,* ed. Nathalie Lebon and Elizabeth Maier, 310–20. Mexico City: Siglo XXI Editores.

Reed, Jean-Pierre. 2004. "Emotions in Context: Revolutionary Accelerators, Hope, Moral Outrage, and Other Emotions in the Making of Nicaragua's Revolution." *Theory and Society* 33:653–703.

Roberts, Kenneth M. 1995. "Neoliberalism and the Transformation of Populism in Latin America: The Peruvian Case." *World Politics* 48 (1): 82–116.

———. 2007. "Latin America's Populist Revival." *SAIS Review* 27 (1): 3–15.

Rousseau, Stéphanie. 2006. "Women's Citizenship and Neopopulism: Peru Under the Fujimori Regime." *Latin American Politics and Society* 48 (1): 117–41.

Schmidt, Gregory. 2006. "All the President's Women: Fujimori and Gender Equity in Peruvian Politics." In *The Fujimori Legacy: The Rise of Electoral Authoritarianism in Peru,* ed. Julio Carrión, 150–77. University Park: Pennsylvania State University Press.

Stein, Steve. 1980. *Populism in Peru: The Emergence of the Masses and the Politics of Social Control.* Madison: University of Wisconsin Press.

Taylor, J. M. 1979. *Eva Perón: The Myths of a Woman.* Chicago: University of Chicago Press.

Weyland, Kurt. 1999. "Neoliberal Populism in Latin America and Eastern Europe." *Comparative Politics* 31 (4): 379–401.

———. 2001. "Clarifying a Contested Concept: Populism in the Study of Latin American Politics." *Comparative Politics* 34 (1): 1–22.

Wirth, John D. 1982. "Foreword." In *Latin American Populism in Comparative Perspective,* ed. Michael Conniff, ix–xiii. Albuquerque: University of New Mexico Press.

Wolfe, Joel. 1994. "'Father of the Poor' or 'Mother of the Rich?' Getúlio Vargas, Industrial Workers, and Constructions of Class, Gender, and Populism in São Paolo, 1930–1954." *Radical History* 58 (Winter): 80–111.

Zabaleta, Marta. 1997. "Ideology and Populism in Latin America: A Gendered Overview." In *Ideologues and Ideologies in Latin America,* ed. Will Fowler, 65–81. Westport, Conn.: Greenwood Press.

Zink, Mirta, and María Herminia Di Liscia. 2007. "Gestar una ciudadanía política: La incorporación de las mujeres al estado peronista, apoyos y resistencias (1945–55)." In *Historias de luchas, resistencias y representaciones: Mujeres en la Argentina, siglos XIX y XX,* ed. María Celia Bravo, Fernanda Gil Lozano, and Valeria Pita, 211–32. San Miguel de Tucumán: Editorial de la Universidad de Tucumán.

THE POLITICS OF OPPORTUNITY

MEXICAN POPULISM UNDER LÁZARO CÁRDENAS AND LUIS ECHEVERRÍA

Jocelyn Olcott

In a ceremony commemorating International Women's Day in 1973, the Communist Party–affiliated Unión Nacional de Mujeres Mexicanas (UNMM) expressed nostalgia for the presidency of Lázaro Cárdenas (1934–40) and his particular attention to incorporating women into politics, and in a rare moment of charity toward the current president, Luis Echeverría (1970–76), the organizers praised him for emulating Cárdenas in this regard. A more common—and less flattering—comparison was made three days later, when UNMM president Martha Portillo de Tamayo lamented that, although Cárdenas had achieved "great benefits and revolutionary advances," they had all collapsed under subsequent regimes, including Echeverría's.[1] Although activists debated how the two presidents stacked up, the comparison itself served a political purpose for UNMM leaders: It held Echeverría accountable to the expectations fostered by Cardenista populism, especially regarding the articulation between gender ideologies and democratic practice.

The comparison does offer some striking parallels.[2] Both administrations began at moments when the regime's legitimacy was on the wane, and both aggressively incorporated (or, put less charitably, co-opted) or repressed dissident groups to shore up their stability. Both pursued policies such as land reform and price supports to improve conditions for rural populations. Both embraced a nationalism that did not entail isolationism but rather situated Mexico as a world leader in promoting a more equitable global distribution of power and

1. Report from March 9, 1973, Archivo General de la Nación (hereafter AGN), Mexico City, Investigaciones Políticas y Sociales (hereafter IPS), box 1152-A, vol. 2, pp. 328–29, 362–63. All translations are my own unless otherwise indicated.

2. Although part of my project here is to trouble the populist label, Cárdenas and Echeverría are the two figures most commonly seen as embodying the first and second waves of Mexican populism.

resources. Cárdenas cooperated with the Mexican Communist Party—the only time in the party's history that it enjoyed such support from the Mexican state—to restructure the ruling party in a way that many on the left saw as the incarnation of the Popular Front, a big-tent strategy to unify leftist organizations in their struggle against fascism (Carr 1992; Olcott 2005). Echeverría, for his part, authored the Carta Echeverría, a foundational document for the UN's 1974 Charter on the Economic Rights and Duties of States, which protected the national sovereignty of all member states and their control over their own resources. Both Cárdenas and Echeverría established their bona fides in this realm by taking controversial positions that antagonized major geopolitical powers. Cárdenas famously nationalized the Mexican petroleum industry, precipitating tensions with the United States and a brief diplomatic break with Britain (Gilly 1994). Echeverría more infamously opposed Zionism—equating it with racism and apartheid—and compared Yasser Arafat to Benito Juárez, precipitating a tourism boycott organized by the U.S. Jewish community and resulting in a humiliating *volte face* the following year (Schmidt 1986).

Among the characteristics that distinguished the Cárdenas and Echeverría administrations from others—and the aspect that made the comparison so apt for the UNMM leaders—was their attention to women's status and, by extension, to gendered representations and practices. Both Cárdenas and Echeverría encountered well-organized, mobilized women's movements based in Mexico City but with sizeable manifestations in other parts of the country, making them important targets for populist incorporation (Lau Jaiven 1987; Olcott 2005). Dominated by educated middle-class women with strong ties to the Communist Party and suspicions of Mexico's political establishment, both movements wove together concerns about political process and everyday practice. Both Cárdenas and Echeverría responded by proposing constitutional amendments to expand women's legal rights: Cárdenas with his unsuccessful effort to reform Article 34 to grant women suffrage and Echeverría with his successful amendment of Article 4—"Man and woman are equals before the law"[3]—establishing the state as a critical agent of women's emancipation.

3. While this amendment may not seem radical, it took effect at the same time that the U.S. feminist movement was losing its battle for passage of the Equal Rights Amendment. As with any legal reform—especially one that emerges from a political calculation rather than a social movement—the extent of the amendment's impact on social and political praxis remains unclear. Neither the scholarship on constitutional reform nor the scholarship on late twentieth-century feminist political activism pays much attention to it. See, for example, Córdova 1989, Barrera Bassols 2000, and Sepúlveda Valle 2000. The legal scholar Mireya Toto Gutiérrez argues that although the amendment was deracinated from feminist organizing, it still marked a "point of departure in the struggle

Such claims of equality, however, provoked intense anxiety among many men and women alike. Official statements of equal rights had to accommodate cultural and social concerns about the annihilation of gender difference as well as practical political concerns about whether women should have separate organizations to represent their interests or simply join existing organizations run by men. Further, whether because of the flapper skirts and bobbed hair of the 1930s or the miniskirts and rock music of the 1970s, the prospect of women's "liberation" conjured the specters of libertinism and lesbianism, corrupting foreign influences that threatened to erode the sanctity of the Mexican home (Zolov 1999; Olcott et al. 2006).

This chapter considers two campaigns that set in relief the gender dynamics of these populist projects as they navigated fraught terrain between claims of equality and difference: Cárdenas's effort to incorporate women into the postrevolutionary polity, and Echeverría's hosting of the UN's 1975 International Women's Year conference. While both of these episodes center on the regimes' stances toward women, the public responses they provoked inevitably reflected concerns about both masculinity and femininity, as debates over women's status fueled anxieties over the most intimate realms of daily life, particularly in such areas as sexuality, household labor, and family relations. Popular groups appealed to state paternalism, and state agents tacked between traditional and modern conceptions of masculinity and femininity. Actors across the political spectrum—from elected officials to everyday activists—drew strategically from these competing gender ideals to take advantage of the opportunities created by the populist aperture.

Mexican Exceptionalism and Populist Politics

Mexico always seems to throw a wrench into discussions of populism, most of which attempt either to periodize the phenomenon—locating the emergence of classic populism in the global economic crisis of 1930s and of neopopulism after the 1982 Latin American debt crisis (Weyland 2001; Leaman 2004; Roberts 2007)—or to enumerate its characteristics. The Mexican case conspicuously defies this periodization, for Echeverría's ascendance predates the onset of

---

for gender equity and initiated a long process of legislative revision and updating [*actualización*] that still demonstrates significant deficits in the federal realm and in state laws" (2002, 402). On the failed suffrage amendment, see Olcott 2005; Cano 2007.

neopopulism. Most scholars of Mexican populism group Echeverría with Cárdenas as a classic populist (e.g., Schmidt 1991; Meyer 1993; Knight 1998; Basurto 1999). Furthermore, the populism of these two men also defies the descriptive definitions. While most populist leaders drew on an urban industrial base, Cárdenas and Echeverría appealed explicitly to the rural masses that had mobilized during the armed struggle of the 1910 revolution. Although Cárdenas certainly possessed a certain kind of appeal, it requires a capacious notion of charisma to accommodate both Cárdenas and Argentina's Juan Perón, and Cárdenas did not demonstrate the adeptness with new communications media that populists such as Perón and Getúlio Vargas exhibited. Whereas some scholars see populism as either the provocation for or the response to military dictatorship, Mexico's worst postrevolutionary episode of repression occurred under Echeverría, and Cárdenas hardly shied away from using force against Catholic rebels in his home state of Michoacán. While Latin American populists purportedly eliminated the political structures that mediated relationships between them and their mass base, Cárdenas devoted much of his presidency to constructing the corporate structures that would foster party loyalty and replace the *caudillismo* and clientelism that threatened the survival of the revolutionary regime. Although Echeverría, buoyed by oil revenues, resorted to significant deficit spending, Cárdenas decidedly did not. And whereas most populist governments came to power with democratic reforms, Mexican populism rode the tide of revolution and waned with the democratic opening.

Confusion only intensifies when we consider the dizzying array of Mexican presidents whom scholars have labeled populists or neopopulists. The roster includes leaders as diverse as the protectionist Cárdenas, the liberal revolutionary leader Francisco Madero, the big spenders of the 1970s Echeverría and José López Portillo (1976–82), and the neoliberal structural adjuster par excellence Carlos Salinas de Gortari (1988–94). Among those who did not succeed in occupying the presidential residency at Los Pinos, the list also, ironically, often includes Cárdenas's son Cuauhtémoc (whom Salinas may or may not have defeated in the 1988 election) and the former Mexico City mayor Andrés Manuel López Obrador (whom Felipe Calderón may or may not have defeated in the 2006 election). With such a wide-ranging lineup, it remains a daunting task to assess the defining characteristics of Mexican populism. In an effort to accommodate this motley array, definitions of populism end up being so elastic that we simply shrug and indicate that, like pornography, we know it when we see it (Laclau 2005a, 3).

To sidestep this analytical difficulty, scholars have offered a host of strategies, most of them divided over whether to assess regimes based on their political approach or their policy outcomes (Viguera 1993). Guillermo Deloya Cobián prefers multiple populisms, while the political scientist David Leaman calls instead for leaning on the adjective "populist" to modify such nouns as nationalism, liberalism, and social democracy (Deloya Cobián 2005, 7; Leaman 2004, 320, 26). The historian Alan Knight has famously suggested that we consider populism a political *style*, but Kurt Weyland cautions us to use the more tangible concept of a political *strategy* (Knight 1998, 226; Weyland 2001, 12). Most of the resulting definitions, however, would apply to one degree or another to every aspiring politician since the advent of mass communications and universal male suffrage (Laclau 2005b, 47–48).

My skepticism about these debates stems from seemingly embedded assumptions about political leaders manipulating the masses. As former Brazilian president Fernando Enrique Cardoso puts it, populist leaders gain support through "manipulation and propaganda rather than deeds and informed opinion when it comes to making use of mass communication. . . . The probability of success is higher if the audience is poor and uneducated and therefore more inclined to accept promises of paradise" (Cardoso 2006, 17). Weyland is less pointed but indicates a similar understanding of "mass" behavior: "A charismatic leader wins broad, diffuse, yet intense support from such a largely unorganized mass by 'representing' people who feel excluded or marginalized from national political life and by promising to rescue them from crises, threats, and enemies" (2001, 14). Political philosopher Slavoj Žižek argues that "populism by definition contains a minimum, an elementary form, of ideological mystification, which is why, although it is effectively a formal frame or matrix of political logic that can be given different political twists . . . it displaces the immanent social antagonism into the antagonism between the unified people and its external enemy, it harbors in the last instance a long-term protofascist tendency" (2006, 557). The expectation, across a range of sympathies and antipathies toward populism, is that this formerly marginal, simple-hearted (if not simpleminded) mass will collaborate in the "routinization" of populist objectives, going along with policies ranging from land reform to structural adjustment and ignoring the political price.

Behind these criticisms lies the assumption that populist politics is more mystified and more cynically motivated than the available alternatives—most pointedly, liberal democracy or revolutionary mobilization (Arditi 2005)—fostering hand-waving dismissals of politicians ranging from Thai prime minister Thaksin Shinawatra, to Venezuelan president Hugo Chávez, to former U.S. president George W. Bush. However, the past ten years of historical scholarship on

Mexico—and I have no reason to believe that Mexicans are any different from other nationalities in this regard—problematizes the assumption of what often amounts to nonelite false consciousness.[4] Although social, economic, and political forms of power clearly remain unequally distributed, those excluded from decision-making circles have generally developed means of working within or around existing structures. In Mexico, where a postrevolutionary populist ethos constrained an increasingly authoritarian corporatist state, nonelites used the corporatist governance structures to claim everything from motorized corn mills and *ejido* plots to political rights and union recognition. Examining the styles and policies of populist regimes offers only a limited sense of how the very people supposedly manipulated by populism actually engaged with it. We must also consider not only the ways in which Cárdenas and Echeverría advanced their own agendas but also how they responded to the discourses and actions of popular actors.[5]

Recent interventions move beyond the definitional debates that dominated earlier scholarship on populism and focus instead on three areas of particular interest for understanding the relationship between gender and populism. First, as the political scientist Francisco Panizza has pointed out, populism "blurs the public-private dividing line and brings into the political realm both individual and collective desires that previously had no place in public life. If the feminist movement shifted the public-private divide by claiming that the personal is political, populism erases it by making the political personal and incorporating into public life issues that were left outside the political realm by hegemonic discourse" (2005, 24). Populism departed from the liberal conception of a masculinized, abstracted political world and entered the realm of what liberals would dub feminized, personalist, and particular (Pateman 1988; Phillips 1991).[6] Second, these scholars insist upon the historical specificity of every populist iteration rather than persisting in the fruitless search for a totalizing or essentialist theory of populism. That is, both strategies (or styles) and policies take

---

4. Gilbert Joseph and Daniel Nugent's collection (1994) on the relationship between state formation and nonelite behavior has encouraged many scholars (myself included) to historicize this relationship so as to understand its complexities.

5. Alan Knight (1994) has argued this point for the Cárdenas period.

6. Although some historians have associated populism with a particularly macho strain of masculinity, that characterization joins many other alleged attributes of populism in failing to apply universally. While Lázaro Cárdenas had served as a general in the revolution, he was a teetotaler and hardly conformed to the caricature of the Mexican macho. Peruvian populist Raúl Haya de la Torre was widely believed to have been homosexual (Pike 1986, 164–65; Mármol and Dalton 1987). Mexican political cartoonists regularly depicted Echeverría as subordinated to his wife, María Esther Zuno de Echeverría (Schmidt 1991, appendix L).

on meaning only within the context of particular political struggles that are informed, in turn, by transnational, national, and local politics. Rather than attempt
to enumerate an exhaustive list of salient characteristics, this approach considers
the ways that populist leaders use narratives and contingent alliances to mobilize marginal or disenfranchised sectors. Finally, the political theorist Ernesto
Laclau (2005a) has shown the usefulness of investigating how the subjects of
populist politics are constituted as political subjects through the articulation,
pursuit, and sometimes denial of demands. This process of defining and insist-
ing upon demands inscribes the political frontier—the us-versus-them ethos—
that most consistently characterizes populism.

The Cárdenas and Echeverría governments both demonstrate the unintended
consequences of populist politics that creates possibilities but ultimately cannot control how political actors exploit them. Most people perceived these two
populist moments not as strategies or styles but as openings, complete with a
sense of both vertigo and opportunity. Particularly for organized groups best
poised to steer debate and to exploit political apertures, it mattered less whether
populist motives were cynical than that the benefits were real. The retention of
populist legitimacy required that the state respond to popular concerns, incorporating them into official agendas.[7] Examining the gender dynamics of populism thus requires particular attention to the push and pull between popular
sentiment and state practice. As popular demands alternate between patronage-
based requests and entitlement-inflected claims, the gendered aspects of populism become particularly pronounced.

"The Small Demands of Daily Life": Cardenismo, Gender, and Citizenship

Although Cárdenas remains in the public imagination the president who best
exemplifies revolutionary ideals, scholars harbor skepticism about his shaping
of gender roles. "Mexico was one of several modernizing nationalist states that
in the 1920s and 1930s adopted policies designed to erode the traditional gender
order and to free women from patriarchal absolutism," explains sociologist Maxine Molyneux. "Through legislation, education, and policies to provide female
employment, Mexico's revolutionary leadership sought to promote the transformation of the 'backward' rural economies. Gender relations therefore became
a matter of state concern as a result of development imperatives rather than the

7. For a similar phenomenon in Argentina, see James 1988.

desire to promote women's emancipation" (2000, 51–52). Cardenismo, like incarnations of corporatist populism elsewhere in Latin America, mobilized women but "sought to guarantee a stable reproduction of gender difference through maintaining sex-typed educational curricula, different employment opportunities, fixed family responsibilities, and standards of sexual behavior" (58). This emphasis on motives, however, elides the possibilities that the Cárdenas government opened up simply by giving considerable attention to issues of women's rights and gender practice. The Cárdenas administration was hardly the first postrevolutionary government to wrestle with gender ideologies and practices. By 1931 changes in Mexican labor and family law allowed relatively easy divorces, granted women greater authority within families, and recognized concubines and children of unmarried parents, and lawmakers actively debated whether to grant women full citizenship rights, including the right to vote.

Opponents of women's political rights trotted out a host of rationalizations for their position. Invoking fears of the Catholic Church's influence, one lawmaker declared, to vigorous applause, "To ask that women be given citizenship rights is a dangerous thing in Mexico because the day that the woman goes so far as obtaining the vote, I think the Archbishop of Mexico would be the President of the Republic."[8] Leaders of the Partido Nacional Revolucionario (National Revolutionary Party, or PNR), including Cárdenas himself, insisted that they could train women to become responsible citizens, pledging in their 1929 constitution "gradually to help and to stimulate the Mexican woman's access to the activities of civic life" (PNR 1929, 3).[9] Nonetheless, observers puzzled over whether women were, as many held, ontologically indisposed to citizenship. "We want to convince the *señoras políticas* [political women]," editorialized the Mexico City daily *Excélsior*, "of the absurdity that they invite upon abandoning the labor appropriate to their sex to deliver themselves to those of the masculine sex. They want to have equal rights with men? How, if nature has not given them the equality they demand? For woman, love is everything in life; for man, it is one incident among many that transpire. They [women] are sentimental by essence; we easily subordinate sentiment to reason and calculation" (April 22, 1933). All of these postures—portraying women as religious zealots, citizens in training, and sentimental sob sisters—conjured an imaginary of masculinity as well as

8. Congreso de los Estados Unidos Mexicanos, *Diario de los debates de la Cámara de Diputados*, 34th legislature, 2d year, no. 24, November 25, 1931, 30–31.

9. The PNR was reorganized in 1938 into the explicitly corporatist Partido de la Revolución Mexicana (PRM), which in turn became the Partido Revolucionario Institucionalizado (PRI) in 1946. The PNR/PRM/PRI dominated Mexican politics from the time of the PNR's creation in 1929 until the presidential victory of Vicente Fox in 2000.

femininity. It did not matter that the vast majority of Catholic insurgents were men, that men could be heard wailing melancholy ballads on any evening in the Plaza Garibaldi, or that by 1930 most girls received the same civic education as boys. If the imagined Mexican woman was pious, emotional, and housebound, the ideal Mexican man was, by implication, secular, rational, and civic-minded. In short, policymakers and public intellectuals alike interpolated Mexican men as exemplars of modernity.

By the 1930s, however, women's political rights had become an important marker of modernity that separated traditional societies from forward-looking ones. In Cárdenas's state-by-state campaign tour—a ploy that hardly seemed necessary, given the certainty of his electoral victory, but one that is frequently cited as evidence of his populist convictions—he repeatedly touted women's rights as part of his modernization program. Two months after taking office, prominent members of his administration participated in a conference on "feminine evolution," one official offering an "exhortation to young men of Mexico to put aside the old prejudices of sexual superiority and help women to elevate themselves to their rightful place" (quoted in *El Nacional*, February 20, 1935).[10]

Although women activists demonstrated a willingness (even an eagerness) to work within party structures, it would be a mistake to read this enthusiasm as a naïve faith in their efficacy. When the PNR granted "working women" the right to vote in party plebiscites, leading suffragists secured a commitment from PNR president Emilio Portes Gil that the category "working women" would include not only factory workers and professionals but also store clerks and housewives (*New York Times*, September 8, 1935). Noted Yucatecan feminist Elvia Carrillo Puerto derided this "passive vote" as "political sweet talk," maintaining that "women have completely different problems from those understood by men" (quoted in *La Prensa*, February 14, 1936). Suffragists picketed Congress and threatened hunger strikes outside the presidential residence at Los Pinos. Others chided the party leadership for its failures to live up to its promises. A group of 157 prominent women activists informed Cárdenas that the PNR's Secretaría de Acción Femenina (Secretariat of Women's Action) "forms an integral part of the [PNR] without satisfying the goals for which it was created" because it remained underfunded. Describing the PNR as an "eminently political party that only airs issues that at bottom have no effective utility," the group argued that "women who need [material resources] for lack of an effective source of aid will resort to prostitution, producing an infinity of painful scenes of miserable

10. *El Nacional* is the ruling party's newspaper.

women that could be remedied."[11] As party leaders contemplated a corporatist reorganization, María del Refugio ("Cuca") García and other Popular Front women wrote even more tartly, "Today we say the following to the PNR: If the new party will contain fundamental vices that mock the will of the popular sectors, from here on out we predict its failure. The mockery of suffrage is corroding the PNR."[12]

We need to read these interventions, however, not only for what they tell us about the regime's shortcomings but also for what they reveal about popular groups' expectations, which were fueled by Cardenista populism. Women's activism coalesced around precisely the chains of demands that Laclau describes as constituting political subjects. "The frustration of an *individual* demand transforms the request into a claim as far as people see themselves as bearers of rights that are not recognized," Laclau contends. "What were requests *within* institutions became claims addressed *to* institutions, and at some stage they became claims *against* the institutional order. When this process has overflowed the institutional apparatuses beyond a certain limit, we start having the people of populism" (2006, 655).

Even more than the possibility of political rights, what characterized Cardenista populism was its commitment to addressing the more immediate, mundane, day-to-day challenges people faced—or, in what Laclau dubs "chains of equivalence," demands for land, schools, potable water, health clinics, and, most emphatically, motorized corn mills. It would be difficult to exaggerate the impact on rural women's lives of the campaign to introduce corn mills; not only did the mills themselves transform women's material conditions, but the campaign instilled a newfound sense of entitlement. *Campesinas* rose before dawn and spent exhausting and tedious hours on their knees, bent over the *metate* (stone grinding tablet). According to historian Arnold Bauer, corn tortillas made up 70 to 75 percent of ordinary people's daily caloric intake by the early twentieth century, giving them "a decreased range of food and, in the case of tortillas, the calories were purchased at the cost of massive inputs of female labor" (Bauer 1990, 9–10; see also Keremitsis 1983; Pilcher 1998).

Thousands of women from throughout Mexico organized themselves into state-sanctioned women's leagues (Ligas Femeniles de Lucha Social) and petitioned and agitated to secure the coveted mills. Groups expressed marked indignation when the government failed to deliver what they increasingly saw as an

---

11. Dolores Magaña et al. to Cárdenas, undated (between May 1936 and March 1938), AGN, Fondo Lázaro Cárdenas del Río (hereafter LCR), file 544/1.

12. María del Refugio García et al. to Cárdenas, February 21, 1938, AGN, LCR, file 544.51/103.

entitlement rather than a boon, and control over the mills became a point of intense conflict within rural communities (Olcott 2005, 146–55). "Before even uttering the phrase 'feminine emancipation' in a town," one Agrarian Department pamphlet explained, "*molinos* must be sent to prevent women from having to prostrate themselves as slaves before the rough *metate*" (Departamento Agrario 1937, 136). In exchange for the mills, the leagues offered state agents a loyal organizing infrastructure that would support other state projects around, for example, education, public health, and temperance.

For *campesinas*, corn mills marked the fulfillment of revolutionary promises to improve their lives—the incarnation of agrarian reform for women. By the end of Cárdenas's *sexenio*, the mechanized corn mills had become the emblem of rural women's emancipation and a focus of women's organizing, and many organizers viewed them as an entitlement. According to the 1940 industrial census, between 1935 and 1940 the number of mechanical corn mills increased from 927 to 6,000 (Bauer 1990, 16).

Agrarian Department organizers and public school teachers, who personified the Cárdenas government in the provinces, repeatedly celebrated the mills as an example of how laborsaving technologies would emancipate peasants and workers and modernize gender relations (see, e.g., Ursúa 1936). Most prominently, the head of the Agrarian Department, Gabino Vázquez, indicated the connections between agrarian reform and postrevolutionary gender roles. The men (*campesinos*) would "forge the spirit of new *ejidatarios,* so that they would be free men who think and work for themselves, who make their *ejidos* prosper, who defend their land, and who respect their homes and dignify the rural family." Woman, armed with her new corn mills, would "give up being a slave" and a "beast only of labor and of pleasure" and would "assume her direct function as mother and element of struggle who participates in acts and assemblies addressing the economic and social issues of the *ejido*" (Vázquez 1937, 37). Agents of the Cardenista state, especially rural schoolteachers and agrarian reformers, celebrated a traditional ideal of womanhood centered on home and family, while situating themselves as modernizers of this femininity through Cardenista policies (Vaughan 2000).

Appealing to the Cardenistas' hybrid concept of traditional and modern femininities, women's organizations insistently took advantage of this opening. One group of fifty-two *campesinas* from the northern town of Estación de Baján, Coahuila, explained that a corn mill would allow them to "abbreviate our housework and allow us to attend more efficaciously to our children, sending them to school with clean clothes and keeping our houses in hygienic conditions."[13] Another group, in the central village of Issac Arriaga, Michoacán, insisted that a mill would improve their children's nutrition, "since they are the future of our Patria."[14] A group of *madres de familia,* concerned that time was running out on Cárdenas's presidency and that "it would be difficult for us to count on another President like you, so good and so generous for the women of the campo," explained that the *metate* absorbed "all our energy and health," which they could otherwise dedicate to their husbands and children.[15] They doubtless calculated that this rhetorical strategy would meet with more success than, say, an appeal based on allowing women more leisure time. But these petitions also reflect the material conditions of most women's lives, in which they expended the vast majority of their time and labor on the unremunerated reproductive or "caring" labors of domestic work, childrearing, caring for elders, and building community networks.

The official support for a modernized patriarchy also allowed women's groups to challenge the not-so-modern patriarchy at home. The Liga Femenil "Nicte-Ha" in Cuncunul, Yucatán, wrote to Cárdenas that they had been "inspired [to request a corn mill] by the extensive revolutionary labor you have developed as the head of the federal government." "Since time immemorial," they explained, "the *campesina* has been the one who has worked hardest in the home, and the man has been very little preoccupied by her improvement and well-being, keeping the woman enslaved all her life in the duties of the home, forgetting that she, too, should be emancipated with her honorable work."[16] Dozens of women in Icacos, Guerrero, wrote to Cárdenas that they had organized themselves, "believing that in unifying our forces we would succeed in achieving emancipation" by "shortening the daily labor of grinding *nixtamal* [lime-treated maize] on a stone."[17] While Cardenista state makers may have seen the mills and other benefits as a paternalist bestowal, in other words, the women themselves claimed these benefits as entitlements earned through their "honorable work," analogous to the benefits men received through agrarian reforms.

13. Tomasa Soto et al. to governor of Coahuila, June 11, 1934, Instituto Estatal de Documentación de Coahuila, box. 1934, file 5-01-1, folder 1, no. 4348.

14. Liga Femenil de Isaac Arriaga to Cárdenas, May 19, 1936, AGN, LCR, file 604.11/64.

15. Madres de Familia de Huerta Grande, Guerrero, August 27, 1939, AGN, LCR, file 136.3/2402.

16. Liga Femenil "Nicte-Ha," August 10, 1937, AGN, LCR, file 136.3/2571. While this petition gives no indication of ethnic self-identification, most of the signatories have indigenous surnames.

17. Frente Unico Pro-Derechos de la Mujer, Icacos, Guerrero, March 14, 1940, AGN, LCR, file 151.1/1592.

Writing in the 1950s, Communist activist Clementina Batalla de Bassols derided this patronage, carping, "The governments, associations, and confessional institutions—under the mask of paternalist help, took special care in making the women's organizations institutions of beneficence, disintegrated organizations, separate from society, from the pueblo. Instead of organizations of struggle, they converted them into associations of very limited aspirations." Rather than incorporate women into the "general struggle for radical agrarian reform," she lamented, state-sponsored women's leagues tried to "distract them with small demands of daily life (such as obtaining a corn mill, sewing machines, and, at most, a school), but that did not convince them to support the better *campesino* struggles of our country."[18]

Batalla de Bassols correctly identified the government's motives in offering these perquisites: Cardenista state agents explicitly understood the distribution of the corn mills as a reward to loyal organizations. Thanking Cárdenas for a recent audience, the secretary-general of the PRM's Women's Coordinating Committee sent him a list of 140 women's leagues slated to receive corn mills because they "should be stimulated for their arduous revolutionary labor."[19] Cárdenas himself exchanged telegrams with his closest advisor, Francisco Múgica, assuring him that he had already given orders to deliver mills to the Michoacán villages of Huecorio and Nocuptzepo "as a stimulus to organize women."[20] The federal government provided explicit guidance about how to petition for mills and sewing machines, establish production cooperatives, and govern these cooperatives. Women's leagues requested these instructions when making their demands, seeking both material support and Cárdenas's imprimatur. They also exceeded these guidelines, using the model of milling cooperatives to establish chicken-farming cooperatives, movie theater cooperatives, and silkworm cooperatives as well.[21]

But Batalla de Bassol's depiction of the women's leagues as duped by populist paternalism into focusing on the "small demands of daily life" grossly underestimates both the material value of these gains and their political implications. Despite the ruling party's conspicuously instrumentalist motives, within the context of Cardenista populism the program also engendered a sense of entitlement

18. AGN, Colección Clementina Batalla de Bassols, vol. 2, file 4, pp. 74–83. Ironically, during the 1930s the Communist Party played an instrumental role in securing corn mills for rural communities.
19. María Guadalupe Sánchez de Rangel to Cárdenas, October 5, 1939, AGN, LCR, file 604.11/121.
20. Múgica to Cárdenas, April 3, 1940; Cárdenas to Múgica, April 5, 1940, AGN, LCR, file 136.3/2936.
21. See, for example, Liga Femenil Josefa Ortiz de Domínguez to Cárdenas, July 6, 1937, AGN, LCR, file 136.3/1223.

not only to the mills but to an array of rights and services ranging from voting rights and land claims to health clinics and child-care facilities. Leagues wrote Cárdenas to remind him that they had not yet received their promised mills. Demanding a mill "to improve our physical and moral conditions, with which no previous authority has ever been concerned," the Unión de Mujeres Revolucionarias explained to Cárdenas, "We come to ensure that the Revolution fulfills its debt that it has contracted with the Pueblo, since other leaders have not understood it."[22] The Unión Femenil "Leona Vicario" similarly insisted that "as an integral part of the Mexican people, with full rights to enjoy the conquests of the Revolution, we have organized ourselves to struggle for our complete liberation." That liberation required, among other things, a corn mill and two sewing machines.[23] In other words, while observers like Batalla de Bassols (and Fernando Enrique Cardoso) saw only a state-run effort to manipulate and contain popular organizing, women involved in these organizations took advantage of such openings to claim what they understood as their rightful revolutionary inheritance.

Programs such as the corn mill distribution took place, of course, within a political context. The decision to devote resources to providing mechanized corn mills to rural women throughout Mexico resulted from several related concerns of the Cárdenas government. First, the intensity of the suffrage struggle by the mid-1930s, combined with the fact that countries throughout the Americas had begun granting women voting rights, convinced Cárdenas of the probability that women would vote by the 1946 presidential election, if not before. Cárdenas pressed hard to grant women full political rights but also took pains to organize and mobilize women within "revolutionary" (i.e., secular and popular) organizations. Cárdenas had governed the Catholic stronghold of Michoacán amid the most violent religious turmoil. He remained convinced that organizing women in state-sponsored leagues would at least mitigate the influence of the Catholic Church and dry up a critical source of its support.[24] As with popular organizations under Juan Perón or Hugo Chávez, however, Cárdenas could not contain the expectations that these women's leagues cultivated. Not only did women come to expect benefits like corn mills as an entitlement rather than as patronage, but they also extended their expectations to a host of other benefits that they understood as due to organized loyal groups under a revolutionary government.

22. Unión de Mujeres Revolucionarias de Acapulco, March 7, 1940, AGN, LCR, file 604.11/95.
23. Unión Femenil "Leona Vicario" to Cárdenas, September 30, 1938, AGN, LCR, file 151.3/1132.
24. On Cárdenas's efforts in Michoacán as a model for his national organizing campaign, see Olcott 2005.

Reconciling the Masculine and the Feminine: Echeverría and International Women's Year

According to political scientist Jorge Basurto, Echeverría sought to emulate Cardenista tactics in implementing his own populist agenda but encountered both a more challenging global context and more consolidated opposition from the business elite (Basurto 1999, 80; see also Hamilton 1982). By some metrics, Echeverría surpassed Cárdenas's populism, at least to the extent that he externalized the enemy, while Cárdenas saw the greatest threats from within, from local *caciques* and Catholic zealotry. And the communications technologies that facilitate populist rule (and the ability of popular audiences to consume those technologies) had certainly matured considerably in the intervening decades. If Cárdenas's efforts to incorporate women harbored the ulterior motives of shoring up the ruling party's control over the postrevolutionary regime, Echeverría seemed to serve the even more personal motivation of serving his own ambition to succeed Kurt Waldheim as secretary-general of the United Nations. After political unrest scuttled plans to hold the UN's International Women's Year (IWY) conference in Bogotá, Echeverría lobbied to host it in Mexico City, pointing to his international leadership in authoring the Carta Echeverría as well as Mexico's strong record in human rights.[25] The IWY conference offered a showcase for Echeverría's brand of populism but once again revealed the limits of state efforts to control popular organizing.

Like Cárdenas, Echeverría came into office amid a small but vocal women's movement with a significant communist faction. By the beginning of Echeverría's *sexenio*, women had voted in three presidential elections but remained at the margins of formal politics. As in the United States and elsewhere, the sexism that permeated New Left movements of the 1968 generation galvanized many women activists to mobilize through women-only organizations (Evans 1980; Lau Jaiven 1987). Much like their U.S. counterparts, Mexican second-wavers came predominantly from the university-educated middle class and participated in the student movements of the late 1960s and early 1970s (Lau Jaiven 1987, 82–83; Lamas 2002, 72). Given the Mexican government's recent history of repression

25. The irony of this claim would not have been lost on the targets of Echeverría's repressive tactics. Secret police records from the IWY conference even include a report confirming a Guerrero woman's story that the Mexican army had occupied her town for three years, detaining, torturing, and raping men, women, and children. AGN, IPS, box 1163-A, vol. 1, pp. 672–73; AGN, Dirección Federal de Seguridad (hereafter DFS), file 100-10-1-75, folder 53, p. 269.

of student organizing, however, feminist activists and government agents viewed each other with suspicion.[26]

The last-minute change of venue for the IWY conference—only in late October 1974 did the organizers express concern about civil unrest in Bogotá—required that the Mexican government act swiftly to prepare for the inauguration of the conference the following June.[27] Echeverría appointed Attorney General Pedro Ojeda Paullada to coordinate the IWY events, giving them a prominent status rarely enjoyed by women activists. The national IWY committee quickly established a press office and arranged logistics not only for the intergovernmental UN conference but also for the parallel NGO tribune, as well as two preconference "encounters"—one for journalists and one on development. In December, Echeverría shepherded through the constitutional amendment granting women equal rights before the law, an achievement doubtless intended to contrast with the U.S. government's failure to amend its own Constitution.

By January the government had produced a glossy monthly tabloid dedicated to publicizing the IWY. The cover of the first issue was dominated by an article on Echeverría's speech inaugurating the year's events, accompanied by a full-color torso shot looking up at the smiling president in three-quarter profile. "Since he was a candidate," the article explained, "the current Head of State has demonstrated a vivid interest in combating any type of social injustice. Now, at the same time that he struggles against other forms of inequality, he has confronted the problem of discrimination against women." The article revealed Echeverría's efforts to define the most salient "women's issues," stressing his commitment to population control to "rescue women from obligatory fertility."[28] Like Cárdenas, Echeverría insisted that the new era would require that notions of both masculinity and femininity be updated. "Mexico and the entire world needs women every day more aware, prepared, responsible, and free, capable of contributing in all social sectors and in all activities, to the construction of a more just future and, thereby, a true peace. But for this to be feasible will also require men capable of eliminating concepts of domination that belong to the past." In an accompanying interview, Ojeda Paullada elaborated that despite

26. For government surveillance reports on feminist groups, see, for example, AGN, IPS, box 1152-A, vol. 2, and box 1157-B, vol. 3; AGN, DFS, file 11-208-71, folder 1, pp. 1, 6.

27. See correspondence in UN Archives, S-0971-0012-05.

28. The IWY conference came on the heels of the UN's 1974 Population Conference, which emphasized population control as critical to economic development. Mexico had experienced a population boom in the preceding decades.

"vigorous national characteristics," Mexico would have to find ways to "recon-cile the masculine and the feminine."[29]

While the official discourse centered on development-related issues—in particular, population control and the incorporation of women into the labor market—women activists, much like their counterparts during the Cárdenas era, sought progress on policies and practices that most immediately affected their lives, often making demands quite distinct from the government's priori-ties. While the IWY conference focused international attention on women's sta-tus, a coalition of left-leaning Mexican women's organizations sponsored a counterconference, offering their own take on the themes of equality, develop-ment, and peace. Official attention to population control opened space for activ-ists to demand legal, state-funded abortion and to express their suspicion of population-control efforts, including involuntary sterilization campaigns in India, the United States, and Puerto Rico. Government efforts to incorporate women into the labor market created an opportunity to discuss women's unpaid labor and to demand the "socialization of domestic labor," including twenty-four-hour public child-care centers as well as public eating and washing facilities.[30]

Even Mexican women activists who disdained the IWY celebrations as the manipulations of an authoritarian regime would later point to 1975 as a water-shed in Mexican feminism (Lau Jaiven 1987; Bartra et al. 2000; Gutiérrez Caste-ñada 2002). The aftermath of the events witnessed the consolidation of two leading feminist organizations as well as the launching of two major feminist magazines, *Revuelta* and *fem*. Between 1976 and 1983 feminists aggressively pur-sued legislation for reproductive rights and sought to establish university-level programs in women's studies. This new climate fostered discussions in Mexico about sexuality in particular. In 1976, *fem* ran a special issue on women's sexu-ality, and in 1977 and 1978, respectively, the first open lesbian organizations, Les-bos and Oikabeth, came onto the scene.

Perhaps most surprisingly—and much to the chagrin of government offi-cials, newspaper editorialists, and leftist women's organizations—the IWY con-ference created space for Mexico's lesbian rights movement. Despite the open hostility toward lesbians of many Mexican feminists, the IWY tribune arguably acted as midwife to Mexico's lesbian rights movement, dragging the issue of women's sexual rights into the arena of public debate (Mogrovejo 2000). In a

29. "Declaración del Presidente Echeverría," *México 75: Año Internacional de la Mujer*, January 1975, 1–2; Blanca Haro, "'Esto es un movimiento de solidaridad humana,' dijo el licenciado Pedro Ojeda Paullada," ibid., 3.

30. AGN, IPS, box 1163-A, vol. 1, pp. 587–90.

standing-room-only session on women's sexuality initiated by participants at the NGO tribune, "participants crowded to the microphones" to express their views about everything from impotence to lesbianism (*El Nacional,* June 24, 1975; *El Universal,* June 24, 1975). While some columnists decried the "pathetic and pathological deviation of lesbianism" and lamented that "some extremists have assumed the exorbitant pretension of converting woman into a *marimacho* [dyke, tomboy], totally repudiating maternity and home," lesbian activists recalled how the episode forced their clandestine movement into public view (*Excélsior,* July 1, 1975). The prominent theater director Nancy Cárdenas "recalled being nearly 'pulled out of the closet' by circumstances [at the IWY tribune] 'which simply surpassed me.' So it was for many lesbians at the time of the Mexico conference" (Bunch and Hinojosa 2000, 6). As the future activist Claudia Hinojosa recalled, "It's true that nobody anticipated that this conference would be converted into the forum for the first public discussion of lesbianism in Mexico. . . . I remember that I observed all those incidents, surprised and confused, from the darkest corners of the closet" (Hinojosa 2002, 175–76).

Cárdenas, disheartened by reports of hostility against lesbians at the IWY, decided to speak up. "They told me that the Communists, my own *compañeras* from earlier in the party, abandoned the conference hall when an Australian girl said, 'I'm a lesbian feminist,'" she explained later in an interview. "They said, 'Throw out the sickos, we're out of here' and abandoned the hall. That seemed to me to give an incomplete image of Mexico, because I was also a leftist militant, was a lesbian, and I had another position and raised my finger" (quoted in Mogrovejo 2000, 67). Cárdenas publicly issued Mexico's first lesbian manifesto, pointing to sexual recognition as a critical form of social liberation, tantamount to struggles against imperialism, apartheid, and racism. "Suddenly, I had forty or fifty reporters around me," she recalled, "like Sophia Loren in Via Appia! I couldn't think. The assault was aggressive: are you a lesbian? Who else is? Why did you agree to come? What does this mean? It was one question after another. I couldn't even answer. The only thing I managed to tell them was: so long as the laws of my country do not offer guarantees for homosexuals, neither I nor anyone can answer your questions" (quoted in Hinojosa 2002, 177). Public discussions about women's sexuality at the IWY provoked countless editorials and cartoons bemoaning the threats to the "national treasure" of Mexican femininity, often eliding lesbianism, feminism, and prostitution and discrediting them as corrupting foreign influences.[31]

---

31. Karen Kampwirth (2003) has found a similar phenomenon in Nicaragua.

Like the Cardenistas, Echeverristas struggled to modernize gender relations without antagonizing popular commitments to such ideals as motherhood and the male breadwinner. First Lady María Esther Zuno de Echeverría, speaking at the inaugural ceremony of an international development conference preceding the UN conference, assured the audience, "Man and woman are not rivals; man and woman do not substitute for one another; man and woman signify unsurpassed complements; man and woman are the very essence of equality, development, and peace" (quoted in *Excélsior,* June 16, 1975). As with the negotiations over corn mills, debates over gender roles had quite tangible implications within the context of 1970s development schemes. Both Marxist dependency theorists and liberal modernization theorists understood the modernization of women's roles to entail their incorporation in the "productive economy." But this emphasis on commodified labor failed to take into account the unpaid labor performed overwhelmingly by women and proposed a dramatic increase in their overall labor burden. Eric Ojala, the director of social and economic policy for the UN's Food and Agriculture Organization, pointed to the "intolerable and colossal waste of human potential that women represent" and argued that the IWY should concentrate on integrating women into agricultural production and rural development (quoted in *El Universal,* June 21, 1975). The Cuban government's recent passage of the "Family Code" underscored the ongoing debates about how modern economies would fulfill reproductive labor needs without exacerbating gender inequalities.

As during the Cárdenas period, the political context of the 1970s defined these debates. By 1975, second-wave feminism had made women's status a critical gauge of modernity and development in different parts of the world, much as women's suffrage had in the 1930s. So long as liberal feminists dominated this agenda, the emphasis remained on issues such as reproductive rights and access to education and employment, but the populist context of these discussions created openings within which more marginal groups could introduce issues such as recognition for lesbians and state support for unpaid reproductive labor. In much the same way that women's expectations had risen with Cárdenas's rhetorical commitment to delivering on revolutionary promises, they also grew with Echeverría's pledge to promote a development strategy that would benefit women.

Ironically, although Cárdenas failed to see through the constitutional reform for women's suffrage and Echeverría succeeded in implementing Mexico's version of an equal rights amendment, it is Cárdenas whom scholars and activists alike remember as the great defender of women's rights. Despite significant historical differences, in both administrations the populist tension between

promoting modernization and honoring traditional cultural practices complicated efforts to shape gender ideologies and promote women's rights. In different ways, Cárdenas and Echeverría both tried to fashion political projects that
would protect women's roles as keepers of cultural tradition and unpaid repro-
ducers of the industrial labor force, while at the same time cultivating Mexico's
image as a forward-looking, modernizing nation.

In the end, however, popular expectations for these populist governments
could not be contained or scripted by state-run programs. Even if we assume, as
many scholars have, that populist leaders act from the basest, most cynical, and
most power-hungry motives, the apertures these governments created yielded
unexpected consequences in terms of popular organizing. Once the Cárdenas
government encouraged women's leagues, women organized and demanded corn
mills and schools. Over time, league members came to see these benefits as an
entitlement the state owed them for their domestic and community labor. Similarly, Echeverría could not discipline women activists to focus on development
that centered on wage labor and population control. Instead, women organized
to demand sexual rights and alleviation of their unpaid labor obligations. In
other words, if we understand populism not only as a state-driven enterprise but
also as an opening for popular organizing, we see a polity that is less tidy and predictable, but also less nefarious, than populism's detractors would have us believe.

References

Arditi, B. 2005. "Populism as an Internal Periphery of Democratic Politics." In *Populism
and the Mirror of Democracy,* ed. F. Panizza, 72–98. London: Verso.
Barrera Bassols, D., ed. 2000. *Mujeres, ciudadanía y poder.* Mexico City: El Colegio de México.
Bartra, E., A. M. Fernández Poncela, and A. Lau. 2000. *Feminismo en México, ayer y hoy.*
Mexico City: Universidad Autónoma Metropolitana.
Basurto, J. 1999. "Populism in Mexico: From Cárdenas to Cuauhtémoc." In *Populism in
Latin America,* ed. M. Conniff, 75–96. Tuscaloosa: University of Alabama Press.
Bauer, A. J. 1990. "Millers and Grinders: Technology and Household Economy in Meso-
America." *Agricultural History* 64 (1): 1–17.
Bunch, C., and C. Hinojosa. 2000. *Lesbians Travel the Roads of Global Feminism.* New
Brunswick: Rutgers University, Center for Women's Global Leadership.
Cano, G. 2007. "Ciudadanía y sufragio femenino: El discurso igualitario de Lázaro Cár-
denas." In *Miradas feministas sobre las mexicanas del siglo XX,* ed. M. Lamas, 151–90.
Mexico City: Fondo de Cultura Económica and Consejo Nacional para la Cultura
y los Artes.
Cardoso, F. E. 2006. "More Than Ideology: The Conflation of Populism with the Left in
Latin America." *Harvard International Review* 28 (2): 14–17.
Carr, B. 1992. *Marxism and Communism in Twentieth-Century Mexico.* Lincoln: Univer-
sity of Nebraska Press.

Córdova, A. 1989. *La nación y la constitución: La lucha por la democracia en México.* Mexico City: Claves Latinoamericanas.

Deloya Cobián, G. 2005. *Perspectivas del populismo en México.* Mexico City: Miguel Ángel Porrúa.

Departamento Agrario. 1937. *¡Despertar Lagunero! Libro que relata la lucha y triunfo de la revolución en la Comarca Lagunera.* Mexico City: Sindicato y el Consejo Técnico de los Trabajadores de los Talleres Gráficos de la Nación.

Evans, S. M. 1980. *Personal Politics: The Roots of Women's Liberation in the Civil Rights Movement and the New Left.* New York: Vintage Books.

Gilly, A. 1994. *El cardenismo, una utopía mexicana.* Mexico City: Cal y Arena.

Gutiérrez Castañeda, G., ed. 2002. *Feminismo en México: Revisión histórico-crítica del siglo que termina.* Mexico City: Universidad Nacional Autónoma de México, Programa Universitario de Estudios de Género.

Hamilton, N. 1982. *The Limits of State Autonomy: Post-Revolutionary Mexico.* Princeton: Princeton University Press.

Hinojosa, C. 2002. "Gritos y susurros: Una historia sobre la presencia pública de las feministas lesbianas." In *Feminismo en México: Revisión histórico-crítica del siglo que termina,* ed. G. Gutiérrez Castañeda, 172–87. Mexico City: Universidad Nacional Autónoma de México, Programa Universitario de Estudios de Género.

James, D. 1988. *Resistance and Integration: Peronism and the Argentine Working Class, 1946–1976.* Cambridge: Cambridge University Press.

Joseph, G. M., and D. Nugent, eds. 1994. *Everyday Forms of State Formation: Revolution and the Negotiation of Rule in Modern Mexico.* Durham: Duke University Press.

Kampwirth, K. 2003. "Arnoldo Alemán Takes on the NGOs: Antifeminism and the New Populism in Nicaragua." *Latin American Politics and Society* 45 (2): 133–58.

Keremitsis, D. 1983. "Del metate al molino: La mujer mexicana de 1910 a 1940." *Historia Mexicana* 130 (2): 285–302.

Knight, A. 1994. "Cardenismo: Juggernaut or Jalopy?" *Journal of Latin American Studies* 26:73–107.

———. 1998. "Populism and Neo-populism in Latin America, Especially Mexico." *Journal of Latin American Studies* 30 (2): 223–48.

Laclau, E. 2005a. *On Populist Reason.* London: Verso.

———. 2005b. "Populism: What's in a Name?" In *Populism and the Mirror of Democracy,* ed. F. Panizza, 32–49. London: Verso.

———. 2006. "Why Constructing a People Is the Main Task of Radical Politics." *Critical Inquiry* 32 (4): 646–80.

Lamas, M. 2002. "Fragmentos de una autocrítica." In *Feminismo en México: Revisión histórico-crítica del siglo que termina,* ed. G. Gutiérrez Castañeda, 71–79. Mexico City: Universidad Nacional Autónoma de México, Programa Universitario de Estudios de Género.

Lau Jaiven, A. 1987. *La nueva ola del feminismo en México: Conciencia y acción de la lucha de mujeres.* Mexico City: Editorial Planta.

Leaman, D. 2004. "Changing Faces of Populism in Latin America: Masks, Makeovers, and Enduring Features." *Latin American Research Review* 39 (3): 312–26.

Mármol, M., and R. Dalton. 1987. *Miguel Mármol.* New York: Curbstone Press.

Meyer, L. 1993. "El presidencialismo: Del populismo al neoliberalismo." *Revista Mexicana de Sociología* 55 (2): 57–81.

Mogrovejo, N. 2000. *Un amor que se atrevió a decir su nombre: La lucha de las lesbianas y su relación con los movimientos homosexual y feminista en América Latina.* Mexico City: Centro de Documentación y Archivo Histórico Lésbico.

Molyneux, M. 2000. "Twentieth-Century State Formations in Latin America." In *Hidden Histories of Gender and the State in Latin America,* ed. E. Dore and M. Molyneux, 33–81. Durham: Duke University Press.

Olcott, J. 2005. *Revolutionary Women in Postrevolutionary Mexico.* Durham: Duke University Press.

Olcott, J., M. K. Vaughn, and G. Cano, eds. 2006. *Sex in Revolution: Gender, Politics, and Power in Modern Mexico.* Durham: Duke University Press.

Panizza, F. 2005. "Introduction: Populism and the Mirror of Democracy." In *Populism and the Mirror of Democracy,* ed. F. Panizza, 1–31. London: Verso.

Partido Nacional Revolucionario (PNR). 1929. *Constitución del P.N.R.* Mexico City: PNR.

Pateman, C. 1988. *The Sexual Contract.* Cambridge: Polity Press.

Phillips, A. 1991. *Engendering Democracy.* University Park: Pennsylvania State University Press.

Pike, F. B. 1986. *The Politics of the Miraculous in Peru: Haya de la Torre and the Spiritualist Tradition.* Lincoln: University of Nebraska Press.

Pilcher, J. M. 1998. *¡Que Vivan los Tamales! Food and the Making of Mexican Identity.* Albuquerque: University of New Mexico Press.

Roberts, K. M. 2007. "Latin America's Populist Revival." *SAIS Review* 27 (1): 3–15.

Schmidt, S. 1986. *El deterioro del presidencialismo mexicano: Los años de Luis Echeverría.* Mexico City: EDAMEX.

———. 1991. *The Deterioration of the Mexican Presidency: The Years of Luis Echeverría.* Trans. Dan A. Cothran. Tucson: University of Arizona Press.

Sepúlveda Valle, C. A., ed. 2000. *Cuestiones constitucionales, 1917–2000.* Guadalajara: Universidad de Guadalajara.

Toto Gutiérrez, M. 2002. "El feminismo en México y su impacto en el discurso jurídico." In *Feminismo en México: Revisión histórico-crítica del siglo que termina,* ed. G. Gutiérrez Castañeda, 401–12. Mexico City: Universidad Nacional Autónoma de México, Programa Universitario de Estudios de Género.

Ursúa, Florencio Encarnación. 1936. "El molino de nixtamal, cuento." *El Maestro Rural,* January 15, 33–36.

Vaughan, M. K. 2000. "Modernizing Patriarchy: State Policies, Rural Households, and Women in Mexico, 1930–1940." In *Hidden Histories of Gender and the State in Latin America,* ed. E. Dore and M. Molyneux, 194–214. Durham: Duke University Press.

Vázquez, G. 1937. *La resolución del problema agrario en la Comarca Lagunera.* Mexico City.

Viguera, A. 1993. "'Populismo' y 'neopopulismo' en América Latina." *Revista Mexicana de Sociología* 55 (3): 49–66.

Weyland, K. 2001. "Clarifying a Contested Concept: Populism in the Study of Latin American Politics." *Comparative Politics* 34 (1): 1–22.

Žižek, S. 2006. "Against the Populist Temptation." *Critical Inquiry* 32 (3): 551–74.

Zolov, E. 1999. *Refried Elvis: The Rise of the Mexican Counterculture.* Berkeley and Los Angeles: University of California Press.

2

CHANGING IMAGES OF MALE AND FEMALE IN ECUADOR

JOSÉ MARÍA VELASCO IBARRA AND ABDALÁ BUCARAM

Ximena Sosa-Buchholz

Classic populism in Ecuador has been influenced by José María Velasco Ibarra, five-time president, who dominated the political arena from the 1930s to the 1970s.[1] While there have been other populist leaders in Ecuador, such as Jaime Roldós (1979–81), Lucio Gutierrez (2003–5), and Rafael Correa (the current president), the short-lived presidency of Abdalá Bucaram (1996–97) marked the beginning of neopopulism in the country. As a neopopulist, Bucaram possessed several characteristics of classic populist leaders, among them his method of appealing directly to common and often excluded people, who now found unity as political actors rather than as isolated individuals (Laclau 2005, 224; Panizza 2005, 3). This style of leadership implicitly divides society into the people, who symbolize the good, and the "other," the established power structure, which represents evil (de la Torre 2000, 15). Such Manichean discourse can be found in both Velasco Ibarra's and Bucaram's campaigns and is designed to mobilize the people, who are united by different sets of demands that are seen to have equal validity. These demands have not been fulfilled by the institutional system but create a widespread identity embodied by a populist leader (Laclau 2005, 74). Populist leaders, often charismatic and personalistic, develop a direct yet hierarchical relationship with the people (Conniff 1982, 1999; Drake 1982; Roberts 1996). The main difference between classic populists and neopopulists is that the latter are neoliberals and promote an agenda of severe economic adjustment, including reductions in government spending, the diminution of state bureaucracy, and the privatization of state enterprises (Roberts 1996, 89; Weyland 1999, 173).

---

1. Velasco Ibarra served five times as president, 1934–35, 1944–47, 1952–56, 1960–61, and 1968–72. This article relies heavily on sources in the Eduardo Lozano Latin American Collection at the University of Pittsburgh, where I was granted a summer research fellowship. All translations are my own unless otherwise indicated.

Ecuador presents an interesting case of the intersection between gender and populism. Women's suffrage, granted in 1929, changed gender relationships by elevating women to equal status in the electoral arena. Unlike other countries in Latin America, Ecuador did not experience a prolonged struggle for women's suffrage, but Ecuadorian women were forced to organize and struggle against efforts to rescind their newly won right. Women's suffrage was instituted by a Liberal government headed by Isidro Ayora, with strong support from the Conservatives. Its first beneficiary was the populist leader José María Velasco Ibarra, in his first democratic presidential election in 1934. Even though literate females were not required to vote until 1968, many women were recruited to vote for Velasco Ibarra. While it cannot be claimed that the female vote was a strong component of his victories, women voters did contribute to Velasco Ibarra's election in 1934, 1952, 1960, and 1968, by organizing women's groups in support of his candidacy. Velasco Ibarra, like other Latin American populist leaders, used political clientelism and "client-ship." While clientelism implies an exchange of goods and services for political favors, client-ship provides not only material benefits but also the possibility of sharing a little power (Taylor 2004, 223). This complex relationship was evident with both sexes at both the community and the personal levels. Both received material benefits (potable water, electricity, and roads) at the communal level. In addition, men were able to get jobs and women, education that could lead to employment.

This chapter explains the changing images of males and females in two historical periods. It concentrates on two major populist leaders, Velasco Ibarra, a classic populist, and Abdalá Bucaram, a neopopulist. It argues three points. First, although both populist leaders appealed to the people, they understood the people in different ways. For Velasco Ibarra, the people represented the literate lower *mestiza* classes (de la Torre 2004, 61). His famous *chusma* (rabble) included artisans, small merchants, small farmers, private and state employees, teachers, bus drivers, and factory workers. The *chusma* excluded the indigenous population because it was illiterate and therefore not eligible to vote. For Bucaram, the people also meant the lower classes, but for him this included the illiterate, because the 1978 constitution introduced universal suffrage. The inclusion of the illiterate expanded not only the breadth of Bucaram's concept of the people but also introduced new demands unique to this previously excluded group. These two conceptions of the people played an important role in the masculine identities of both leaders. Velasco Ibarra embodied a traditional masculine ideal, which the *chusma* wanted to emulate. Bucaram personified the popular[2] masculine ideal, with which the illiterate poor identified. Second, because educated Ecuadorian women already had the right to vote, the relationship between gender and populism was geared toward encouraging female voter turnout. Velasco Ibarra used two strategies to attract the female vote; he encouraged women's education so that they would become eligible to vote, and he promoted women's associations whose goal was to elect him president. These two strategies were linked by Velasco Ibarra's presentation of himself as a Catholic Liberal[3] with the primary goal of renewing the country's morality. This was an image that appealed to both sexes. Bucaram also needed to draw from the newly enfranchised illiterate, who were incredibly poor and were either unemployed or barely employed in the formal or informal sectors. Bucaram appealed to these voters not only by using the popular masculine image but by using his running mate, Rosalia Arteaga, as an image of the unification of classes, regions, and genders. Finally, populism traditionally has been considered a threat to democracy. But, even though they have often become dictators later, most if not all populist and neopopulist leaders have been elected democratically. Velasco Ibarra was elected president four times and appointed by the National Assembly once. He declared himself dictator three times, in 1935, 1945, and 1970, each time, he claimed, in the name of the people.

Bucaram also came to power in a democratic election. His six-month presidency was filled with authoritarian behavior while maintaining a democratic front. His neoliberal policies, including his attempt to peg the country's exchange rate to the dollar, combined with his attempts to appeal to the masses through gifts of material benefits, his constant bypassing of laws, and his political behavior, which included verbal aggression, acquiescence in the plagiarism of the minister of education, and the exclusion of essential groups, provoked a massive backlash that drove him from power.

Historical Background

Velasco Ibarra and Bucaram entered politics by dissimilar routes with different political landscapes. It is useful to understand the differences between the two

2. "Popular" refers here to what are known in Latin America as the *clases populares*, meaning the lower economic classes.

3. Historically, liberalism in Latin America has been identified with anticlericalism. By openly identifying himself with the Catholic Church, Velasco Ibarra was consciously changing the commonly accepted notion of what it meant to be liberal.

eras in which they governed before describing how gender and populism intersected during their terms. Velasco Ibarra began his political career by writing
controversial editorials in *El Comercio,* a major newspaper in Quito. After earning his law degree at the Universidad Central and divorcing his first wife, Esther
Silva,[4] he studied at La Sorbonne in Paris. Even though Velasco Ibarra did not
belong to the Conservative Party, while he was in Europe, this party appointed
him to Congress. Velasco Ibarra was also a critic of the presidential fraud con-
tinually perpetrated by the Liberal Party, which had held power since 1895. In
1933, in one of his first interviews, he declared that "the only possibility of sav-
ing the country was through free and clean presidential elections, with no favor
to any political party" (*El Comercio* [Quito], August 14, 1933). Velasco Ibarra thus
became a new type of political figure, independent of any traditional party.

Velasco Ibarra ran for president six times, losing only once, in 1940. In 1944
he was appointed after the May revolution, or La Gloriosa,[5] against the Liberal
government of Carlos Arroyo del Rio, who not only had won the election by
fraud but contributed to military defeat in a war with Peru, causing Ecuador to
lose half of its territory. Velasco Ibarra represented democracy and the national
unity that had been betrayed by the Liberal government, the symbol of the evil
that needed to be destroyed (de la Torre 2000, 55–56). This Manichean view
contributed to the belief that Velasco Ibarra was the only person who could save
the country. In the words of Pedro Saad, a leftist leader, Velasco Ibarra "was the
battering ram of democracy; without this battering ram we could not have bro-
ken down the walls of Arroyo's despotism" (quoted in Ordenana Trujillo 1984,
59). After La Gloriosa, Velasquismo became consolidated as a political movement headed by this populist leader.

Velasco Ibarra was able to stay in power only once, during his third presidency (1952–56), mainly because of the banana boom. He was overthrown by
the military four times and assumed dictatorial powers three times (the exception was his fourth presidency). Twice he remained dictator for almost two
years, in his second and fifth presidencies. He justified the pattern of assuming
dictatorial powers by claiming that it was necessary "in order to preserve the
country's social justice and peace" (Velasco Ibarra 1970, 598). The most famous
of such statements was made in 1945, when he declared that "the country had

---

4. His divorce did not affect his political career for two reasons. First, he did not draw support
from the mainstream of the Conservative Party, whose members were the most likely to look askance
at a divorced candidate. Second, he campaigned during a period in which private and public lives
were kept separate. Therefore his divorce was not the subject of public discussion.

5. The main coalition behind La Gloriosa was the Alianza Democrática Ecuatoriana, created in
1943. It included conservatives, communists, socialists, and independent liberals.

fallen into chaos and there were rumors of coup plots"; therefore, he said, he was issuing a decree proclaiming the need to protect the country from anarchy. "Confronting the current emergency demands the maintenance of the peace and the security of citizens and families; the government will, through this proposition, have the power to employ all necessary and indispensible means and will not permit any direct or indirect interference with the government's maintenance of order and regularity" (Registro Oficial, March 30, 1946).

Velasco Ibarra formed no political party until his last campaign, in 1968. Becoming the champion of clean and free elections, Velasco Ibarra also expanded his constituency by encouraging those previously excluded from voting to exercise their new right. He repeatedly appealed to the people with the statement "the people know what is good for themselves; they have the right to clean elections and they know who is best suited to govern" (*El Comercio* [Quito], August 16, 1933). In all of his campaigns, Velasco Ibarra was able to recruit a multiclass coalition that included professionals, schoolteachers, merchants, manual laborers, university students, artisans, and bus drivers.[6] While most of these coalitions were formed for electoral purposes, the only one that endured was the Concentración de Fuerzas Populares (CFP).[7] Velasco Ibarra also went into self-imposed exile, mainly to Argentina, the native land of his second wife, Corina Parral. He cultivated the image of the Gran Ausente (Great Absent One), which allowed him to present himself as an outsider who was free from corruption and traditional party ties and therefore best understood the needs of his *chusma*. Many controversial books and articles have argued for and against his authoritarian and demagogic style, which has deepened popular distrust of political parties and encouraged a cult of political personalities. When he died in 1979, Velasquismo died with him, but his enduring public works keep his legacy alive in the minds of many Ecuadorians.[8]

Abdalá Bucaram Ortiz became involved in politics through his work on the campaigns of Carlos Guevara Moreno and his uncle, the congressman and regional populist Assad Bucaram, known as Don Buca. Like Velasco Ibarra, Bucaram is a lawyer; he earned his degree at the Universidad Estatal de Guayaquil. He also has a master's degree in physical education and has won some athletic awards. Unlike Velasco Ibarra, who disapproved of organizing political parties, Bucaram founded the Partido Roldosista Ecuatoriano (PRE) in 1982, almost a

---

6. During his short presidencies, Velasco Ibarra had confrontations with many groups, especially students and workers.

7. The CFP was headed by Carlos Guevara Moreno, another regional populist leader.

8. For more discussion of this point, see Sosa-Buchholz 2006.

year after President Jaime Roldós (1979–81) and his wife and Bucaram's sister Martha died in a plane crash.

After serving as superintendent during Roldós's presidency, Bucaram was elected mayor of Guayaquil in 1984. His difficult relationship with President León Febres Cordero (1984–88), another native of Guayaquil, together with the accusation that he had misappropriated municipal funds, forced him to flee to Panama. After trying twice, in 1988 and 1992, to win the presidency, he finally succeeded in 1996. Bucaram began his neoliberal government by declaring that "privatizations will be accomplished through the sale of concessions, the system of exchange rate control will continue, all debts will be honored, there will be an agreement with the IMF" (*El Comercio* [Quito], August 7, 1996). In order to implement his economic plan, Bucaram relied on two major advisors, Augusto de la Torre and former Argentinean minister of finance Domingo Cavallo. De la Torre was a neoliberal technocrat who had served in the previous government as head of the central bank and was fixated on managing inflation, downsizing the public sector, and renegotiating the foreign debt. Cavallo brought with him the idea of convertibility, a fixed currency pegged to the U.S. dollar. Eager to keep his populist promises, Bucaram created a series of programs that were seen as his attempt to build a cult of personality (ibid., October 5, 1996). He promised to create four hundred thousand houses for low-income citizens, froze the price of cooking gas, distributed free school supplies with his name on them, and produced his famous milk, Abdalact. But these efforts were not enough to keep him in power. His austere economic plan, coupled with his aggressive behavior and accusations of corruption, contributed to his ouster by the people, whose chant was "Leave!" (*¡Que se vaya!*). Like his tenure as mayor, his presidential term did not last long; he remained in power for only six months.

Two Types of the Masculine Ideal

Building on the idea that masculinity is a socially constructed quality that must be demonstrated in such social contexts as the home, the workplace, and all-male associations (Tosh 1994, 184), I argue that Velasco Ibarra and Bucaram created two different types of masculine ideal, both of which attracted followers. Both leaders appealed to the people's emotions. Velasco Ibarra did this in a cerebral fashion and projected an image of a father-protector wise in the ways of the world, while Bucaram's masculine type was more that of the intimidator, someone good to have on your side but dangerous as an enemy. Although both leaders came from middle-class families, Velasco Ibarra belonged to a distinguished family in Quito. His father, Alejandrino Velasco, was one of the first engineers in Ecuador, and his mother, Delia Ibarra, was a descendant of an aide de camp to Simon Bolivar. Bucaram belongs to a lower-middle-class family from Guayaquil. His parents, like many Lebanese in Ecuador, were in the import-export business (Valenzuela 1997, 104). Both Velasco and Bucaram were lawyers, a traditionally masculine profession, although neither of them practiced law. They proved their masculine identities through power and competition in politics (Viveros 2001, 245; Gutman 1997, 397).

They had different perceptions of their masculinity, however (Connell 1995, 205; 2005, 846). They constructed their self-images in different political contexts, but both sought public approval. Velasco Ibarra saw himself as a different kind of political leader, an outsider uncorrupted by either the Liberals or the Conservatives. He represented a traditional masculine ideal because he symbolized higher moral attributes "above political ideologies, parties and programs of government" (de la Torre 2000, 66). While Bucaram was also an outsider, he challenged the traditional masculine model of the politician. Bucaram represented *el pueblo*, the people, but in a different sense than Velasco Ibarra. Bucaram was one of the people. He dressed like, acted like, and had the same tastes as the people; he belonged to the same community that they did (de la Torre 1996, 41). He was the incarnation of the popular masculine ideal. Both men sought validation from the people and found it in their successful presidential campaigns.

Velasco Ibarra also represented a traditional aristocratic masculine type in the way he excluded himself from men's associations such as sport clubs and bars. According to Julio Pazos, an editor of one of Corina Parral's books, the president was known for maintaining a friendly but distant presence at public events. He did not usually stay long at receptions, ate and drank very little, and never danced or smoked (Pazos 2004). Bucaram was the opposite; he represented the popular masculine type. Not only did the president sing and dance but he produced his own CD, *Un Loco que Ama* (A Crazy Man Who Loves), and released it while in office. Because the president believed that sports were a good way to eliminate stress, he was an active participant. His favorite sport was soccer and he became president of Barcelona, the most popular soccer club in Ecuador, while still in office (Sosa-Buchholz 1999, 154). Moreover, he allowed himself to be photographed while sweating and adjusting his gym shorts, dancing with showgirls, and auctioning off his mustache in order to raise money for the poor.[9]

9. De la Torre says he raised $1 million for this cause (2000, 102).

These two masculine ideals attracted different types of voters. From the beginning of his political career, Velasco Ibarra represented clean presidential elections. He broke the tradition of closed-door elections by touring the country. Liberals and Conservatives could no longer elect their candidate without the participation of the rest of the literate constituency. This was the beginning of mass politics, which was consolidated by the May revolution, or La Gloriosa, in 1944, that returned Velasco Ibarra to power as the savior of the country. He gave his followers a sense of being participants by reminding them of their rights as citizens (de la Torre 2000, 36). Bucaram also represented mass politics, but in a more comprehensive sense, because by this time all Ecuadorians were eligible to vote. Like Velasco Ibarra, Bucaram embodied hope. He knew that people had lost faith in traditional politicians. Both leaders exploited people's disillusionment. Nevertheless, Velasco Ibarra campaigned at a time when only the literate (and thus more affluent) were allowed to vote. It was natural, then, that his image as a gentleman would have more appeal. By the time Bucaram ran, however, the illiterate were allowed to vote, and his cruder, more ill-mannered image appealed to those in the lowest economic strata.

In spite of these different types of masculinity, Velasco Ibarra and Bucaram had similar populist characteristics. Both of them used a Manichean discourse that divided the society into the people, who were represented by the populist leader, and the other, that is, the established power structure. At the end of his political career Velasco Ibarra declared that he was the only one who had represented the good in society because he detested electoral fraud, religious sectarianism, administrative corruption, and governmental inaction (Cuvi 1977, 209). Bucaram also equated the established power structure with evil when he described himself as "the whip of the oligarchy" (*El Telegrafo* [Guayaquil], April 1, 1996). When he was overthrown, in 1997, he stated that his "failure represents the failure of the poor" (*Hoy* [Quito], February 3, 1997, quoted in Valenzuela 1997, 109).

Once both populist leaders established that they were fighting against the status quo, the evil, they were able to present themselves as saviors of the country. In 1969, during his last presidential term, Velasco Ibarra reaffirmed his belief that "the nation requires guidance based on a moral context so that we may be saved from chaos. The dangers are many. Now that I am seventy-six years old, I hope I have fulfilled my duty to the people and the state" (Velasco Ibarra 1969). Bucaram shared this belief, claiming that "the governments of the Right have destroyed so much of Ecuador; therefore, Abdalá [Bucaram] is seen as a great hope. This fills me with satisfaction" (*El Universo* [Guayaquil], May 23, 1996).

These two types of masculinity appealed to two different electorates and called forth two distinct types of leader whose presidencies had dissimilar outcomes. Velasco Ibarra, embodying the traditional masculine ideal, enjoyed a continuity, albeit unstable, that allowed him to return to office time after time over a period of twenty-four years. Although Velasco Ibarra was able to continue his political dominance for forty years, his terms were unstable, as he was overthrown four times by the military (Sosa-Buchholz 1999, 144). While he may have lost his office, he never lost the respect of a broad range of Ecuadorian socioeconomic classes, as evidenced by his ability to return to office repeatedly. Bucaram, representing the popular masculine ideal, served as president for six months, from August 1996 to February 1997, before being overthrown by a massive popular demonstration. He had lost the respect of the Ecuadorian electorate, even the illiterate sector, and this resulted in the pronouncement by the Congress of his mental incapacity. To date he has been unable to return to the presidency, or for that matter to the country.

Velasco Ibarra is remembered in the collective memory as the essence of honesty, integrity, and high moral standards (Sosa-Buchholz 2006). One of his followers, Fausto Cordovez Chiriboga, in an interview in September 1995, described him thus: "Velasco frenetically honored his obligations, moral, civic, and patriotic. He could not conceive of the idea of a citizen not making every effort, even sacrifice, to serve the homeland and its people. He was the embodiment of pure honesty and economic disinterest" (SEVI 1995).

Bucaram was seen as the person who helped the poor. For example, a leader from Guasmo, a poor neighborhood in Guayaquil, confessed that he knew that he and his people did not have any possibilities with the right-wing party, the Social Cristianos, so he supported Bucaram because he might give him and his people access to economic resources (de la Torre 1996, 59). Bucaram encouraged such expectations with his statements of support for the poor. "The only thing I can say," he told the press in 1996, "is that I am an antioligarch, antiimperialist, antimonopolist, pro-poor, antirightist man, who does not believe in this dehumanizing neoliberalism" (*Hoy* [Quito], February 9, 1996).[10]

While Velasco Ibarra was seen as a strong father figure, Bucaram embodied a lower-class masculinity and was therefore labeled the "repugnant other" (de la Torre 1996, 17), by whom the upper classes were embarrassed. Velasco Ibarra was an excellent orator and writer. As the author Consuelo Yánez Cossio pointed out, "When he used the radio, it was almost possible to see him, because he

---

10. Despite claiming that he opposed neoliberalism, he in fact pursued neoliberal policies.

dominated the medium. He spoke in order to convince. He knew that radio was unique, that it reached the people, that the people were fundamentally oral, and for Velasco Ibarra the word was still a commitment, a promise, the truth, the norm" (SEVI 1995).

Bucaram was the opposite. Not only his obscene vocabulary but also his poor taste in clothing as well as his expensive but kitschy home represented everything that the higher Ecuadorian classes disdained. For Bucaram and his followers, however, his physical appearance and his belongings signified that Bucaram wanted to communicate with the people. He had in abundance what the *pueblo* had only in small quantities. Violeta Molina, a PRE activist, referred to Bucaram's gold necklaces. He had two hundred and wore them all, while most people might have only one (de la Torre 1996, 27). Subconsciously, people believed that some-day they too could enjoy such abundance.

Populists and Feminists

Velasco Ibarra, as a classic populist, wanted to attract the newly available women's vote. Since his five presidencies were during the first wave of feminists, who were either Liberals or Communists, Velasco Ibarra needed to appeal to women, so he expanded female education and upheld women's right to vote in 1946. Ecuadorian women were the first in Latin America to be granted the right to vote, in 1929, but efforts continued to rescind the right of suffrage. In contrast with the rest of Latin America, after females were given the right to suffrage, feminism basically diminished (González and Kampwirth 2001, 13). Ecuadorian women continued to be visible in two ways. They maintained their tradition of writing, which had begun in the nineteenth century, in order to defend their right to vote (see Handelsman 1978; Sosa-Buchholz 2008). In addition, since the female vote was not legally obligatory, feminists, or Velasquista women, who saw their role as helpers in the electoral campaign needed to persuade literate females to exercise this political right. Velasco Ibarra played a crucial role in attracting female voters. Not only did he expand women's education, but he portrayed females as moral guardians of society (like himself). The expansion of education enlarged the number of women eligible to vote, while simultane-ously changing the class composition of the female electorate from primarily upper class, through the inclusion of upper-middle and middle-class women. This obviously expanded Velasco Ibarra's electoral base.

Once President Carlos Arroyo del Rio was toppled in 1944 and Velasco Ibarra was in power, he upheld the female vote in 1946, in accordance with his liberal principles. As a lawyer, the president believed that women should have the same rights as men and should be treated as equals under the law. "Women must have the same position as men," he said. "There is no legal reason why women should be inferior to men. That is to say, women have the right to vote, to sell their own properties; the married woman has the right to maintain ownership of property that was hers before the marriage, she has the right to buy and sell what she wants. This is a legal fact. To be a congresswoman is quite acceptable" (quoted in Cuvi 1977, 198).

Knowing that educated women were more likely to be treated as equals in fact and not just in law, the president supported the establishment of women's schools. During his five presidencies, Velasco Ibarra built nearly one thousand schools, many of them women's schools, because he believed that education was the foundation of equality.[11] He wanted "to place women in harmony with the legislation that allowed them to vote; women must also be given the opportunity to study, to think and to work" (Velasco Ibarra 1974, 65). His biggest accomplishment was the creation, in 1934, of a lay public school, the Gimnasio Educacional Femenino, which later became the all-girl high school 24 de Mayo. This school was the first to give girls the opportunity to get a high school diploma, which opened the possibility to higher education.[12] In 1952, during his third presidency, Velasco Ibarra oversaw the creation of a new building for 24 de Mayo. In his speech at its opening, he emphasized that women must obtain the same knowledge and develop their intellectual capacity to the same level as men but that their education must also offer them specific preparation appropriate to their sex and their function in life (*El Comercio* [Quito], October 30, 1952). The school thus offered different diplomas for graduates specializing in teaching, secretarial work, accounting assistance, business accounting, nursing, domestic economics, sewing, and textiles or embroidery (ibid., November 15, 1952).

Because of Velasco Ibarra's Catholic beliefs, women's education was linked to the idea of converting women into moral guardians of society, as mentioned above. The president saw education as a means of solving the economic and political crises the country faced. These crises had a common thread: the lack of high moral standards. His immediate solution was to instill morality by his

11. I calculated this number on the basis of presidential speeches.

12. It should be noted that 24 de Mayo was a public school and represents further evidence of Velasco Ibarra's reaching out to middle-class women. As in most societies, Ecuadorian elites tend to be educated in private schools. Before the establishment of 24 de Mayo, females who wanted a high school diploma had to do it in a boys' school and were often discouraged from doing so.

own example, but he saw education as the long-term solution. Women's education was particularly important, he argued, because "women represent above all the sentimental force; [they are] intellectual, . . . a giving power, a generous power, an intensely loving power, a power that is willing to sacrifice" (quoted in Cuvi 1977, 97). Women were Velasco Ibarra's natural moral allies because, as he said in his speech at 24 de Mayo, "in this time of demoralization, women of this school are building the soul of a pure and great homeland" (*El Comercio* [Quito], October 30, 1952).

Velasco Ibarra identified himself as liberal, but Ecuadorian historiography has labeled him a conservative leader (Cuvi 1977; Quintero 1980; Quintero and Silva 1995; Ayala 1996). The president was a liberal Catholic, which meant that he held firm liberal beliefs combined with a strong sense of Catholic morality. For Velasco Ibarra, politics was a chapter of morality, and so both sexes had to be educated in good morals. This was especially true for women, for they were the moral guardians not only of their own children but of the whole society (Lionetti 2001, 222–23; Yeager 2005, 212). Women not only became Velasco Ibarra's allies but reinforced his image as moral savior of the country. Velasquista women saw their role as supporters of the electoral campaigns; they were not interested in further participation in politics. As Judith de Teran, one of his supporters, put it, "We, the Velasquista women, believe that Dr. Velasco is the defender of clean suffrage, of freedom of education and the renewal of morality" (*El Comercio* [Quito], April 7, 1968). Their task was "to be the support, the nourishment, the intermediary between the base and the president" (Rodriguez Castelo 2006, 69).

Just as male supporters of Velasco Ibarra reached out to the male electorate, Velasquista women—mostly schoolteachers or relatives of Velasquista men—organized committees whose only task was to attract female voters. For schoolteachers, Velasco Ibarra represented the possibility of secondary education, which was a prerequisite for university admission. In an interview in March 1995, Elena Cortez, a teacher at 24 de Mayo, spoke for many when she said, "I can only say that Dr. Velasco, with his vast culture, projected a broad future for women, shattering the myth that women belong only in the home and were limited to their family environment" (SEVI 1995). Zoila Yánez de Carrillo, a Velasquista schoolteacher known as *la jefa de la chusma* (the rabble's leader), organized campaign committees, distributed campaign leaflets, and glued posters.

Female relatives of Velasquista men saw their efforts as part of the family's commitment to Velasquismo. Although there was no official female Velasquista party, many campaign committees were created by upper- or upper-middle-class women whose husbands were active Velasquistas. These committees were either of mixed gender or female only. For example, Lola Crespo de Ortiz, the wife of Luis Alfonso Ortiz Bilbao, a friend and follower of Velasco Ibarra, organized a committee in 1960 named after the president's father, Alejandrino Velasco, which was composed of shopkeepers, carpenters, tailors, and people from different social classes from the neighborhood of San Marcos and its environs (SEVI 1995; see also Ortiz Bilbao 1989). Judith Terán de Terán Varea, another Velasquista woman from a conservative family, also married to a collaborator of Velasco Ibarra, organized Velasquista women in her home. Like Lola Crespo, Judith Terán welcomed women from different social classes who were literate and interested in voting.

Some of these women were also crucial in raising funds for Velasco Ibarra's campaigns and for his support during his periods of exile. For example, Victoria Samaniego de Salazar, the daughter of Carlos Samaniego Alvarez, a close friend of the president and his secretary during his fourth term (1960–61), was in charge of selling the president's belongings during his last two periods of exile (1962–68 and 1972–79). In one of his letters the president asked her, "I beg you to sell the painting for the amount that they had offered and sell everything that can be sold. You know that this is the only means of subsistence that I have" (Velasco Ibarra 1962). Victoria herself was also a benefactor. She and her husband, Augusto Salazar, bought three hundred honorific medals given to Velasco Ibarra during various presidential terms.[13]

Some conservative female politicians have argued that the president became an advocate of women's rights thanks to the example of his wife, Corina Parral. Gloria de Carbo, for example, recalled, "The fact that he accepted that his wife worked, which broke with the traditional role of First Ladies, and that he supported her founding of the National Institute of Children and the Family, shows that Dr. Velasco promoted the values and rights of women" (SEVI 1995).[14]

Although Parral was the ideal First Lady and did not intervene in politics, she was conscious that women who wanted to participate in the public sphere needed to be better than men in order to succeed. "For a woman to be part of the public life of a nation," she said, "she has to be very capable. I will also add that she has to be more capable than a man, because if a mediocre man becomes

13. The majority of these medals are in the Velasco Ibarra Museum, where I served as a historical consultant.
14. The Patronato del Niño (National Patronage for Children), later the Instituto Nacional del Niño y la Familia (National Institute of Children and the Family, or INNFA), the main goals of which were to provide services like day care, medical and social assistance, rehabilitation, and medicine, was founded by Corina Parral in 1960, during Velasco Ibarra's fourth presidential term. The Ciudad del Niño was built in 1971, during his final term.

a congressman and he is criticized, nobody is surprised, but if a woman is in the same position, she will be severely attacked" (SEVI 1995). Parral knew that "qualifications or merit . . . are harder for women to gain [because] of a rich variety of informal biases and assumptions that work in favor of men" (Connell 1995, 205). While Velasco Ibarra was not the only Ecuadorian president who worked to incorporate women into the public sphere through education, he was the first, and he set the tone for those who followed.

Before Abdalá Bucaram took office in 1996, the second wave of feminists fought to create a more equal relationship between men and women, in particular by eliminating all forms of discrimination against women and creating a national women's office, the National Council of Women (Consejo Nacional de la Mujer, or CONAMU), during the presidency of the populist Jaime Roldós (1979–81).

Bucaram's presidency inaugurated the participation of women in politics at the national level. Recognizing that feminists had gained ground, Bucaram acknowledged the involvement of women to gain not only their support but also the support of the broader society. He thus appointed women to high-ranking positions in his government, beginning with the selection of Rosalia Arteaga as his vice president. He also appointed the feminist Guadalupe León as labor minister and honored Lorena Bobbitt as a national hero.[15]

Arteaga was the first female to occupy the position of vice president. A lawyer and writer, Arteaga is from Cuenca and belongs to the upper middle class. She entered politics in 1978 but achieved prominence when she resigned as minister of education under Sixto Duran Ballen (1992–96) because he wished to mandate religious education in public schools (Sosa-Buchholz 1999, 154). Her resignation marked Arteaga as a politician with principles. She capitalized on this image to found the short-lived Independent Movement for an Authentic Republic (Movimiento Independiente para una República Auténtica, or MIRA). Knowing that this movement was not strong enough to win the presidential election of 1996, she agreed to run for vice president with Bucaram. "The social arena will be captured through the effort and leadership in education, health, and work by a great woman," Bucaram announced, "a great fighter, Dr. Rosalia Arteaga, the first female vice president in the history of our country" (*El Comercio* [Quito], August 11, 1996). Once in office, however, Arteaga was hardly allowed to participate in the areas that Bucaram had promised she would.

The association between Bucaram and Arteaga represented unification at

15. Lorena Bobbitt became famous in 1993 when she cut off her husband's penis in response to his repeated acts of violence against her.

several levels. First, it symbolized the union between two rival regions that were necessary to win the election. Bucaram represented the coast, and Arteaga, the highlands. Second, it signified a union between two social classes, Arteaga representing the upper middle class and Bucaram, the popular or lower classes. Finally, it cemented Bucaram's concept of masculinity. Bucaram represented a popular masculine ideal of capturing an educated, higher-class woman who knew how to behave. This was evident in the way he conducted his electoral campaign, particularly in the way in which it incorporated dance. Arteaga looked faultless in her clothes, hairstyle, and makeup, whereas Bucaram wore more informal clothes that appealed to lower classes. When Bucaram and Arteaga danced, Bucaram embodied the lower-class male fantasy of seducing an upper-middle-class woman; such a conquest symbolized the ultimate proof of masculinity (de la Torre 1996, 33–34).

In an effort to win the support of feminists, Bucaram nominated Guadalupe León as his labor minister and declared Lorena Bobbitt a national hero, but this strategy did not work. León resigned after four months, and Bobbitt was never seen as a hero. Feminists were not willing to accept female violence against men any more than they would male violence against women. Bucaram's relationship with feminists became even more tense when the Political Directorate of Ecuadorian Women (Coordinadora Política de Mujeres Ecuatorianas, or CPME), founded in 1996, issued a statement explaining why it could not support the president.[16] The CPME objected to Bucaram's appropriation of legal reform proposals by feminist groups, in particular the reform of rape legislation, and condemned the modification of the presidential succession such that Arteaga could not succeed to the presidency. In addition, the group criticized the aggressive behavior of state officials, especially Alfredo Adum, toward women (Lind 2005, 117–18).[17]

Velasco Ibarra and Bucaram both contributed to and reflected changes in gender relations. Both sought to incorporate women into the public sphere as voters. Velasco Ibarra wanted to educate female voters, and he maintained a strong relationship with them by fostering female education as a primary means of renewing the country's morality. Bucaram, like all politicians, also needed

16. The CPME is composed of feminists from political parties, NGOs, and popular women's movements. While it was established to address the political crisis during the Bucaram administration, its two main goals have been to institute a quota for women in politics and to obtain political party status for the women's movement. For more detail, see Lind 2005, 121.

17. One of Adum's more scandalous statements was that the only difference between him and Cro-Magnon man was their dress. Both, he said, would like to drag women by the hair back to their caves and eat them, both literally and figuratively. See Araujo 1997, 56.

female voters, and he attempted to include women in politics both by nominating them and through legislation. But his often vulgar masculine image eventually met with widespread disapproval from men and women alike and contributed to his ouster before the end of his term. Other causes, such as convertibility, labor legislation that weakened workers' rights, and price increases for cooking gas, also played a role.

Populism, Gender, and Democracy

The intersection between populism, gender, and democracy needs to be seen in historical context. Both classic populism and neopopulism are inclusive in terms of gender, but the relationship between populism and democracy is a contested one.

The role of gender in populist politics changes the relationship between the two sexes. The images of males during Velasquismo and Bucaramato stand in contrast to each other. Velasco Ibarra represented a traditional masculine ideal because he appealed to literate constituencies, whereas Bucaram embodied a popular masculine ideal because he needed to attract not only educated voters but also illiterate ones. Nevertheless, politics is still a man's affair, and women are still fighting for their share. Different groups of women became involved in Velasquismo and Bucaramato. Velasquista women were interested in participating in politics to support Velasco Ibarra through the vote. They either formed women's committees to endorse Velasco Ibarra or they worked for the president. Velasquista women saw their involvement as many Latin American feminists did, as a complementary task that did not challenge but understood patriarchal values (Lavrin 2002, 38–39). Women were interested in a system of equality, and this could only be obtained through education with a high component of morality, a perspective that was also advocated by males, including the president.

Women involved in Bucaram's government had predecessors who had participated in politics either in Congress or as ministers.[18] Women participated not only as voters but in political posts as well. Arteaga was the first woman to win executive power at the national level. But even when women win, as in her case, men still find ways to reclaim their domain.[19] Women must thus work

18. Ester del Campo (2005, 1703) estimates that 28.5 percent of positions in Ecuador's government ministries and secretariats were held by women in 1999, the highest percentage in Latin America.

19. Once Bucaram was overthrown in 1997, Congress decided that Rosalia Arteaga was not qualified to become president on the grounds that she was part of Bucaram's government. She was able to stay on as vice president, however, for the unexpired portion of his term.

harder to prove that they can be active participants in politics. Initially, women worked either in grassroots organizations or at other institutional levels. In the case of Bucaram, most feminist organizations were against his policies; it thus seemed to them natural to participate in his overthrow. It is interesting that lower-class women have participated in demonstrations for a leader like Velasco Ibarra, but this was the first time that middle- and upper-class women joined males to oust a populist leader, Bucaram. Women fight in several ways for what they perceive as their rights. The question remains how equal the two sexes are when it comes to the struggle for democratic rights.

It has been argued that populism presents a threat to democracy. In the Ecuadorian case, as we have seen, Velasco Ibarra broke the rules of democracy by declaring himself a dictator in the name of the people, and not once but three times. In tolerating corruption and plagiarism, Bucaram also bypassed the law.[20]

Both men, however, were elected democratically, and both claimed to represent the people. Velasco Ibarra embodied the fight for clean elections, and Bucaram represented the most excluded class of Ecuadorian society, the illiterate. If it is in the nature of populism to advocate for the people, the other, the excluded, then, as Peter Worsley has argued, "populism is profoundly compatible with democracy" (quoted in Panizza 2005, 30; see also Canovan 1981). Moreover, as de la Torre argues, for populists, "democracy is understood as crowd action and mobilization on behalf of a leader rather than as the respect for liberal democratic norms and procedures" (2000, 141). In the Ecuadorian case, the people have been mobilized both for the leader (as in La Gloriosa for Velasco Ibarra) and also against the leader (as in the case of Bucaram).

The will of the people is only one component of democracy. As Mény and Surel note, democracy must be constitutional, as a counterweight to the power of the people. It must institute "enforceable human rights, constitutional courts, territorial and functional division of powers and the autonomy of the central banks" (2002, 10). The problem is that when these constitutional safeguards, and the larger government behind them, are perceived as dysfunctional, as no longer representing the people, the people will find channels through which to express their discontent, which may take the form of populism. Populism is therefore a reminder that democracy is not working, or, as Panizza says (2005, 30), it is the mirror in which democracy is reflected.

---

20. The press discovered that Sandra Correa, the minister of education, had plagiarized her doctoral dissertation, yet Bucaram supported her.

References

Araujo, Diego. 1997. "Adum y Correa: Los rostros del bucaramismo." In *Que se vaya! Crónica del Bucaramato*, ed. Diego Cornejo Menacho, 56–65. Quito: Hoy.

Ayala, Enrique, ed. 1996. *José María Velasco Ibarra: Pensamiento político.* Quito: Banco Central del Ecuador and Corporación Editora Nacional.

Canovan, Margaret. 1981. *Populism.* New York: Harcourt Brace Jovanovich.

Connell, R. W. 1995. *Masculinities.* Berkeley and Los Angeles: University of California Press.

———. 2005. "Hegemonic Masculinity: Rethinking the Concept." *Gender and Society* 19 (6): 829–59.

Conniff, Michael. 1982. "Introduction: Toward a Comparative Definition of Populism." In *Latin American Populism in Comparative Perspective*, ed. Michael Conniff, 3–30. Albuquerque: University of New Mexico Press.

———. 1999. "Introduction." In *Populism in Latin America*, ed. Michael Conniff, 1–21. Tuscaloosa: University of Alabama Press.

Cuvi, Pablo. 1977. *Velasco Ibarra: El último caudillo de la oligarquía.* Quito: Instituto de Investigaciones Económicas.

De la Torre, Carlos. 1996. *Un solo toque: Populismo y cultura política en Ecuador.* Quito: Centro Andino de Acción Popular.

———. 2000. *Populist Seduction in Latin America: The Ecuadorian Experience.* Athens: Ohio University Press.

———. 2004. "Un balance crítico a los debates sobre el nuevo populismo." In *Releer los populismos*, ed. Kurt Weyland et al., 53–78. Quito: Centro Andino de Acción Popular.

Del Campo, Esther. 2005. "Women and Politics in Latin America: Perspectives and Limits of the Institutional Aspects of Women's Political Representation." *Social Forces* 83 (4): 1697–726.

Drake, Paul. 1982. "Conclusion: Requiem for Populism." In *Latin American Populism in Comparative Perspective*, ed. Michael Conniff, 217–45. Albuquerque: University of New Mexico Press.

González, Victoria, and Karen Kampwirth. 2001. "Introduction." In *Radical Women in Latin America: Left and Right*, ed. Victoria González and Karen Kampwirth, 1–28. University Park: Pennsylvania State University Press.

Gutman, Matthew. 1997. "Trafficking in Men: The Anthropology of Masculinity." *Annual Review of Anthropology* 26:385–409.

Handelsman, Michael. 1978. *Amazonas y artistas: Un estudio de la prosa de la mujer ecuatoriana.* Vol 1. Quito: Casa de la Cultura Ecuatoriana.

Laclau, Ernesto. 2005. *On Populist Reason.* London: Verso.

Lavrin, Asunción. 1995. *Women, Feminism, and Social Change in Chile, Uruguay, and Argentina, 1890–1940.* Lincoln: University of Nebraska Press.

———. 2002. "Creating Bonds and Respecting Differences Among Feminists." *Latino(a) Research Review* 5 (1): 37–50.

Lind, Amy. 2005. *Gendered Paradoxes: Women's Movements, State Restructuring, and Global Development in Ecuador.* University Park: Pennsylvania State University Press.

Lionetti, Lucia. 2001. "Ciudadanas utiles para la patria: La educación de las 'hijas del pueblo' en Argentina (1884–1916)." *The Americas* 58 (2): 221–60.

Mény, Yves, and Yves Surel. 2002. "The Constitutive Ambiguity of Populism." In *Democracies and the Populist Challenge,* ed. Yves Mény and Yves Surel, 1–21. New York: Palgrave.

Neira, Mariana. 1995. "Zoila Yánez Gómez de Carrillo: La jefa de la chusma." *Vistazo* 8 (June): 20–23.

Norris, Robert. 2004. *El gran ausente: Biografía de Velasco Ibarra.* Quito: LibriMundi.

Ordeñana Trujillo, José Vicente. 1984. "Un revolución traicionada." In *El 28 de Mayo de 1944: Testimonio,* ed. Rafael Mendoza Aviles, 55–73. Guayaquil: Universidad de Guayaquil Press.

Ortiz Bilbao, Luis Alfonso. 1989. *La historia que yo he vivido: De la guerra de los cuatro días a la dictadura de Páez.* Quito: Corporación Editora.

Panizza, Francisco. 2005. "Introduction: Populism and the Mirror of Democracy." In *Populism and the Mirror of Democracy,* ed. Francisco Panizza, 1–31. London: Verso.

Pazos, Julio. 2004. Interview by author. June.

Quintero, Rafael. 1980. *El mito del populismo.* Quito: FLACSO.

Quintero, Rafael, and Erika Silva. 1995. *Ecuador: Una nación en ciernes.* Quito: Editorial Universitaria.

Registro Oficial (Administración del Sr. Dr. Dn. José María Velasco Ibarra, Presidente Constitucional de la República), Quito, March 30, 1946.

Roberts, Kenneth. 1996. "Neoliberalism and the Transformation of Populism in Latin America: The Peruvian Case." *World Politics* 48 (1): 82–116.

Rodriguez Castelo, Ruby. 2006. *La participación de la mujer en el Ecuador.* Quito: Identidad.

Sociedad de Estudios Velasco Ibarra (SEVI). 1995. *José María Velasco Ibarra: La historia de un pueblo.* Compact disc. Interviews with various people about Velasco Ibarra. Quito: Sociedad de Estudios Velasco Ibarra.

Sosa-Buchholz, Ximena. 1999. "The Strange Career of Populism in Ecuador." In *Populism in Latin America,* ed. Michael Conniff, 138–56. Tuscaloosa: University of Alabama Press.

———. 2006. "La memoria colectiva de Velasco Ibarra y su legado en la cultura política." In *Estudios ecuatorianos: Un aporte a la discusión,* ed. Ximena Sosa-Buchholz and William Waters, 79–102. Quito: FLACSO/Abya Yala.

———. 2008. "Mujeres, esfera pública y populismo en Brasil, Argentina y Ecuador, 1870–1960." *Procesos: Revista Ecuatoriana de Historia* 27 (1): 81–105.

Taylor, Lucy. 2004. "Client-ship and Citizenship in Latin America." *Bulletin of Latin American Research* 23 (2): 213–27.

Tosh, John. 1994. "What Should Historians Do with Masculinity? Reflections on Nineteenth-Century Britain." *History Workshop Journal* 38:179–202.

Valenzuela, Oscar. 1997. *Mi lengua me boto.* Quito: Abya Yala.

Velasco Ibarra, José María. 1962. Velasco Ibarra to Victoria Samaniego, Memorial Velasco Ibarra, Pontificia Universidad Católica del Ecuador, September 28.

———. 1969. Interview by Xavier Benedetti, *El Universo* [Guayaquil], December 19, reprinted in *La Hora* [Quito], March 22, 1993, 53–56.

———. 1970. "Proclama pronunciada el 22 de Junio [1970] al asumir los plenos poderes: Mensajes Presidenciales." In *Obras Completas,* ed. Juan Velasco Espinosa, 597–99. Quito: Ediciones Lexigrama.

———. 1974. "La mujer francesa." Originally published 1931. In *Impresiones al pasar,* in *Obras Completas,* ed. Juan Velasco Espinosa, 63–65. Quito: Ediciones Lexigrama.

Viveros Vigoya, Mara. 2001. "Contemporary Latin America Perspectives on Masculinity." *Men and Masculinities* 3 (3): 237–60.

Weyland, Kurt. 1999. "Populism in the Age of Neoliberalism." In *Populism in Latin America,* ed. Michael Conniff, 172–90. Tuscaloosa: University of Alabama Press.

Yeager, Gertrude. 2005. "Religion, Gender, Ideology, and Training of Female Public Elementary School Teachers in Nineteenth-Century Chile." *The Americas* 62 (2): 209–43.

3

GENDER, CLIENTELISTIC POPULISM, AND MEMORY

SOMOCISTA AND NEO-SOMOCISTA WOMEN'S
NARRATIVES IN LIBERAL NICARAGUA

Victoria González-Rivera

General [Somoza] . . . by pulling us from the shadows, you have situated us in front of the light.
—*Olga Núñez de Saballos, Somocista leader, February 20, 1956*

For me, a president must get close to his people, and Tacho Viejo [Anastasio Somoza García]
knew how to get to the people and share with them.
—*Mary Coco Maltez de Callejas, former Somocista leader, May 2007*

In 1990 the unexpected happened in Nicaragua: The leftist Sandinista National Liberation Front (FSLN), which had come to power in 1979 as the result of an armed insurrection, peacefully gave up power in light of its electoral loss at the polls.[1] Violeta Barrios de Chamorro, the candidate backed by the U.S. government, won the election and went on to serve for six years as Nicaragua's first woman president. Although Chamorro had opposed the right-wing Somoza dictatorship overthrown by the Sandinista revolution, many Somoza supporters, both men and women, who had fled the country after the revolution began to return to Nicaragua after 1990. By the mid-1990s many Nicaraguans were speaking openly of their support for the former dictators and for the Somozas' Nationalist Liberal Party (Partido Liberal Nacionalista, or PLN).

This chapter addresses the life stories and memories of women who identified

An earlier (and shorter) version of this chapter was published in Spanish in *Mujeres, género e historia en América Central durante los siglos XVIII, XIX y XX*, ed. Eugenia Rodríguez Sáenz (San José, Costa Rica: Unifem y Plumsock, 2002).

1. The first epigraph to this chapter is from a speech by the president of the Ala Femenina honoring Anastasio Somoza García on February 20, 1956, quoted in Baltodano Marcenaro 2008. The second epigraph is from Ramos 2007, 2. All translations are my own unless otherwise indicated.

as Somocistas in the postrevolutionary (post-1979) period, before the FSLN's return to power in 2006. I also address the narratives of "neo-Somocista" women, working-class women who were teenagers in the late 1970s and who, in the late 1990s and the early years of the twenty-first century, with the resurgence of Liberalism in Nicaragua, claimed they were Somocistas even though they had only recently become involved in Liberal Party politics.[2]

Historical Background

The Liberal and Conservative parties that arose in the postindependence (post-1821) period came to dominate Nicaraguan politics for most of the next two centuries. Conservatives ruled Nicaragua from 1857 to 1893 and from 1910 to 1926. Liberals governed the country from 1893 to 1909 and later on between 1933 and 1979. For much of the nineteenth and twentieth centuries Nicaragua was plagued by civil wars between these two parties. While the differences between Liberals and Conservatives on some issues were miniscule, they did diverge significantly on some important issues. The Liberals, for instance, as early as 1837 wanted women to be "enlightened" members of an ever-changing secular society, according to the *Aurora de Nicaragua,* a León newspaper. Conservatives, by contrast, believed that women's lot, like men's, was enriched by religion, tradition, and stability. The Conservative Party's slogan in the 1910s was "God, Order, and Justice" (Walter 1993, 20).

In addition to internal strife, Nicaraguans dealt with several periods of military occupation by the U.S. Marines (1909, 1912–25, 1926–33). Before their departure in 1933, the Marines created and trained a National Guard to replace the local partisan armies. Anastasio Somoza García, a Nicaraguan loyal to the United States, was named head of the new military/police force. With the National Guard under his command, Somoza took control of the Nicaraguan government in 1936 and ruled the nation until his assassination, in 1956, by a twenty-seven-year-old poet.

Anastasio Somoza García, a Liberal and a fierce anticommunist, had the full support of the United States during his twenty-year reign. His two sons, Luis Somoza Debayle and Anastasio Somoza Debayle, followed in their father's footsteps and also became U.S.-backed dictators. Luis died of a heart attack in 1967, and Anastasio Somoza Debayle ruled Nicaragua from 1966 through 1979.

2. Presumably there were also middle-class women of this age group who can be classified as neo-Somocistas, but I did not come across any of these women in my fieldwork.

The Somozas were violent and corrupt. They also were heirs to the Liberal tradition, which had heralded women's rights since the mid-nineteenth century. Moreover, the Somozas fit the populist mold, which has been characterized as one that includes personalistic and paternalistic leadership, multiclass support, top-down politics, an amorphous yet antielitist ideology, and clientelism (Roberts 1995, 88).

Somocismo started to unravel in the aftermath of the 1972 earthquake that left most of Managua, the capital, in shambles. The rampant corruption in the earthquake relief efforts exposed the regime's flaws to many who had previously supported the dictatorship. As unemployment soared and society became increasingly militarized in response to uprisings by leftist guerrillas, it became more and more difficult to tout the regime's biggest achievements: Nicaragua's modernization and the growth of the middle class.

The 1979 left-wing Sandinista revolution that ended the right-wing Somoza dictatorship of more than four decades was supported by the vast majority of the Nicaraguan population, including a huge majority of women, many of whom were politically active in the armed insurrection that toppled Nicaragua's last dictator. This fact led many outside the country to believe that few Nicaraguans had supported the dictatorship over the course of its years in power and that Nicaraguan women became politically active for the first time in the revolutionary struggle. Moreover, the level of violence that characterized the dictatorship's final years led many to believe that the Somozas had governed only through terror. This was not the case at all.

Historian Jeffrey L. Gould argues that the Somozas at points embraced populism, and that "peasant activists engaged politically and ideologically with Somocista populism."[3] I have argued elsewhere that urban Nicaraguan women have been politically active in traditional politics at least since the nineteenth century and that, as a group, like the urban workers and peasants Gould describes, they too "shaped and transformed" Somocista populism (González 2001, 55). From the mid-1950s through the early 1970s, women were involved at every level of Somocismo except the highest one, which was reserved for the Somozas themselves. They helped shape, transform, *and create* Somocismo, working especially hard to win over other women through populist rhetoric and clientelistic promises.

Somocista women were organized primarily in the nonfeminist Ala Femenina del Partido Liberal Nacionalista, the women's wing of the Nationalist Liberal

3. See http://www.iub.edu/~lahist/index.php?page=gould (accessed January 6, 2010). See also Gould 1990.

Party. This group, the largest and most influential Liberal women's group under the Somozas, actively incorporated women into Somocista politics and into the workplace. For these women, Somocismo was synonymous with clientelism and populism.

The Somozas, like other classic populists, "promised inclusion without revolution, an inclusion that was material as well as symbolic" (Kampwirth 2003, 1). Somocista women as a group probably took the greatest advantage of this inclusion for the longest period of time, and they achieved some real gains: the vote, urban women's massive entrance into the workforce, and middle-class women's election to political posts. In turn, women's support for the dictatorship gave it much needed credibility.

Urban Somocista women of all social classes became particularly active within Somocista populism as client-citizens after the Somozas co-opted the independent feminist movement of the 1940s and women won the right to vote in 1955. Somocista women's roles as client-citizens solidified as the state hired thousands of women to staff the expansion of social services that accompanied Nicaragua's economic and social modernization. Although men also played a role as client-citizens within Somocista populism, their experiences differed from those of women.

Somocista populism depended on the co-optation of political movements made up of peasants, urban workers, and feminists, and rested on clientelism, understood as "a system of patron-broker-client ties and networks that dominate a society's politics and government" (Kettering 1988, 419). Moreover, Somocista populism was inexorably gendered and classed. In particular, the high percentage of female-headed urban households in Nicaragua (approximately 30 percent throughout the second half of the twentieth century) (González 2002)[4] shaped the way in which Somocismo intersected with gender and class inequalities.

Many working-class and lower-middle-class women became Somocista client-citizens in order to fulfill their economic obligations as single mothers. In other words, they supported the Somozas and voted for them in exchange for jobs and goods. These single mothers worked within a long-standing societal consensus that held that, for single mothers, working for wages was in fact good mothering.[5] Since the best and sometimes only way to get a job was through participation in a Somocista political organization like the Ala Femenina, the

---

4. For more on female-headed households in Nicaragua, see also "Nicaragua, Just the Facts: A Poor Country, Part I," http://www.envio.org.ni/articulo/2838; and Dore 1997.

5. Linda J. Seligmann, among others, has noted that "in many societies [women's] work is not conceptualized as physical caretaking, but rather as the economic maintenance of children" (2001, 3).

line between employment and political participation was often blurred. Becoming a Somocista or pretending to be one was often the only way in which a poor woman could fulfill her mothering obligations.

While most working-class and lower-middle-class men also worked to support their families, they sought employment as men, whether or not they were supporting children financially. For men, the link was between masculinity and employment, not fatherhood and employment. In fact, the low rates of child support on the part of noncustodial fathers contributed to the high number of female heads of household in the workforce. Surprisingly, perhaps, the Somozas, while seemingly concerned, did not actively seek to lower the number of female heads of households in Nicaragua so that more women could stay at home and take care of their own children. Instead, they sought to provide jobs for the women who needed them in order to support their children. In a 1966 speech to the town of Masaya, Anastasio Somoza Debayle told the crowd, "I am determined to . . . assist [women] so that they can work and help sustain their homes economically, and in that way help aggrandize the home and the homeland" (. . . *hacia la meta*, n.d., 35, 36).

The Somozas also offered jobs and political participation to middle-class women who did not have families to support (women who could depend financially on their husbands, and unmarried women without children). The pressures these women confronted were different from those of their working-class counterparts. Many Somocista women leaders who held high positions within the Somoza administration were born in the 1920s and came from middle-class backgrounds. They were part of the generation of "firsts" in Nicaragua: They were the first women attorneys, the first women pharmacists, the first women mayors, and so on. Given their pioneer status, many felt social pressure to choose between a family and a high-level career in politics. Faced with that choice, a large percentage remained single and childless. Maritza Zeledón, for instance, an Ala leader, believed that ideally "women should get married and have children." But she had a hard time meeting a man who would support her political and professional aspirations: "The boyfriends I had wanted me to stop studying." Additionally, Zeledón was unable to find a man "who knew more" than she did, another social expectation. In the end, Zeledón never married or had children, but her professional and political career flourished.[6]

Once they were employed and thus became integrated into Somocista populist clientelism, women's experiences, regardless of their class background, were

6. In order to protect my informants, I have used pseudonyms.

different from those of men. Working women—mothers or not—had to deal with the long-standing stigma attached to women in public life, a stigma not applied to working men. Working women had to worry constantly about their sexual reputations. One Ala leader told me, "I always had to be careful so that I wouldn't be slandered." None of the men I interviewed expressed this concern.

Somocista and Neo-Somocista Women: Heretical and Distributional Memories of Dictatorship in the Postrevolutionary Years

Based on archival research and on dozens of oral interviews I conducted between 1994 and 2006 with female and male supporters of the Somoza regime, I argue that Somocista women simultaneously support and subvert the official stories of Somocismo in their narratives. It is necessary to speak of official stories in the plural because there are at least two official versions of Somocismo: the one promoted by the Somozas before 1979 and the one promoted by Liberals in Nicaragua after they returned to power in 1996. Additionally, I contend that Somocismo, like Peronism, is remembered in "heretical" and "distributional" terms (Auyero 2001, 186, 187).

In his study of contemporary Peronism in Argentina, Javier Auyero notes that "to be a Peronist means, and has always meant, many different and competing things. . . . These different meanings are anchored in different relational settings, entailing diverse narratives and memories." Auyero goes on to argue that "in ideal-typical terms, there are not one but two memories of Peronism. On the one hand, the *heretical memory* narrates the history of Peronism in terms of social justice. The *distributional memory,* on the other hand, narrates the history of Peronism in terms of 'what we got from the government.' . . . These different memories and narratives are neither clear-cut nor mutually exclusive: the difference is mainly a matter of emphasis within a master narrative of Peronism as a 'wonderful time'" (2001, 186, 187).

Auyero's analysis is very useful in my study of the Somozas. The emphasis on progress, equality, and modernization, as well as on social justice and the rise of the middle class, constitutes the basis for the heretical memories of my informants. The distribution of goods, services, and jobs is emphasized in the distributional memories.

The heretical memories of Somocismo are those that focus on the Somozas' nineteenth-century Liberal heritage and the (largely unmet) ideals of progress, equality, and modernization embedded in that heritage. The distributional memories are those that focus on the clientelistic aspects of the dictatorship. These memories are crucial to the depiction of Somocismo as a populist praxis that can be resurrected. In turn, the portrayal of the Somozas as populists fuels the ongoing nostalgia for them.

Although heretical and distributional stories were sometimes told by the same person, an informant's class background, her position within the dictatorship, and her current economic situation greatly affected which aspect of Somocismo she emphasized. Working-class Somocista "clients" and neo-Somocistas tended to emphasize the distributional aspects of the dictatorship. By contrast, middle-class Somocista leaders, the "patrons" in the clientelistic pyramid, like middle-class Somocista men, generally focused on the heretical aspects of Somocismo.

Organizationally, the rest of this chapter is divided into five sections. The first summarizes an extensive interview I conducted with Antonia Rodríguez, a middle-class Somocista national leader. Her narrative is important, for it demonstrates how Somocista women's lives intersected with the official history of Somocista populist Liberalism promoted in the 1950s, '60s, and '70s. The second section tells the story of Rosa Alvarez, a seamstress who was a grassroots Somocista leader. Alvarez's narrative reveals the ways in which Liberalism was masculinized under the Liberal administrations of the neopopulist Arnoldo Alemán, elected in 1996 and in power between 1997 and 2002, and Enrique Bolaños, in power from 2002 through 2006. It also demonstrates the importance that "distributional" memories have for working-class Somocista women. The third section describes my encounter with neo-Somocista women. These women's narratives demonstrate the existence of a new official history of Somocismo, one that ignores the political participation of women before 1979. The fourth section deals with market women and the new Liberal women's movement that arose with the Liberals' return to power in 1996. While this new movement included neo-Somocistas and non-Somocista Liberals (a small but significant group that identifies as Liberal but not as Somocista), it excluded, for the most part, women who had been Somocista leaders before 1979. The final section addresses in greater detail the ways in which Somocista populism is remembered by Somocista Nicaraguans today.

This study gives readers an in-depth picture of women's roles under the Somozas and their roles in right-wing Liberal Nicaraguan politics after Conservative president Violeta Chamorro's son-in-law Antonio Lacayo and FSLN general secretary Daniel Ortega were defeated at the polls by the Liberal Arnoldo Alemán in 1996. The Liberals' return to power after a seventeen-year absence was unexpected by many anti-Somocistas, who had fought against the Somozas precisely to prevent this from happening. It was, however, a welcomed change by those who voted for Alemán, although, as this chapter explains, many did so expecting something different.

I do not address what happened to gender relations within Liberalism after 2006, when a pact signed between Daniel Ortega, Nicaragua's former Sandinista president, and Arnoldo Alemán, former president and convicted felon (he was convicted of stealing one hundred million dollars from state coffers), paved the way for Ortega's re-election that year. The pact proposed amendments to the constitution and the electoral law that effectively divided government posts, and thus political power, between the FSLN and the Liberal Constitutionalist Party, the heir of Somocista Liberalism (Hoyt 2004). The constitutional changes and the changes in the electoral law led to the sharing of power between the FSLN and the Liberal Right, making it possible for Ortega to win the 2006 elections with only 38 percent of the popular vote.

An Ala Leader: Antonia Rodríguez's Story

Between 1994 and 1999 I interviewed seven Somocista leaders who had great political visibility at the national level before 1979. Three of these women were co-founders of the Ala Femenina del Partido Liberal Nacionalista, the women's wing of the Somozas' Liberal Party. The other four leaders also participated in the Ala, but they did not occupy the highest posts. Antonia Rodríguez belongs to the latter group.

Rodríguez is unique because she never fled Nicaragua in response to the Sandinista revolution, nor was her house confiscated. Instead, she remained at her nonpartisan yet high-level government post after the revolution and worked for the new administration until her retirement. Her story is important not because it departs from the other leaders' stories but because it is so similar. All of these women's stories fall back on and intersect with the official story of the rise of Liberalism in twentieth-century Nicaragua, a story very much about "the people" and about women's work, a theme central to Somocista populism.

Certain themes stand out in the stories of Somocista women leaders as well as in the first official history of Somocista Liberalism. Hard work, for instance, is a constant in female Somocista leaders' stories, as is women's work and the intersection between larger political events and family life. As a group, the women I interviewed did well financially under the Somozas, and their families appreciated the relative peace that prevailed in the aftermath of Anastasio Somoza García's assassination of the anti-imperialist hero Augusto C. Sandino in 1934.

In the extensive interview I conducted with Antonia Rodríguez, she shared her family history with me. Rodríguez was a first-generation university graduate and came from a family that had been able to make the transition from working-class to middle-class status. Her maternal grandfather had been a bricklayer and her maternal grandmother sold homemade soap for a living: "She made soap with one of her sons . . . in the yard." Her grandmother's family also sold *mondongo* (tripe soup) in the market. "I don't remember much about my grandmother, but I know that she was thin, tall, very active, very friendly. I've been told she knew all sorts of things, how to make things. She was always trying to improve her [economic] situation."

Politics, economics, and family are intertwined in Rodríguez's life story: "My grandfather went off to fight in Mena's war, on the Atlantic coast [in the early twentieth century] and got lost over there. . . . My grandmother's oldest brother went to look for him . . . until he found him. . . . He had stayed on the Atlantic coast. At that time my grandmother was pregnant and gave birth in his absence. My grandmother then died during Chamorro's war. She died in the Chinandega fire."

Rodríguez's paternal grandfather had been "a very distinguished gentleman, and the entire town respected him a lot. He was . . . very fond of the church and all that." He died when Rodríguez's father was about fourteen years old. "Then my grandmother, widowed, with two sons, and poor . . . took her two sons to León. In León she put them in school and got them to learn a trade. My grandmother [meanwhile] sold clay pots in the market."

Rodríguez's father became a musician at an early age, and her mother earned a living as a seamstress. "My dad earned sixty *centavos* playing at the church. And a dozen bananas cost five *centavos*. So my mom said to him [in order to alleviate our poverty], 'the day I have some money, I will open up a store.'" A priest then helped her get a loan.

> That is how my mom's store started, buying vegetables, bananas, pieces of cheese, and things like that. My father says that he was embarrassed when my mom opened the store [because it was so small]. My mom was the one in charge of the store. She loved business.
>
> Politically speaking, all [of my family members] were Liberal. I've been told that during the war in [the late 1920s], Aunt Heriberta would carry pistols in her basket under the soap she took to market to sell. They were

obsessed Liberals. All of them. All of them. All of them. On the other hand, since they lived in León, there were no Conservatives around.

My mother was very liberal and so was my dad. So, when they moved to the central highlands during the war with Sandino and Moncada in 1926, my poor father had to hide because the Conservatives forced people to display green flags. My father [also] hid because the Conservatives would stop by my mother's store, which was very small, and asked for everything: "Give us vegetables for the troops' soup, give us such and such a thing." And since the Conservatives were backed by the Yankees. . . . Yes, young lady, that is the way it happened. That is the way history is written.

Eventually, Rodríguez became the first person in her family to obtain a university degree. She then left her hometown and moved to the capital in search of employment. She was successful in her field and eventually secured a high-level post in the ministry where she worked.

Rodríguez's story sounds similar to the one Anastasio Somoza Debayle himself told in his campaign speeches during the 1960s. Certain themes are stressed: women's work, women's suffering, childbearing in difficult circumstances, and husbands being persecuted by the Conservatives. "My grandfather, Luis H. Debayle, told me how, a few days before my mother was about to give birth to me, the Conservatives broke into my family's home at night and took my father away to kill him. If it had not been for his schoolmates [they would have done so]. . . . My mother gave birth to me without the assistance of my grandfather [who was a very famous medical doctor] or a midwife, which almost caused her death and mine" (. . . hacia la meta, n.d., 88).

Generational and regional commonalities are two important themes in both Rodríguez's and Somoza Debayle's stories. Born a year apart, both believed they were part of the generation that was reaping the benefits of Liberalism. Moreover, although they lived in Managua, they identified as Leoneses, which made them true Liberals, for the city of León was considered "the cradle of Liberalism" in Nicaragua. In the speech quoted above, Somoza noted, "I, along with all other men of my age in Nicaragua, and especially those of León, owe a debt to all Liberal heroes. . . . We owe those men the peace, the tranquility, and the high level of socioeconomic development that our nation has achieved and will achieve with the revolutionary ideals of the Nationalist Liberal Party" (88).

Antonia Rodríguez's life coincided in many important respects with this first official version of Somocista Liberalism. Many Nicaraguans of Anastasio and Luis Somoza Debayle's generation could relate on a personal level to the

Somocista discourse, and the Somozas knew this. That the Somozas and their followers—particularly Ala leaders—believed they had life stories in common explains in part why Somocismo made sense to those who supported the dictatorship. It also helps to explain its populist appeal.

A Grassroots Somocista Leader: Rosa Alvarez's Story

In July 1998 I attended the convention of the Liberal Constitutionalist Party (Partido Liberal Constitucionalista) in Managua. Important political deals were being forged at this convention, and therefore many attendees were too busy to grant me extended interviews, although they proudly admitted they had been supporters of "the General." Some women, however, were very willing to talk, and Rosa Alvarez was one of them.

When I approached potential informants, I normally began the conversation by stating that I was interested in interviewing women with long trajectories within Liberalism. Alvarez's response surprised me, for she clearly interpreted my inquiry as a compliment. She asked me, "How did you know I have dedicated my life to Liberalism?" I admitted that I had not known but had approached her quite randomly. She seemed disappointed by this but was intent on demonstrating that she had indeed played an important lifelong role within Liberalism. She invited me to sit down with her and began a conversation that would lead her to tears.

Alvarez began by telling me that she came from a poor family and had always been poor. She told me of physical ailments she had been unable to treat owing to her financial situation, and of her dilapidated home. She was proud of the fact that she had never benefited financially from her political activism, that she was a real Liberal, a "heart Liberal," a *liberal de corazón,* unlike others who were in it for the money. And yet she expected some recognition, at least, of her commitment to the party, something she felt she had not received. But this was just the beginning of her story.

Alvarez told me that the FSLN had jailed her, along with seventy other women, in 1982. Then, in 1985, she was fired from her job because she was politically active against the Sandinistas. Her husband and children disapproved of her political activism. Defying them had never been a problem, since she felt so strongly about her political principles, until now. She had never been ashamed of being a Liberal until 1998. It was at this point in the conversation that Alvarez began to cry. "How can I support a man who is starving his country?" she sobbed. She repeated the question several times and wondered out loud how she could reconcile her Liberalism with support for the Alemán administration. In her view, Alemán was not a *liberal de corazón*. His heart was not in the right place and he was in politics for the money, using the Liberal Party to profit from the people. Equally upsetting, in her view, was Alemán's disregard for local political players. Alvarez felt that he did not respect or acknowledge grassroots Liberals like her who had given their lives to their local communities. Instead, he imposed outside leaders on communities, with disastrous political results for grassroots Liberalism. The damage she felt Alemán was doing to the Liberal Party pained Alvarez deeply. "They call themselves Liberals," she told me, "but they are opportunists. . . . If they were truly Liberals, the country would not be in bad shape [*desgracia*] as it is today."

Inevitably, Somocista women's views of the Somoza years are mediated by their experiences since then. For Alvarez, Somocismo was everything the Alemán government was not. She could not help but contrast the two regimes. In her view, the Somozas took care of their people. Alemán, meanwhile, was letting them starve. Under the Somozas she had held political power and had been recognized as a local leader; under Alemán she felt she had no power and no recognition: "today they name [the leaders] from above [*los eligen de dedo*]. In the past they earned [their posts] . . . [and] women participated more."

Several aspects of Alvarez's story need to be stressed. First, her complaint about women with long-standing Liberal trajectories not being taken into account by Alemán was a very common one among the Somocista women I interviewed. It does appear that Alemán did not take women into account to the extent that the Somozas did. But Alvarez's complaint about the imposition of outside leaders on local communities was one that was made often during the Somoza dictatorship as well. Moreover, corruption under the Somozas was commonplace.[7]

Alvarez's positive recollections of the Somoza era do not correspond to established historical facts, which present a rather negative picture of the dictatorship once the violence and corruption are taken into account. Nonetheless, Alvarez was not alone in her positive assessment of the Somozas and her negative assessment of the Alemán administration. A great number of the Somocista women I interviewed shared her view. Moreover, Alvarez's version of the past

---

7. See, for example, a letter written to Anastasio Somoza Debayle by Liberals in El Realejo, Chinandega, dated January 15, 1972, in which they complain of corruption. Archivo Nacional, Palacio Nacional, Managua, box 306, código 1.5, Relación Junta Nacional y Legal del PLN, Fondo Presidencial, Sección Partidos Políticos.

(the version she shared with me) was based on a selective memory that is still being used to critique contemporary Nicaraguan Liberalism.

Ironically, Alvarez's selective memory, and that of thousands of other women like her, helped bring Arnoldo Alemán to power. Like Alvarez, many working-class Somocistas voted for Alemán because they wanted a return to the Liberal clientelistic populism of the 1950s and 1960s, a return that never took place. This yearning was felt not only by established Somocistas like Alvarez but also by "new" Somocistas: a new generation of Somocista Liberal women who do not necessarily come from Liberal families and who, in the late 1990s, were in their thirties and forties and had not experienced the "golden era" of Somocismo as adults. Like Antonia Rodríguez, Alvarez noted that Liberalism was "deeply ingrained" in her. As an eight-year-old child she had accompanied her grand-father to political events in Managua. And her grandmother was the first woman to vote in her community, in 1957, the year women first got the chance to vote—albeit in fraudulent elections. Moreover, Alvarez told me that her grandmother was "the most famous Liberal in [her] town. She is proud that her granddaughters are Liberals."

Neo-Somocistas at a Liberal Women's Assembly: Margarita Chávez's and Maribel López's Stories

More than a thousand women gathered at the Liberal women's assembly that took place in Managua's Olof Palme Convention Center in May 1998. I wanted to speak to older women, so I decided to interview the oldest-looking women in the group. I first approached a woman who appeared to be in her eighties. Her hair was completely white, she was very petite, and she could barely walk on her own. It turned out that she was only sixty-eight and was not even a Liberal. Her story, however, like that of all Nicaraguans, is intertwined with the history of Somocismo and politics in general. Margarita Chávez had been a grade-school teacher in southern Nicaragua during the Somoza years. She was a Conservative and was eventually fired because of her political beliefs, never to be employed again, for she refused to vote for the Somozas.

I continued my conversation with Chávez in her home, located in a poor Managua neighborhood, several days later. I visited her there at the insistence of her daughter, Maribel López. López, a very vocal woman in her early forties, identified herself as a Somocista and had invited her mother to the Liberal assembly. What these two women had in common was their anti-Sandinismo, fueled in part by their opposition to the draft instituted by the FSLN in the 1980s. The family's opposition to the FSLN was so great that one of Chávez's sons had joined the Contras in the 1980s, a fact Chávez mentioned with pride.

After I had talked at length with Margarita Chávez, Maribel López went out of her way to introduce me to Liberal women in her working-class neighborhood. We spent almost an entire day visiting homes and talking to Liberal women. They all told the same story: The Somozas had been good for the people; under the Sandinistas, Somocistas had suffered a great deal, but they were happy to have the Liberals back in power. While it is hard to know how genuine these women's stories were, given that López was the Liberal representative in her neighborhood, they appeared to be sharing their true opinions. A couple even brought out Somocista magazines from the 1970s to prove to me that they were long-standing Liberals.

Although I do not doubt the sincerity of Maribel López and the women to whom she introduced me, it turned out that hardly any of them had been politically active during the dictatorship, in large part because they were teenagers in the 1960s and 1970s. These women were truly reactionaries in the sense that they were reacting against the Sandinistas and wanted to go back in time to Nicaragua's supposed golden age, an era they lived through as children. Interestingly, they claimed as theirs a past that they believed was masculine, since, like the leadership of the Liberal Party in Nicaragua in the 1990s, they believed that Liberal women were "just in the process of becoming organized."

Maribel López and her cohort represent the continuity of Somocismo in Nicaragua's right-wing politics. These neo-Somocista women were transforming and re-creating Somocismo to satisfy their late twentieth- and early twenty-first century needs. Since Somocismo was never an established, coherent ideology, it is quite malleable and thus quite useful for neo-Somocistas, who emphasize only certain aspects of the dictatorship, for instance, the growth of the middle class or the creation of the social security system. Somocismo is also useful when the dictatorship is spoken about in general terms, as in "the Somozas provided for the people."

Unlike Rosa Alvarez, whose selective memory of her own personal experiences shapes her worldview, neo-Somocista women must rely on the memories of others in order to make sense of the Somoza years. Under no circumstances, however, should we underestimate the importance of childhood and adolescent experiences in the political formation of these women, a topic that deserves further attention elsewhere. Whatever the origins of neo-Somocista women's nostalgia for the dictatorship, it is important to note that they had more power

under Liberalism between 1996 and 2006 than the Somocistas of Alvarez's generation had during that same period. In other words, while "real" Somocista
women were largely excluded from Alemán's government, neo-Somocista women
were highly visible. The way in which neo-Somocistas understand the past—
particularly women's roles in the Liberal Party—will undoubtedly influence the
future of Nicaraguan Liberalism and their own role in politics.

Market Women: Another Group of Neo-Somocistas

Liberal market women were also part of the new generation of Liberal women
active in politics during the Liberal Party's return to power between 1996 and
2006. These women were highly vocal at the Liberal women's assembly. They
were also easy to spot, since they were wearing their trademark aprons with the
frilly pockets. I spoke to a few market leaders briefly at the assembly. Then, in
June 2000, I spoke at length to several market women at the Mercado Oriental,
Nicaragua's largest open-air market. I was searching for Liberal female activists
in their sixties and seventies and did not find them, presumably because of working women's short life expectancy rates. (Average life expectancy for Nicaraguan
women was fifty-seven in the late 1970s and sixty in the early 1980s [García and
Gomariz 1999, 392].)

Most Liberal market women were in their thirties and forties and were becoming politically involved in Liberalism for the first time under the Alemán
administration. Like Maribel López's neighbors, however, what motivated them
was their anti-Sandinismo and the belief that they could turn back the clock to
the 1950s and 1960s. While contemporary issues fueled their political participation, many were building on female Liberal market family traditions. Rocío Cruz,
a market vendor in her late thirties who came from a Liberal family, told me, "I
was practically born in the market. My mother brought me here six days after
I was born. . . . Liberalism for me is freedom, unity. There is a sisterhood [*her-
mandad*] that I myself have experienced. We are always united [*estamos unidas
siempre*]." Cruz's use of the feminine "estamos unidas" is not coincidental, for
market vendors have traditionally been women. Even today, most of the approximately twenty thousand people working in Managua's Mercado Oriental are
women, as are most of the thousands of vendors working in open-air markets
throughout the nation.

Market women were among the staunchest supporters of the Somozas. They
were also some of the Sandinistas' harshest critics. Karen Kampwirth, in her

study of Contra women, says of the small merchants who became counterrev-
olutionaries in the 1980s:

> Rationing was one of the Sandinista actions that particularly angered the
> women who became contras. . . . Several mentioned particular resentment
> at the periodic shortages of white sugar that forced them to buy "black
> sugar," something that never happened before: "General Somoza gave that
> sugar to animals."
>
> Sandinista rationing, and rules against hoarding, created particular
> hardships for small merchants. . . . The purpose of the Sandinistas' rule[s]
> was to ensure that meat [and other goods were] available at affordable
> prices for all. But the same rule that made life easier for some who had
> not been able to afford meat under Somoza, made life harder for [other]
> women. . . . Moreover, by forcing them to make illegal purchases, it turned
> them into enemies of the state. . . . [It was then] not such a great leap to
> join the Contras. (Kampwirth 2001, 93)

Small merchants tended to disapprove of the economic policies instituted by
the FSLN. For Liberal market women in particular, the freedom to purchase and
sell the products they wished in the quantities they wished whenever they wanted
to was an essential component of their economic and political "freedom," a
freedom they associated with the Somoza period. Given such political and economic priorities, it is understandable that many market women welcomed the
Alemán administration and its neoliberal economic policies at the turn of the
century.

Surprisingly, perhaps, given their constant references to the golden age of
Somocismo, the younger women of the new Liberal women's movement (a movement that includes neo-Somocistas as well as non-Somocista Liberals) did not
establish strong links with the women of the "old" Liberal women's movement
and instead, as noted above, promoted the idea that they were the first Liberal
women to be involved in politics. This is understandable if one realizes that
Liberal women in the late 1990s and early 2000s had different priorities from
their foremothers. Unlike the Somocista women of the Ala Femenina, the "new"
Liberal women did not emphasize citizenship (women's suffrage) or populist
clientelism as the primary appeal of Liberalism for women. Instead, one of their
major goals was to prevent the Sandinistas from achieving power again. This
goal, of course, was ironic, since Arnoldo Alemán's hunger for power made it
possible for Daniel Ortega to return to office in 2006.

The situation is more complicated, however, as the Liberal women's movement did include a few long-standing Somocistas in its leadership, although
very few, to my knowledge, were high-level Ala leaders. Although I attempted
to interview these women, I never got beyond their secretaries once I told them
that my research project was on "women with long trajectories in the Liberal
Party." Presumably, they did not want to stress the links between the Somozas
and the Alemán administration for political reasons.

Heretical or Distributional? Somocista and Neo-Somocista Women Remember Somocismo

Depending on their personal circumstances and experiences, different informants emphasized different aspects of Somocismo in their interviews. Perhaps
because of their working-class background and their concern over basic needs
like food and shelter, Rosa Alvarez and Maribel López focused on the part of
the official story that contends that the Somozas provided for the people in the
1950s and 1960s. That is the mythical Nicaragua they wish to return to, and they
are willing to work hard in order to re-create a populist clientelistic system that
in their view functioned fairly. Although the heretical and distributional categories are not mutually exclusive, Alvarez's and López's accounts can be considered distributional memories of Somocismo.

Marta García, a middle-class Ala co-founder, identified with a different aspect
of Somocismo: the rise of the middle class. "Before Liberalism, only the upper
and lower classes existed. Liberalism founded institutes [high schools] and the
middle classes were created through them. . . . Somocismo can be defined as the
era in which the middle classes developed in Nicaragua."

Eugenia Robleto, another Ala leader, emphasized the importance of progress
and social justice in Somocista politics. She noted that she became involved in
mayoral electoral politics under the Somozas because of the poverty she saw in
her hometown: "The poverty motivated me to participate." In an effort to alleviate her constituents' destitution, she oversaw the installation of drinking water
in her region.

Lucrecia Noguera Carazo, another Ala co-founder, also focused on progress
in an article she wrote for *Novedades,* the Somocista newspaper, in 1969: "The
Liberal Party in all periods has been the one which has given the Nicaraguan
people their most precious achievements: the Labor Code [*Código del Trabajo*],
Social Security, Labor Reforms, Constitutional Rights, the freedom to work,

university autonomy, the Agrarian Reform, under the wing of peace. That is why the Nicaraguan people do not need the siren song of the Communists, because the PLN has given, and continues to give, all that is necessary to the people so as to live democratically" (1969, 6).

The Somozas themselves often emphasized the "heretical" aspects of Somocismo that these Somocista women stressed, aspects that were central to their populist strategy and style. The following passage from an antielitist speech given by Anastasio Somoza Debayle in 1967 focuses on social justice and the elimination of class differences:

> In 1946, when I arrived at a hacienda in Chontales to buy cattle, the peons greeted me with their hands joined together [in sign of reverence]. . . . I felt profoundly depressed to see human dignity so trampled by customs imposed by Conservative families, the owners of that hacienda. I protested to the men, asking that they not disrespect their God, because I was equal to them, and such reverence is reserved for God, not for men.
>
> Let not Nicaraguans be surprised by my Nationalist Liberal fervor! For it is our party which holds the principle that "all Nicaraguans, in civil and political matters, are equal before the law."
>
> That is why I am not impressed by family lineages, or transitory titles or posts like those used by the speaker of the Conservative Party. It is time that we, the Nationalist Liberals, and all the workers who are treated feudally by Conservative capital, that we make Conservatives comply with these principles of National Liberalism, for their own happiness and for the happiness of the people of Nicaragua. Here I repeat what I said before the Great Convention: "In my eyes there are no social classes!" (. . . *hacia la meta*, n.d., 97, 98)

Because female Somocista national leaders were policymakers, they had to think in broader political terms than Somocista women who were not national leaders. They also had to fashion populist appeals to the population. These are some of the reasons why the former emphasized the "heretical" aspects of Somocismo and the latter did not. But other issues are involved. The national leaders I interviewed could not be open about the material goods they had received from the Somozas, if any, because their public identities were based on a narrative that said they had worked hard for whatever posts and goods they had. Moreover, several were attempting to reclaim properties that had been confiscated by the Sandinistas. If they claimed that Somocismo was about "what we

got from the government" (Auyero's phrase), they would undermine their political strategy.

In spite of the differences between national Somocista leaders and working-
class rank-and-file Somocista women, their understanding and experience of
Somocismo intersect at many points, especially at the personal level. They all
had to find a balance between politics and family matters, often confronting
unsupportive husbands and parents. Marta García, for instance, like Rosa Alvarez,
faced a reluctant husband. Unlike Alvarez, however, García came from a middle-
class Liberal family, but, she told me, "I was not rich." She married in 1960 and
had a child soon thereafter, and then her husband left her for another woman.
Although García's husband was in the Somozas' army, he did not want her to
participate in politics. This did not keep her from participating, however, and
after her separation she devoted herself completely to Somocismo and to her
child. "I had two children," she explained; "the other one was the Ala." Even during her marriage, she noted, "my husband was not able to dominate me completely." For example, she refused to use his last name as her own, something he
had wanted her to do.

Another commonality between working-class and middle-class Somocista
women is that they see themselves as the heroines and the true Somocistas. On
the one hand, they are the "liberales de corazón," the ones who follow all the
rules. On the other hand, they are the ones who broke established societal rules
by struggling against unsupportive husbands and parents in order to forge a
new nation. They are also the ones who were slowed down in politics by maternity, who had to watch what they did so as not to damage their sexual reputations, and who implicitly had to work harder than Somocista men and later
generations in order to advance in Liberal politics. Eugenia Robleto commented
during our interview, "My daughter says, 'I'd like to be just like my mom.' But
she doesn't like to struggle."

As other scholars have noted about oral histories with women elsewhere in
Latin America, "'tales of resistance against ingrained male stereotypes of femininity' may be placed alongside 'narratives of obedience' and 'conformity'" to
party lines (French and James 1997, 299, quoting Ann Farnsworth-Alvear). It is
in this apparent contradiction in the discourse of Somocista women of different classes that we find that they both support and subvert the official versions
of Somocismo.

It is important to reiterate that Somocista women (those active in Somocista
politics before 1979) are largely absent from the story contemporary Liberals
tell of Somocismo—the second official version of Somocismo. Regarding the

creation of a dominant popular memory, England's Popular Memory Group wrote in the early 1980s,

> It is useful to distinguish the main ways in which a sense of the past is produced: through public representations and through private memory (which, however, may also be collective and shared).... Certain representations achieve centrality and luxuriate grandly; others are marginalized or excluded or reworked. Nor are the criteria of success here those of truth: dominant representations may be those that are most ... obviously conforming to the flattened stereotypes of myth.... There is a second way of looking at the social production of memory which draws attention to quite other processes. A knowledge of past and present is also produced in the course of everyday life.... Usually this history is held to the level of private remembrance. (Popular Memory Group 1998, 76–77)

After 1979, Somocista women's memories of Somocismo survive only at the level of private remembrance. They do not form part of the contemporary Liberal version of Somocismo, for that story holds that Somocismo was largely a masculine endeavor. Women's past contributions to Liberalism have not been acknowledged by Liberal leaders in the post-Somoza era, and, with a few exceptions, older Somocista women have not been invited to participate in contemporary Liberalism. Marta García, the former Ala leader, felt that the Alemán administration did not take women into account, even though she knows Alemán personally and, like many other Somocista women who spent the period 1979–90 in exile, she raised funds for Alemán's 1996 campaign. "They say that today women are taken into account," she commented, "but I don't see it." Indeed, the Liberal propaganda between 1996 and 2006 hardly mentioned women's longstanding participation in Somocismo, something Luis and Anastasio Somoza Debayle considered one of their greatest achievements. The Liberal officials I spoke to in the late 1990s and early 2000s knew nothing about the history of Liberal women. They told me only that "Liberal women are in the process of being organized." Ironically, neo-Somocista women also disregard women's contributions to Somocismo, although if these contributions were known, they might help broaden the appeal of Somocismo among those who cherish populist and clientelistic policies.

Somocista women's memories coincide with the Somocista discourse of thirty and forty years ago, but not with the contemporary Liberal version of Somocismo. Given this state of affairs, it is no wonder that Marta García says, "History might have been erased, but we are [still] here [to tell our story]." García sought to disrupt the contemporary official story of Somocismo as it is told today, proposing as an alternative the official version of Somocismo that was popular before 1979. But hers seemed to be a difficult endeavor.

The Liberal women's movement of the late 1990s and early 2000s was much more in line with traditional right-wing women's movements in other parts of the world than Somocista women ever were. While Somocista women before 1979 looked to the future, Liberal Nicaraguan women in the late twentieth century consistently looked backward to "better times," just as fascist women in Europe and right-wing women in other Latin American countries did. In addition, unlike the discourse of the Ala Femenina, the new Liberal women's movement stressed "a return to family values," even though these "traditional" values were not in fact characteristic of Nicaraguan families, then or now. Nicaragua's "New Right" emphasizes the nuclear family, procreation, and marriage, and that emphasis has only been strengthened by the pact between Daniel Ortega and Arnoldo Alemán. Indeed, with the full backing of the Catholic Church, the New Right, in collusion with Daniel Ortega's Sandinista Party, was able to pass a law in 2006 that, for the first time in Nicaraguan history, prohibits abortion under all circumstances, even if it would save the life of the mother.

Conclusion

While we await research that specifically compares and contrasts the Somoza and the Alemán administrations, my research thus far reveals that the shift within Nicaraguan Liberalism in relation to gender policies—in particular its recent masculinization and its new emphasis on "the family"—may be attributed to at least three factors, and probably more, some of which are discussed above and some which I've discussed elsewhere (González 2002). Unlike the Somozas, who consolidated the modern Nicaraguan state and incorporated urban women into that process by offering them state employment, the Alemán administration was charged with dismantling the state in the context of neoliberal global economic policies that led to high levels of unemployment. Unlike the Somozas, then, Alemán had no economic incentives to offer women and no need to involve them in formal sectors of the economy. Second, the Nicaraguan Right has been heavily influenced by socially conservative (and Catholic fundamentalist) right-wing forces in the United States over the past thirty years, forces that place great importance on the family and family values. The Somozas, too, were influenced by the Right in the United States, but they adopted U.S. anti-communism, not necessarily their views on women and the family. A third factor to consider is the militarization of Nicaraguan politics in the 1970s and 1980s, which diminished women's role in the Nicaraguan Liberal Right. In exile during the 1980s, many Somocista women retreated into domestic affairs and apolitical employment, while Somocista men took over the task of envisioning the type of government that would eventually replace the Sandinistas. A possible fourth factor is that Alemán had to contend with a politically and economically strong feminist movement, while the Somozas were able to co-opt and weaken the early twentieth-century feminist movement in Nicaragua when they came to power in 1936.

An additional point to keep in mind is that even today many Somocista Liberals in Nicaragua are embarrassed by the Somozas' mobilization of prostitutes and the regime's support of prostitution for its own financial gain. Ironically, this legacy makes it hard for some contemporary neo-Somocistas to embrace their foremothers, some of whom were labeled prostitutes regardless of their actual economic/sexual endeavors, but not their forefathers, some of whom administrated and profited from the sex industry.

In short, it is by examining Somocista women's narratives that we can begin to trace some of the ways in which the official story of Somocismo has changed over the years and learn how Liberal politics in Nicaragua became masculinized in the Alemán years (as compared to the 1950s, 1960s, and 1970s). Through Somocista women's narratives we also learn more about the Somozas' populist appeal and the ways in which women in particular make sense of their support for the dictatorship. Neo-Somocistas' narratives also shed light on these processes. In addition, interviews of neo-Somocista women reveal that women often actively participate in erasing their foremothers' accomplishments and failures. Most important, perhaps, the interviews with both of these groups of women help us to understand political culture—including clientelistic populism—as a dynamic endeavor in which both men and women participate, even if they sometimes do so only in ways that might be considered "private." More specifically, from these interviews we learn why Somocismo still plays a role in contemporary Nicaragua. It is the measuring stick against which many compare all other governments. In short, Somocismo's malleability allows it to be used to praise *or* criticize the Sandinistas, to praise *or* criticize Arnoldo Alemán, depending on whether the focus is on the violence the Somozas instituted through the National Guard, or on their successful appeals to "the people." At the dawn of the twenty-first century, the Nicaraguan nation continues to stand in the shadow of complex populist clientelistic politicians who were also violent anticommunist dictators. Disentangling the different components that made up Somocismo might help us to escape from the dictators' grip.

References

Auyero, Javier. 2001. *Poor People's Politics: Peronist Survival Networks and the Legacy of Evita.* Durham: Duke University Press.
Baltodano Marcenaro, Ricardo. 2008. "Ciudadanas por y para la dictadura: El Ala Femenina Liberal de Juventud Liberal Nicaragüense, 1954–1961." Asociación para el Fomento de los Estudios Históricos en Centroamérica, boletín no. 34, February 13. http://afehc-historia-centroamericana.org/index.php?action=fi_aff&id=1826.
Dore, Elizabeth. 1997. "The Holy Family: Imagined Households in Latin American History." In *Gender Politics in Latin America: Debates in Theory and Practice,* ed. Elizabeth Dore, 101–17. New York: Monthly Review Press.
French, John D., and Daniel James. 1997. "Oral History, Identity Formation, and Working-Class Mobilization." In *The Gendered Worlds of Latin American Women Workers: From Household and Factory to the Union Hall and Ballot Box,* ed. John D. French and Daniel James, 297–313. Durham: Duke University Press.
García, Ana Isabel, and Enrique Gomariz. 1999. *Mujeres centroamericanas: Ante la crisis, la guerra y el proceso de paz.* Vol. 1, *Tendencias estructurales: Información estadística por sexo.* San José: FLACSO.
González, Victoria. 2001. "Somocista Women, Right-Wing Politics, and Feminism in Nicaragua, 1936–1979." In *Radical Women in Latin America: Left and Right,* ed. Victoria González and Karen Kampwirth, 41–78. University Park: Pennsylvania State University Press.
———. 2002. "From Feminism to Somocismo: Women's Rights and Right-Wing Politics in Nicaragua, 1821–1979." PhD diss., Indiana University.
Gould, Jeffrey L. 1990. *To Lead as Equals: Rural Protest and Political Consciousness in Chinandega, Nicaragua, 1912–1979.* Chapel Hill: University of North Carolina Press.
. . . *hacia la meta . . . : Mensajes políticos del Gral: Anastasio Somoza Debayle, presidente constitucional de Nicaragua 1967–1972; Ante la gran convención del Partido Liberal Nacionalista y durante su campaña presidencial.* N.d. Managua: Editorial San José.
Hoyt, Katherine. 2004. "Parties and Pacts in Contemporary Nicaragua." In *Undoing Democracy: The Politics of Electoral Caudillismo,* ed. David Close and Kalowatie Deonandan, 17–42. Lanham, Md.: Lexington Books.
Kampwirth, Karen. 2001. "Women in the Armed Struggles in Nicaragua: Sandinistas and Contras Compared." In *Radical Women in Latin America: Left and Right,* ed. Victoria González and Karen Kampwirth, 79–109. University Park: Pennsylvania State University Press.
———. 2003. "Arnoldo Alemán Takes on the NGOs: Antifeminism and the New Populism in Nicaragua." *Latin American Politics and Society* 45 (2): 133–58.
Kettering, Sharon. 1988. "The Historical Development of Political Clientelism." *Journal of Interdisciplinary History* 18 (3): 419–47.
Noguera Carazo, Lucrecia. 1969. "¿Hasta cuando se convencerán los comunistas?" *Novedades* (Managua), August 6.
Popular Memory Group. 1998. "Popular Memory: Theory, Politics, Method." In *The Oral History Reader,* ed. Robert Perks and Alistair Thomson, 75–86. London: Routledge.

Ramos, Helena. 2007. "Mary Coco Maltez, 'El General no supo a que hora retirarse.'" *7 Días On Line,* edition 520, http://www.7dias.com.ni/ (accessed May 30, 2007).

Roberts, Kenneth M. 1995. "Neoliberalism and the Transformation of Populism in Latin America: The Peruvian Case." *World Politics* 48 (1): 82–116.

Seligmann, Linda J., ed. 2001. *Women Traders in Cross-Cultural Perspectives: Mediating Identities, Marketing Wares.* Stanford: Stanford University Press.

Walter, Knut. 1993. *The Regime of Anastasio Somoza, 1936–1956.* Chapel Hill: University of North Carolina Press.

$$\boxed{4}$$

FROM WORKING MOTHERS TO HOUSEWIVES

GENDER AND BRAZILIAN POPULISM FROM GETÚLIO VARGAS
TO JUSCELINO KUBITSCHEK

Joel Wolfe

Beginning with the end of slavery in 1888 and the founding of the republic in 1889, Brazilian elites struggled with the issue of political incorporation for the vast majority. Debates about citizenship rights in many ways defined twentieth-century Brazil. Indeed, the franchise was not fully extended to all Brazilians of voting age until 1988, a full century after the end of slavery. Fear or at least apprehension of popular participation in electoral politics led to a variety of experiments to refashion the poor as whiter, more pliant, and even middle class. These ran the gamut, from an embrace of Lamarckian eugenics (Stepan 1991) to the military's efforts to make a Brazil worthy of its army (McCann 1984).

It should come as no surprise that two of twentieth-century Brazil's most important political leaders grappled with the issue of popular incorporation and the meaning of citizenship. Both Getúlio Vargas (1930–45, 1951–54) and Juscelino Kubitschek (1956–61) embraced forms of populism in order to bring the majority into politics without destabilizing the political system or the country's economic development. Because neither man simply granted full, equal citizenship rights to all Brazilians, their programs promoted workers and the poor as new political actors with unique attributes. The process of political classification often rested on competing notions of how men and women acted, and should act, in society. In other words, gender was an often overlooked linchpin in Vargas's and Kubitschek's programs. The ways in which these men relied on gender became an important part of how and why their attempts at political incorporation ultimately failed, despite affecting Brazilian politics in fundamental ways.

Getúlio Vargas took power in Brazil at the conclusion of the brief revolution of 1930. The political maneuvering and armed conflict over the results of the 1930 presidential election resulted more from interstate rivalries over power and the exhaustion of the liberal economic model of the old republic (1889–1930) than from popular pressure for major changes in Brazilian society. Given the absence of any revolutionary program, Vargas's first period of rule (1930–45) was marked by a series of experiments in economic policy, state making, and the inclusion of the popular classes in politics. Although incomplete and hardly Vargas's most significant contribution to Brazilian history, his attempts to fashion populism in the early 1940s have largely shaped his legacy. The nuclear family was the central organizing trope for the populism that was to shape Vargas's new Brazil. He fashioned himself the "father of the poor" who would personally guarantee social justice for the majority of Brazilians. In his radio addresses on the Hora do Brasil, Vargas spoke directly to the nation's poor as their protector (McCann 2004, 19–40; Knight 1998). Such appeals marked Vargas's populism as highly gendered, emphasizing his masculine role as the father or protector of the nation.

Juscelino Kubitschek (1956–61) was, like Vargas, one of twentieth-century Brazil's most significant political leaders. He is remembered for his successful developmentalist program, the major achievements of which were the establishment of the national automobile industry and the building of Brasília. Although very different on the surface, Kubitschek's and Vargas's policies, which were both ultimately expressions of Brazilian populism, shared as one of their key goals the peaceful political incorporation of large segments of the Brazilian population. Vargas sought to bring workers as workers into the state, while Kubitschek attempted to incorporate workers through the social transformation of the working class itself. Gender shaped Kubitschek's policies as they had Vargas's. Instead of representing himself as the father of Brazil's poor, he promoted the development of a middle-class ethos for all Brazilians. One of the key differences between Vargas's and Kubitschek's policies lay in how they thought about the Brazilian family. Vargas saw himself as a national paternal figure who would protect and advance the interests of the poor. Kubitschek sought to empower Brazilians to create their own middle-class, consumer-oriented families. This difference revealed the divergent views of Brazilian citizenship in these two strains of populism.

Neither program succeeded fully, but they both fostered deep changes in national politics. Vargas and JK (as Kubitschek was widely known) crafted policies specifically to address the incorporation of new groups of urban and rural workers, both male and female. Vargas's focus on the poor usually emphasized women's status as workers, and so his gendered policies reflected concerns about the status of working women. Kubitschek, on the other hand, attempted to transform workers into consumers as a form of political incorporation. His policies shifted the emphasis from women as workers to women as housewives, even though the majority of Brazilian women continued to work outside the home. Ultimately, neither program achieved its aim of bringing working people into a political system capable of peacefully reproducing itself. The military ousted Vargas in 1945 and he committed suicide in 1954, in the midst of his presidential term, which he had won by election. The years immediately following JK's administration were marked by such political turmoil that they ended with the military's seizure of power in 1964 and the establishment of a dictatorship that lasted until 1985. Still, an examination of the gendered components of Vargas's and Kubitschek's policies not only provides new insights into how Brazilian populism worked in practice but also reveals the limits of top-down attempts at popular political incorporation and social transformation.

In many ways, Vargas was an accidental populist. Although a group of young military officers (the *tenentes*) pushed a radical agenda of economic and social unification, Vargas assumed office in November 1930 as a traditional politician who had learned his craft in an environment of hypercronyism in the Republican Party of Rio Grande do Sul, which had long been dominated by the classic *coronel*, Antônio Augusto Borges de Medeiros (Axt 2002). At first, Vargas experimented with different forms of governance. He promised to write a constitution, which he did (the constitution of 1934) and hold presidential elections, which he did not (he instead declared the establishment of the Estado Novo dictatorship in November 1937). In the years between seizing power and promulgating the new constitution, Vargas experimented with a number of policies that could be described as "populist." Indeed, the constitution of 1934 finally reflected some measure of political liberalism by expanding the franchise to women and guaranteeing the secret ballot in all elections (Levine 1980; da Costa 2000, 53–77). The new constitution also codified Vargas's initial labor legislation, which had, among other things, led to the creation of the Ministry of Labor, Industry, and Commerce in 1931 (Castro Gomes 1988).

Although there is no generally accepted definition of Latin American populism, scholars often associate Vargas's populism with his policies toward Brazil's urban workers. The most significant aspects of this political orientation are (1) an attempt to expand the franchise to garner support from newly incorporated groups; (2) a reformist set of policies that could redistribute wealth from at least some segment of the dominant classes to those newly enfranchised supporters; (3) a careful balancing of reformism with support for the extant economic system; and (4) the articulation of a highly nationalist discourse of rights and responsibilities. In a later period, that discourse would focus on elites who were seen as too close to foreign economic interests and those interests themselves.

From afar, Vargas's labor policies in the early 1930s seemed to be quite populist. He fashioned a corporatist labor structure of category-based unions (e.g., metalworkers, glass workers, textile workers, etc.) in cities and towns (*municípios*), which were then linked to state-level labor confederations and national federations. Individual unions had to be part of this government structure and owed their legitimacy to approval by the newly created Ministry of Labor. Wage and work disputes were to be settled by tripartite labor courts, with one representative of labor, one of industry, and one from the government (Mericle 1974). At first, before the government in Rio could fully implement this corporatist structure, strikes and wage disputes were handled by whatever parts of the new labor bureaucracy had been put in place, but this haphazard execution of labor policy quickly ended Vargas's initial experiment with populism.

By 1931 Vargas's desire to centralize political authority in the capital, Rio de Janeiro, was apparent to all. As provisional president, Vargas removed most of the states' governors and replaced them with "Interventors," some of whom were not even from the states they now governed on Rio's behalf. For example, Vargas placed northeastern *tenente* João Alberto Lins de Barros in charge of São Paulo. More than his moderate to progressive views on labor, João Alberto's status as an outsider made him anathema to São Paulo's (or Paulista) elites. A series of strikes by industrial workers in São Paulo—the nation's industrial heartland— brought the first opportunity for the new industrial relations system to settle disputes through government intervention, and so brought the first tentative experiments with populism.[1] When, in late 1930, João Alberto ordered São Paulo city's factory owners to provide their employees with a forty-hour workweek and a 5 percent wage increase, the Paulista elite began to worry about the implications of Vargas's initial embrace of Brazilian workers (Wolfe 1993, 49–62).

João Alberto's intervention on behalf of São Paulo's striking workers provided the state's industrialists their first glimpse of what the new populist government might bring. Factory owners, first and foremost, wanted to be left alone

1. Vargas led all Brazil, and so his policies reverberated throughout the nation. In this chapter I emphasize the impact of his policies on São Paulo, for several reasons. It was Brazil's most industrial state, and the city of São Paulo and its industrial suburbs had the greatest number of industrial workers in the nation. Moreover, São Paulo's elites and working people were of more concern to Vargas than the population of any other state or region, and much of his program was drafted with São Paulo in mind (Woodard 2006). I do nevertheless discuss the impact of his populism, and of Kubitschek's developmentalism, throughout Brazil in passing. All translations are my own unless otherwise indicated.

to run their businesses as they chose. If there were to be any new regulations or ways of organizing work—and some forward-looking industrialists believed moderate reforms of work and living conditions were needed—they should not be imposed by the central government in Rio (Weinstein 1996). Paulistas' loud objections to João Alberto's role not only led Vargas to sack him but also made up one more piece of the state's evolving animus toward the government in Rio. The revolution of 1930 was more than anything else the overthrow of Paulista dominance by Minas Gerais, Rio Grande do Sul, and assorted states in the Northeast (Fausto 1970). Although São Paulo lost the presidency in 1930, many of the state's elites refused to accept their new inferior status. Their grievances coalesced into the so-called constitutionalist revolution of 1932, which led to outright civil war on July 9, 1932. Although combat lasted only until October 2 of that year, the conflict played a key role in the unfolding of Vargas's populism (Weinstein 2003).

The central government won the civil war but ended up ceding control of the federal labor bureaucracy in São Paulo to the state's elites. This unique relationship, whereby Jorge Street—a Paulista textile industrialist—ran the state Department of Labor, which had the ultimate authority in industrial relations until 1951, certainly limited the impact of Vargas's program in Brazil's industrial heartland (Wolfe 1993, 168–69). Despite this unique arrangement, the 1932 civil war became a key moment in the development of Vargas's populism. João Alberto's attempted intervention in the strikes showed everyone what a powerful government could potentially do for workers, but the quick withdrawal of support and the surrender of power to Paulista industrialists also revealed the fickle nature of such a potential alliance with political figures. It was, however, the actions of São Paulo's industrialists that revealed the latent opportunities a populist program could hold for both male and female workers. During the conflict, Paulistas relied on increased industrial productivity to supply the troops with uniforms, weapons, vehicles, food, and other essentials. Factory owners, who had recently resisted granting modest wage increases during the strikes, provided elaborate benefits to keep their employees working the long hours the war effort required. In addition to discounted food sold in working-class neighborhoods, the industrialists provided free medical and dental care in hastily opened clinics. They further targeted women workers with extensive obstetric care (ibid., 62).

The civil war confronted workers in the nation's industrial heartland with a confusing state of affairs. Vargas was increasingly acting like a dictator and would not hold the elections that had been agreed upon, but he seemed to support their interests. In practice, however, he provided them with no real material benefits. The industrialists who had reacted so violently to João Alberto's nascent populism embraced some forward-looking benefits when they needed to curry favor with Paulista workers. In the final analysis, the first decade of Vargas's rule provided few real benefits to Brazilian workers. It was during this period, however, that Vargas crafted his populism, largely in response to worker appeals (Wolfe 1994). In the 1930s, opposition from Paulistas, as well as the weak nature of the central state itself, forced Vargas to rely more on rhetorical support for workers and other poor Brazilians than on policies that would have a positive material impact on their lives. Although he did not offer many real benefits, Vargas did begin to outline what would become the first sustained populist message in Brazil.

Part of Vargas's populist project involved elevating workers and others to full-fledged citizenship, at least rhetorically. Vargas had extended the franchise to women and, early in his administration, had had close ties to reformers who sought to replace the cronyism of the old republic with modern, democratic elections. As he moved to consolidate his rule and eventually declare a dictatorship—with the establishment of the Estado Novo in November 1937—Vargas's rhetoric about citizenship pivoted away from the franchise and toward notions of state-guaranteed rights for urban workers and other traditionally excluded groups, such as Afro-Brazilians (Andrews 1991, 146–56; Butler 1998). The policies specifically oriented toward urban labor were highly gendered in the ways in which they differentiated between male and female workers.

Thousands of the nation's poor responded directly to Vargas and his populist appeals by asking for his assistance with everything from school tuition, to neighborhood sewage problems, to annoying foremen. Their letters, many of which Vargas read himself, often brought some sort of relief to their writers. In order to get Vargas's attention, the letter writer usually used a vocabulary of rights, patriotism, and populism—not infrequently referring to the dictator as the self-styled "father of the poor"—that would validate their petition in the eyes of the government. These letters gave Vargas a sense of how his policies were being received, and granted him the unique opportunity to craft his rhetoric in response to popular interests (Wolfe 1994). Moreover, given the weak nature of the federal government at this time, this back-and-forth between Vargas and Brazilian workers provided a key tool for the crafting and implementation of policy.

Rhetorically, Vargas's populism offered a great deal to workers, particularly to women, but in practice the Estado Novo years presented Brazilian families with new challenges. Given the tight control on labor organizing and the de facto ban on any sort of organized protest, workers had to rely on the government for wage increases in the late 1930s and early 1940s, a period of high inflation, especially for staples such as food, transportation, and housing. The government was the final arbiter in wage issues because Vargas's Ministry of Labor had created a tripartite labor court to determine wages. Union representatives tended to support increases, while industry representatives opposed them. This stalemate left the power to decide with the labor bureaucrat. During most of the Estado Novo era, government officials opposed wage increases. Careful study of wages and food consumption among workers throughout Brazil at this time has found that despite a national campaign to fight malnutrition, workers rarely earned enough to feed themselves and their families (Crocitti 2006, 143–71). The high cost of living affected all Brazilians, but the structure of working-class households and gender ideologies that made women responsible for the reproduction of their families' labor power meant that women bore the brunt of high food costs.

Women, although singled out for praise in the regime's rhetoric, fared poorly during the 1930s and early 1940s. Vargas's labor policies elevated womanhood, and especially motherhood, to goods that needed state protection. In the early 1930s, both unions and the state promoted the idea that women's work was in the home and that when women had to work for wages, employers and the government should provide for their needs as mothers. Large-scale factories that employed women of childbearing age, for example, had to provide separate spaces where they could nurse their babies. Other protective measures included limits on women's night-shift work, something women workers had never sought (Wolfe 1991). Moreover, industrial unions—one of the centerpieces of Estado Novo populism—reproduced problematic gender discourses and practices. The union for all textile workers in São Paulo city (Sindicato dos Trabalhadores nas Indústrias de Fiação e Tecelagem de São Paulo), though it represented an industrial sector dominated by women, was run by and for men. Beyond its all-male directorate, the union used the mandatory union tax (*imposto syndical*) from all the city's textile workers to fund activities (e.g., a soccer team and a well-stocked bar at union headquarters) that served the interests of only the small number of workers who bothered to join the union formally (i.e., to become *sindicalizado*). In 1942, the year before Vargas issued his consolidated labor laws, or CLT—considered a high point of this era's populism—only 1.72 percent of São Paulo's textile workers joined the union, although every textile worker had paid the compulsory union tax (Wolfe 1993, 70–93).

Other programs addressed working-class concerns during this period as well, but in deeply traditional ways. Vargas's establishment of the Ministry of Education and Public Health could have provided real benefits to Brazil's working class and poor had government budgets provided even a fraction of the funds needed to implement policy. When the federal government did support public education, there was nothing liberating in the curriculum for girls. Not surprisingly, the education system mirrored social gender ideology and so reinforced ideas about appropriate roles for men and women (Dávila 2003). Industrial training for young women also failed to challenge traditional ideas about gender roles (Weinstein 1996, 219–50). In other words, Vargas's populism, although gendered, did not address directly many women workers' concerns. Populism offered some female-centric policies, but it was far from feminist in any way. Part of the reason for this state of affairs was that Brazil had very few avowedly feminist activists at this time, and those who thought of themselves as such were focused on gaining the franchise. After winning the right to vote, their movement lost momentum (Hanher 1990; Alvarez 1990). Vargas's turn toward dictatorship further eroded the power of Brazil's nascent feminist movement. At its best, Vargas's program offered uplifting rhetoric about the central role not only of workers but of all previously excluded groups as Brazil moved toward national unity and development. At its worst, this populism reinforced gender inequality, treating women workers less like men than like children.

The one truly emancipatory component of Vargas's initial populist program was the combination of universal suffrage and the elevation of workers and other traditionally excluded groups as key players in Brazil's ongoing national development. The absence of elections in the aftermath of the promulgation of the 1934 constitution limited the full impact of these measures until Vargas returned to presidential politics in the election of 1950.[2] Upon being sworn in as the democratically elected president of Brazil in January 1951, Vargas finally began to implement at least some minor components of his populist project. The problem for Brazilians who supported Vargas was that, by the early 1950s, his populism was less a coherent program than a jumble of proposals and promises. In an era of ostensibly open politics, various segments of the populist alliance competed with each other for the regime's favor and resources (Soares d'Araújo 1982; Skidmore 1967, 81–142).

2. After his ouster by the military in November 1945, Vargas was elected to the Senate from both Rio Grande do Sul (his home state) and Rio de Janeiro (the state that benefited most from the programs of the 1930–45 period, with the steady expansion of the federal bureaucracy). He chose to serve as a Gaúcho (a native of Rio Grande do Sul).

Vargas's problems were reflected in the details of his election. Although he received a commanding plurality of the vote (48.7 percent in a three-way race), he did so with an increasingly conflicted alliance of populist and developmentalist political factions, represented by his two political parties. The Labor Party (Partido Trabalhista Brasileiro, or PTB) represented Vargas's turn toward workers and his growth in popularity with workers, as the government lessened its control over unionization at this time (Wolfe 1993, 160–88). The Social Democratic Party (Partido Social Democrático, or PSD) was considered a middle-class party that reflected the interests of the growing bureaucracy Vargas had established (Owensby 1999, 186–202). In practical terms, though, the PSD came to represent the developmentalist component of Vargas's politics. Although he sought to weave nationalist policies into his populism, nationalism was never a major concern of the Brazilian working class—as opposed to the often dire situation they faced at the hands of industrialists. In practice, the government's developmentalist policies, such as the establishment of the National Steel Company (Companhia Siderúrgica Nacional, or CSN) in Volta Redonda, the creation of Petróleo Brasileiro, or Petrobras, and the broad developmentalism outlined in the Joint United States–Brazil Technical Commission, at least in the short term, threatened the interests of Vargas's working-class constituents (Wolfe 2008, 347–64).

Each component of Vargas's developmentalism had costs for Brazilian working people. Although the CSN offered a broad range of social benefits and relatively high-wage jobs in the growing complex at Volta Redonda, the town was a focal point of government surveillance and labor control (Dinius 2006). Petrobras fanned the flames of nationalist political discourse at a time when the vast majority of Brazilians already worked for Brazilian employers. Focusing on the perfidy of foreign corporations in such an environment did little for the nation's working people other than elevate the status of Brazilian employers, even when they had done nothing to earn nationalist praise. And the recommendations of the Joint U.S.–Brazilian Commission focused on breaking bottlenecks in transportation, energy production and transmission, and the production of industrial inputs. Improvements in these areas would no doubt have long-term positive implications for the health of the economy and could eventually bolster workers' conditions and compensation, but such gains were years away (Tibirica Miranda 1983; Randall 1993; Joint United States–Brazil Technical Commission 1949; Sikkink 1991). The contradictory goals and policies of the second Vargas era played themselves out in a messy jumble of events that at their worst brought allegations of extraordinary corruption and even charges of a conspiracy to murder a political opponent of Vargas. The personal and political toll on Vargas became so great that he famously remarked, "I have the impression of being in a sea of mud." The president ended his personal misery and helped Brazil turn the page historically by committing suicide in the presidential palace on August 24, 1954 (Rogers 2006).

Although supporters in the PTB, detractors on the political right (especially in the União Democrática Brasileira, or UDN), and the military officer corps felt the long shadow of Vargas's rule after his death, the president's suicide did not usher in a period of nostalgia or a long succession of political heirs.[3] Indeed, the 1955 presidential election brought the young, innovative governor of Minas Gerais, Juscelino Kubitschek, to prominence. Although he was a candidate on the PSD-PTB ticket, JK had a radically different view of the popular classes from Vargas's that differentiated his developmentalism from his predecessor's populism. Whereas Vargas saw himself as the "father of the poor" who would mobilize the people, Kubitschek ultimately sought to transform the people. Developmentalism was more than a set of specific goals, or "targets," as JK called them, that would obliterate economic bottlenecks and improve productivity. The ultimate goal of Kubitschek's target plan (Programa de Metas) was the refashioning of the Brazilian poor into middle-class citizens. He would achieve this goal through an expanded economy that would produce advanced consumer goods (e.g., automobiles and domestic appliances), and by reshaping the physical spaces of Brazil and, in the case of his new, modernist capital city, Brasília, even transform residential patterns (Wolfe 2010).

The differences between the ways in which Vargas and JK imagined how men and women fit into their programs are instructive. Vargas sought to protect women, particularly in motherhood, and often did so in infantilizing ways. Although Kubitschek's policies seemed to promote a U.S.-style nuclear family, he ultimately sought to give more real power to individual families by raising their standard of living. Whether that would alter gender relations within families, and more broadly in society, was not considered as a component of JK's developmentalism.

Kubitschek was trained as a physician who specialized in urology. He studied

---

3. Comparisons to two other Latin American populists reveal the shallow nature of Vargas's legacy. He created neither a lasting political movement (as Juan Perón did in Argentina) nor a sense of nostalgia (which continues to define the administration of Lázaro Cárdenas in Mexico and helps explain, in part, the popularity of his son Cuauhtémoc Cárdenas) (Suárez 2003). A sober assessment of Cárdenas's legacy can be found in Knight 1994. Daniel James (1988) provides a thorough review of the complex ways in which Peronism was read by a wide variety of political actors in the post-1955 period. For a dissenting view of Vargas's legacy, see Dávila 2006.

and worked in Europe during an era of significant medical advances. When he returned to Brazil, his interests turned to politics, but he brought his training and experience in medicine to his new craft (Bojunga 2001). As mayor of Belo Horizonte and later governor of Minas Gerais, JK often spoke about development issues in medical terms, providing the "diagnosis" of a problem and offering "prescriptions" for its "remedy." This was more than a simple rhetorical sleight of hand, for Kubitschek had come of age professionally during the heyday of Lamarckian eugenics in Brazil (Stepan 1991; Skidmore 1974). Rather than embrace Vargas's corporatism, which categorized people by socioeconomic class and occupation, Kubitschek sought to change Brazilian working people into middle-class citizens capable of participating in a democracy.

JK embraced such a program because he well understood populism's limits. The ultimate weakness of Vargas's program had been demonstrated by the workers themselves when they launched large-scale, debilitating general strikes. After Vargas's ouster in late 1945, workers throughout Brazil initiated broad strikes for improved wages and better conditions in their factories. In January 1946 a general strike organized outside the corporatist unions revealed the obvious weaknesses in the system. Ongoing industrial conflicts and urban bus and trolley riots and burnings (known as *quebra-quebras*) in August 1947 further demonstrated to all that Brazil's working people had not been brought peacefully into the political system (Wolfe 1993, 117–59). Vargas's return as the elected president in 1951 created even more uncertainty in the minds of Brazilian elites and middle class. The 1953 "Strike of the 300,000" not only shut down the city of São Paulo (with a population of about 2.2 million) for five weeks, it also involved the very public presence of women workers in a variety of roles. Women organized the initial strike committees, and key demands grew out of their experiences in the city's textile factories. Women led many of the most visible protests, and union leaders sometimes had to plead with striking women to avoid violent clashes with the police (Wolfe 1997). Such broad, destabilizing industrial conflicts revealed the very real limits of populism and provided fertile ground for Kubitschek's developmentalism. The visible leadership role of women in these strikes and protests also shaped the decision by policymakers to attempt to return to a nostalgic state of allegedly traditional gender roles by domesticating women workers and creating high-paying industrial jobs for their husbands.

Although JK's developmentalism rejected laissez-faire capitalism and embraced activist state planning, it did emphasize close working relationships with private industry (Sikkink 1991). A centerpiece of Kubitschek's program was the role multinational automobile companies would play in remaking the Brazilian working class into domesticated middle-class consumers and citizens. First and foremost, modern auto factories would be sites not only of industrial discipline but, more important, of education. Ford do Brasil and Willys-Overland do Brasil (WOB, a subsidiary of Kaiser Industries) instituted literacy programs along with industrial education in the mid-1950s. Men were trained to work in the factories and women were taught how to become secretaries and perform other clerical tasks in the multinationals' expanding administrative offices. The Brazilian media proudly noted the expanding skilled workforce created by and for the new auto sector. In their advertisements, the auto companies in turn trumpeted the growing number of skilled Brazilian workers (Wolfe 2010).

The auto companies' industrial training programs quickly proved to be effective. An internal report to the WOB board of directors took note of their new workers' skills: "It is with pride that we can affirm that, in spite of the fact that the great majority of our employees had little or no previous training or experience in the automotive field, work standards and production per man hour are the equal of those in other countries with generations of industrial training" (quoted in ibid., 129–30). Brazilians came to view the auto factories as sites for the transformation of country folk from Brazil's interior into modern citizens. The factories were in fact seeking migrants from the rural sector, who came to São Paulo on the new roads built during this period, as another key component of Kubitschek's developmentalism. By the late 1950s people from throughout Brazil, but especially the Northeast, migrated on the backs of flatbed trucks (known as *pau de arara*, or "macaw's perches") to São Paulo, looking for work, primarily in the foreign auto factories or the nationally owned auto parts companies.

New, modern factories boasting the latest equipment elevated male factory workers' status as a positive force for change. The auto plants seemed to provide the perfect environment for remaking Brazilians from all corners of the nation and every race and ethnicity, and even both sexes, into modern citizens. Volkswagen declared that "in a modern factory there is also room for women." While men operated huge stamping equipment, women sewed seat cushions. Despite this traditional sexual division of labor, VW described all its employees as "modern workers." Willys referred to its workers as "today's pioneers," expert in using the latest machinery (Wolfe 2010, chapters 5 and 6). The auto companies defined modern, forward-looking workers in ways that served corporate interests and at the same time appealed to Brazilians of all social classes. The sexual division of labor, which elevated male over female workers, lessened the widespread gender anxieties that followed the massive, women-led general strikes of the mid-1940s and early 1950s. Indeed, women's very appearance and self-presentation reassured many Brazilians. The foreign-owned plants required that workers wear uniforms in the factories; foremen in some sections wore ties. The foreign executives in charge of these facilities valued order and cleanliness on the shop floor and believed that industrial training and discipline were the keys to high productivity and profitability. A U.S.-based corporate official who inspected Willys' Brazilian plants concluded, "The whole operation had a feeling of soundness. The plant was clean, the tempo was very good, and the morale was high. I think you should be very proud of your organization" (quoted in ibid., 131). Kubitschek's targets of foreign investment and internal migration seemed to hold the key to solving Brazil's social problem by transforming workers into middle-class citizens. Unlike Vargas's paternalistic populism, JK's developmentalism offered workers a form of liberation. They would be free to become temperate and hardworking consumers who would never dream of striking or challenging the established authority. Developmentalism and its showpiece auto factories produced cars that Brazilians wanted to own and workers they seemed to respect, or at the very least did not have to fear. Kubitschek's developmentalism seemed to have domesticated Vargas's populism.

Underlying the rhetoric about the transformative power of work in the auto factories were the highest working-class wages and best benefits available in Brazil, paid primarily to male autoworkers. Training and experience determined wage levels, but even the lowest-paid assembly line workers (who made up a quarter of the labor force in the auto sector) earned significantly more than the vast majority of other urban laborers in the 1950s and early 1960s. General Motors do Brasil noted that by the early 1960s the auto factories provided a "high employment level . . . a praiseworthy quality of life and the highest per capita income in the country" (General Motors do Brasil 1995, 75). In addition to the highest industrial wages in Brazil, the foreign auto companies also provided comprehensive benefits. Ford do Brasil had been offering its workers health care at work and medical and accident insurance since 1937, with far better benefits than the plans created by the Vargas government could offer. Ford expanded its health care services dramatically as it built new industrial facilities over the course of the 1950s. According to Ford's employment manual, all workers received access to company-run infirmaries and company dentists and barbers. They could eat subsidized meals at company restaurants and take industrial training and literacy classes. Workers were automatically enrolled in Ford's sporting club and given access to a wide variety of athletic facilities. The company practiced a central tenet of Fordism by selling Ford vehicles, along with Philco radios and televisions, at a discount and making company financing available to its workers.

Employees who did not yet have their own cars could get around São Paulo and its industrial suburbs on either company-owned or subsidized buses. Discounted cars, appliances, and other benefits helped Brazilian workers live as consumers, much like their counterparts in the United States, whom they often consciously sought to emulate (Wolfe 2010). A key aspect of this arrangement depended on male workers' earning high enough wages to be the sole breadwinners for their families, which allowed women to stay at home and care for their families. Some Brazilian autoworkers did achieve this idealized, highly gendered status during this period.

By the early 1960s, between six and seven hundred thousand Brazilians worked in the auto sector. The city's industrial suburbs grew and prospered along with the auto plants, as migrants from throughout the country made their way to São Paulo for the high industrial wages and extensive benefits. All the foreign manufacturers followed Ford's lead and offered their employees cars at discounted prices with special financing. Volkswagen even helped workers buy houses by subsidizing mortgages and providing other assistance (Wolfe 2010). The wages and benefits so outpaced anything else available to poor and working-class Brazilians that work in the auto factories became nearly synonymous with social mobility. The press frequently wrote about autoworkers who not only had their own cars but owned modest homes. In the case of Willys, many were also depicted as modest shareholders.[4]

Social mobility, consumerism, and stay-at-home mothers made up the dominant public themes in the lives of São Paulo's autoworkers in the late 1950s and early 1960s. José Soares de Oliveira Irmão, for example, came to São Paulo from a small town in the northeastern state of Bahia. After seven years at Volkswagen, he was able to buy a car and his own house, which he filled with appliances sold at a discount at the company store. In the stories told about autoworkers, whether raised in a *favela* (urban slum) or on a plantation, they almost always had a car, and their wives did not work outside the home (Wolfe 2010). Luís Inácio Lula da Silva, who was born in rural Pernambuco and would go from work in an auto factory, to a prominent role in the labor movement, to the presidency of Brazil, recalled how affluent autoworkers seemed to be in the early 1960s: "At that time, the people in the automobile industry got something like ten raises a year. They were the elite—they had houses, they were the first to buy televisions, the first to buy cars. I saw the people at VEMAG pass, because it was close

---

4. Willys-Overland do Brasil incorporated in Brazil and sold stock there. It also made shares available to its employees at discounted prices.

to where I lived, at Christmastime, loaded down with boxes of toys for their kids" (quoted in Keck 1992, 73). Whether the reality jibed with Lula's recollection, it is clear that JK's developmentalism had succeeded in creating the ideal, at least, of the Brazilian worker as the male, practically middle-class breadwinner who earned enough not only to own his own house and car but also to allow his wife to stay at home as a housewife.

The state sought to accelerate this social transformation and move it beyond São Paulo's auto plants with the creation of a new interior capital that would use modernist models of housing, consumption, and sociability to create a progressive mentality among Brazilians of all social classes. Brasília's housing was designed to be democratic and to foster a sense of equality among all residents. According to James Scott, "Brasília was to be an exemplary city, a center that would transform the lives of the Brazilians who lived there—from their personal habits and household organization to their social lives, leisure, and work. The goal of making over Brazil and Brazilians necessarily implied a disdain for what Brazil had been. In this sense, the whole point of the new capital was to be a manifest contrast to the corruption, backwardness, and ignorance of the old Brazil" (1998, 119). The new families that would inhabit Brasília were to be a curious mix of modern citizen and gendered nostalgic throwback. The city's planners assumed that most residents, no matter their social class, would own a car, for the modernist apartments included garages. It was further assumed that mothers would drive their children and do errands in Brazilian-made station wagons and other cars. In turn, men would hold good, high-paying jobs so that their wives would not have to work outside the home. That Brasília did not deliver on its promises is well known, but this should not obscure the fact that its design reflected important, highly gendered components of Kubitschek's developmentalism.[5]

Vargas's 1945 ouster and 1951 suicide mark the failure of his populism. The political chaos under Jânio Quadros (1961) and João Goulart (1961–64) and the twenty-one-year military dictatorship that followed (1964–85) can also be read as evidence of Kubitschek's inability to remake Brazil's working people into middle-class consumers and citizens. But, whereas populism had reached its structural limits by the early to mid-1950s, JK's policies needed a great deal of time

---

5. Scott 1998 is the best-known critic of Brasília, but his analysis is largely based on James Holston's (1989) pathbreaking study, which argues convincingly that the new capital failed to meet its stated goals, although it did boast the highest overall wages in Brazil. Architect Farès el-Dahdah (2005), on the other hand, has argued that modernism is defined by its contingent nature and that Brasília can be considered a failure only if one misinterprets the nature of modernism itself.

to bear fruit. Several significant aspects of his program did eventually alter consumption and living patterns, and the foreign auto sector in time transformed the working class into active and vocal citizens who played an important role in bringing down the twenty-one year military dictatorship and in shaping Brazil's subsequent democracy (Keck 1992). The election of Lula, the former autoworker and labor leader, to the presidency in 2002 (and his re-election in 2006) provides stark proof of the unintended but positive impact of Kubitschek's developmentalism.

One of primary reasons why Vargas's populism failed is that he sought a static solution to Brazil's closed political system. That is, Vargas opened participation slightly, but in ways that put people into preexisting class categories, thus freezing their status in the state bureaucracy and beyond. In doing so, Vargas celebrated workers as workers, which often emphasized extant gender ideologies. Women workers were to be protected, not emancipated or considered true equals.[6] JK's developmentalism, by contrast, attempted to remake the working class through a fundamental transformation of industry, urban spaces, and the workers themselves.[7] Kubitschek's developmentalism embraced the most conservative and seemingly traditional gender roles for Brazil's working class: Men were to earn high enough wages for women to stay at home (in houses the families owned) to raise the children and care for their husbands. The unintended consequence of these policies, however, was the creation of a working class that pressured its employers and the state for the wages and benefits Kubitschek and others had so often promised. In pressing those demands, male and female workers brought about real change in Brazil, although it was slow in coming and was often obscured during the oppressive years of the dictatorship. In other words, although Kubitschek's developmentalism relied upon traditional ideals of womanhood and motherhood, it ultimately allowed a key segment of the working class to experience true social mobility. While very few Brazilian workers earned enough to become the sort of middle-class citizens JK imagined, the working class as a class was able to use the ideals of developmentalism to promote bottom-up democracy in place of top-down programs of political incorporation or economic and social transformation.

6. It is important to note that in practice women workers carved out political spaces that fostered de facto equality with men (Wolfe 1993).

7. Another way to differentiate between Vargas's populism and Kubitschek's developmentalism is through an analysis of social, economic, and political spaces. Vargas ultimately sought to rearrange society within existing spaces, while JK created new ones (Wolfe 2010; Harvey 2006).

References

Alvarez, Sonia. 1990. *Engendering Democracy in Brazil: Women's Movements in Transition Politics.* Princeton: Princeton University Press.

Andrews, George Reid. 1991. *Blacks and Whites in São Paulo, Brazil: 1888–1988.* Madison: University of Wisconsin Press.

Axt, Gunter. 2002. "Contribuições ao debate historiográfico concernente ao nexo entre estado e sociedade para o Rio Grande do Sul castilhista-borgist." *Métis: História e Cultura* 1 (1): 39–70.

Bojunga, Claudio. 2001. *JK o artista do impossível.* Rio de Janeiro: Objetiva.

Butler, Kim D. 1998. *Freedoms Given, Freedoms Won: Afro-Brazilians in Post-Abolition São Paulo and Salvador.* New Brunswick: Rutgers University Press.

Castro Gomes, Angela Maria. 1988. *A invenção do trabalhismo.* Rio: IUPERJ/Vértice.

Crocitti, John J. 2006. "Vargas Era Social Policies: An Inquiry into Brazilian Malnutrition During the Estado Novo (1937–1945)." In *Vargas and Brazil: New Perspectives,* ed. Jens R. Hentschke, 143–71. New York: Palgrave Macmillan.

Da Costa, Emília Viotti. 2000. *The Brazilian Empire: Myths and Histories.* Rev. ed. Chapel Hill: University of North Carolina Press.

Dávila, Jerry. 2003. *Diploma of Whiteness: Race and Social Policy in Brazil, 1917–1945.* Durham: Duke University Press.

———. 2006. "Myth and Memory: Getúlio Vargas's Long Shadow over Brazilian History." In *Vargas and Brazil: New Perspectives,* ed. Jens R. Hentschke, 257–82. New York: Palgrave Macmillan.

Dinius, Oliver. 2006. "Defending Ordem Against Progresso: The Brazilian Political Police and Industrial Labor Control." In *Vargas and Brazil: New Perspectives,* ed. Jens R. Hentschke, 173–205. New York: Palgrave Macmillan.

el-Dahdah, Farès. 2005. *Case: Lucio Costa: Brasilia's Superquadra.* Munich: Prestel.

Fausto, Boris. 1970. *A revolução de 1930: Historiografia e história.* São Paulo: Brasiliense.

General Motors do Brasil. 1995. *General Motors do Brasil: Seventy Years of History.* São Paulo: Prãemio Editor.

Hanher, June. 1990. *Emancipating the Female Sex: The Struggle for Women's Rights in Brazil, 1850–1940.* Durham: Duke University Press.

Harvey, David. 2006. *Spaces of Global Capitalism: Towards a Theory of Uneven Geographical Development.* New York: Verso.

Holston, James. 1989. *The Modernist City: An Anthropological Critique of Brasília.* Chicago: University of Chicago Press.

James, Daniel. 1988. *Resistance and Integration: Peronism and the Argentine Working Class, 1946–1976.* Cambridge: Cambridge University Press.

Joint United States–Brazil Technical Commission. 1949. *Report of the Joint United States–Brazil Technical Commission.* Washington, D.C.: U.S. Government Printing Office.

Keck, Margaret E. 1992. *The Workers' Party and Democratization in Brazil.* New Haven: Yale University Press.

Knight, Alan. 1994. "Cardenismo: Juggernaut or Jalopy?" *Journal of Latin American Studies* 26 (1): 73–107.

———. 1998. "Populism and Neo-Populism in Latin America, Especially Mexico." *Journal of Latin American Studies* 30 (2): 223–48.

Levine, Robert M. 1980. "Perspectives on the Mid-Vargas Years, 1934–1937." *Journal of Inter-American Studies and World Affairs* 22 (1): 57–80.

McCann, Bryan. 2004. *Hello, Hello Brazil: Popular Music and the Making of Modern Brazil.* Durham: Duke University Press.

McCann, Frank D. 1984. "The Formative Period of Twentieth-Century Brazilian Army Thought, 1900–1922." *Hispanic American Historical Review* 64 (4): 737–65.

Mericle, Kenneth S. 1974. "Conflict Resolution in the Brazilian Industrial Relations System." PhD diss., University of Wisconsin–Madison.

Owensby, Brian. 1999. *Intimate Ironies: Modernity and the Making of Middle-Class Lives in Brazil.* Stanford: Stanford University Press.

Randall, Laura. 1993. *The Political Economy of Brazilian Oil.* Westport, Conn.: Praeger.

Rogers, Thomas D. 2006. "'I Choose This Means to Be with You Always': Getúlio Vargas's Carta Testamento." In *Vargas and Brazil: New Perspectives,* ed. Jens R. Hentschke, 227–55. New York: Palgrave Macmillan.

Scott, James. 1998. *Seeing Like a State: How Certain Schemes to Improve the Human Condition Have Failed.* New Haven: Yale University Press.

Sikkink, Kathryn. 1991. *Ideas and Institutions: Developmentalism in Brazil and Argentina.* Ithaca: Cornell University Press.

Skidmore, Thomas E. 1967. *Politics in Brazil, 1930–1964: An Experiment in Democracy.* New York: Oxford University Press.

———. 1974. *Black into White: Race and Nationality in Brazilian Thought.* New York: Oxford University Press.

Soares d'Araújo, Maria Celina. 1982. *O segundo governo Vargas, 1951–54: Democracia, partidos e crise política.* Rio de Janeiro: Zahar.

Stepan, Nancy Leys. 1991. *The Hour of Eugenics: Race, Gender, and Nation in Latin America.* Ithaca: Cornell University Press.

Suárez, Luis, ed. 2003. *Cuauhtémoc Cárdenas: Política, familia, proyecto y compromiso; tres generaciones, un mismo destino.* México City: Grijalbo.

Tibirica Miranda, Maria Augusta. 1983. *O petroleo é nosso: A luta contra o "entreguismo" pelo monopolio estatal, 1947–1953.* Petrópolis, Brazil: Vozes.

Weinstein, Barbara. 1996. *For Social Peace in Brazil: Industrialists and the Remaking of the Working Class in São Paulo, 1920–1964.* Chapel Hill: University of North Carolina Press.

———. 2003. "Racializing Regional Difference: São Paulo Versus Brazil, 1932." In *Race and Nation in Modern Latin America,* ed. Nancy P. Appelbaum et al., 237–62. Chapel Hill: University of North Carolina Press.

Wolfe, Joel. 1991. "Anarchist Ideology, Worker Practice: The 1917 General Strike and the Formation of São Paulo's Industrial Working Class." *HAHR* 71 (4): 809–46.

———. 1993. *Working Women, Working Men: São Paulo and the Rise of Brazil's Industrial Working Class, 1900–1950.* Durham: Duke University Press.

———. 1994. "'Father of the Poor' or 'Mother of the Rich'? Getúlio Vargas, Industrial Workers, and Constructions of Class, Gender, and Populism in São Paulo, 1930–1954." *Radical History Review* 58 (Winter): 80–111.

———. 1997. "There Should Be Dignity: São Paulo's Women Textile Workers and the Strike of the 300,000." In *Workers' Control in Latin America,* ed. Jonathan Brown, 189–216. Chapel Hill: University of North Carolina Press.

———. 2008. "Populism and Developmentalism." In *A Companion to Latin American History,* ed. Thomas H. Holloway, 347–64. Malden, Mass.: Blackwell.

————. 2010. *Autos and Progress: The Brazilian Search for Modernity.* New York: Oxford University Press.

Woodard, James P. 2006. "'All for São Paulo, All for Brazil': Vargas, the Paulistas, and Historiography of Twentieth-Century Brazil." In *Vargas and Brazil: New Perspectives,* ed. Jens R. Hentschke, 83–107. New York: Palgrave Macmillan.

5

WOMEN AND POPULISM IN BRAZIL

Michael Conniff

During the heyday of populism in Brazil, the so-called populist republic, women played some key parts in politics. This period, as defined by Brazilian analysts, spans the period from the failed bid of Getúlio Vargas to remain in office in 1945 until the overthrow of the last classic populist, João "Jango" Goulart in 1964. This chapter looks at preliminary evidence about the roles several women played as they related to populism, culled from a larger study of nine populist leaders of the era.[1] The evidence suggests that women played important roles in populist campaigns, just as they did in ordinary politics. In three examples studied here, women campaigned for themselves or for others using populist techniques. These cases indicate that populism is not necessarily masculine in Brazil, as it is in other countries, and that female populists are more likely to be found at lower echelons of government than at the top. Their scarcity in the upper ranks is most probably a symptom of the great difficulties women face in competitive politics in general. Two other cases, involving women as followers and voters, speak to the ways in which populists successfully appealed to feminist issues. In short, populism and gender interacted in Brazil in complex ways.

Our first case concerns Getúlio Vargas's daughter, Alzira, who worked closely with him on the campaign of 1950 that solidified his reputation as a classic populist. Getúlio had a long and varied career in politics that spanned more than three decades. From his initiation into Rio Grande do Sul politics in the 1920s, he vaulted into a fifteen-year presidential run on the strength of the 1930 revolution, which he led. Then, in 1950, he came out of retirement to run an amazing campaign in which he won a landslide victory in a three-way race. This last election, his undoubted charisma, and his ability to cater to unions, business

---

1. An early analysis appeared as Conniff 1991. All translations in this chapter are my own unless otherwise indicated.

groups, and even rural voters, have led historians to label him a quintessential populist. Alzira Vargas served as his campaign chief of staff and, in her words, his "second conscience." Alzira also directed the political career of her husband, Ernani, a former naval officer and uninspiring politician. Alzira's was a variation on the general experience of spouses who share or inherit the charisma of populist leaders (see Navarro 1982). I call her the campaign manager-spouse.

In our second case, Getúlio's great-niece, Ivete Vargas, defied norms of feminine behavior for her generation and entered politics, following her famous uncle's lead. Although many tried to don the mantle of Getúlio's successor, Ivete was a legitimate heir by both blood and politics. She may also be considered the model for a female populist, fairly unusual in Latin America.

In our third case, populism in contemporary Brazil may have its leading practitioner in a young politician from the Northeast, Alagoas's Heloísa Helena. Heloísa's background fits the pattern of other populists, except for her gender. Her career invites comparisons with those of Miguel Arraes, Leonel Brizola, and Ivete Vargas, and she definitely warrants watching.

Some evidence suggests that as followers of populist leaders, women behave differently from men. We have valuable information about the differing voter intentions of men and women because of an extraordinary polling organization, the Instituto Brasileiro de Opinião Pública e Estadística, or IBOPE. Getúlio Vargas had given women the vote in 1932, making Brazil the second country in Latin America to do so. He did so because of his deep devotion to equality, but it also helped to associate populist politics with women's rights and votes, as happened elsewhere. Happily, we have the opportunity to track the preferences of women voters from the mid-1940s on because of IBOPE polls.

Finally, in the case of Rio de Janeiro's Carlos Lacerda, his image and rhetoric were especially appealing to mature women. Like Vargas, Lacerda had a long and storied career, beginning as a leftist allied with Luis Carlos Prestes in the 1930s, migrating toward the Catholic Right in the 1940s and '50s, and ending up with a very productive term as the first governor of the new state of Guanabara (today Rio de Janeiro) in the early 1960s. Lacerda might have been president had the military not taken power in 1964. His female followers tended to see him as a surrogate son and were called his "Mal-Amadas," or unrequited lovers, a phrase used ironically. As a result of this gendered appeal, Lacerda usually scored some ten percentage points higher among women than men in polls of voter intentions. He could be called the "good son" politician.

This chapter is based on archival research and interviews, mostly done in the late 1980s, but it also revisits work I did in the early 1970s in Rio. Most of the populist leaders had died by then, but I was able to consult dozens of oral histories deposited at the Centro de Pesquisa e Documentação de História Contemporánea (CPDOC) in Rio. I also met with scores of family members and colleagues of the populists. Finally, I consulted the papers of Getúlio Vargas, Adhemar de Barros, Carlos Lacerda, and others, as well as the archives of IBOPE.

Alzira

Getúlio's only daughter, Alzira, was born in 1914, when the family lived in São Borja, Rio Grande do Sul. Although small in stature (which often matters in a male sport like politics), she showed strong intellectual promise. She attended Catholic school in Rio de Janeiro and stayed close to home. Much of what we know of Getúlio's personality is based on her writings and her stewardship of his archives. As his wife, Darcy, did not seem to care for politics, Alzira served as his personal secretary between 1937 and 1945. She watched over his daily work and managed his voluminous correspondence; presumably she typed many of his letters. She also shared intimate conversations with him and knew virtually everyone who circulated through his life.

Alzira selected and preserved the most sensitive correspondence from Getúlio's two administrations, separating it from the daily flood of paper that crossed his desk. This treasure later formed the core of the CPDOC, founded by her daughter, Celina, in the mid-1970s. The CPDOC has evolved into the largest and best presidential library in Latin America today. In 1939 Alzira married Ernani do Amaral Peixoto, a naval officer who had served as a military aide to Getúlio in the 1930s. Although Alzira had earned her law degree at the University of Rio de Janeiro, she did not stray far from household acquaintances.

For several years after his overthrow in 1945, Getúlio stayed in Rio and served in the Senate, to which he had been elected from the states of Rio Grande do Sul and Rio de Janeiro. He attempted to keep current on politics, which he had managed almost single-handedly for a decade, and to defend his administration from attacks by critics and opportunists. Eventually he became discouraged and withdrew to Rio Grande do Sul, where the family owned ranches named Itú and Santos Reis. There he lived alone in seclusion, as a *solitário,* a kind of recluse and martyr. This withdrawal thrust Alzira into the role of his eyes and ears in Rio de Janeiro. Getúlio did have an extensive network of relatives and friends who wrote to him about current affairs, yet Alzira gradually became his main correspondent.

In 1950 the country had to choose a president to replace the lackluster Eurico Dutra, who had been elected largely thanks to Getúlio's endorsement. Getúlio's potential role in the election was huge, because he still enjoyed enormous popularity with the masses. Yet the political elite went about selecting a candidate largely without him. Alzira, by now his most intimate confidante, began guiding and encouraging him to take up the campaign that would revive his career and vindicate his sacrifices. He would in this way become the true *pai dos pobres,* or father of the poor. She organized his correspondence, guided the dense traffic of people who came to Rio Grande do Sul to consult with Getúlio, and counseled him on what to say and how to remake himself for an eventual election. She insisted that he remain above the fray, uninterested in the presidency unless the masses demanded his candidacy. He should appear to be retired from politics and content in that role. Father and daughter decided that the "draft Getúlio" movement should begin on his birthday, April 19, less than six months before the election. The rest is history. He won the 1950 election handily.

Other politicians realized that Alzira was Getúlio's chief campaign manager and later advisor, and she herself acknowledged that they considered her a Rasputin, an "eminence parda . . . destruidora de ministros," that is, a gray eminence and destroyer of cabinet officers. Once he decided to run, Getúlio worked with Alzira to assemble a speech-writing team for a marathon campaign tour in a DC-9 airplane. He wanted each speech to be tailored to the region in which he would deliver it, touching on issues and problems of local interest. He instructed the writers to speak to the people and to avoid the appearance of addressing only intellectuals and elites, or *grãfinos.* They also worked on the image he would attempt to project to the electorate. He wished to be seen as a statesman who had been hounded by ungrateful politicians and sought vindication. At the same time, his team disseminated images of him as the warm, congenial grandfather, relaxed and at home in the world. One caricature portrayed him in *gaúcho* clothing, smoking a cigar and smiling with visitors.

Alzira's apartment on Rua Rui Barbosa in Flamengo Beach became a headquarters for Getúlio, Ernani (who ran for senator), and the Brazilian Labor Party (PTB). Alzira did not set up women's auxiliaries, as other populists did (e.g., the Peróns and Adhemar de Barros), but along with her mother she did support a number of charities, as was usual for political spouses.

Vargas's indifferent appeal to women voters is surprising, because he had supported legislation giving them the right to vote in 1932, making Brazil the second Latin American nation to grant women's suffrage. He did so at the urging of the feminist leader and scientist Bertha Lutz, who represented the Brazilian

Federation for Feminine Progress (Conniff 1981, 56–57). Still, his image and demeanor were those of a traditional politician from the rural South, whereas the feminist movement was rooted in cities and a few northeastern states. Finally, Vargas did not preside over many elections before 1950 because of his dictatorship from 1937 to 1945. In sum, Alzira managed an extremely successful election campaign in 1950, in which her father won recognition as a classic populist. Although Alzira did not believe her father was a populist, historians and political scientists disagree.[2]

Alzira's role as confidant and political agent for her father fits nicely with our understanding of populists in Latin America. Alzira was certainly not a populist herself but rather an astute campaign manager for her father's populist triumph. Populists generally do not allow aides to become too influential or knowledgeable, for fear they might become rivals. Getúlio, however, could trust Alzira never to challenge him, because she was a woman, his daughter, and the family caretaker. Such arrangements may have discouraged other females with political aptitude from launching public careers that might rival their male relatives.

Ivete

Getúlio's niece Ivete Vargas was in some ways his most fervent admirer and the leading heir to his populism. Born in São Borja in 1927, she grew up in Rio Grande do Sul within the highly political Vargas family. Her grandfather was Viriato, Getúlio's brother. In 1947, when she was only twenty, she became engaged in politics with João Goulart and helped found the Labor Party's branch in Rio Grande (PTB-RS). She moved to Rio de Janeiro to work as a reporter for her grandfather's newspaper and used that position as an entrée into politics; Getúlio and Alzira involved themselves in her career. Eventually Ivete moved to São Paulo and ran for Congress on the PTB ticket, which was dominated by Hugo Borghi, a wealthy manufacturer who dabbled in politics. She enjoyed name recognition as a Vargas and displayed considerable electioneering skills herself. She won election in October 1950 at age twenty-three, the youngest woman ever elected to Congress. That year São Paulo populist Adhemar de Barros, a physician and former governor, and parties in six other states tried to get her to run on their tickets (CPDOC 2001; Vargas 1979)!

2. Alzira Vargas do Amaral Peixoto, interview by author, May 21, 1987 (also May 28 and June 2, 1987; September 14 and 28, 1972); see also CPDOC 2001; Vargas 1979; Peixoto 1981; Peixoto 2002; and Ernani do Amaral Peixoto, interview by author, May 13, 1987.

Ivete embraced the PTB's pro-labor ideology, called *trabalhismo*, and made it the centerpiece of her long political career. In 1945 Getúlio had created two parties to handle the disparate sectors that supported him, the Social Democratic Party (PSD) for the older, rural, traditional politicians, and the PTB for up-and-coming labor representatives who had to be brought into electoral politics. Ivete had no such divided loyalty—she was a PTBista first and foremost—and that made her the heir to Getúlio. Her vote totals rose from 20,000 in 1950 to 265,000 in 1982.

Ivete gained a huge following among labor voters in São Paulo and routinely received the highest number of votes of any candidate nationwide. She did this by sticking to the labor platform and using her prodigious speaking skills. She had guts. She also trod a delicate path between Borghi, Jânio, and Adhemar. By 1958 she had won election as president of the PTB–São Paulo.

Many other politicians tried to capture the mantle of Getúlio after his suicide—Jango, Juscelino, and Brizola in particular. But only Jango was 100 percent pro-labor and was recognized as Getúlio's heir (he was even rumored to be his illegitimate son). Apart from Jango, Ivete had the strongest claim to the *trabalhista* banner.

Ivete took part in opposition to the military government in 1965 and joined the Brazilian Democratic Movement (MDB). She was *cassada* (banned from politics) in 1965 because of her association with the PTB. She remained on the sidelines until the ban expired in the late 1970s. The twenty-one years of military dictatorship, in which top generals ran the government for the twin purposes of economic growth and national security, deprived Ivete of a longer and more productive career in politics.

When the military regime ended the two-party system in 1978, Ivete immediately petitioned the national electoral authorities to reestablish the PTB under her leadership. Leonel Brizola, Jango's brother-in-law and a longtime militant in the PTB, also fought for the designation. The tribunal decided in Ivete's favor, so Brizola formed his own PBT, playing on the name. The two rivals attempted to mediate their differences but became bitter enemies. The acrimony was driven partly by the fact that Ivete had become friendly with the military regime's authoritarian strategist, Golbery e Couto. This fits the pattern of populists' inability to collaborate, because their charisma and vote-getting power depends upon undivided loyalty from followers. Close collaborators always dilute a populist leader's aura (Conniff 1999, 1–21).

Ivete's credentials were also tarnished by the fact that Jânio Quadros joined the party in 1982 and ran for mayor of São Paulo. Quadros was a quintessential populist, but he had no labor credentials. Instead, his appeal grew out of his eccentricity, his bizarre personality, and his rhetorical brilliance in public forums. He was also a fierce loner who often shared the hustings only with his mother.

Ivete moved to the middle of the political spectrum, even joining the legislative coalition that supported the last military president, João Figueiredo, in his bid for re-election. Such ideological drift is, of course, common among populists—witness Vargas's drift to the left, Lacerda's to the right, and Perón's from fascism to democracy. In Ivete's case, it involved reinventing herself, after years of enforced absence from politics, in a new context that included Brizola's re-emergence and the appearance of well-established leftist parties. As the leader of a small party, Ivete felt obliged to seek alliances when they presented themselves, in this case with supporters of the regime that had banned her from office!

Ivete fell victim to cancer in 1984 and died at the age of fifty-six, at the peak of her career. By that time, ironically, the labor vote had been more effectively captured by the newly formed Partido dos Trabalhadores (Workers' Party, or PT) of Luis Inácio "Lula" da Silva. Ivete had served continuously in the Congress from 1950 until her death, missing only the years when she was banned from public office by the military. I think she deserves to be remembered as a populist and as one of the most important labor heirs to Getúlio.

Heloísa Helena

In Brazil today, the only woman who seems to fit the definition of populist is Heloísa Helena, the forty-eight-year-old senator from the state of Alagoas. Heloísa was born into a poor family but managed to gain an education as a nurse. In 1992 she first ran for political office, winning the vice mayoral post in the capital, Maceió. From the start, she joined the Partido dos Trabalhadores out of a conviction that it offered the best chance of leading the country toward socialism. She bills herself as a nurse, a Christian, and a Marxist. She is a fiery public speaker and charismatic leader (Decker 2009).

Heloísa Helena should be called a radical populist, as she differs from most of the neopopulists of the region in her rejection of neoliberal economic policies. The term "neopopulism" is used to describe politicians who employ the same techniques to win office as their predecessors but embrace the market-oriented, capitalist economic policies advocated by the International Monetary

Fund, the World Bank, and the U.S. government, the so-called Washington consensus (see Weyland 1999, 172–90). Fernando Collor de Mello, who served a truncated term as president from 1990 to 1992, stands out as a Brazilian neo-populist, while Alberto Fujimori and Carlos Menem are good examples from Peru and Argentina, respectively. They and others enjoyed some policy successes in the 1990s before being widely discredited after 2000.

Heloísa, however, has not succumbed to the temptation to embrace free-market reforms. Instead, she supports agrarian reform, the Movimento dos Sem Terra (the landless movement), suspension of foreign debt, Hugo Chávez's Alternativa Bolivariana para los Pueblos de Nuestra América (Bolivarian Alternative for the Peoples of Our America),[3] reduction in the length of the workday, and banning genetically engineered crops. With regard to the foreign debt, she pronounces an eminently populist line: "To fill the bellies of the bankers it's necessary to empty the plates of the Brazilians!"

Heloísa Helena gained much greater prominence when she was elected a federal senator from Alagoas in 1998, at age thirty-six. When Lula won election as president in 2002, it seemed that she would play a major role in his government. Almost immediately, though, Lula shifted toward the center and reassured the domestic and international business communities that he would preserve the economic status quo. Heloísa Helena protested vociferously and was expelled from the PT in 2003. The following year she gamely formed her own party, the Partido Socialismo e Liberdade (Party of Socialism and Liberty, or PSOL). It has formed an alliance with two other parties on the left, the PC do B and the PSTU.

Heloísa Helena ran for president in the October 2006 elections and came in third in the first round of voting, with 7 percent, a respectable showing for a young woman from a splinter party. Throughout 2009 national polls showed her running in third or fourth place as a presidential candidate in the 2010 elections. But then she surprised observers in late 2009 by announcing that she would run for senator from Alagoas, throwing her party's support to Marina Silva, another female politician from a poor family who recently left the PT to run for president on the Green Party ticket. At her age, and with continued stamina and pluck, Heloísa Helena should have a long and successful career as a populist.

---

3. Hugo Chávez, another radical populist who shuns neoliberal economics, has formed a loose alliance of Latin American leaders opposed to U.S. leadership in the hemisphere. His movement harks back to Simón Bolívar, leader of Latin American independence in the early nineteenth century, hence the term "Bolivariana."

Women as Populist Voters

In 1944 some very innovative thinkers formed an opinion-polling organization called the Instituto Brasileiro de Opinião Pública e Estadística, known universally today as IBOPE. It would be decades before other Latin American countries created such organizations. And it dominated market and opinion surveys in Brazil for the second half of the twentieth century.[4]

According to early IBOPE polls, women in Rio and São Paulo did not have strong differences from men in candidate preferences. A significant percentage (15 percent) of women did, however, express less interest in politics than men. Voters in those days reported getting most of their news from newspapers (66 percent), as compared to radio (44 percent) and acquaintances (25 percent).

In the 1950 election cycle in Rio and São Paulo, IBOPE found that Vargas had an uncanny ability to make statements in line with public preferences, and they mistakenly believed that he must have his own polling organization. They also found that female voters in those two markets were more likely to vote for the UDN candidate, Eduardo Gomes, than for Vargas. They speculated that Gomes, a retired air force general, appealed to women because of his dark good looks. In this case, then, Vargas's granting women the vote and his extraordinary populist campaign bought him no favor among women voters.

In the early 1950s IBOPE polled in 10 cities, trolling for indications of who would win the 1955 presidential election. Women's preferences varied from city to city and often were very similar to men's. The results by gender remained inconclusive in 1955. Two years later a poll in São Paulo found that men registered to vote in higher proportions than women (72 percent versus 50 percent) and actually voted more often as well (90 percent versus 80 percent).

The general experience among women voters in the populist republic was mixed at best. In a few markets, one or another populist fared better with women

---

4. This section is based on research in the IBOPE archive in Rio and the Arquivo Adhemar de Barros in São Paulo in 1987, and on interviews I conducted with Homero Sánchez (March 18, 1987) and IBOPE officials Orjan Olsen and Neysa Furgler (June 23, 1987). A Panamanian, Homero Sánchez, and two Brazilians were given scholarships to study at the Gallup organization in Chicago in 1944. There they learned the basics of sampling, polling, and statistical projections. They set up shop in Rio de Janeiro in 1945 and began seeking clients for market surveys, at first among the U.S. companies operating there. In 1948, however, they decided to branch out into political opinion work and did some polls in Rio and São Paulo, the largest cities in the country. At first they controlled for socioeconomic status, occupation, and gender, but as time went on they added new categories to build stratified samples and also extended their polling to as many as a dozen cities. They frequently checked their projections against actual election outcomes and achieved remarkable results, usually getting within a few percentage points of actual outcomes.

voters than with men, but only Lacerda was consistently favored by women. Major populist figures like Vargas, Adhemar de Barros, João Goulart, and Jânio Quadros enjoyed no exceptional support from women polled. Thus women do not seem to have been particularly susceptible to populist appeals. This may be because candidates in general, including populists, addressed themselves primarily to male voters. After all, despite gaining the right to vote in 1932, few women participated in elections before the 1946 presidential contest, so the system had barely adjusted to their presence in the electorate.

The Mal-Amadas

The one case in which women did heed the call of populism was that of Carlos Lacerda, who had a large following among women, called the Mal-Amadas, or unrequited lovers, because Lacerda could not return their love.[5] Something in his passion, claims of integrity, zeal for reform, and underdog status in campaigns against the ruling parties appealed to women. Moreover, according to activists in the 1950s, Lacerda's demeanor resembled that of the good son who charges into the world to improve it. Some women apparently saw him as that son and supported him disproportionately in elections. I cannot be sure whether the two groups overlapped.

In the 1960 race for governor of the new state of Guanabara (formerly the Federal District), women showed a marked preference for Lacerda. In two Rio polls in 1960 and 1961 (gubernatorial and looking ahead to 1965), Lacerda had a six-point advantage among women as compared to men. In 1963 Lacerda led in presidential preferences in sixteen cities. In a 1964 poll, his advantage among women grew to 11 percent, where it remained through 1965.

Lacerda was a very effective speaker in Congress and other public forums, and he was the only populist in my study who was born and raised in a big city, Rio de Janeiro. He was sophisticated, articulate, and always on his toes. The Mal-Amada phenomenon seems to have been limited to Rio, where he had much exposure over a long period of time. It probably did not hurt that Lacerda was handsome, poised, and physically fit.

5. One of the Mal-Amadas recalled that the term came from a popular song of the era, whose lyrics went, "ninguem me ama, ninguem me quer" (nobody loves me, nobody wants me). This section is based on Dulles 1991, 1996, on private correspondence with Dulles, and on the Carlos Lacerda Papers at the University of Brasília.

Analysis

When discussing populist leadership during our interviews, many Brazilians made family analogies in which the president was represented as the father of the country and the citizens as the children. Vargas's slogan *pai dos pobres* (father of the poor) certainly fit this pattern. My informants, especially the women, suggested that Vargas was a strong father figure, or, by the 1950s, a grandfather figure, while Lacerda fit the model of the beloved son. They did not believe that one could differentiate a "voto feminino" as such, a doubt that was largely borne out in the polling data. They also concurred that physical appearance does sway voters, perhaps more among women. Lacerda, Gomes, and Juarez Távora were examples of handsome candidates who polled somewhat better among women voters than among men.

Gender and populism interacted in several ways. Gender characteristics (masculinity, femininity) definitely influenced how the public perceives populists. They also influenced men's and women's voting patterns, as we saw in the IBOPE surveys, but in ways we understand only imperfectly half a century later. Women voters represented a large potential electorate for populist candidates, but not all populists tried to attract their votes or succeeded in doing so. Finally, the mothers, wives, and daughters of populists influenced their election campaigns in a variety of ways. Alzira, more than most, became an alter ego for Getúlio as they molded his 1950 campaign. Most of the populists I studied made reference to their mothers and wives, often taking them along on campaigns.

In Brazil it is risky to compare classic populists with neopopulists with respect to gendered politics, because there has been only one example of the latter, Fernando Collor de Mello. Collor's manifestation of gender was fairly flamboyant, moreso than that of traditional populists. His second wife was a beauty queen, and he showed her off, exercised, exuded physical health and vitality, and generally displayed machismo in his public persona.

Populism in Brazil tended to promote democracy by encouraging more voters to register and participate in elections. After gaining the franchise, women voters gradually rose as a percentage of the electorate, and higher turnouts tended to legitimize public authorities. As role models, Ivete Vargas and Heloísa Helena probably attracted women voters and opened spaces for them in party leadership, elective office, and election administration. Because the military coup of 1964 targeted leading populists, along with their female officeholders and followers, authoritarianism was the enemy of democracy while feigning to save it. I have referred to this pretense elsewhere as the "macabre dance," which really originated in the 1930s with the Estado Novo coup (Conniff 1981, chapter 8). Finally, the populist leadership instituted the official ballot in 1955, assuring all voters, including women, that their votes would be tallied honestly.

The most important feminist goals of women populists were related to labor rights, for in major cities women approached half the labor force yet received far lower wages and benefits than men. The national-level populist Ivete pursued these goals through the PTB, while Heloísa Helena did so first in the PT and later in the PSOL. In the three-quarters of a century since they won the vote in Brazil, women have penetrated the male bastion of political power in many ways. This chapter has traced their involvement in populist campaigns in the post–World War II years, focusing in particular on two women who were elected to high office using classic populist techniques, and another who helped her father win the biggest election of his career. I have endeavored to demonstrate that populism was not so male-oriented that women could not play important roles. Perhaps women's most important contribution to populism in Brazil has been ensuring that issues women consider crucial, and that would stir them to action, have found a place in the political world.

References

Centro de Pesquiza e Documentação em História Contemporánea (CPDOC). 2001. "Ivete Vargas." In *Dicionário histórico-biográfico brasileiro pós 1930*. 2d ed. Rio de Janeiro: Fundação Getúlio Vargas.

Conniff, Michael. 1981. *Urban Politics in Brazil*. Pittsburgh: University of Pittsburgh Press.

———. 1991. "The Populists of Brazil, 1945–1966." *Review of Latin American Studies* 4 (1): 44–65.

———, ed. 1999. *Populism in Latin America*. Tuscaloosa: University of Alabama Press.

Decker, Michelle. 2009. "Partido Socialismo e Liberdade: The Evolution of the 2010 Elections." Paper presented at the Midwest Association for Latin American Studies conference, Dallas, Texas, November 2009.

Dulles, John W. F. 1991, 1996. *Carlos Lacerda, Brazilian Crusader*. Vols. 1–2. Austin: University of Texas Press.

Navarro, Marysa. 1982. "Evita's Charismatic Leadership." In *Latin American Populism in Comparative Perspective*, ed. Michael Conniff, 47–66. Albuquerque: University of New Mexico Press.

Peixoto, Alzira Vargas do Amaral. 1981. *Depoimento, 1979*. Rio de Janeiro: CPDOC.

Peixoto, Celina Vargas do Amaral. 2002. "O Getúlio Populista." *O Globo*, December 27.

Vargas, Ivete. 1979. *Depoimento, 1977–78*. Rio de Janeiro: CPDOC.

Weyland, Kurt. 1999. "Populism in the Age of Neoliberalism." In *Populism in Latin America*, ed. Michael Conniff, 172–90. Tuscaloosa: University of Alabama Press.

6

POPULIST CONTINUITIES IN "REVOLUTIONARY" PERONISM?

A COMPARATIVE ANALYSIS OF THE GENDER DISCOURSES OF THE FIRST PERONISM (1946–1955) AND THE MONTONEROS

Karin Grammático

Peronism set the tone for Argentine history. The political movement led by Juan Domingo Perón, a military figure who emerged on the political scene in 1943 as a member of the Grupo de Oficiales Unidos (Group of United Officers, or GOU), overturned the conservative government of Ramón Castillo and shaped twentieth-century Argentine history, because of both its innovations and its skill in appropriating past political practices.[1]

One of the most important changes brought about by Peronism was the integration of the working class into the national community and the corresponding recognition of its civil and political status. This was the result of the Peronists' ability to recast citizenship in a new mold, one with a social character. But this success was not limited to workers; other social sectors that had previously been excluded also enjoyed a new position in Argentine society thanks to Peronism.

> The question of citizenship itself, and that of full access to political rights, was a powerful element of Peronist discourse, forming part of the language of popular protest against political exclusion. . . . Peronist discourse denied the validity of liberal ideas of separation between the state and politics, on the one hand, and civil society, on the other. . . . Citizenship was redefined in terms of the economic and social sphere. . . . By constantly emphasizing the social dimension of citizenship, Perón explicitly challenged the validity of a concept of democracy that was limited to formal political rights, and he stretched the concept to the point of including participation in the social and economic life of the nation. (James 1990, 27–29)

---

1. This chapter, including quotations from Spanish-language sources, was translated from the Spanish by Karen Kampwirth. I would like to thank her for this enormous translation job.

Women participated in, and benefited from, these profound changes, gaining the same civil rights under Perón that men enjoyed. The notable attachment of women to Peronism was one of the reasons that it was so successful.

In this chapter I analyze images of women and gender in Peronist discourse between 1946 and 1955, comparing them to images promoted by the guerrilla organization the Monteneros in the 1970s. Perón's government was overthrown in a military coup on September 16, 1955, sending Perón into exile and creating a de facto government headed by General Pedro E. Aramburu (1955–58). According to Marcelo Cavarozzi, the Aramburu government's banning of Peronism (which remained in effect until 1973) introduced a deep division into Argentine society and politics. For example, between 1958 and 1966 "parliamentary mechanisms co-existed, in conflictual and sometimes antagonistic ways, with extra-institutional politics. The result was the division of society into two main 'blocs'— that is, a popular sector [largely Peronist] and an anti-Peronist front made up of bourgeois and middle-class groups—these two blocs rarely used the same political spaces for resolving conflicts and reaching agreements based on compromise" (1997, 20).

From exile in Madrid, where he lived from 1960 to 1973, Perón strengthened his ties with Peronist sectors in opposition to the labor movement, and above all with the youth sector that had recently joined the Peronist movement; many members of that sector would support the future armed wings of Peronism. During the 1960s, radicalization was fed by the example of the Cuban Revolution (1959) as well as by the growing political, social, and cultural presence of young people. These teenage boys and girls, many of whom were from affluent and middle-class families, joined the very Peronist movement that their elders had repudiated and fought against in earlier years.

It was in this context that the Montonero organization was officially born, in May 1970, with the kidnapping and assassination of the former de facto president, Pedro E. Aramburu. The Montoneros identified themselves as Peronists (although they conflated various ideologies, including integral Catholicism, nationalism, and Marxism) and believed that armed struggle—supported by grassroots organizing—was the only way to bring about the return of Perón. For them, Perón was the clear leader of the national liberation movement, and he would make it possible for socialism to triumph in Argentina.

In addition to the words of the Montoneros, I analyze the words of members of Agrupación Evita (Evita Group), a political front for women that the Montoneros created in September 1973. The continuities and ruptures in these words shed light on the ideological and political basis of Montonero thought and its possible links with the Peronism of the 1940s and 1950s. Although there is new interest in the political ideology of the Montoneros, few studies analyze their discourse in terms of classic Peronism (Sigal and Verón 2003), and those that consider gender issues remain largely unpublished.

Agrupación Evita repeated the themes of Peronist populism and reproduced some of its practices regarding women and their participation in politics. The key point is that the Peronist Left made few innovations in the area of women and politics, and in fact there were no women in the national leadership of the Montoneros, with the brief exception of Norma Arrostito, who participated in Aramburu's kidnapping and assassination in 1970. Nonetheless, the women of Agrupación Evita managed to do some questioning of their political roles, but they did it as a result of their experiences as political activists.

This study is based on written and oral sources. The written sources include various speeches given by Juan and Eva Perón, documents produced by the Montoneros and Agrupación Evita, and the mainstream and Montonero press. The study also draws upon interviews I conducted between 2003 and 2007 with women who held leadership positions within Agrupación Evita; the interviewees are identified by initials only.

Agrupación Evita: "Radical Movement Within the Feminine Branch"

On September 19, 1973, Agrupación Evita was officially presented to the public during the closing act of the "Perón for president" campaign, coordinated by Region I of the Juventud Peronista (Peronist Youth, or JP). Calling itself the "radical movement within the Feminine Branch of the Justicialista[2] movement" (*La Opinión,* September 19, 1973, 6), Agrupación Evita was one of the final mass organizations, as they were called at the time, formed by the Montoneros that year. In addition to the JP—which was the first Peronist organization to join the Montoneros, in June 1972—a series of mass organizations affiliated themselves with the Montoneros: the Juventud Universitaria Peronista (Peronist University Youth, or JUP), the Juventud Trabajadora Peronista (Peronist Worker Youth, or JTP), the Unión de Estudiantes Secundarios (Union of High School Students, or UES), the Movimiento de Villeros Peronistas (Peronist Shantytown Dwellers' Movement, or MVP), and the Movimiento de Inquilinos Peronistas (Peronist Tenants' Movement, or MIP).

2. "Justicialista" (or pro-justice) was the official name of Perón's party (translator's note).

Agrupación Evita was created, as were the other Montonero front organizations, with two goals: on the one hand, a greater influence in the social movements of the time, and on the other hand, to challenge the "orthodox" sectors for control of the Peronist movement. In this way, through the actions of its women's front, the Montoneros hoped to displace the authorities of the Feminine Branch, whose leaders maintained close relations with the political groups and unions of the Peronist Right. Even though the Feminine Branch—one of three sections of Peronismo, along with the union movement and the masculine section—did not seem to make major decisions and was less politically important than in earlier periods, there were reasons why the Montoneros were interested in that organization. The Montoneros were determined to break up any group that could present an obstacle to their agenda, and the leadership of the Feminine Branch was one such obstacle. Despite its problems, it was one of the institutionalized sectors of Peronism, and it still had a right to representation when decisions were made. Finally, the Montonero leaders recognized the symbolic value of the Feminine Branch and its founder, Eva Perón, within Peronist memory. So Montonero leaders hoped that through the Agrupación Evita they would be able to recreate one of the most distinctive Peronist achievements: providing their female followers with their own organizational structure. In its own way, it replicated this Peronist characteristic (having an institutional space dedicated to women), and so reinforced the idea that the Montoneros were truly Peronist.

Agrupación Evita and the other front organizations played fundamental roles in Montonero politics following the triumph of the Frente Justicialista de Liberación (Justice Liberation Front, or FREJULI) in the March 1973 general election. The Montoneros, whose activities had been limited to clandestine work and armed struggle, decided to participate in legal political activities, and so had to practice politics in a new way. The mass organizations were the means by which the Montoneros intended to start participating in legal politics. All together, the various groups of the Peronist Left formed the Tendencia Revolucionaria, or Revolutionary Tendency (Gillespie 1998, 169–70).

At this time two Peronist currents were vying for Perón's exclusive recognition and for control of the movement. On the one hand, the right-wing, or orthodox, Peronists fought for a *patria Peronista* (Peronist fatherland). Headed by union leaders, this faction defended the idea that "class alliance" was fundamental to Peronism and rejected the possibility of an anticapitalist revolution in Argentina. On the other hand was the Peronist Left (also known as the "Tendency") which fought for a *patria socialista* (socialist fatherland) and promoted "revolutionary" change under the leadership of Juan Perón.

Perón, who had benefited from playing the protest-oriented Peronist Youth off against the Peronist union bureaucracy and other political allies, successfully repeated this game so as to put an end to the already weak military dictatorship (1966–73). Playing the role of a "pyromaniac firefighter" (to use Alan Rouquie's expression), Perón went back and forth between endorsing the guerrilla movement's actions and presenting himself as the only one who could control that movement and make the country governable.

And so once again Perón made himself into the indispensable figure of Argentine politics. Although he succeeded with this maneuver, Perón chose not to run for the presidency in March 1973, instead designating Héctor Cámpora to run in his place. Cámpora won with 49.5 percent of the vote.[3]

The new political situation caused by the Peronist win created challenges for the Montoneros. They responded by pulling back from clandestine politics, rethinking the wisdom of armed struggle, and beginning new political practices. As mentioned above, these new practices involved creating mass political organizations with the goal of participating more in grassroots politics. At the same time, these organizations played important roles in the struggle against right-wing factions—which the Montoneros denounced as the principal enemies of "popular government"—for control of the Peronist movement. Nonetheless, they soon began to lose this gamble, in part because of problems with the mass organizations, but mainly because of changes in the relationship between the left-wing factions and Perón himself. From March 1973 until Perón's death in July 1974, when they decided to go underground again, the Montoneros, along with the Tendency, rode a roller coaster in which the initial euphoria over Cámpora's victory—for which they thought they were largely responsible—and their participation in his government gave way to worry about Perón's apparent support for right-wing groups. The Montoneros ended up losing ground to the Right, both in the national government and in the Peronist movement.[4]

---

3. On July 12, 1973, Cámpora and Vicente Sola Lima resigned from the presidency and the vice presidency, respectively. Raúl Lastiri, president of the Congress, became the interim president, and new elections were announced for September 23. This time, Juan Perón was eligible to run; he was elected president, and his wife, Isabel Perón, vice president, by an overwhelming majority. They took office on October 12, 1973.

4. The first indication that Perón was withdrawing his support from the left wing of his movement came in April 1973, when he fired Rodolfo Galimberti from his position as youth delegate to the Supreme Peronist Council because he publicly supported the creation of popular militias. From that point on, the disagreements between Perón and the Peronist Left grew. In January and February 1974, eight congressmen from the JP resigned, and governors close to the Tendency were fired. Finally, on May 1, during the celebration of May Day (Labor Day) in the Plaza de Mayo, any chance of reconciliation ended when an argument between Perón and left-wing demonstrators concluded

Constructing the Political Identity of Peronist Women

In an effort to expand their base of support, the Peronists promoted the mobilization of broad sectors of the population that had previously been at the margins of social and political life in Argentina. This helps to explain the painstaking attention the Peronist government devoted to women. The mobilization of women began early. In 1944, when he was secretary of labor, Perón arranged for the creation of the División de Trabajo y Asistencia de la Mujer (Women's Labor and Welfare Division), which, in addition to overseeing welfare initiatives, became the political office that did much of the work of promoting women's suffrage.

Once Perón was elected president, his government continued to promote political rights for women. Eva Perón headed the intense campaign, which culminated in law 13,010, giving women the right to vote, on September 23, 1947. This victory was decisive in consolidating ties between women and the Peronist government, and it was Eva's "baptism by fire," in which she became responsible for mobilizing women. After that time, politicians began appealing to women as political actors. Along with the law giving women the vote, the other milestone in the political mobilization of women occurred two years later, with the formation of the Partido Peronista Femenino (Feminine Peronist Party).

At the same time, the Perón administration enacted a series of measures that benefited women socioeconomically. The state demanded women's help in promoting national development, which would happen if family economies—for which housewives were responsible—were overseen correctly. In 1952 the Ministry of Finance declared in an official publication, "Housewives are the ones who have to care for the domestic economy, providing for the home, controlling household spending and the family budget. If they take on this responsibility . . . , there is no doubt that every family economy will be well organized, since mothers and wives are the ones who best understand what is necessary, and they understand when and why things get wasted and how and where to find savings" (quoted in Bianchi and Sanchís 1988, 53–54). Demands of this sort can also be found in Perón's two Five-Year Plans (1947–52 and 1952–57) and in the Economic Emergency Plan of 1951 (Novick 1993, 22).

---

with the exit of the leftists, leaving the plaza half empty. After Perón's death, on July 1, 1974, the situation became unbearable for the Left. Attacked by the Alianza Anticomunista Argentina (Argentine Anticommunist Alliance, or Triple A), a paramilitary organization headed by the minister of social welfare, José López Rega, the Montoneros again went underground. As a result, the open political organizations ceased to exist.

Linked to the political relevance it gave to the institution of the family and women's roles, Perón's government saw motherhood as one of the most important ways in which women could commit themselves to the state and to the development of "national greatness" (Di Liscia 1999). To this end, it gave insistent pronatalist sermons and deployed a series of measures to protect mothers and newborns. It is worth noting that in addition to health measures, the Perón administration gave women subsidies for giving birth, reduced taxes for big families, enforced strict repression of abortion, provided training for women in modern child-care norms through radio programs and the print media, and otherwise supported mothers and children through *unidades básicas femeninas* (the political meeting spaces for Peronist activists). All of these efforts were due, on the one hand, to the population policies of the Perón government, which saw population growth as beneficial geopolitically and, on the other hand, to its interest in promoting public health policies to guarantee a healthy working class.

Government support for women was linked to a discourse dedicated to women, which helped to create a political identity for Peronist women. Women's identity arose from the conditions working-class women faced, and if they were women of the people, they were Peronists (Palermo 1997–98). Being a Peronist implied being part of the people, and being part of the people in turn guaranteed that one was part of the nation. It was this identity of Peronists with the people and the nation that made it possible to incorporate women, who until then had been excluded from political life, into a broad-based political movement that identified as Argentine (Bianchi and Sanchís 1988, 57).

As part of "the people," Peronist women exhibited values like self-abnegation, sacrifice, love, and selflessness, all of which were tied up with the image of mother. In a note published in the party magazine *Mundo Peronista* in 1952, Perón explained, "*I have faith in women, because I have faith in mothers.* We Peronists want women to educate their children from the time they are in the cradle, so they may raise prudent men who are motivated by their profound affection for the country and their deep respect for society, who are motivated by the basic citizenship virtues. . . . If anything is important, it certainly is to conserve and defend the family, for it is the true building block of the nation" (quoted in Zink 2000, 17, emphasis added). The behavior and expectations that the Peronist discourse laid out for women were intimately tied to the model of the traditional family, in which men were breadwinners and women, homemakers.

This discourse called into question whether women could work outside the home. As Bianchi and Sanchís note with respect to Eva Perón's speeches, "women who worked outside the home were practically excluded. Though there were references to them, that was mainly during the campaign for women's suffrage. . . . Slowly these references began to disappear until the point when women's work outside the home was explicitly condemned. If as late as 1949 the fact that some women worked outside the home was recognized—along with the difficulties they faced—that was presented as an exceptional response to circumstances and needs that would force a woman to compete with a man. . . . But this acknowledgment had disappeared by [the time of] *La razón de mi vida* (1951), where Evita affirmed without any doubt that women's place is in the home, condemning those who would distance themselves from their 'destiny and mission'" (1988, 60). Nonetheless, it is worth noting that the gender expectations promoted by the Peronist state contrasted with what was actually happening in Argentine society. According to census data, from 1900 until at least 1950 there was a steady increase in the number of women who worked outside the home (Lobato 2007, 46, 49).

The link between promoting women's roles as wives and mothers and the decision to promote women's participation in the public sphere was less problematic. In fact, their role as wives and mothers qualified them to take part in political life. For the Peronists, women's political participation was based on the "extension of women's home responsibilities into ever wider networks, especially the largest network: that of the national community" (Palermo 1997–98, 166).

By classifying women as belonging to the domestic world and at the same time promoting their participation in public life, the Peronists erased the border between public and private, at least rhetorically. This was not because of a break between daily life and political action but rather their continuity. As a result, there was nothing radical about incorporating women into political life; it reaffirmed all the attitudes, feelings, and values that were supposedly typical of women.

The language of Agrupación Evita preserved this compatibility between women's political activism and their roles as wives and mothers. Its discourse also used the home and motherhood to justify women's participation in politics. As a spokesperson for Agrupación Evita put it in an editorial in *El Descamisado,* the Montoneros' newspaper, "Going out from our homes, our families, through her daily life each woman makes sacrifices which ennoble her" (November 6, 1973, 28–31). Women's actions "revolve around a series of demands, which are of concern to all the people but which are taken on more by women because they concern their roles as mothers, housewives, and workers" (ibid., February 12, 1974, 16–19).

Agrupación Evita does not seem to have questioned the grouping *woman-mother-political action*. It nonetheless added the figure of *worker* as a building block of the identity of Peronist women. Along with the fight for "milk and vaccines," the group demanded "equal pay for equal work . . . preschools and day care centers so we may work without worry" (ibid., September 26, 1973, 25). "We need a labor union that would advocate for women who devote themselves to domestic service" and laws that "would protect . . . women who dedicate their time and life to taking care of their homes" (ibid., November 6, 1973, 28–31).

For its part, the Montonero organization blurred the implications of gender for political action—it repeated in different ways the idea that "here there are no men and women, there are exploiters and exploited"—and gave priority to class struggle instead. It referred to women's particular political qualities only in the context of insistently and exclusively underlining their maternal roles: "*but there was a higher calling that led them to give themselves to the Peronist cause: the lives of their children;* when they nursed them they reminded them that there had been a great leader, that a beautiful woman had accompanied him, and that we all belong to that people. . . . So behind every person fallen in battle, behind every imprisoned and tortured comrade, *there was a mother who had inculcated that consciousness*" (*El Descamisado*, November 6, 1973, emphasis added).

More than Agrupación Evita, the Montoneros took their ideas about gender relations and women's roles in political struggle directly from the Peronism of the 1940s and 1950s. Their political analysis did not seem to critique relations between men and women at all. And in their excessive insistence on associating women with the figure of the mother, they erased the political content from women's participation in public life.

Populist Tensions: Feminism

Part of constructing an identity involves clearly defining the "enemy." In the case of Peronism, the feminist played this role. Peronist identity was constructed in opposition to the feminist and also to the "woman of the oligarchy." These two "enemies" carried the weight of the foreign and "disloyal" (*vendepatria*) views that Peronists accorded them.

Feminists were part of the opposition, minority, and anti-Argentine cast of characters. For Eva Perón, they belonged "to another race of women. To say they are like men is to unfairly insult men. . . . We have seen the rise of a class of female leaders who are frivolous and of little use to the nation, women who have never thought about the well-being of their men, but only about squandering their lives, with little concern for morals. These are not the sort of women that the nation needs. The people, the country, the nation require women who struggle to perfect the species: women who are good mothers, who are good companions to their men and not so outrageous as to kill time, just waiting for death, without doing anything worthwhile" (quoted in Bianchi and Sanchís 1988, 58–59).

One of the most decisive issues in the relationship between Peronism and the Argentine feminist movement was women's suffrage. During the first three decades of the twentieth century various feminist groups promoted a series of initiatives—ranging from mock elections, petitions, public meetings, even draft laws—with the goal of securing the franchise for women. These efforts failed, and when women finally got the vote, it was associated with Peronist politics. In this way the Peronists cleverly pushed to the side the feminist struggles that preceded this legal change, replacing them with the image of Eva Perón, whom they represented as the one who had brought about this political victory for Argentine women. For their part, "the great majority of feminists did not celebrate the victory . . . they found that the right they had fought so hard for would now surely be a way to manipulate [women]. Female voters would respond to the maneuvers of the regime, which would subjugate the female will. . . . Disconcerted, feminists returned to the stubborn old idea that the women's vote was a right-wing vote, an idea that was heard throughout anti-Peronist circles, and not just among men" (Barrancos 2007, 182–83).

In recent years we have finally seen some analysis of the relationship between Peronism and feminism that goes beyond mutual condemnation. Silvana Palermo, for example, argues that Peronist discourse on feminism must be understood in terms of the way in which it recovered and redefined elements of maternalistic feminism—which valued femininity and sexual differences, emphasized the complementarity of men and women, and saw maternity as playing a key role in women's demands for equity—incorporating maternalistic feminism into populist rhetoric (Palermo 1997–98). Palermo's interpretation, with its emphasis on the selective way in which the Peronists took elements from one of the most important schools of thought within feminism, opens new doors for thinking about this issue.

Rather than diminishing over time, the differences between Peronism and feminism only deepened. Agrupación Evita maintained the distance from the feminists that Peronists had always maintained. Nonetheless, the silence of the Montonero front group was surprising given the era—a time when feminism was receiving a great deal of international attention and when there was also a local feminist presence in groups like the Unión Feminista Argentina (Argentine Feminist Union) and the Movimiento de Liberación Femenina (Women's Liberation Movement).[5]

The members of Agrupación Evita believed that women's participation should "be part of the struggle of all exploited people, because there is no such thing as women's liberation without national and social liberation, and their problems will be resolved as part of the people as a whole" (*El Descamisado,* February 12, 1974). The idea that female liberation would be an inevitable and even a natural result of the revolutionary change that Peronism would bring about was repeated by the former members of Agrupación Evita I interviewed.

> I knew a few feminist comrades [*alguna compañera*] at that time; obviously they questioned us and said that we were just throwbacks, just helpers, and they hurt my pride, but we responded very proudly that first we had to make social revolution and then we could concern ourselves with that. The thing is, those were the 1960s, when women went to college, and we thought that was how we were going to resolve everything, but that isn't so. (N. B., interview by author, October 6, 2003)

> Despite our making demands as a women's group, we didn't feel that feminism, which was already well known at an international level, could represent our interests as women comrades in the struggle for national liberation. (D. G., interview by author, June 14, 2006)

These ideas, held by members of Agrupación Evita, were shared with other female Peronist leaders who did not participate in Agrupación Evita. The interpretations put forth by Nilda Garré, a sympathizer with the left-wing Tendency, and Virginia Sanguinetti, from the more orthodox Peronist group Guardia de Hierro (Iron Guard), are significant. In 1973 both young women were members of Congress who took part in a series of congressional debates on the "woman question." Garré observed, "One should not address this issue as a problem of divisions between the sexes. Women's liberation is part and parcel of the liberation of the people. In that way our proposal is different from that of the feminist movement, which makes just demands but uses sectarian criteria." Similarly, Sanguinetti noted, "These proposals form part of a political plan: to incorporate women

5. On the Argentine feminist movement in the 1970s and its ties to the political and armed Left, see Grammático 2005.

into productive work. . . . The goal of the laws is to resolve the supposed contradiction between the mother and the working woman; the nation needs both
of them. . . . The Peronist feminine movement was never feminist because it knew
how to address women's issues within the context of liberating all the people"
(quoted in *La Opinión*, November 6, 1973, 21).

In these statements one sees the enduring mistrust of the feminist agenda,
without distinction between different currents of Peronism. Although, according to Garré, feminism made "just demands," both legislators—from mutually
antagonistic currents within Peronism—emphasized how wrong feminists were
not to frame women's struggles within the struggle for "national liberation"
that Peronism embodied.

Arguing for a Separate Structure

Upon his return to the country on June 20, 1973, Perón set out to complete and
deepen the process of reorganizing and controlling the Peronist movement that
had begun in the latter years of the military dictatorship. With this goal in mind,
he held a meeting on August 27 with hundreds of female Peronists from all over
the country in the Teatro Nacional Cervantes to revive the Feminine Branch of
the party. This was one of the few events that he presided over following his
return, prior to his becoming president.

In his speech Perón emphasized the importance of women in national development. "If we are not capable of incorporating women into productive positions in this country," he said, "we will be giving up on half of our chances for
attaining future greatness. . . . From this it is clear that we need to incorporate
women into the active life of the country. Women have the same abilities as
men, and they should not be reduced to inferior jobs, for they can compete
with men in the areas of technology, scientific work, research, and every sort of
study" (Perón 1973).

Recognizing women's productive abilities was something new for Perón, but
he made clear that it was not at odds with women's main role: taking care of the
home and children. "At this moment," he continued, "Argentine women carry
responsibilities that are as great as those of men, or even greater, for because of the
moral decline that has occurred, a woman's hand and word have a decisive influence, much more decisive than those of the man who heads the household. . . .
We have to save the family, which is in danger, because when communities fall
apart and their morals loosen, the first to suffer is the family. Shoring up this

institution will create the basis for our future, but it is also the most serious responsibility of the Argentine woman. . . . To rebuild the country, women are more important than all institutions and all the moral associations and that sort of thing."

All of these tasks required an organization, whose "natural" setting was none other than the Feminine Branch: "Women in our movement must be loyally organized to carry out this task: uniting and organizing is necessary because of this task. . . . The political organization Feminine Branch has a decisive importance, because in the future this organization is going to produce groups to serve in social welfare organizations, so that women may defend their own families and their communities" (ibid.).

Validating themselves through this message from Perón, the Montoneros promoted and justified the creation of their own women's front: "Agrupación Evita has been created in response to the needs of General Perón. Our leader has pointed out the necessity of women's active participation in this stage of the process of National Liberation and Reconstruction. And this participation should happen within the natural framework that Peronist women have created and developed: the Feminine Branch of the movement" (*El Descamisado*, November 6, 1973). The Montoneros appealed to Perón's language, not only to legitimize the existence of the Agrupación but also to endorse its status as an internal current within the Feminine Branch.

The Feminine Branch had been created on July 26, 1949. That day, in the same theater that Perón would choose twenty-four years later for his meeting with female delegates to his movement, Eva Perón presided over an important political event that concluded with the founding of the Partido Peronista Femenino (Feminine Peronist Party, or PPF, which later became the Feminine Branch). Having been designated president of the new party by acclamation, Evita gave a long speech that established the goals of the PPF and the ways in which its members would participate in politics.

With the end of "the unacceptable period of civil guardianship" over Argentine women, and thanks to the women's suffrage law, a new era had begun. "We gather in the first national assembly of the feminine Peronist movement," she told her audience, "to *trace our own steps,* to search for *our own path* as women and citizens who have accepted and feel responsible for the future of the Nation. . . . The fact that we are prepared to trace our own path as women and citizens does not mean, nor could it mean, breaking off from the national Peronist revolution or dividing the movement" (Perón 1952, 4, 8, emphasis added).

Although some Argentine political parties, like the Socialist Party, had made a place for women, only the Peronist movement included a women's division on the same footing as the other "branches," the masculine party and the labor union sector. For the Peronists, the creation of the PPF was, on the one hand, compensation for the hardships and humiliation that women had suffered in the pre-Peronist era; on the other hand, it was a sort of political recognition of their status as wives and mothers: "We women *have not just been witness to social drama. We have been actors* and we will continue to be [actors] in the future even more intensely. We insist on a place in the struggle because we have suffered as much as or more than men and because, as we always say, *our essential mission is not just to give children to the Fatherland, but rather to give men to humanity*" (ibid., 4, emphasis added). Evita added that women's first and most important mission was to "spread and popularize Perón's doctrine . . . beginning in the home, where we are the inspiration and spirit, so that its material and moral life will be filled with the ideas and works of General Perón," and so to obtain "happiness for all workers, an essential precondition for the greatness of the Fatherland, because there is no great fatherland without happy people. And the only path that is open to Peronist women, who enjoy full political rights, is to organize and unify the feminine Peronist movement in the service of its Leader and its nation" (7).

Just as the PPF had dedicated itself to the service of Perón's project and worked toward "the happiness of the people" and "the greatness of the fatherland," Agrupación Evita presented its work as a contribution to the policies of reconstruction and national liberation that the Peronists set forth in May 1973. In their first public communications, its leaders declared that they should "unite the feminine sector of the Movement to really promote its essential work, following the instructions of General Perón, who has called on us to organize and rebuild" (*La Opinión,* November 3, 1973, 15).

The areas in which the members of Agrupación Evita worked were fundamentally linked to helping children, mothers, and families. They engaged in a wide variety of activities, including organizing camps for children, cleaning and channeling streams in poor neighborhoods, repairing schools, and giving talks on women's and children's health. At the same time, they promoted the political education of their followers and reenergized the campaign to repatriate Evita's remains.

The political tasks that members of Agrupación Evita carried out do not seem to have differed much from the tasks carried out by other Peronist women organized within other currents of the Movement, including those who worked directly under the leadership of the Feminine Branch. One can even trace certain continuities between the jobs that Eva Perón thought up for the *unidades bási-cas femeninas* at the end of the 1940s and those that the Montonero women's front proposed. Nonetheless, Agrupación Evita framed its activities within the context of a "revolutionary project." Although the first public event organized by Agrupación Evita was dedicated to the "Peronist Mother," it was presented as an event far different from typical festive events dedicated to motherhood. "It is not going to be a traditional show," wrote one of its leaders, but "rather a festival that does not contradict the spirit of struggle to which we are devoted" (*La Opinión*, November 3, 1973, 15). The same criterion informed the organiza-tion of children's camps. For Agrupación Evita, recreational activities expressed "the dynamic presence of the people along with the People's Government, which for us is a way of being with General Perón in the path toward the National Lib-eration that we seek" (*El Descamisado*, December 18, 1973, 30–31).

Agrupación Evita reflected upon the reasoning that led female Peronists to organize themselves separately from men:

> It is worth asking ourselves why we have to organize as women within the Feminine Branch of the Movement. In truth, we are the equals of Peronist men, we have the same rights and the same duties toward our people. So then, if we are equal, why do we have to create a separate organization? [It is because] we are not at the same level as men in terms of conscious-ness and political organization. That can be seen in the fact that, of all the ways in which our people organize themselves, there are always more men doing active work. . . . But there are reasons why that happens. We have had less political training and education than men because, in addi-tion to working, we have to carry out our obligations as wives and mothers, working at home and educating our children. (*El Descamisado*, Septem-ber 26, 1973, 25)

Upon founding the PPF, Evita spoke proudly of the possibility that Peronist women could trace their "own path" in a structure devoted exclusively to women. In the words of Agrupación Evita, by contrast, one detects a certain disappoint-ment in having to organize this way, despite women's having the same rights and responsibilities as men. The difference was rooted, the Agrupación explained, in women's lack of preparation for a political fight. This educational deficit—from which men did not seem to suffer, as they were always the majority in-volved in "active work"—could be attributed to women's responsibilities for their children, which placed serious limits on their political activism.

The roles of wife and mother were crucial in the construction of Peronist women's political identities, and Agrupación Evita took on that position as its own, but in its discourse there is some tension between domestic and political work. That tension—responding to the subordinate position that women are assigned in the gendered division of labor—was not thoroughly analyzed. In fact, Agrupación Evita actually reinforced the gendered division of labor in its acceptance of the classic populist vision of women slaving away for the well-being and happiness of the people: "our goal is for our *unidades básicas* to be our organizing and mobilizing tasks for the happiness of our people and the defense of women's rights" (*El Descamisado,* September 26, 1973, 25).

Concluding Thoughts: Inheriting and (Re)Creating Political Identities

The work of noted Agrupación Evita leader Susana Sanz did not begin auspiciously. "When she was assigned the role of leading Agrupación Evita in the Cuyo region, Susana Sanz felt like a bomb had gone off. . . . At that time, for many activists, being sent from the Peronist Youth [JP] to the Agrupación Evita was a sort of demotion. . . . The JP attracted more people all the time. So when they sent her to Agrupación Evita she felt like she had been relegated to something less important" (Anguita and Caparrós 1998, 155). Some weeks later, Sanz told the Montonero leadership, "Please do not send me just any *compañera.* For the Agrupación I only want those *compañeras* who, first, are content with being women, and, second, who love women. Because if they do not feel that the marginalization of women is unjust, and [if] they don't understand that to fight against all of that requires certain kinds of work and that women can learn . . . it would be of no use, it would not help to send those sort of *compañeras* to the Agrupación" (157). These two statements reflect two very different moments in the life of this activist. Among other things, they illustrate how significant political learning changed how she saw herself as a leader and her thinking about women's political action.

The awakening of doubts regarding the traditional role of women in politics and the increasingly positive view of political work with women were evident in the experiences of other Agrupación Evita activists I interviewed.

> Always in my experience of women's meetings, women always talked about issues of daily life. We talked about personal issues or about our boyfriends or sexual questions. We women never acted like we could only talk about

politics, strictly speaking. That is, I think that in fact, regarding the dichotomy of public and private—a dichotomy that shouldn't exist—in our
meetings, although we didn't yet have any gender consciousness, I think
that came out right away: the problems we had, we worried if a woman
had a drunkard husband, and we tried to think about what could be done
about it. And we told our personal stories as well. That is why we found
those meetings to be so valuable, because collectively we came to realize
that I am not the only one who goes through these things. (N. B., interview
by author, October 6, 2003)

For example, it seems like a silly thing but it is an indicator: on the first
of May [1974], when we went to the Plaza we marched in organized col-
umns. . . . I remember that there was a big fight because the *compañeros*
from the JP wanted to go to the head of the line, and those of us from
Agrupación Evita also wanted to head the line. And we were still arguing
as we marched into the Plaza de Mayo. . . . It isn't that we had the same
sort of gender consciousness that we have today . . . but women's issues
were on the table, just not very well theorized. . . . We did not have a feminist agenda as it is understood today, and no understanding of gender,
but we did talk about women's issues, just not from a theoretical perspective, which came along a little later. We always talked about how women
were fighting, leading, and then we were not represented within the top
leadership, and that happened everywhere. I'll tell you how it happened in
the neighborhood. And also, one thing happened: we women got together
and when women get together, issues come up, things come up. (P. A., interview by author, July 5, 2006)

In this way Agrupación Evita unintentionally opened doors to rethinking relations between men and women in daily life and in politics. It was a space for
analyzing the roles that women played within the Montoneros, and it also permitted the reevaluation of political work for and with women.

With more or less consciousness of the changes, with more or less difficulty
in naming them and accepting their consequences, the questioning of inequality between men and women began to gnaw at the organization's structures and
beliefs. Although national liberation continued to be their priority, female activists began to question why they had been forced into particular places and
roles. And so it was that, from within the very heart of Agrupación Evita, a
number of its members began to think of daily life and intimate relations as

political, to question authority, and to find conflict where before there had been only indifference.

References

Anguita, Eduardo, and Martín Caparrós. 1998. *La voluntad.* 3 vols. Buenos Aires: Editorial Norma.

Barrancos, Dora. 2007. *Mujeres en la sociedad argentina: Una historia de cinco siglos.* Buenos Aires: Editorial Sudamericana.

Bianchi, Susana, and Norma Sanchís. 1988. *El partido peronista femenino.* Buenos Aires: CEAL.

Cavarozzi, Marcelo. 1997. *Autoritarismo y democracia (1955–1996): La transición del estado al mercado en la Argentina.* Buenos Aires: Ariel.

De Riz, Liliana. 2000. *La política en suspenso, 1966–1976.* Buenos Aires: Piados.

Di Liscia, María Herminia. 1999. "'Ser madre es un deber' (maternidad en los gobiernos peronistas, 1946–1955)." In *Historia y género: Seis estudios sobre la condición femenina,* ed. Daniel Villa et al., 33–51. Buenos Aires: Biblos.

Gillespie, Richard. 1998. *Soldados de Perón: Los Montoneros.* Buenos Aires: Grijalbo.

Grammático, Karin. 2005. "Las mujeres políticas y las feministas en los tempranos setenta: Un diálogo (im)posible." In *Historia, género y política en los '70,* ed. Andrea Andujar et al., 19–38. Buenos Aires: FFyL-UBA/Feminaria.

———. 2007. "La Agrupación Evita: Apuntes de una experiencia política de mujeres." In *Historias de luchas, resistencias y representaciones: Mujeres en la Argentina, siglos XIX y XX,* ed. María Cecilia Bravo, Fernanda Gil Lozano, and Valeria Pita, 267–82. San Miguel de Tucumán: Editorial de la Universidad de Tucumán.

James, Daniel. 1990. *Resistencia e integración: El peronismo y la clase trabajadora argentina, 1946–1976.* Buenos Aires: Editorial Sudamericana.

Lobato, Mirta Zaida. 2007. *Historia de las trabajadoras en la Argentina (1869–1960).* Buenos Aires: Edhasa.

Navarro, Marysa. 2005. *Evita.* Buenos Aires: Editorial Edhasa.

Novick, Susana. 1993. *Mujer, estado y políticas sociales.* Buenos Aires: CEAL.

Palermo, Silvana. 1997–98. "El sufragio femenino en el Congreso Nacional: Ideologías de género y ciudadanía en la Argentina (1916–1955)." *Boletín del Instituto de Historia Argentina y Americana Dr. Emilio Ravignani* 16–17:151–79.

Perón, Eva. 1952. *Discurso de Eva Perón ante la 1ª asamblea nacional del Partido Peronista Femenino, 26 de julio de 1949.* Buenos Aires: Presidencia de la Nación, Subsecretaría de Informaciones.

Perón, Juan Domingo. 1973. *Perón convoca a la mujer: Discursos del teniente General Juan Perón ante las delegadas del movimiento nacional justicialista.* Buenos Aires: Confederación General del Trabajo.

Sigal, Silvia, and Eliseo Verón. 2003. *Perón o muerte: Los fundamentos discursivos del fenómeno peronista.* Buenos Aires: Eudeba.

Zink, Mirta. 2000. "Madres para la patria: 'Mundo Peronista' y la interpelación a las mujeres." In *Mujeres, maternidad y peronismo,* ed. María Herminia Di Liscia et al., 12–37. Santa Rosa: Fondo Editorial Pampeano.

7

POPULISM FROM ABOVE, POPULISM FROM BELOW

GENDER POLITICS UNDER ALBERTO FUJIMORI AND EVO MORALES

Stéphanie Rousseau

Presidents Alberto Fujimori of Peru (1990–2000) and Evo Morales of Bolivia (2005–present) are two contemporary cases of populism in the Andes. Fujimori's rule is a famous case of neopopulism typical of the neoliberal swing in Latin America, while Morales is sometimes depicted as representing a resurgence of old-style populism in the era following the "Washington consensus," and sometimes as a successful case of "ethnopopulism."[1] If they differ on several counts, their leadership styles share important features. Both illustrate the rise to power of new political actors, including a significant number of women. Both personally embody socially significant experiences affecting the poor, which accounts for their populist appeal. They exemplify new political leadership models that, by virtue of their social and ethnic origins, contradict the common imagery of powerful elites in the Andes as invariably *criollas* (i.e., "white").

In analyzing these two leaders' politics, this chapter evaluates to what extent and on what basis they are populist.[2] In order to avoid normative definitions of populism that associate it with irrational collective behavior, or historicist definitions that point to particular development models, I use Laclau's approach, which is theoretically wider in scope and more sociologically grounded (Laclau 2005). For Laclau, populism is a specific mode of political articulation that emanates from and is consolidated in the context of a highly unstable institutional order. Instead of being processed "individually" through the normal workings of

---

1. On Fujimori's (neo)populism, see, among others, Roberts 1995; Weyland 1996, 1999, 2001; Rousseau 2006, 2009. On Morales's populism, see Castañeda 2006; Madrid 2006; Molina 2006; Laserna 2007; Seligson 2007. All translations are my own unless otherwise indicated.

2. In this chapter, for the sake of stylistic considerations, the present tense is sometimes used when comparing Fujimori and Morales, even though Fujimori's rule ended in 2000.

political institutions, frustrated and neglected social demands become subsumed under a new unifying category, the "people," whose identity is fundamentally negative, that is, opposed to the dominant political order. The "people" are pitted against a common enemy, usually the oligarchy, imperialist forces, the political elite, or, more recently, neoliberalism. The "people" are created in the act of political representation. As a result, populism can be found in various contexts and the political ideologies of populist leaders can vary (Laclau 2005).

If both Fujimori and Morales conform to populist practice, they differ in terms of policy content and the dynamics of mobilization. I locate the core of this difference in the historical process of each leader's rise to power. Fujimori is a case of populism constructed from above, whereas Morales is a case of populism constructed from below. Yet both men are very popular leaders with whom the poor in particular have come to identify strongly.

Both the practice and the content of populism are consequential for gender relations, and this chapter focuses on the relationship between gender and populist politics. Populism in general does not imply a particular understanding of gender relations, but "women" is a generic political category often used to enhance popular identification with the leader. Populism builds its power in part on a gendered discourse that resonates with popular understandings of gender roles and symbolism. Because Fujimori implemented one of the harshest structural adjustment and liberalization plans, while Morales assumed state power at the crest of a massive anti-neoliberal mobilization, they pursued different political agendas in relation to distinct female constituencies, and their discourse on gender differs. More surprisingly, though, their gender politics shares common features. Both of their populist projects clash with the feminist movement at some level. In contrast to most cases of classic populism, however, each of these new populist leaders also insisted on promoting women's political leadership, even at the highest levels.[3]

This chapter is based on extensive research in Peru (2000–2001), where I conducted more than forty interviews with women activists, NGO workers, members of popular organizations, academics, and politicians (see Rousseau 2009), and on more recent fieldwork in Bolivia (May 2007), where I interviewed some fifteen women and men elected to Bolivia's Constituent Assembly, NGO workers, members of popular organizations, and academics.

---

3. Eva Perón and the reforms she promoted (women's suffrage) in Argentina are an exception to classic populist leaders' tendency to avoid opening central political positions to women.

Fujimori: Populism from Above

Fujimori is the son of a poor Japanese immigrant. As a math professor who became dean of Lima's Agrarian University in the mid-1980s, he symbolized popular hopes of upward social mobility. Prior to becoming president he had not been involved in politics. In his first, successful, electoral bid for the presidency, in 1990, he relied on his links with evangelical churches and the Association of Small and Medium-Size Businesses, comprising many informal entrepreneurs (Bowen 2000, 17–18). His success resided in great part in the fact that he was an "outsider" in Peruvian politics. Fujimori campaigned on a pragmatic platform (his first slogan was "Honesty, Technology, and Work"). Popular sectors were convinced by his promise that he would not adopt a structural adjustment plan, even though a few months after assuming power, Fujimori did exactly that. As Bowen reports, when facing a choice between world-famous writer Mario Vargas Llosa and Alberto Fujimori, "many poor Peruvians with indigenous or mestizo background were saying, 'I don't vote for a *pituco* (Rich White Man): *El Chino* is just like us" (2000, 25).

Once in power, Fujimori built a new style of politics based on direct and regular links with urban and rural popular sectors. He was the first president to travel to the most isolated villages, often wearing traditional indigenous clothes in his propaganda photos, in great contrast with the Peruvian political elite's style. His electoral strategies revolved precisely around showing himself as "A President Like You," a slogan used widely (Conaghan 2005, 17). His way of speaking Spanish, typical of a son of immigrants who spoke Japanese at home, resembled the accent of Quechua people from rural areas. He also introduced very successfully more modern popular culture references in his public appearances, such as techno-cumbia songs shouting the merits of *El Chino* (The Chinese, a popular way of describing people of Asian descent).

At the same time, he cultivated a masculine image by surrounding himself with very lightly dressed female dancers onstage during his political rallies. His *machista* outlook was enhanced by the "strong hand" he advocated in his government's counterinsurgent strategy against the Shining Path and the Tupac Amaru Revolutionary Movement (MRTA), two guerrilla groups that have been active since the early 1980s. The Shining Path in particular had managed to sustain a treacherous war against the Peruvian state, causing one of the highest numbers of civilian deaths in all of Latin America's internal conflicts.[4]

4. The Truth and Reconciliation Commission's report, released in 2003, found that at least 69,280 people were killed between 1980 and 2000. It estimated that the Shining Path was responsible for

As a result, Peruvians saw insecurity as the top political issue to be addressed in the early 1990s. Fujimori's image as a tough leader was crafted carefully on several occasions—for example, when he personally participated in the final operation led by special military forces against the MRTA, who held hostages in the Japanese embassy in 1997.

After winning the presidency in a democratic election, Fujimori performed a "self-coup" in 1992 with the help of the military, shutting down Congress and the judiciary and only reinstating controversial democratic institutions, with a new constitution, in 1993 under heavy international pressure. This institutional rupture allowed Fujimori to concentrate political power in his hands, and he used it to accelerate the pace of neoliberal reforms and adopt special laws to suspend fundamental freedoms in the name of his counterinsurgency plan. Under the authority of Fujimori's ally Vladimiro Montesinos, the SIN, a state intelligence agency, was used to control opponents and corrupt authorities. Fujimori also retained control over the judiciary, including the electoral tribunal, throughout the rest of the decade.

Fujimori remained a highly popular political leader until the late 1990s. He was voted into power mainly by the popular sectors and some of the middle class, who saw in him the possibility for change (Lynch 1999). When he assumed power, the country was facing a dramatic crisis not only on the security front but politically and economically. Hyperinflation and state debt were endemic and both left-wing and right-wing parties were discredited (Carrión 2006). As a result, the Peruvian state was on the verge of collapsing.

Populist Discourse and the Creation of an Enemy

Fujimori justified his drastic neoliberal reforms and the state's enhanced use of repressive force against insurgents with a populist discourse that pitted the people's interests against that of the political class. That is, he constructed the "enemy" as the established political parties and unions. Not surprisingly, he promised "solutions" in the area in which the majority of Peruvians expressed the most anxiety and saw as the country's most pressing need: order and security. "I will pacify the country before finishing my mandate, there is no doubt," he said in a 1992 interview. "This is a key problem, and for this reason I will manage it

---

54 percent of the deaths and the MRTA for 1.5 percent, state security forces and paramilitary groups being responsible for the rest. See http://www.cverdad.org.pe/ingles/ifinal/conclusiones.php (accessed January 16, 2008).

personally" (quoted in Bowen 2000, 91). Fujimori justified Peru's turn to neo-liberalism as a way to end "corporatist" privileges. In his address to the nation on April 5, 1992, he justified the extraordinary measures of shutting down democratic institutions and suspending the constitution by claiming that Congress was "irresponsible, sterile, antihistorical and antinational." He described these measures as "the starting point of the quest for an authentic transformation" (quoted in ibid., 116).

Sustaining Populist Support

Alberto Fujimori's leadership style is an example of populism constructed from above, where a politically astute individual uses the context of extreme political discontent to present himself as the only solution to the people's needs. His political charisma was reinforced in the first five years of his rule, when he effectively managed to curb hyperinflation and jail the Shining Path's leader. Popular hopes invested in him explain, among other things, why the vast majority of Peruvians accepted Fujimori's coup, even if it meant the suspension of democratic rights and freedoms (Kenney 2004).

And yet, given that he implemented one of the toughest structural adjustment packages in Latin American history, Fujimori's popularity remains paradoxical. Adjustment measures such as the end of price subsidies on basic food staples hit the poorest sectors the hardest. Collective self-help organizing became the only way to survive the adjustment. Women in shantytowns were central in this process, drawing on their long experience of collective action to face hunger on a daily basis.

Not long after the "FujiShock," Fujimori set up a range of social programs to "compensate" the poor for the effects of structural adjustment. These compensatory schemes were then transformed into more permanent state programs, focusing mainly on food aid delivered through popular organizations led by women. These programs became one of the key instruments of Fujimori's populism (Rousseau 2006 and 2009). After 1992, all of his main social programs were administered by the Ministry of the Presidency, thus allowing him to retain a close link to the people.

Fujimori's Gender Politics

Fujimori sought to project the image of a modern leader seeking his nation's progress through Peru's renewed participation in the global economic system

under neoliberal precepts. In his speeches, he regularly referred to the incorporation of women in development as one of the key pillars of his government's
policies, pledging to raise women's economic contribution to Peru's productivity. His official discourse indicates a formal adherence to the principle of gender
equality from a basic liberal standpoint. In reference to his government's new
family-planning program, for example, he said, "Women can have at their dis-
posal, with full autonomy and freedom, the tools necessary to make decisions
about their own lives" (Fujimori 1995). At the same time, though, his numerous
references to women's allegedly "unique virtues," echoed even more strongly by
many congresswomen from his party and others, ended up creating a discourse
full of gender essentialism (Blondet 2002; Rousseau 2009).

Fujimori appointed an unprecedented number of women to high political
positions. From the beginning of his political career and increasingly up to the
end, Fujimori appointed more women as ministers, vice ministers, and to high
executive positions within state agencies, and gave congresswomen and women
ministers in his government a higher profile, than any past Peruvian ruler. Directly
following the 1992 coup, he appointed Blanca Nelida Colán chief public prosecu-
tor. In 1995 Martha Chávez became the first woman to be appointed president
of Congress, followed some time later by Martha Hildebrandt (Schmidt 2006,
157–58).

These women became Fujimori's most outspoken defenders against repeated
accusations of corruption and abuse of power by the political opposition and
the media (Blondet 2002; Schmidt 2006; Rousseau 2009). They all referred repeatedly to the opposition as "terrorists" or "defenders of terrorists," and to Peruvian
women's "motherly" concerns about insecurity. Martha Chávez used dramatic
language to describe poor women's heroic role in confronting political violence:
"Amid this difficult and painful context, our women, especially those living in
poor areas of Peru, in a decided and courageous attitude turned themselves *into
the most fearsome opponents* of the criminal actions of terrorist groups . . . defying them every day" (1995, emphasis added). That they themselves were women
allowed these politicians to claim that they really understood mothers' needs.
They consistently expressed their complete trust in the president and called on
citizens to do the same.

Gendered Policies

In 1995 Fujimori made a significant turn toward developing a set of policies that
would appeal to women in particular. In the context of the World Conference

on Women held in Beijing that year, the "promotion of women" became one of the centerpieces of Fujimori's politics. He began by being the only male head of state to attend the Beijing conference, a strong political statement in itself.

Some critics saw Fujimori's new orientation toward women as an attempt to counter the negative effects of his marital problems on his credibility (Schmidt 2006). Early on in his presidency, his wife, Susana Higuchi, publicly denounced her husband's government's corruption. Later, she publicly declared her opposition to her husband's coup. The couple finally divorced in 1996. Higuchi reported having been harassed by intelligence agents. After their divorce, Fujimori was quoted as saying that he was looking for another bride who should "have good legs." He later commented that miniskirts on female public servants "were a good thing for state offices' décor" (quoted in Schmidt 2006, 157, 165).

It is difficult to know how large a part these issues played in Fujimori's decision to build a "women's agenda." In any case, Fujimori's new agenda coincided with his need to refurbish his image in his second term (1995–2000), after his success in fighting subversive groups and introducing a structural adjustment reform package. He had by then jailed the leader of the Shining Path and other insurgents and had managed to stabilize the economy. The World Conference on Women provided an opportunity to advance a whole new agenda that would legitimize his rule both internationally and at home.

Some of Fujimori's new policies on women were used as central pieces of his populist project. The most controversial of these was the creation of a reproductive health program with universal free access to family-planning counseling and contraceptives. For the first time, surgical sterilization was included in the list of approved contraceptive methods in Peru, henceforth offered free of charge to all Peruvians. While this program met with outraged opposition from the Catholic Church, Fujimori emphasized the positive impact it would have on gender and class equality in access to health care. At the World Conference on Women in Beijing, he promoted his new program and openly criticized the Catholic Church's reaction: "Peruvian women are not going to remain confined or constrained by the intransigence of ultraconservative mentalities that pretend to turn into a dogma their incapacity to accept social change" (Fujimori 1995).

Another key piece of his women's agenda was the creation of a government ministry for the promotion of women and human development (PROMUDEH) in 1996. PROMUDEH was the first cabinet-level ministry of its kind in Latin America, and Fujimori transferred many social programs targeting poor women from the Ministry of the Presidency to PROMUDEH. Fujimori also reformed the electoral code, mandating that 25 percent of party candidates for Congress and municipal elections be women. This controversial reform provoked strong opposition from key political parties, including his own, but Fujimori openly and consistently supported it. Some of Fujimori's female candidates won the largest number of votes in the 1995 and 2000 elections. Congresswomen, the media, and some women's NGOs supported electoral gender quotas partly on the grounds that women were more honest than men and more dedicated to the public good (Rousseau 2009, 133–34).

Fujimori's promotion of women proved to be a fruitful political strategy. Election polls revealed that after 1995 the percentage of female voters supporting Fujimori increased consistently in relation to the percentage of male voters who supported him. In 1995 Fujimori won 65 percent of the female vote as compared to 61 percent of male voters; in 2000, in the first electoral round, he won 53.8 percent of women's votes versus 46.8 percent of males, and in the second round 79.7 percent of female voters supported him, as opposed to 67.7 percent of males (Schmidt 2006, 163).

Fujimori and the Feminist Movement

The feminist movement was critical of Fujimori by and large. Disagreements emerged over Fujimori's authoritarian practices, his *machista* behavior, and the abuses of women's rights alleged against some of his policies and programs. The feminist movement in Peru is primarily a middle-class urban movement that arose out of the left-wing protest movement of the 1970s. Fujimori's neo-populism targeted working- and middle-class women not generally associated with the feminist movement. That said, his policies often divided the feminist movement because Fujimori appeared to respond to some of its demands.

At several crucial junctures, sectors of the movement organized opposition campaigns against Fujimori's politics. In 1993, for example, several feminist organizations put together an advocacy campaign called Women for a Vote of Conscience to oppose the newly drafted constitution. One of the feminist coalition's key concerns was the inclusion in the constitution of a provision that recognized the legal personhood of the fetus.[5] The new constitution was adopted intact over the protest of the feminist campaign.

5. Political constitution of Peru, Article 2.1, http://www.tc.gob.pe/legconperu/constitucion.html (accessed September 1, 2007).

While Fujimori's government adopted some policies long advocated by the feminist movement, there were fundamental disagreements over how the government handled women's rights. The best example was the importance that Fujimori gave at Beijing to his new family-planning program. Peru also sided with the most conservative Latin American governments and the Vatican on the issue of abortion in the final documents that came out of the conference (Cornejo 1995). Fujimori clearly did not share the feminist argument that women should have full control over their bodies. These discrepancies notwithstanding, most Peruvian feminists supported the president's bold move to broaden access to family-planning services and contraceptive choice.

This support carried great risks. Not long afterward, in 1997, one of the major scandals surrounding Fujimori's government was prompted by investigations carried out by a feminist lawyer who reported more than a hundred cases of women who had allegedly been coerced by public health-care providers into being sterilized, or had been sterilized without their consent. This presented the feminist movement with a serious dilemma: how to respond to these abuses without siding with the Catholic Church, which fiercely opposed the family-planning program. This issue divided the movement for some time, one side advocating a quiet effort to reform the program through constructive dialogue, the other protesting in the streets and filing legal complaints on behalf of the victims. Fujimori denied the abuses and took the opportunity to attack the feminist movement, claiming that it was undermining the interests of the majority of poor women who needed public family-planning services (Barrig 2000; Rousseau 2007 and 2009).

Although the feminist movement had advocated the creation of a high-level state agency on women's issues for several years before PROMUDEH came into being, the ministry's mandate was designed without feminists' input, and its successive ministers came from outside feminist circles. During Fujimori's rule, PROMUDEH's main activities concerned managing clientelistic social programs. That said, some feminist NGOs entered into contractual relations with PROMUDEH to carry out several projects in the field of reproductive health, domestic violence, and training for women police officers. This was also a conflict-ridden field for the feminist movement because of Fujimori's controversial use of PROMUDEH as a linchpin of his populist politics (Barrig 2000). Despite the divisions within the feminist movement on how to handle its relationship with Fujimori's government during the 1990s, it was a key actor in organizing the mass protests against Fujimori at the end of his rule.

Organized Women in Popular Movements: The Populist Use of Hunger

Grassroots survival organizations in Peru's shantytowns are known internationally for setting up collective kitchens and other initiatives revolving around the provision of food.[6] Peruvian political parties have long attempted to control these women-led organizations, but a powerful Federation of Collective Kitchens emerged in the 1980s as an independent social movement led by poor women pressing claims on the state.

In the 1980s food staples came mainly from the United States as in-kind aid and were channeled through church-based organizations and other NGOs that collaborated with the federation. In the 1990s the United States ended this form of assistance, and food aid was left in the hands of the Peruvian state. This allowed Fujimori's government to centralize and institutionalize food aid programs by creating a powerful state agency, the Programa Nacional de Asistencia Alimentaria (PRONAA). The PRONAA is responsible for managing the delivery of food staples to grassroots self-help organizations led by women. Although it initially signed an agreement with the Federation of Collective Kitchens, the PRONAA often bypassed the federation and dealt directly with individual kitchens; it gradually convinced many members that they did not need the federation to represent them (Rousseau 2009).

Fujimori used control over food aid for political manipulation. PRONAA staff intervened even to the point of selecting women leaders of the kitchens, threatening them or bribing them with gifts to ensure their political obedience. The federation's long battle for autonomy and recognition was finally lost through the erosion of its leadership's independence.[7] Faced with very difficult conditions, most leaders became extremely pragmatic. As Relinda Sosa, a former president of the federation, told me in justifying her collaboration with PRONAA, "Those women who are far away from political power have to solve their problems, they have to eat. . . . I would have liked to be in the newspapers' headlines to denounce [PRONAA's political manipulation], but the question was whether this would really change the life of people." The extreme violence in Lima's shantytowns, where some key women leaders had been attacked by the Shining Path, suggests some of the difficult choices facing women and their

6. The first *comedores populares* were set up in the late 1970s; their number increased throughout the 1980s and 1990s. See Lora 1996 and Rousseau 2009.

7. This information is based on my interviews, in Lima in 2001, of the people who served as president of the *junta directiva* of the Federación Nacional de Comedores Populares Autogestionarios between 1990 and 2001.

leaders in the collective kitchens.[8] Shining Path guerrillas strategically targeted the leaders of popular organizations who it claimed were acting against the "true interests of the people" by not joining its ranks. Fujimori's attacks on the Shining Path in the early 1990s, which reduced their strength significantly, was particularly welcomed by most of these women.

Fujimori's politics vis-à-vis the popular sectors included the appointment of several women leaders in his party. Some managed to become municipal councilors or members of Congress. One of these new political recruits, Marta Moyano, is the sister of Maria-Elena Moyano, who was assassinated by the Shining Path in 1992. Marta became one of Fujimori's fiercest defenders in Congress. She was still defending Fujimori in 2007, even as he was being tried in court for his part in extrajudicial killings. "The legacy of Alberto Fujimori in today's Peru is peace," she has said, "constructed on the basis of community development under a new concept of democracy that calls for the state to be present where people need it" (quoted in Schipani 2007).

The inclusion of women leaders from poor neighborhoods in municipal government and Congress is a remarkable result of Fujimori's populist politics. This was a giant step forward for women's political representation. By the end of Fujimori's reign, however, socioeconomic inequality had increased, and the poor's dependence on food aid from the government remained high (Rousseau 2006 and 2009). In 2009, at the end of a long legal trial, Fujimori was convicted on several counts of torture, kidnapping, and forced disappearances committed during the early 1990s. Supporters who rallied around his daughter, Keiko, elected to Congress in 2006, rejected the verdict and pledged to continue defending El Chino's legacy.

Morales: Populism from Below

Evo Morales is a peasant leader from a poor mining zone who moved to the coca-growing region of Chaparé and became the leader of the highly repressed coca-grower federation. As "vanguard" of the new peasant struggle in Bolivia, facing the Bolivian armed forces funded by the United States specifically to eradicate coca farming, this federation inspired many other social organizations that grew in strength throughout the 1990s. Because of his indigenous (Aymara)

8. Juana López and Maria-Elena Moyano were killed in 1991 and 1992, respectively. Emma Hilario was attacked twice; the second attack involved being shot at.

descent, Morales has also come to represent the ascent of indigenous peoples to power, reversing centuries of *criollo* control over the state. While the exact number of indigenous citizens in Bolivia is still hotly debated, it is generally accepted that more than 60 percent of the population identifies as indigenous (Canessa 2006).

Morales's political genius and that of his party, the Movimiento al Socialismo (MAS), has resided in the ability to attract both indigenous and nonindigenous followers, which has given Morales a strong rural and urban popular base (Madrid 2006). Morales emerged as a leader in the context of sustained popular mobilization that began in the mid-1990s and has grown ever since, and that has used both electoral strategies and street blockades to force political elites out of power. Mobilized masses saw deepening socioeconomic inequality as the consequence of neoliberal policies pursued by successive democratic governments from the late 1980s onward. In 1999, 62 percent of the total population lived in poverty; that figure had grown to 64.6 percent by 2002. Those living in extreme poverty made up 35.8 percent of Bolivia's population in 1999 and 36.8 percent in 2002 (Arias and Bendini 2006).

The repressive measures adopted by the Bolivian state in the 1990s against one of the only lucrative activities available to peasants, coca growing, was among the main incentives behind the launching of a new political party that eventually became the MAS. Created as a "political instrument," the MAS became a springboard for social organizations' direct access to state institutions. In the second half of the 1990s, the party made its first gains at the municipal level; in 1997 four of its candidates—one of them Evo Morales—were elected to Congress (Dunkerley 2007; Komadina and Geffroy 2007). In the early 2000s the party decided to broaden its appeal both by developing a much clearer indigenous identity, thus allying itself with regional indigenous organizations, and by embracing an agenda of regaining state control over key natural resources such as gas and petroleum, an issue that attracted the support of nonindigenous working- and middle-class voters as well (Madrid 2006).

Evo Morales was elected president in 2005 with 54 percent of the vote. Since assuming power in January 2006, his government has increased the scope of health-care coverage, tripled the state taxation rate on natural gas production, and promoted regional indigenous self-government. A national Constituent Assembly was set up in 2006, its members elected through universal suffrage. The MAS held the majority of seats in the assembly, but its numbers were insufficient to adopt a new constitution without negotiations, which were fraught with tension and plagued by disagreements. The draft constitution was adopted in late 2007 over the opposition of most of Bolivia's other political parties, which launched violent street protests in response. Nevertheless, the new constitution was approved by national referendum in January 2009, with 61.43 percent of the vote.

Morales and many of the newly elected MAS politicians mark a rupture in political representation by enabling the majority of indigenous Bolivians to hold important government positions. In the 2002 electoral campaign the MAS's official slogan was "Somos Pueblo; Somos MAS" (We are the People; we are MAS," the party's acronym also meaning "more," or "more numerous," in Spanish). The MAS attempted to reinforce this self-identification among the people by launching a publicity campaign, in the early months of Morales's reign, on the theme of "Evo soy yo" (I am Evo), featuring typical Bolivian men and women of different backgrounds (Pinto and Navia 2007, 177).

Also notable is Evo Morales's decision not to wear the traditional suit and tie expected of a man of his rank, preferring instead a sweater or, more recently, a dark jacket on which colorful indigenous weavings are sewn in an elegant fashion. Morales also has a very manly outlook. The courage he demonstrated as a union leader fighting against military repression, and his reputation for seducing women, enhance popular myths about Morales's strength (Pinto and Navia 2007; Canessa 2008).

Populist Discourse and the Creation of an Enemy

If many ideologies coexist within the MAS, from traditional Marxism to post-colonial indigenous views, the political inclusion of popular sectors, notably by adopting the discourse of indigenous peoples' empowerment, is the main thrust of the MAS project. Morales defines the "enemy" of the people as multifaceted: It includes neoliberal policies, the paternalism, corruption, and clientelism of the "traditional" party system, and Bolivian agribusiness and multinational gas and oil interests. In his inaugural presidential speech in January 2006, Morales said, "They were talking about 'democracy.' . . . But in 1997, when I arrived in this Congress, what have I seen personally? . . . Corruption pacts, a pact on how and where to get money from. . . . Tricks and more tricks to fool the people. . . . These economic policies implemented under external instructions, what have they left us with? Unemployment. . . . What have these politicians done? Is it that they don't feel what our nation's majority suffers?" (Morales 2006, 25–27).

Evo Morales is not a typical populist leader in the sense of mobilizing the masses from above. To the contrary, he rose as a leader by popular organizing. In late 2009, Morales was re-elected with 64 percent of the vote. I would argue that Evo Morales represents populism constructed from below, where an extremely popular leader is indispensable to the formation of a power bloc made of a vast constellation of social and political actors. As Raul Madrid (2006) has observed, the key difference between Morales's brand of populism and classic populism is the strong rural base of support on which Morales's power relies. Peasant and indigenous organizations in Morales's populism are the "functional equivalent" of urban labor unions in the heyday of classic populism.

While I agree with Roberts that Morales is accountable to a broad range of social organizations, I disagree that this excludes him from the category of populist phenomena altogether (Roberts 2007, 9). The key question is whether social movements can retain their autonomy under the MAS government. Unlike many traditional left-wing parties in the region, the MAS is not an institutionalized political party. This creates tension for the autonomy of social movements, as there is no intermediary between the state and the social movements that form the core of the MAS. While the government is regularly submitted to "approval" meetings in which Morales justifies his decisions and is exposed to the criticism of his followers, those who lose out are the cabinet members drawn from these social organizations, as a result of infighting between them. Moreover, Morales himself is the cement that holds the distinct forces together (Komadina and Geffroy 2007).

Sustaining the Populist Project

Morales's redistributive schemes are much broader in scope than Fujimori's. The resources generated by the partial nationalization of gas and petroleum, which allowed the state to set a much higher tax rate on private extractive and export activities, have been invested in several new social programs, including greater health-care coverage, educational "vouchers," and a new universal pension plan for the majority of uninsured Bolivians, to name a few of the most important. Evo Morales's redistribution plans rely on the support of Cuban and Venezuelan cooperation to provide direct social services, such as medical and literacy campaigns, to the poorest.

Morales's government is also seeking to enhance political participation among the poorest sectors of Bolivia. It created a program to register undocumented Bolivians and provide them with birth certificates. This is particularly crucial for indigenous women's citizenship, as a high proportion of indigenous women lack official identification documents and are therefore prevented from voting and other acts of citizenship.

Thus Morales has shown his commitment to improving the lives of the majority. One of the instruments he created in 2006 to reflect this vision and hear
popular organizations' demands was the Coordinadora Nacional por el Cambio (CONALCAM), through which twenty-five or thirty of the main social organizations sympathetic to the MAS meet regularly with the president. In January
2008 the CONALCAM was further strengthened when Morales announced that
it would "become the highest decision-making body, over and above the Cabinet, in order to deepen changes" (*La Razón* 2008).

Morales's Gender Politics

Morales's discourse on gender is apparently consistent with traditional Latin
American gender norms. As he said in a speech given on International Women's
Day (March 8, 2006), "To see a woman is always to see a symbol of affection and
honesty. . . . To talk about women is always to talk about family unity. Personally, when I see a woman I see my mother, and when her name is Maria, I think
that all Marias are my mothers" (Morales 2006, 119). Morales's reference made
to the Virgin Mary reflects the traditional Catholic view of women as sacrificing
their personal interests for the sake of the family. What is more novel is that
later in the speech Morales paid tribute to the central role of organized women
from popular sectors in the struggle against injustice and oppression that he
seeks to represent. Bolivian women are known for their combativeness at key
junctures in contemporary political history—for example, the mining women
who led a hunger strike against authoritarianism in the 1970s, prompting the
fall of the dictatorship, or the women who played a central role in the "gas war"
of 2003, which led to Sanchez de Lozada's resignation from the presidency.

What is also striking in Morales's discourse is his reference to the negative
impact of colonialism on gender relations and the need to return to "authentic"
indigenous norms that allegedly embodied more legitimate gender relations.
Morales has even gone so far as to suggest that machismo is a foreign import
and is not indigenous to Andean culture (Morales 2006, 120). One important
current of the MAS consists of indigenous organizations that propose to "decol-
onize" Bolivian society by rediscovering Aymara and other indigenous social
systems. Morales has adopted its main discursive elements and symbolism.

A basic component of the Aymaran worldview is the concept of *chachawarmi,* whereby one becomes a fully adult person only upon entering marriage.
Chachawarmi implies that political authority is exercised at both micro- and

macrocosmic levels, within the heterosexual couple and through its replication at the community level, where both a man and a woman are to lead together. *Chachawarmi* is an important conceptual element of the project for the foundation of a new social order, according to many MAS politicians, both female and male, elected to the Constituent Assembly.[9] If representative democracy is seen as an imported liberal ideal that is likely to disrupt community solidarity, gender equality, for some of them, is also seen as a Western value foreign to indigenous traditions, "imported" to Bolivia through international cooperation agencies.

In the speech he gave on International Women's Day in 2006, Morales felt compelled to justify his unmarried status, which goes against the principle of *chachawarmi,* by emphasizing his total commitment to political struggle; having a wife and family, he explained, would divide his attention and compromise his political dedication (Morales 2006, 125). Morales's sexual behavior is nonetheless a matter of great interest in the Bolivian media. His many affairs with women and the children produced by these affairs endow him with a rather typical Latin American sense of machismo. In August 2008 he appeared publicly with two of his children on the day of a national referendum, arguably to appease critics who charged him with paternal irresponsibility. Morales plays on the gossip surrounding his sexual affairs with women of diverse backgrounds (and the affair of his vice president with a former Miss Bolivia) to underline the fact that women from all social classes like him and his allies (Canessa 2008).

Gendered Policies

When he assumed power, Morales made it clear that his government would dismantle the Ministry on Indigenous Affairs and the Subministry on Gender, Generations, and Family created in 2002. The president justified his decision by claiming that these were "forms of discrimination" and that in his government the "indigenous and women would be appointed ministers."[10] Under intense pressure from some organized women's circles, the government was forced to relent and created a Subministry on Gender and Generations within the Justice Ministry. In 2007 this new subministry was seen as very weak both politically and financially, especially as compared to its predecessor (Carafa 2007).

9. I rely here on interviews I conducted with constituents elected with the MAS in Sucre, Bolivia, May 2007.

10. "Villegas aclara que el viceministerio de la mujer no desaparecerá," http://funsolon.civiblog .org/blog/_archives/2006/1/20/1716339.html.

It is nevertheless the case that Evo Morales has increased women's presence in politics. In his first cabinet, four of the sixteen ministers he appointed were women (one each in the ministries of government, justice, economic development, and health). In a highly symbolic gesture, Morales appointed Casimira Rodríguez, an experienced leader of the domestic workers' movement, as minister of justice. Rodríguez, a *mujer de pollera* (a woman who dresses in typical indigenous multilayer skirts), has emphasized that her appointment contributed to "decolonizing the state." But she has also confessed that her one-year term was extremely difficult because of discrimination against her within the bureaucracy, especially from one of her deputy ministers, a man appointed by Evo Morales (Rodríguez 2007). She did expect these difficulties to come though: "When the president told me, 'you will be justice minister,' the first thing I said to him was, 'I am not a lawyer,' and I saw him really motivated, saying, 'No, but I also don't know how to govern. How does one govern a country? I will learn, we will learn'" (Rodríguez 2007).

In terms of electoral strategy, Morales's gender policy was put in place for the Constituent Assembly elections, where gender parity was adopted as a principle and imposed on party lists (there were two candidates, one male and one female, for each district). The result was that 34 percent of the assembly's members were women, the MAS leading the other parties in terms of women's presence. Nearly half (47 percent) of the MAS seats were filled by women, while the main opposition party, PODEMOS, could count only 27 percent of its seats filled by women.[11] Evo Morales also appointed a woman as president of the Constituent Assembly installed in August 2006: Silvia Lazarte, a peasant leader with years of experience at the Federación de Mujeres Campesinas "Bartolina Sisa," Bolivia's primary rural women's union.

In terms of broad policy orientation, if one is to judge the MAS on the basis of the constitution adopted in 2009, many significant advances have been made in establishing legal grounds for progress in gender equity and equality, two principles central to the new text. The new constitution separates the state from the Catholic Church and proclaims its secular nature and its respect for all religions. It also recognizes sexual and reproductive rights as constitutional rights for the first time. A leading coalition of Bolivian women's organizations, the Articulación de Mujeres por la Equidad e Igualdad (AMUPEI), applauded the new constitution and called the state's mandates to eliminate all forms of discrimination

---

11. Unpublished paper, data compiled by a project led by Cecilia Salazar at the Postgrado Multidisciplinario en Ciencias del Desarrollo at the Universidad Mayor de San Andrés, La Paz.

against women, and to recognize the economic value of domestic labor, "historic gains" (*La Razón* 2007). The new constitution forbids discrimination based on sex, gender identity, sexual orientation, color, and pregnancy, among other categories.

Relationship with Feminist Movements

The victory claimed by feminist groups regarding the 2009 constitution is somewhat paradoxical in light of their ambiguous relationship to the MAS. The rise of the MAS to power corresponds to what Karin Monasterios has called "indigenous nationalism," where "indigenous women's groups (both rural and urban) have come to be perceived as the legitimate representatives of large women's majorities" (2007, 33). As Monasterios argues, this important shift calls into question past patterns of women's representation, in which urban *mestizo* middle-class women, whether closely allied with the feminist movement or not, were the main actors. The feminist movement in particular has come under fire for having been too involved in the NGO gender technocracy promoted by the United Nations and the Bolivian state in the 1990s, seen as foreign to indigenous women's interests. Professional women who identify themselves as feminist and who have worked extensively in NGOs or state offices to develop legal or policy reforms have reported feeling extremely estranged by the new political context. They feel that their contribution has been disregarded and their ideas associated with Western imperialism (e.g., Carafa 2007).

Outside the NGO sector, the radical feminist group Mujeres Creando and the Feminist Assembly created in 2004 criticize Evo Morales and his vice president, Alvaro Garcia-Linera, for being *machistas* who use women as political clients but fail to recognize them as citizens. Maria Galindo, founder of Mujeres Creando, in an article entitled "No saldrá Eva de la costilla de Evo" (Eve will not come out of Evo's rib), emphasized the patriarchal character of the MAS victory and the celebrations surrounding it, in which the vice president was quoted as saying that "el poncho y la corbata" (the poncho and the tie) both won in the 2005 elections. "In other words," writes Galindo, "the Indian man and the gentleman represent the nation. Where are the many women coca growers who struggled as hard as Evo to resist state repression?" (2006).

Relationship with Organized Women in Popular Movements

Feminist estrangement from MAS politics seems to be connected more to ethnic and class cleavages than to fundamental ideological opposition. But feminist

views differ to some extent from the priorities of organized women in indigenous and peasant organizations who are central pillars of the MAS. Women
coca growers, leaders of neighborhood organizations, the National Federation
of Peasant Women "Bartolina Sisa," and the Federation of Domestic Workers
have a number of their leaders elected or appointed to various political positions,
whether to Congress, the Constituent Assembly, local government posts, or elsewhere. Evo Morales's gender discourse, emphasizing women's full inclusion in
all areas of society, is based on a strong belief in gender complementarity and
associates women strongly with indigenous culture and community values. In
contrast to the feminist movement, which emphasizes women's individual rights
and autonomy, many organized women in the MAS are struggling in unison with
male-dominated organizations for enhanced power and better living conditions
for peasants and other indigenous people.

Disagreements among women from different ethnic and class backgrounds
are also due to the history of power relations between them. Many indigenous
women leaders are suspicious of the work of feminist NGOs. For example, Teodora Tapia, an Aymara social communicator who was elected with the MAS to
the Constituent Assembly, told me, "There are a lot of NGO proposals going
around. Obviously they are being financed, they have professionals. . . . I see that
they use us women as commodities, they do a project in the name of women.
Why? To get rich. I already had problems with [some key feminist NGOs] because I don't like to be treated as a commodity or see my sisters treated as such"
(Tapia 2007).

Most peasant women leaders and women who have migrated to poor urban
neighborhoods define their role in politics as an extension of their maternal
duties. As Bertha Blanco, an executive member of the National Federation of
Peasant Women "Bartolina Sisa," put it, "I believe that, as women, we have struggled and suffered a lot. We feel validated through our participation as women.
Because before having other ambitions, we are mothers first, and we have to see
to where our children are going to grow up. That is why we are persevering in the
struggle to protect all our natural resources" (Blanco 2007). Rosalia del Villar, a
young member of the Constituent Assembly elected with the MAS to represent
one of El Alto's districts, explained that although she is not a feminist, she seeks
to redress inequalities between men and women, whom she sees as complementary: "I am grounded in a community logic, to be together with [my hus-
band]. I mean, I do not want to compete with him. The feminist logic competes
with man, and I don't want to compete with my husband" (del Villar 2007).

Conclusion

The two cases explored here do not exhaust the possibilities in terms of combining different political and policy orientations with populist dynamics. Populism from above in the case of Fujimori's Peru led to severe human rights violations, widespread corruption, and blatant disrespect for the rule of law and the principle of separation of powers central to liberal democracy. Populism from below in Evo Morales's Bolivia is associated with a cycle of social movement mobilization and indigenous empowerment that seeks to reform the state and redistribute resources democratically. Both processes entail highly conflictual politics centered on the populist opposition between "the people" and "its enemy," however defined. The many contrasts between these two cases notwithstanding, the charismatic leadership exhibited by Fujimori and Morales is grounded in their capacity to represent excluded majorities and legitimize their actions on that basis.

Morales's populism is more clearly articulated around the question of ethnic difference. It politicizes ethnicity to the point of proposing indigenous norms as an alternative to liberalism. This has direct consequences for the way in which gender relations are defined. Referring explicitly to gender complementarity, Morales values women's political participation on the basis of the historical and current record of ordinary women's combativeness in confronting conservative elites. Significantly, his policy of increasing social programs may benefit women in a more long-term fashion, through increased literacy and better health care, for example. Fujimori, by contrast, projected the image of a modernizing leader who sought to include women in the market economy yet also institutionalized food aid activities based on women's volunteer work. Women's fundamental rights were not always respected under his rule, and some key women politicians resorted to essentialist views of women's roles and values in order to mobilize Peruvians to support Fujimori's countersubversive measures.

A striking similarity between the two men is the importance both have given to promoting and recognizing women's political leadership, in accord with the progress made by women throughout Latin America in the past few decades. But this goes hand in hand with the fact that neither of them has strong links with the feminist movement, and in fact both have had difficult if not openly hostile relations with feminists, a rather paradoxical finding.

References

Arias, Oscar, and M. Bendini. 2006. "Bolivia Poverty Assessment: Establishing the Basis for Pro-Poor Growth." *En Breve* 89 (May): 1–4.

Barrig, Maruja. 2000. *La persistencia de la memoria: Feminismo y estado en el Perú de los 90.* Lima: Cuadernos de Investigación Social de la Pontificia Universidad Católica del Perú.

Blanco, Bertha. 2007. Interview by Nic Paget-Clarke. *In Motion Magazine,* February 25, http://www.inmotionmagazine.com/global/bb_int_2eng.html (accessed January 31, 2008).

Blondet, Cecilia. 2002. *El encanto del dictador: Mujeres y política en la década de Fujimori.* Lima: Instituto de Estudios Peruanos.

Bowen, Sally. 2000. *El expediente Fujimori: El Perú y su presidente, 1990–2000.* Lima: Perú Monitor.

Canessa, Andrew. 2006. "Todos somos indígenas: Towards a New Language of National Political Identity." *Bulletin of Latin American Research* 25 (2): 241–63.

———. 2008. "Sex and the Citizen: Barbies and Beauty Queens in the Age of Evo Morales." *Journal of Latin American Cultural Studies* 17 (1): 41–64.

Carafa, Yara. 2007. Interview by author, May 23, La Paz, Bolivia.

Carrión, Julio. 2006. *The Fujimori Legacy: The Rise of Electoral Authoritarianism in Peru.* University Park: Pennsylvania State University Press.

Castañeda, Jorge. 2006. "Latin America's Left Turn." *Foreign Affairs* 85 (3): 28–44.

Chávez, Martha. 1995. Speech given before the Fourth World Conference on Women, September 6, Beijing, China. http://www.un.org/esa/gopher-data/conf/fwcw/conf/gov/950907164545.txt (accessed January 21, 2008).

Conaghan, Catherine. 2005. *Fujimori's Peru: Deception in the Public Sphere.* Pittsburgh: University of Pittsburgh Press.

Cornejo, María Elena. 1995. "El imperio invadido." *Caretas* no. 1382, http://www.caretas.com.pe/1382/imperio/imperio.html (accessed September 1, 2007).

Del Villar, Rosalia. 2007. Interview by author, May 16, Sucre, Bolivia.

Dunkerley, James. 2007. "Evo Morales, the 'Two Bolivias,' and the Third Bolivian Revolution." *Journal of Latin American Studies* 39 (1): 133–66.

Fujimori, Alberto. 1995. Speech given before the Fourth World Conference on Women, September 15, Beijing, China. http://www.un.org/esa/gopher-data/conf/fwcw/conf/goc/950915131946.txt (accessed January 21, 2008).

Galindo, Maria. 2006. "No saldrá Eva de la costilla de Evo." http://www.nodo50.org/mujeresred/spip.php?article1355 (accessed September 1, 2007).

Kenney, Charles. 2004. *Fujimori's Coup and the Breakdown of Democracy in Latin America.* Notre Dame: University of Notre Dame Press.

Komadina, Jorge, and Céline Geffroy. 2007. *El poder del movimiento político: Redes organizativas, identidad y política del MAS en Cochabamba (1999–2005).* Cochabamba: Centro de Estudios Superiores–UMSS and PIEB.

Laclau, Ernesto. 2005. "Populism: What's in a Name?" In *Populism and the Mirror of Democracy,* ed. Francisco Panizza, 32–49. London: Verso.

Laserna, Roberto. 2007. "El caudillismo fragmentado." *Nueva Sociedad* 209:100–117.

Lora, Carmen. 1996. *Creciendo en dignidad: Movimiento de comedores autogestionarios.* Lima: Instituto Bartolomé de las Casas-Rimas and CEP.

Lynch, Nicolas. 1999. *Una tragedia sin héroes: La derrota de los partidos y el orígen de los independientes; Perú, 1980–1992.* Lima: Universidad Nacional Mayor de San Marcos.

Madrid, Raul. 2006. "The Rise of Ethno-Populism in Latin America: The Bolivian Case." Paper given at the 2006 meeting of the American Political Science Association, Philadelphia, August 31–September 3.

Molina, Fernando. 2006. *Evo Morales y el retorno de la izquierda nacionalista.* La Paz: Eureka.

Monasterios, Karin. 2007. "Bolivian Women's Organizations in the MAS Era." *NACLA Report on the Americas* 40 (2): 33–37.

Morales, Evo. 2006. *La revolución democrática y cultural: Diez discursos de Evo Morales.* La Paz: Editorial Malatesta and Movimiento al Socialismo.

Olea, Cecilia. 2001. Interview by author, April 25, Lima, Peru.

Pinto, Darwin, and R. Navia. 2007. *Un tal Evo: Biografía no autorizada.* Santa Cruz: Editorial el Pais.

La Razón (La Paz). 2007. "Defendamos lo que ganamos las mujeres." December 21, http://www.la-razon.com/versiones/20071221_006127/nota_264_523265.htm.

———. 2008. "Conalcam será el máximo nivel de decisión política." January 24, http://www.la-razon.com/versiones/20080124_006161/nota_247_538205.htm.

Roberts, Kenneth M. 1995. "Neoliberalism and the Transformation of Populism in Latin America: The Peruvian Case." *World Politics* 48 (1): 82–116.

———. 2007. "Repoliticizing Latin America: The Revival of Populist and Leftist Alternatives." Woodrow Wilson Center's *Update on the Americas,* November.

Rodríguez, Casimira. 2007. Interview by author, May 29, Cochabamba, Bolivia.

Rousseau, Stéphanie. 2006. "Women's Citizenship and Neopopulism: Peru Under the Fujimori Regime." *Latin American Politics and Society* 48 (1): 117–41.

———. 2007. "The Politics of Reproductive Health in Peru: Gender and Social Policy in the Global South." *Social Politics: International Studies in Gender, State, and Society* 14 (1): 93–125.

———. 2009. *Women's Citizenship in Peru: The Paradoxes of Neopopulism in Latin America.* New York: Palgrave Macmillan.

Schipani, Andrés. 2007. "El legado de Fujimori." BBC Mundo.com, December 10. http://news.bbc.co.uk/hi/spanish/latin_america/newsid_7135000/7135782.stm (accessed January 29, 2008).

Schmidt, Gregory. 2006. "All the President's Women: Fujimori and Gender Equity in Peruvian Politics." In *The Fujimori Legacy: The Rise of Electoral Authoritarianism in Peru,* ed. Julio Carrión, 150–77. University Park: Pennsylvania State University Press.

Seligson, Mitchell. 2007. "The Rise of Populism and the Left in Latin America." *Journal of Democracy* 18 (3): 81–95.

Tapia, Teodora. 2007. Interview by author, May 21, Sucre, Bolivia.

Weyland, Kurt. 1996. "Neopopulism and Neoliberalism in Latin America: Unexpected Affinities." *Studies in Comparative International Development* 31 (3): 3–31.

———. 1999. "Neoliberal Populism in Latin America and Eastern Europe." *Comparative Politics* 31 (4): 379–401.

———. 2001. "Clarifying a Contested Concept: Populism in the Study of Latin American Politics." *Comparative Politics* 34 (1): 1–22.

8

POPULISM AND THE FEMINIST CHALLENGE IN NICARAGUA

THE RETURN OF DANIEL ORTEGA

Karen Kampwirth

Nicaragua has a long history of *caudillo,* or strongman, politics, of politicians drawing on the populist tradition to make, and remake, their own images.[1] President Daniel Ortega (1984–90 and 2007–present) acted within that tradition in the years leading up to his re-election, but he did not begin his political life as a populist. Instead, he first participated in politics as a member of a revolutionary organization, the Juventud Patriótico Nicaragüense (Nicaraguan Patriotic Youth, or JPN). Because of his work with the JPN, he was first arrested by the Somoza family's National Guardsmen in 1960, when he was fifteen years old. In 1961 the Frente Sandinista de Liberación Nacional (Sandinista Front for National Liberation, or FSLN) was founded to oppose the Somoza dictatorship, and Ortega was one of its first recruits, joining in 1963. During the long years between the founding of the FSLN and the overthrow of the Somoza dictatorship in 1979, Ortega endured seven years of torture and imprisonment (Cockcroft 1991, 40–41, 44, 61).

After the Somoza dictatorship fell, the revolutionaries made efforts to avoid replicating the Nicaraguan tradition of strongman rule, setting up several bodies to govern the country by coalition. Ortega served on the five-member Junta de Gobierno de Reconstrucción Nacional (National Reconstruction Governing Council), which had been created months before the fall of Somoza. With guidance from the nine men of the Sandinista National Directorate, of which Ortega was the liaison (as the only person who belonged to both bodies), the members

This chapter draws on a total of about two years' worth of fieldwork conducted between 1988 and 2006 in Managua, including hundreds of interviews with Sandinistas and former Sandinistas.

1. On populism and the Somoza family, see Gould 1990 and González-Rivera's chapter in this volume; on populism and Arnoldo Alemán, see Kampwirth 2003. All translations are my own unless otherwise indicated.

of the Junta ruled by decree until May 1980. At that point, the Council of State, or legislative branch, came into being, sharing power with the Junta until 1984, when a national election was held. Daniel Ortega, the candidate of the revolution, won what was widely seen as a clean election with 67 percent of the vote, despite the presence of opposition parties to his left and right (Booth 1985, 29–32, 41; LASA 1985).

That political feat would not be repeated, and he would lose presidential races in 1990, 1996, and 2001. Whether as a cause or as an effect of these repeated defeats, Ortega's strategies became increasingly personalistic and decreasingly revolutionary. In other words, Daniel Ortega reverted to the Nicaraguan tradition of *caudillo* rule. This tendency to portray himself as one man, one savior, rather than as a representative of a collective movement can be seen in his campaign strategies and in internal party dynamics. Over the course of the 1980s and early 1990s, "Daniel Ortega's faction assumed greater and greater control within the Directorate. Ortega's status had evidently been greatly strengthened during his years as Nicaragua's president—he was now the *primus inter pares*" (Luciak 2001, 119).

"Daniel," as he was always called by his followers, certainly drew on the populist tradition of justifying his authority in terms of defending an excluded and impoverished "people" against an "other" that could vary with the political moment (Knight 1998, 229). In Daniel's case, that "other" typically included Somocistas, the oligarchy, the imperialists (especially of the U.S. variety), and the elite, an elite that included feminists. But in keeping with the ideological flexibility of populism, and with the focus on maintaining the power of the charismatic leader (Conniff 1982, 21–22), Daniel was quite willing to make temporary alliances with many of the traditional enemies of his party, often at the same time that he denounced those new allies when speaking to his followers. And despite Daniel's political and personal scandals, his followers remained loyal.

The story of this transformation from revolutionary to populist (or perhaps populist revolutionary) was highly gendered at key moments. And the models of masculinity and femininity projected by Daniel Ortega and his wife, Rosario Murillo, shifted as Sandinista politics became increasingly populist. Daniel Ortega can tell us a great deal about the relationship between gender, feminism, populism, and revolution. The case of Nicaragua suggests the strong likelihood that the linking of a revolutionary agenda, an agenda of social change and social justice, to one individual (normally one man) will undermine feminist gains within a revolution.

A revolutionary agenda is inevitably narrowed as the movement becomes less collective and more individual. Although debate was sometimes stifled during Ortega's first term in office, there was debate within the party—among both leaders and followers—and a wide range of positions regarding the revolutionary goal of "emancipating" women. As Maxine Molyneux put it, "While few were against some form of women's emancipation, the conceptions of what constituted this emancipation varied considerably, from a limited, traditional 'protection' of women, and mobilization of them behind certain national campaigns (employment, defense of the revolution, mass education and health), to policies informed by feminism, which saw an alteration of gender relations and the full implementation of reproductive rights as the goal toward which the revolution should have been moving" (2001, 73–74).

Another reason why the shift from collective revolutionary leadership to the leadership of one man and his immediate family may have negative implications for feminists is that the fate of women depends on the views of that one man. And one of the themes that ran through Ortega's career, from 1979 onward, was conflict with Nicaraguan feminists. For Ortega, women's emancipation meant the "protection" model that Molyneux described, with goals consistently framed in terms of enhancing women's ability to carry out their traditional roles effectively, what some scholars have called an agenda of feminine interests over feminist interests, or practical gender interests over strategic interests (Alvarez 1990, 24; González and Kampwirth 2001, 11–17; Molyneux 2001, 43–45, 152–60).

Ortega, Gender Politics, and Revolution, 1979–1990

As noted above, the FSLN (like most political parties) was a coalition party whose leaders and followers embraced a range of positions on gender politics. From the beginning, women played a significant role in Sandinismo, constituting about 30 percent of the combatants in the struggle to overthrow the Somoza dictatorship (Kampwirth 2002, 2). Nonetheless, once the Sandinistas came to power and the Contra war had begun (requiring that they initiate a military draft), they did not include women in the draft, despite lobbying efforts for their inclusion by the Sandinista women's organization, the Asociación de Mujeres Nicaragüenses Luisa Amanda Espinosa (Luisa Amanda Espinosa Association of Nicaraguan Women, or AMNLAE). Women were permitted to serve in the army as volunteers, however (Molyneux 1985, 149–50).

Hazel Fonseca was one of those volunteers. In 1981 Ortega spoke to her all-female battalion, a speech that made an impression on her. "Daniel Ortega practically said to us: Go give birth! Now women should dedicate themselves to supporting their husbands, et cetera." In 1985 the women's battalion was eliminated completely and "many women in the EPS [the Sandinista army] ended up in more administrative positions" (Fonseca, interview by author, June 10, 1991).

At about the time that the women's battalion was dissolved, in the mid-1980s, the first signs of an autonomous feminist movement began to emerge within the Sandinista-affiliated labor unions, and especially in the debates regarding the role of gender equality in the new constitution, which was ratified in 1987 (Kampwirth 2004, 30–36). One feminist, Marta Júarez, was very involved in revolutionary politics: as a literacy volunteer, as a member of the neighborhood watch group (the CDS), in the Sandinista youth, as a member of a reserve battalion, and in a group called Christians for the Revolution. By the mid-1980s Júarez was active in the Asociación de Mujeres Ante INIES (Women's Association of INIES, or AMPRONIC), a small Sandinista women's discussion group, and in the women's secretariat of CONAPRO, the association of professionals.

Abortion was one of the many issues these groups addressed. In 1984, "we had spent time reflecting on the issue of abortion," Júarez told me, "since at that point there were demands to provide care in the hospitals. I even understood that legally there was not a problem, it was already codified. In the mass media there was a lot of debate about how women were dying because they did not go to the hospital until the last minute." The women's groups invited doctors and lawyers to talk to them, and they went to events where they could introduce the topic. At one event for professional women, they asked Daniel Ortega about the problem of illegal abortion and the correspondingly high death rates. "Daniel said, 'And if there is a wounded soldier [*cachorro*] and a woman comes along who had an abortion, who are they going to prioritize?' We said, 'Both of them.' I was so offended by his idea that the hospital had to give priority to the wounded man . . . I remember that I got up and left. And he has not changed his way of seeing things, of seeing women with such contempt" (Júarez, interview by author, December 1, 2006).

More evidence that the Sandinistas were deeply divided over whether "women's emancipation" should be understood as feminine or feminist came in September 1987. That month, more than a thousand women met at a "face-the-people" meeting marking the tenth anniversary of the founding of the Sandinista women's organization AMNLAE. At this meeting, President Ortega and the minister of health, Dora María Téllez, answered questions about abortion, birth control, sterilization, and other issues (Molyneux 2001, 68).

Téllez was one of the most prominent Sandinista women, a former guerrilla commander who went on to found the Sandinista dissident party, the Movimiento de Renovación Sandinista (Sandinista Renewal Movement, or MRS), in 1995. As minister of health, she was a strong advocate for women's health issues, including an expansion of therapeutic abortion (abortion in cases of rape, incest, or threat to the woman's life) to include abortion for some socioeconomic reasons (Wessel 1991, 542–43). Moreover, her remarks at the face-the-people meeting in 1987 suggested a feminist interpretation of women's emancipation. One audience member, a worker at a shoe factory, complained "that not only were sterilizations very difficult to get, but that they even required the husband's permission" (Molyneux 2001, 68). Téllez promised to address this problem immediately. She concluded her remarks with the argument that "the solution was 'not to defend the right to abortion but to prevent abortions.' This was being tackled by simultaneously improving the availability of birth control devices and by maintaining public education campaigns" (ibid.).

Ortega's comments were framed by a different understanding of gender politics. He suggested that efforts to promote birth control or abortion might be seen as imperialist, or as a way for the United States to stop movements for social justice in southern countries before they had a chance to begin. According to Ortega, U.S. policy had been to "freeze the population growth in these countries, to avoid the risk of an increase in population that could threaten a revolutionary change." He suggested that the U.S.-funded Contra war should be seen as "a policy of genocide," suggesting that women who were interested in controlling their fertility were guilty of disloyalty and of undermining the revolution. "One way of depleting our youth is to promote the sterilization of women in Nicaragua . . . or to promote a policy of abortion. . . . The problem is that the woman is the one who reproduces. The man can't play that role." A woman who, out of a desire to be "liberated," decides not to have children "negates her own continuity, the continuity of the human species" (quoted in ibid., 69).

Certainly the large family that Daniel Ortega and Rosario Murillo raised together (depending on the source, they have seven to nine children) is consistent with Ortega's remarks on the political importance of giving birth.[2] Murillo was already involved in revolutionary politics when she first met Ortega in Havana in the mid-1970s (Cockcroft 1991, 63–64). But when they returned to Nicaragua

2. According to James Cockcroft (1991, 90), they have nine children. Duncan Kennedy (2006) says Ortega has seven children. Most sources (e.g., Ríos 2007) say that Ortega and Murillo have eight children. Part of the confusion is no doubt due to the fact that Murillo had children from a previous relationship. It also could be due to the common belief among some rank-and-file Sandinistas (which I have not seen in print sources) that one or more of their children were adopted.

upon the overthrow of Somoza in 1979, she played the role of the supportive partner, without a formal role in politics. Her choice of clothing contributed to her image as a hippie earth mother who pursued her interests in poetry, literature, and having babies.

Though she did not play the sort of decision-making roles she was to play the second time Ortega was elected president, in 2006, she played an important symbolic role, that of the fertile woman. People sometimes joked that each year of the revolution was marked with a new pregnancy. This was an exaggeration, perhaps, but the symbolism was consistent with the idea that "women were passive bystanders in the revolutionary process and therefore must discharge their debt to the nation by having babies" (Molyneux 2001, 69).

Ortega ran as the presidential candidate of the party of the revolution in 1984 and 1990. In 1984 he and his running mate, Sergio Ramírez (who would later become a founder of the MRS), won 67 percent of the vote. But when Daniel Ortega ran for president again in 1990, the U.S.-funded Contra war had been raging for most of the previous decade. The war was the central issue in the 1990 presidential campaign, and the language in which both sides spoke of war and peace was highly gendered.

Daniel Ortega, the "fighting cock," was portrayed simultaneously as a loving father, hugging his baby daughter, Camila, and as a horse-riding cowboy leading other men on horses. At a rally in Chontales, Ortega accused the Contras of continuing "to assassinate and threaten the people" and promised to "respond to their threats with the arms of peace, with this cavalcade of peace" (*Barricada*, January 5, 1990, 1). These masculine images were tied together with the slogan "everything will be better," a very poor choice for a party that had already governed for ten years. And in fact Daniel lost the election to Violeta Barrios de Chamorro, who ran as an apolitical mother who could reunite the Nicaraguan family (for more on gender images and the 1990 election, see Bayard de Volo 2001, 157–61; Kampwirth 2004, 40–43; Lancaster 1992, 290–93).

By 1990 Daniel Ortega had already moved toward a populist style of politics and away from his origins in revolutionary politics. Although I have never seen a study of the symbolism employed in the 1984 election, the occasional posters I have seen from that period show a much more revolutionary, much more collective set of images. The same Daniel Ortega had been the presidential candidate in 1984, but he was presented then as the representative of the revolution rather than as "Daniel." By 2006 Daniel seemed to have stripped himself of much of that collectivist revolutionary ideology and he did not even formally represent the party of the revolution, but rather a coalition that included many of the historic enemies of the revolution, along with the FSLN. But I am getting ahead of the story. I now turn to the years Ortega spent out of power.

Governing from Below, or the Years of the Pact, 1990–2006

When Daniel Ortega and the FSLN lost the 1990 election, they did something rather unusual in the history of armed revolution: They peacefully handed power over to the winner of the election, Violeta Barrios de Chamorro, representative of the fourteen-party UNO coalition. While giving up formal power, Ortega promised that his party would continue to "govern from below." That is, as the best-organized political party in the country, and the only one with a significant base of organized supporters, the FSLN would continue to shape the course of Nicaraguan politics, even after losing the presidency.

But the strategy of "governing from below," despite the appeal of that rhetoric from a revolutionary perspective, was highly flawed. Activists in what the Sandinistas called "popular organizations" were demoralized at the end of the revolution and constrained economically, both because they no longer had access to state resources and because of high unemployment rates and low wages. The Sandinista women's movement was an exception to this general pattern. While feminists were also often demoralized by the Sandinista electoral loss in 1990, within a year they were reenergized by the freedom they enjoyed as they cut their formal ties to the FSLN. Although feminist voices had been heard within the Sandinista-affiliated women's movement in the 1980s, it was not until 1991 that a large, diverse, and well-organized autonomous feminist movement transformed social movement politics (Bayard de Volo 2001; Criquillón 1995; Kampwirth 2004).

In the wake of the 1990 election, Sandinista leaders were also divided over other questions, including alliances with other parties and internal party democracy. In the early 1990s women served on the National Directorate for the first time, and Daniel's status as leader of the party and perpetual candidate was challenged. But Daniel's faction eventually won that dispute and the party divided in 1995, with the new party, the MRS, taking most Sandinista intellectuals, social democrats, and feminists with it, while the FSLN kept most of the party's rank and file (Smith 1997).

Following the FSLN's loss of many of its most prominent members to the MRS, and after Daniel Ortega's electoral loss to Arnoldo Alemán in 1996, Ortega sought to consolidate the power of his party and his own personal power through a series of pacts with Alemán (Dye 2004; Hoyt 2004). It was quite remarkable that he would enter into political pacts with Alemán, head of the Partido Liberal Constitucionalista (Liberal Constitutionalist Party, or PLC), a party that traced its roots to the Somoza dictatorship. The PLC and Alemán himself were historic enemies of the FSLN and Daniel Ortega. Even as they entered into private pacts, both men often denounced each other in public. But the alliance becomes less of a mystery in the context of the FSLN's steady movement from a collective revolutionary party to a vehicle for the personal power of Daniel Ortega. And it is not the first time that populists have entered such pacts; the agreements between the FSLN and the Liberals are reminiscent of coalitions that Peruvian Victor Haya de la Torre's APRA party made over the decades with its historic enemies (Collier and Collier 1991, 695–706).

One feature of the first pact was an attempt to convert Nicaragua to a two-party system, a system in which both parties would share in the spoils of power, regardless of which one had won the presidency. It was also a way to strengthen the personal power of Arnoldo Alemán and Daniel Ortega. Both men had strong reasons to put their animosity aside through the pacts. Alemán feared that at the end of his term as president he would face trial and imprisonment for embezzling hundreds of millions of dollars. He was protected from this fate by one feature of the pact: former presidents and former presidential candidates were automatically granted a seat in the National Assembly, giving them parliamentary immunity (although eventually his immunity was stripped and he was convicted and sentenced to twenty years in prison, most of which he served on his luxurious ranch). Daniel Ortega also had reason to want parliamentary immunity, for he faced charges of a much more personal sort.

In March 1998 Daniel Ortega's stepdaughter, Zoilamérica Narváez, publicly accused Ortega of having sexually abused her from the age of eleven, and of raping her from the age of fifteen. Mere hours after Zoilamérica made her accusation, Rosario Murillo, her mother and Daniel's common-law wife, denounced her in a press conference, calling the accusation a "blow to our family" that should be treated as "a family affair" (*Envío* 1998, 6). Daniel stood silently at her side, a silence that he would maintain in the following years. With support from the autonomous feminist movement (especially the Red de Mujeres Contra la Violencia), Zoilamérica pressed her case in national and international courts for three years, while Daniel enjoyed immunity from prosecution through his position in the National Assembly (Bayard de Volo 2001, 247–48; Huerta 1998; Kampwirth 2004, 73–74; Luciak 2001, 175, 179–81; Narváez 1998).

Throughout this crisis, Daniel kept the loyalty of the rank and file. Instead,

Daniel's followers were furious at Zoilamérica. And they often expressed that anger through populist categories. One of the central characteristics of populism is a discourse of us and them, a struggle against the other. For Daniel and his followers, imperialists were always a central enemy. Feminists were another "other," often implicitly and sometimes explicitly. In the figure of Zoilamérica, the imperialist and the feminist were rhetorically united. I was told that the CIA was behind her accusations, or that Zoilamérica was a Somocista, or that nothing of the sort could have happened because Daniel was a good leader. Months later, these beliefs were still strong: When tens of thousands gathered to celebrate the July 19 anniversary of Somoza's overthrow, many of the young men (but not the women) in the crowd sported Daniel's image on T-shirts that read, "Daniel, estoy con vos" (Daniel, I am with you).

Some of Daniel's followers saw Zoilamérica not as a pathological liar or a tool of the CIA but as a woman scorned. Yes, Zoilamérica and Daniel had had a sexual relationship when she was a teenager living in his household, but it was "consensual"; the trouble was that she did not "get what she wanted," and so later claimed that he had forced himself on her. This version of events was consistent with the well-known secret in Sandinista circles since the early 1980s (Randall 1998, 69). It also assumed that it was reasonable for Daniel to have sexual access to anyone he wished, including a young teenager living under his roof. But the view that there had been a sexual relationship was much less common than the outright denial. And over the years, although Daniel's followers rarely mentioned Zoilamérica, I did occasionally hear references to the sexual accusations, typically used as an example of how much Daniel had suffered for the good of his people.

In December 2001, to the surprise of many, Ortega voluntarily gave up his parliamentary immunity so as to face Zoilamérica before a judge. The judge, Juana Méndez, had been a loyal supporter of Ortega's faction within the FSLN since the 1970s, according to her own testimony. To the surprise of few, Méndez threw out the case almost immediately. For Daniel Ortega, the costs of years of pact making with Arnoldo Alemán were all repaid at that moment. Thanks to the pact (which gave him effective control over the judiciary), Ortega could count on judges to come through when he most needed it.

Not only did the pact free Daniel from his stepdaughter's legal challenge, but a later version of the pact (combined with the fact that the Liberals were divided) arguably gave him the presidency in 2006. After the 1984 election Daniel had never won more than a large minority of votes, typically in the range of 40 percent. Under the rules devised in the pact, a candidate could win the first round with only 40 percent or even 35 percent, as long as the runner-up was at least five points behind (and in fact Ortega ended up winning with 38 percent of the vote). In exchange for the electoral rules that he wanted, Ortega arranged for Alemán's release from prison and his being placed under house arrest, later extended to "arrest" within the boundaries of the country (Torres-Rivas 2007, 7). In this case, it is hard to argue that populist politics served to consolidate the rule of law or electoral democracy.

The New and Improved Daniel, or the 2006 Election

During the 2006 campaign, the new vision of what it meant to be a revolutionary was traditional Catholic rather than liberation-theology Catholic, antifeminist rather than feminist. On the billboards that sprang up everywhere in Nicaraguan cities, there was little of the FSLN's traditional red and black, replaced instead with an array of brilliant colors, especially hot pink. Daniel Ortega, the Marxist-Leninist in military uniform in the early years of the revolution, was replaced with Daniel the practicing Catholic in white shirt and jeans. The rhetoric of anti-imperialism and class struggle was replaced with the rhetoric of peace and reconciliation. In fact, many historic enemies of the FSLN were incorporated into the Gran Unidad Nicaragua Triunfa coalition (the electoral coalition in which the FSLN was the largest member), most prominently vice-presidential candidate—and former Contra commander—Jaime Morales Carazo.[3]

Increasingly, Daniel and his followers described the candidate in almost religious terms, as someone who was above the dirtiness of normal politics. A few weeks after the election, I interviewed sixteen voters in Managua's working-class Altagracia neighborhood, five men and eleven women, ranging in age from nineteen to eighty-three. All were Sandinistas. They consistently praised the new Daniel, who, in the spirit of forgiveness, silently turned the other cheek. "Today we can see a Daniel who is different from the one at the time of the triumph of the revolution. . . . He showed it throughout the campaign, he was attacked so hard but he did not respond to those offenses. Instead he spoke of peace, of reconciliation" (Oscar, interview by author, December 2, 2006). "The propaganda against Daniel was dirty, dirty . . . [but] he did not respond to the

---

3. Ortega and Morales were historic enemies, and not only for having been on opposite sides of the Contra war: Morales's house was expropriated early in the revolution and given to Ortega, who lives there to this day (but who has since apparently paid for the house). Many other former Contras, and even members of the Somoza family's National Guard, joined the Sandinista electoral coalition in 2006 (see, e.g., EFE 2006; Pantoja 2006; Silva 2006; Vanegas 2006).

attempts to provoke him" (don Miguel, interview by author, November 26, 2006). Ortega himself spoke of the dirtiness of the campaign against him in religious terms, indirectly comparing himself to Christ. "They defamed Christ, they slandered him, they whipped him . . . and finally, when he was being crucified, that was when He said: Forgive them, Father, for they know not what they do. And it is those people who carry the weight of those grudges and those dirty campaigns; for that reason we should forgive them, for they do not know the harm that they themselves are doing in their hearts" (quoted in González Siles 2006).

Pointing to the new role of Catholicism in his image, and the diverse nature of the Gran Unidad Nicaragua Triunfa coalition, much of the press coverage of the election asserted that Daniel had changed (e.g., Kennedy 2006). Thinking that the rhetoric of change was aimed at attracting the votes of non-Sandinistas rather than at long-term loyalists, I asked the Sandinistas I interviewed to tell me what Ortega is like and whether he had changed. I was surprised that almost all said he had changed.

But there were some differences in how men and women understood change (though, since my numbers are quite small, this can only be suggestive). The five men I interviewed all asserted that he had changed, explaining, for instance, that he was now more experienced, or more of a statesman (uniting many former enemies in his electoral coalition). For example, one man in his twenties explained, "[He is] a very intelligent guy, he is even well educated, he is a lawyer. That is something that I like, the intelligence that he has. [He has changed so much, it is] a turn of 180 degrees in his politics. In his way of politics. He now uses another psychology to win. Before I suppose he used the leftist prototype a lot" (Salvador, interview by author, November 26, 2006). Ten of the eleven women, like the men, said he had changed (the eleventh said it was too soon to tell). Change, for most of them, was framed as a new situation (especially that the war was over), that he was more experienced, and that he could govern on his own rather than as part of the nine-member National Directorate. Three of the women brought up the question of his public embrace of Catholicism.

> As I see it, Daniel Ortega is very good, very good. He has done well for me. And now I see a future for young people, it is a triumph for them. . . . Yes, he has changed, from heaven to earth. Because he is in the Catholic Church. (Doña Mirna, interview by author, December 2, 2006)

> He is a sincere person, very sincere, a humane person who identifies with the poor. He has attained moral and religious values. Before, he did not

have religious values; now he does. I think he has changed, and the proof is in his accepting the church and recognizing his errors, because before he was a hard person. Upon accepting God he asked for forgiveness for his sins, and before, he wouldn't have done that. He is a person who seeks out peace, reconciliation. (Carla, interview by author, December 3, 2006)

I am a Sandinista . . . because I believe in Daniel. Daniel is a great person, he is a man who is with the people. He is the president of all the poor. Daniel Ortega is a charismatic man. Some people don't want to realize what a sensitive person he is, that Daniel is a man who loves the people, who loves Nicaragua. Daniel Ortega is a man that, what can I tell you, that always has told the truth. . . . For those reasons I believe in Daniel. And he carries through with his promises. . . . Yes, he has changed, because everything changes. Daniel has changed in that sense, because politics can't be like in previous years. He has advanced, but he always has his sensibilities. He has always been Catholic. He has always loved his people, he has always told the truth. He knows that the political situation in the world has changed and so he has to change. But he has always looked for ways to help. (Alejandra, interview by author, November 27, 2006)

Daniel's followers almost all embraced the view that Daniel had changed. But because they had all voted for him in previous elections (with the exception of those who had been too young to vote), it seemed that they would have voted for Daniel whether he had changed or not. With the exception of some of the women, they did not focus on one of the central themes of the campaign: Daniel's new religious identity.

In the press coverage of the campaign, one of the main signs that Daniel had changed was his formal marriage to Rosario Murillo, his partner of twenty-seven years, in a Catholic ceremony presided over by former archbishop Miguel Obando y Bravo, a little more than a year before the 2006 election (Ríos 2007). Not only did he marry Murillo, but he often allowed her to speak for him. Daniel was silent when his wife—who also headed his electoral campaign—advocated the abolition of therapeutic abortion, firmly allying herself with the Catholic Church.

In an interview on Radio Ya, Murillo was asked about the position of the Gran Unidad Nicaragua Triunfa coalition, to which the FSLN belonged, with respect to therapeutic abortion.

Precisely because we have faith, because we have religion, because we are believers, because we love God above all things. . . . For those reasons we also defend, and we agree completely with the Church and the churches, that abortion is something that affects women fundamentally, because we never get over the pain and the trauma that an abortion leaves us! When people have had, or have had to resort to that, they never get over it. And this pain is something that we don't want for anyone.... The [Sandinista] Front, the Great Nicaragua Unified Triumph, says, "No to abortion, yes to life!" (Murillo 2006)

With these words Murillo cemented the new alliance with the Catholic Church and with the former archbishop in particular (whom she praised elsewhere in the interview). These words represented a real shift in the position of the Sandinista party regarding therapeutic abortion. It also represented a shift for Rosario Murillo herself, as she wrapped herself in the fold of the Catholic Church. It was a fold to which she had only recently returned, as Gioconda Belli noted. "Her words, which would not be at all startling coming from someone who had lived within the Church for many years, cannot fail to surprise coming from someone who, until a few months ago, signed her opinion pieces according to the phases of the moon and who was openly influenced by lights, stars, and all the magical paraphernalia of the Age of Aquarius" (Belli 2006).

The words of Gioconda Belli, herself a former Sandinista guerrilla, reflect long-standing hostility between Rosario Murillo and her husband, on the one hand, and many women who trace their political roots to the Sandinista guerrilla struggle, on the other. After the Sandinistas lost the 1990 election, long-simmering disagreements first led Sandinista feminists to seek autonomy from the FSLN, and then led the FSLN itself to break up, with most of the historic leaders, intellectuals, and feminist Sandinistas joining the new party, the MRS. For most feminists, the final nail in the coffin for their relationship with Ortega was the sexual abuse accusation made by his stepdaughter. That breakup with the feminists and the MRS made Daniel Ortega more powerful than ever within the FSLN, and it left him free to promote the feminine model of women's emancipation that he had espoused from at least the early 1980s.

But despite long-standing tensions, I think it is highly unlikely that the FSLN would have voted to abolish the life-of-the-mother exception if not for the fact that the election was days away. In other words, the FSLN's newfound opposition to therapeutic abortion does not indicate an ideological shift to the right. What it does show is that, after a decade and a half out of power, and after nearly a decade of political pacts with the Right, the FSLN was quite willing to oppose its former base in the women's movement, to say nothing of the vast majority of Nicaragua's medical establishment, if that is what it took to return to power.[4] It was part and parcel of the FSLN's long-term evolution from a revolutionary party to one that was often a personal vehicle for Daniel Ortega and his family.

But the vote to abolish therapeutic abortion in October 2006 cannot be understood exclusively in terms of formal politics. It was also due to important changes in social movement politics, specifically the evolution of the feminist and antifeminist movements after the Sandinistas' electoral loss in 1990. The rise of the autonomous feminist movement, followed by the antifeminist movement, goes far beyond the scope of this chapter and has been analyzed elsewhere.[5] While the feminist movement was far bigger than the antifeminist movement, it was divided in 2006 and was often alienated from its former allies in the FSLN, to the point that it was unable to stop the move to eliminate the right to abortion to save the woman's life. By contrast, sixteen years of sympathetic governments had allowed the antifeminist movement to grow and organize effectively. It had probably never before been as united, especially across Catholic and evangelical lines.

Conclusion

As the Sandinista Front evolved from a revolutionary party to one that was largely controlled by Daniel Ortega and his family, the gender content of what it meant to be a Sandinista also evolved. Women's emancipation, which had a feminist meaning for many revolutionaries during the 1980s (though its meaning was always contested), took on less feminist content within the FSLN during the final decade of the twentieth century and the first decade of the twenty-first. This may seem ironic, as this was the same period that saw the emergence of a massive autonomous feminist movement in Nicaragua, one of the most significant in Latin America.

---

4. One of the many ironies of this story is that the abolition of therapeutic abortion, which Daniel Ortega and the FSLN supported in a cynical attempt to win the 2006 election, almost certainly contributed nothing to the eventual Sandinista win. Ortega was reelected in 2006 because the law was changed to allow a candidate to win the first round with as little as 35 percent of the vote, and because the major right-wing party was divided in two. For an analysis of the electoral math, see Kampwirth 2008, 131–32.

5. On the Nicaraguan feminist movement, see, e.g., Babb 2001; Bayard de Volo 2001; Isbester 2001; and Kampwirth 2004. On the antifeminist movement, see Kampwirth 2006, and on the role of feminists and antifeminists in the abolition of therapeutic abortion, see Kampwirth 2008.

Similarly, the models of masculinity and femininity projected by Daniel Ortega and Rosario Murillo shifted with time. When the Somoza dictatorship was overthrown, Daniel was a young man in heavy glasses, always in a military uniform. When he first ran for president in 1984, he "seemed incapable of the usual behavior of politicians. . . . He smiled only when he meant it, and he neither kissed babies nor hugged young women" (Cockcroft 1991, 85). By 1990 Daniel had traded his glasses for contact lenses and his military uniform for jeans and brightly colored open-collar shirts. And he sought to be all sorts of men at once: hugging children, dancing with young women, leading a cavalcade of men on horseback. In 2006 a new masculine model was layered over the older images of Daniel: pious, married, Catholic, unbending opponent of abortion, always dressed in jeans with a collarless white shirt.

By 2006 Daniel and Rosario's children were grown and Rosario's role had changed dramatically. Still dressed in hippie-ish style, she was now Daniel's campaign manager, and once he took office in 2007 she became, by many accounts, the most powerful individual in the new government, second only to her husband (e.g., Envío 2007, 5; Sandoval 2007). Rosario Murillo seemed to offer herself as proof of the great strides women had made under her husband's government.[6]

As a leader in the era of radical populism, in the poorest country on the mainland of the Americas, Daniel Ortega might not have had much more, in material terms, to offer to women. During the age of classic populism, the Somoza family had the ability to co-opt women through the vote and, at least in the case of female Somocistas, through state largess, especially state employment. In the era of the crushing debt and neoliberal policies, populists like Ortega have found it harder to incorporate women into their coalitions through jobs and other material resources.

While there was always hope that Nicaragua's economic desperation could be resolved with the help of oil-rich Hugo Chávez (thus funding national patron-client relations through the help of an international patron), this had not yet

6. In honor of International Women's Day, Rosario Murillo asserted that "we women are returning to hold power," but she offered no evidence of this beyond the promised 50 percent of government positions, a promise that had not yet been fulfilled (EFE 2007; to get a sense of popular response to Murillo, it is worth looking at the many pages of reader comments that follow this article in the online version of El Nuevo Diario). Also see Rosario Murillo's remarkable Web site, http://www .conamornicaragua.org.ni/index.html, on which are posted many years' worth of documents (speeches, articles, poems) and what may be a comprehensive set of speeches given by Rosario and Daniel during their time in office. The graphics change occasionally, but when I looked at the site in August 2007 it was headed with a crowd scene celebrating the July 19 overthrow of Somoza (tinted hot pink). Rosario Murillo herself appears in the upper-left corner, her arm raised in a victory sign, surrounded by red and yellow daisies.

happened months into the most recent Ortega administration. Instead, Nicaraguans have had to settle for the symbolism of gigantic billboards marking May Day. Against a background of hot pink, Daniel lifted his fist in the air, promising, in the words of the Internationale, "Arriba los pobres de la tierra" (Arise, ye wretched of the earth).

But Daniel Ortega's problems have not been only economic. Unlike some earlier populists, he has faced a significant feminist movement, a movement of the second wave, with a focus on personal politics, including reproductive rights, domestic violence, and incest, issues that at best made him uncomfortable. It is not surprising, then, that Daniel would construct feminists as part of "the other," as women alienated from their own true natures, who could be ignored or attacked depending on the political moment. And when abolishing therapeutic abortion seemed an expedient way to help guarantee Daniel's return to power, his party unanimously supported that dramatic change in policy, despite the projected cost in lives.[7] There is evidence to suggest that most rank-and-file Sandinistas opposed the abolition of therapeutic abortion; nonetheless they voted for Daniel (Kampwirth 2008, 129–31).

In some sense, they had no choice. For Sandinismo is a major source of personal identity for a large minority of Nicaraguans. Forged in the Sandinista revolution, which Daniel Ortega has increasingly come to personally embody, voting against Daniel would be voting against their own personal histories. It would be voting against the many sacrifices rank-and-file Sandinistas made over the years, sacrifices that often included the deaths of loved ones in the struggle against the Somoza dictatorship or the Contra war. Despite the many sins of Daniel Ortega, voting against him—voting against themselves—would be too much to ask.

References

Alvarez, Sonia. 1990. *Engendering Democracy in Brazil: Women's Movements in Transition Politics.* Princeton: Princeton University Press.
Babb, Florence. 2001. *After Revolution: Mapping Gender and Cultural Politics in Neoliberal Nicaragua.* Austin: University of Texas Press.
Bayard de Volo, Lorraine. 2001. *Mothers of Heroes and Martyrs: Gender Identity Politics in Nicaragua, 1979–1999.* Baltimore: Johns Hopkins University Press.
Belli, Gioconda. 2006. "De la era de acuario a la Inquisición." http://www.socialismo-o-barbarie.org/america_latina/060827_nicaragua_sandinistasiglesia.htm (accessed September 8, 2006).

7. Six months after therapeutic abortion was abolished, forty-two women had died as a result of that legal change (Brenes 2007).

Booth, John. 1985. "The National Governmental System." In *Nicaragua: The First Five Years,* ed. Thomas W. Walker, 29–43. New York: Praeger.

Brenes, María Haydee. 2007. "Plantón de mujeres ante Corte Suprema." *El Nuevo Diario,* May 18.

Cockcroft, James. 1991. *Daniel Ortega.* New York: Chelsea House.

Collier, Ruth Berins, and David Collier. 1991. *Shaping the Political Arena: Critical Junctures, the Labor Movement, and Regime Dynamics in Latin America.* Princeton: Princeton University Press.

Conniff, Michael. 1982. "Introduction: Toward a Comparative Definition of Populism." In *Latin American Populism in Comparative Perspective,* ed. Michael Conniff, 3–30. Albuquerque: University of New Mexico Press.

Criquillón, Ana. 1995. "The Nicaraguan Women's Movement: Feminist Reflections from Within." In *The New Politics of Survival: Grassroots Movements in Central America,* ed. Minor Sinclair, 209–37. New York: Monthly Review Press.

Dye, David R. 2004. *Democracy Adrift: Caudillo Politics in Nicaragua.* Brookline, Mass.: Hemisphere Initiatives.

EFE. 2006. "Partido somocista se adhiere al FSLN." *El Nuevo Diario,* August 26.

———. 2007. "Murillo confirma su poder." *El Nuevo Diario,* March 7.

Envío. 1998. "A Test in Ethics for a Society in Crisis." March, 3–9.

———. 2007. "The Ortega-Murillo Project: Personal, Family, National, or International?" *Envío* 26 (312): 1–8.

González, Victoria, and Karen Kampwirth, eds. 2001. *Radical Women in Latin America: Left and Right.* University Park: Pennsylvania State University Press.

González Siles, Silvia. 2006. "Daniel Ortega ahora se compara con Cristo." *La Prensa,* October 31.

Gould, Jeffrey L. 1990. *To Lead as Equals: Rural Protest and Political Consciousness in Chinandega, Nicaragua, 1912–1979.* Chapel Hill: University of North Carolina Press.

Hoyt, Katherine. 2004. "Parties and Pacts in Contemporary Nicaragua." In *Undoing Democracy: The Politics of Electoral Caudillismo,* ed. David Close and Kalowatie Deonandan, 17–42. Lanham, Md.: Lexington Books.

Huerta, Juan Ramón. 1998. *El silencio del patriarca: La linea es no hablar de esto.* Managua: Talleres Gráficos de Litografía el Renacimiento.

Isbester, Katherine. 2001. *Still Fighting: The Nicaraguan Women's Movement, 1977–2000.* Pittsburgh: University of Pittsburgh Press.

Kampwirth, Karen. 2002. *Women and Guerrilla Movements: Nicaragua, El Salvador, Chiapas, Cuba.* University Park: Pennsylvania State University Press.

———. 2003. "Arnoldo Alemán Takes on the NGOs: Antifeminism and the New Populism in Nicaragua." *Latin American Politics and Society* 45 (2): 133–58.

———. 2004. *Feminism and the Legacy of Revolution: Nicaragua, El Salvador, Chiapas.* Athens: Ohio University Press.

———. 2006. "Resisting the Feminist Threat: Antifeminist Politics in Post-Sandinista Nicaragua." *NWSA Journal* 18 (2): 73–100.

———. 2008. "Abortion, Antifeminism, and the Return of Daniel Ortega: In Nicaragua, Leftist Politics?" *Latin American Perspectives* 35 (6): 122–36.

Kennedy, Duncan. 2006. "Second Chance for Nicaragua's Ortega." BBC News, November 8. http://news.bbc.co.uk/1/hi/world/americas/6129994.stm.

Knight, Alan. 1998. "Populism and Neo-Populism in Latin America, Especially Mexico." *Journal of Latin American Studies* 30 (2): 223–48.

Lancaster, Roger. 1992. *Life Is Hard: Machismo, Danger, and the Intimacy of Power in Nicaragua*. Berkeley and Los Angeles: University of California Press.

Latin American Studies Association (LASA). 1985. "A Summary of the Report of the Latin American Studies Association Delegation to Observe the Nicaraguan General Election of November 4, 1984." In *Nicaragua: The First Five Years*, ed. Thomas W. Walker, 523–32. New York: Praeger.

Luciak, Ilja. 2001. *After the Revolution: Gender and Democracy in El Salvador, Nicaragua, and Guatemala*. Baltimore: Johns Hopkins University Press.

Molyneux, Maxine. 1985. "Women." In *Nicaragua: The First Five Years*, ed. Thomas W. Walker, 145–62. New York: Praeger.

————. 2001. *Women's Movements in International Perspective: Latin America and Beyond*. New York: Palgrave.

Murillo, Rosario. 2006. "FSLN con Dios y contra el aborto." (Extracto de la entrevista ofrecida por Rosario Murillo, jefa de campaña del Frente Sandinista de Liberación Nacional, a la emisora Nueva Radio Ya), August 21. http://www.izquierda.info/modules.php?name=News&file=print&sid=1498 (accessed September 8, 2006).

Narváez, Zoilamérica. 1998. "'Quisiera que me entedieran . . .': Entrevista con Zoilamérica Narváez." *La Boletina*, supplement, October, 1–39.

El Nuevo Diario. 2007. "PRN critica a los CPC: Talavera dice que no son partido de oposición." August 6. http://www.elnuevodiario.com.ni/2007/08/06/politica/55574.

Pantoja, Ary. 2006. "Más ex somocistas en FSLN." *El Nuevo Diario*, August 27.

Randall, Margaret. 1998. "Margaret Randall escribe al FSLN." In *El Silencio del Patriarca: La línea es no hablar de esto*, ed. Juan Ramón Huerta, 69–71. Managua: Talleres Gráficos de Litografía el Renacimiento.

Ríos, Julia. 2007. "Rosario Murillo, el poder tras el 'orteguismo.'" *El Nuevo Diario*, January 10.

Sandoval, Consuelo. 2007. "Gran poder a Murillo causa alarma." *El Nuevo Diario*, February 2.

Silva, José Adán. 2006. "Ortega insiste en perdón y olvido." *La Prensa*, September 4.

Smith, Steve Kent. 1997. "Renovation and Orthodoxy: Debate and Transition Within the Sandinista National Liberation Front." *Latin American Perspectives* 93 (2): 102–16.

Torres-Rivas, Edelberto. 2007. "Nicaragua: El retorno del sandinismo transfigurado." *Nueva Sociedad* 207 (January–February): 4–10.

Vanegas, Leoncio. 2006. "'Tal vez Ortega nos cumple': Contras decepcionados de los liberales." *El Nuevo Diario*, September 22.

Wessel, Lois. 1991. "Reproductive Rights in Nicaragua: From the Sandinistas to the Government of Violeta Chamorro." *Feminist Studies* 17 (3): 537–49.

9

WAKING WOMEN UP?

HUGO CHÁVEZ, POPULISM, AND VENEZUELA'S "POPULAR" WOMEN

Gioconda Espina and Cathy A. Rakowski

This is a revolution of women.
—*María León, Minister for Women's Affairs,* Ultimas Noticias *(Caracas), March 8, 2008*

In June 2007 George W. Bush referred to Hugo Chávez's administration as "shallow populism," to which Chávez responded "shallow populism, no—radical populism!" (Traynor 2007). Chávez has not explained what he means by "radical populism," however. In this chapter we explore one interesting aspect of "Chavista-style" populism—the ways in which it is gendered. We focus on the construction of Chávez's image as leader and the construction of his "people," on calls for men and women to mobilize, and on the discourse of public service programs known as *misiones*. All are strategies that Chávez and others use to organize support for his "Bolivarian revolution," which is designed to move Venezuela toward a new form of "XXI Century Socialism." We also briefly discuss Venezuela's National Institute of Women (Inamujer) and the Women's Development Bank (Banmujer), both important mechanisms for the ideological training and mobilization of women. Revolutionary discourse and symbols, Inamujer and Banmujer, and the *misiones* are important components of Chávez's version of radical populism—also known as "Chavista populism" or "Chavismo" (Hawkins 2003).

Some political leaders—among them María León,[1] president of Inamujer and minister of state for women's affairs, and Nora Castañeda, president of Banmujer—claim that the revolution has "woken women up" and empowered them.

This chapter builds on long-term research by the authors on women's rights organizing in Venezuela. Our research has included participant observation, interviews with activists and politicians, and documentary research. All translations are our own unless otherwise indicated.

1. In 2009, Leon was appointed head of the new Ministry of Popular Power for Women and Gender Equality.

They point to women's community activism and legislative advances as proof. The 1999 constitution is nonsexist and was the first reform achieved during Chávez's first term as president. The gender content of the constitution and other women's rights legislation passed since he was first elected in 1998 (a revised law against domestic violence, pensions for housewives, breastfeeding protection, a revised equal opportunity law)—while having roots in initiatives that date back to the 1940s and in legislation of the 1990s—often are credited mistakenly to Chávez alone.[2] Venezuelan women also have a long history as community leaders and activists and have been important to the success of clandestine political movements (see Espina 1994; Friedman 2000).[3] Women outside the revolution (autonomous feminists and members of opposition parties) worked closely with members of the Constituent Assembly on the new 1999 constitution, and many continued to collaborate with key allies in the National Assembly on other legislative projects (Espina and Rakowski 2002; Rakowski and Espina 2006).

Following his re-election in December 2006, Chávez intensified efforts to speed up the pace of revolutionary change in the direction of a socialist state modeled in part on Cuba; these efforts included his failed proposal to reform the constitution. Important roles were assigned to the *misiones*, urban land committees, and the newer *consejos comunales* (communal councils) that are rapidly displacing other community organizations.[4] All emphasize "ideological training," as do Inamujer's *puntos de encuentro* (encounter points) women's groups and Banmujer's user groups. At the same time, there are blatant contradictions between Chávez's discourse on participation and co-management and real practices; decisions and control originate at the top and are reinforced by financial incentives (Hawkins, Rosas, and Johnson forthcoming; Penfold-Becerra 2007, 2005; Corrales and Penfold 2007). All of these practices are key features of Chavista populism.

The chapter is organized into four sections. First, we present an overview of the origins of Chavista populism and the construction of its symbols and practices. Second, we consider briefly the discourse of the *misiones*, important

2. Chávez was reelected in 2000, following approval of the new constitution, and again in 2006; he also won a recall referendum in 2004. In 2007 voters rejected his proposed reforms to the constitution, some of which would have expanded his powers and ended presidential term limits. In 2008, however, voters approved the suspension of presidential term limits for Chávez.

3. See Sujatha Fernandes's chapter in this volume for a discussion of popular women's activism in Chávez's Bolivarian revolution.

4. *Consejos comunales* and urban land committees receive funding directly from the national government, bypassing municipal and state governments that are supposed to work with local citizen organizations according to the constitution. This is an important strategy for recentralizing power and control in the national government.

redistributive mechanisms for advancing the populist project. Third, we focus on discourses that target women, particularly the concept of "revolutionary motherhood." We conclude with a brief discussion of challenges facing Chavista populism and women's continued importance as voluntary labor.

Populism and the "Bolivarian Revolution"

Chavista populism is *not* a return to an old-style, so-called Latin American classic populism of the 1930s and '40s, nor is it an example of more contemporary "neopopulism," though it shares features of both (Cammack 2000; Ellner 2006; Laclau 2006a, 2006b).[5] This includes the goal of seeking "the destruction of the old ruling groups and the institutional basis for their authority" (Kornhauser 1960, 132; Laclau 1980, 1987, 2006a). As Garretón has observed for Chile, Cammack argues that the outcomes of Chavista-style populism "will depend on its ability to move from a reactive or 'defensive' posture to a foundational project which gives rise to the creation of a new institutional order" (Garretón 1986, 145–48, quoted in Cammack 2000, 152). Although Chávez's foundational project (i.e., XXI Century Socialism) is under construction through ideological training and institutional reforms, including some that are unconstitutional, he also clearly retains a defensive posture—for example, through numerous and persistent claims of plots against his life, of an impending invasion by the United States, by Colombia, and so on. He makes direct appeals to the people for support, thus bypassing existing institutions. This strategy is frequently employed when political systems are in crisis (Cammack 2000, 154).

In the historical conjuncture that paved the way for Chávez's rise to power, the most important factors were a steady increase in poverty since 1979; citizen frustration with the failure of promised outcomes of neoliberal structural reforms; rampant political corruption that led to the loss of confidence in and the eventual collapse of traditional political parties; the exclusion of workers and investors from an adverse market; and citizens' inability to have their concerns heard. These factors affected not only poor and working-class citizens but also the middle classes (Paramio 2006, 66; Raby 2006). Like other newly emerging populist governments in Latin America, Chavista populism emerged in the "wake

5. Chávez's discourse is not "neopopulist" because he preserves the anti-imperialist and redistributionist rhetoric of classical populism, but he does share the "outsider" status of neopopulist leaders (he had no prior political career) (Arenas 2005).

of a successful neoliberal challenge . . . at a moment when both the foundational project and ideological hegemony of neoliberalism seem[ed] well established" (Cammack 2000, 155).[6]

To this context must be added "facilitating events" such as the 1989 *caracazo*, during which the poor revealed a readiness to act on their frustration by coming down from the hills surrounding Caracas, where they rioted and looted in response to an announcement by President Carlos Andrés Pérez of an increase in transportation fares as part of a package of IMF measures to be implemented by his government. A group of young military officers (who already had been working on plans for a socialist future and an end to corrupt parties) were utterly disgusted by the role the military was forced to play in repressing the uprising, including the death and disappearance of more than a thousand citizens. On February 4, 1992, these officers led the first of two failed coups that year.

It was at this time that the Venezuelan public was introduced to coup leader Hugo Chávez Frías through television and radio. People were impressed by Chávez's behavior, his articulation of their frustrations and concerns, and the dignity with which he assumed responsibility for the failure of the coup and asked co-conspirators to put aside their weapons to avoid further bloodshed. This "important heroic gesture" marked the political birth of a leader who demonstrated "decisive actions," "identification with the popular cause," and a "capacity to lead" (Raby 2006, 69–71; Arenas 2005; Espina and Rakowski 2007), and who "looks out for" the people (*cuida de ellos*) (Paramio 2006, 68–72).

What, then, are the specific features of Chávez's self-proclaimed "radical populism"? First, it takes the "traditional redistributive form" of classical populism and is heavily dependent on oil revenues. Second, abundant oil revenues have bolstered Chávez's "exaggerated vision" of his potential regional political role and his penchant for donating Venezuela's oil money to other countries and forgiving their debts (Paramio 2006, 62–65). In the meantime, Venezuela's public services are in crisis, public infrastructure has seriously deteriorated, food shortages have become endemic, and poverty and unemployment are still widespread. Declining and fluctuating international prices for oil since 2008 have led to reduced public budgets in Venezuela, further decline in infrastructure and services, high inflation rates (over 30 percent in 2008 and higher projected for 2009) and protests

6. It is important to note that Chávez maintains an uneasy relationship with the Left in Venezuela and throughout Latin America. Although he initially enjoyed the support of coalitions of leftist parties, this support has fragmented as his plans and practices have evolved. When he demanded that all supporters join the United Socialist Party of Venezuela (PSUV), a number of parties refused, and a few have even joined coalitions with opposition parties.

on the part of workers in oil, medicine, education, state-owned industries, public administration, and other fields.

Third, Chavista populism is "statist" (Ellner 2006) and "authoritarian" (Paramio 2006). In spite of a discourse that emphasizes "a participatory and protagonistic democracy" (consecrated in the 1999 constitution) and a socialism based on co-management and people-centered decision making, the Chávez government and locally based programs like the *misiones* are "very top down, heavily dependent on funding and decisions made by national leaders," and there continues to be a strong tendency to increase recentralization (Ellner 2006, 73–79; Hawkins, Rosas, and Johnson forthcoming; Penfold-Becerra 2007; Rodriguez 2006).[7] Remarkably, much of Chávez's discourse attacks bureaucracies even as his actions strengthen the executive branch and himself as the "main guardian of national sovereignty" (Ellner 2006, 73–75).

Fourth, Chavista populism is based on a direct relationship between a *caudillo* (boss) and the popular classes (Ellner 2006), which, given the importance of a discourse of confrontation, suggests the potential for creating followers rather than autonomous citizens (Paramio 2006, 72). Chavista populism brings with it expectations for obedience in return for the distribution of services and funds to the popular classes (Krauze 2005). Recent studies of urban land committees, communal councils, and citizen groups reveal resistance to central control and support for local control (see, e.g., Fernandes 2007a, 2007b; García-Guadilla 2007).

Discourse, Symbols, and Collective Identity

Discourse is the central element in the relationship between the leader and his people (de la Torre 1994, 51–52; Laclau 1980, 1987). Chávez's discourse during his first presidential campaign (1997–98) and preceding his second election in 2000 (following approval of a new constitution) had broad appeal across classes because of widespread political corruption and the devastating impact of the neoliberal economic policies of the 1990s. He did not yet use what Laclau (1980) calls the "ideological symbols of popular resistance" (see also Espina and Rakowski 2007). Following his second election, his discourse changed. It became more

---

7. In particular, Chávez has used centralization as a strategy to prevent state and local elected officials from exercising their responsibilities as mandated by the constitution. Following the election, in 2008, of opposition and independent candidates as governors and mayors of the most populous states and municipalities, he ordered that their authority over public services and infrastructure be transferred to federal agencies. In April 2009 he denied constitutionally guaranteed federal funds (*situado constitucional*) to the new mayor of the Caracas metropolitan area and transferred the responsibilities of the mayor's office to federal agencies.

nationalist, more populist and socialist, more focused on the idea of a great struggle and on the construction of enemies. He deliberately associated his new "Bolivarian revolution" with Simón Bolívar and other heroes from the war for independence. He also drew on religious symbolism and a strong sense of moralism. Some followers even refer to him as a "messiah"; he often appears in photos at his desk next to a statue of Christ carrying the cross.

Chávez christened the campaign against the presidential recall referendum of 2004 "the Battle of Saint Inés" (in reference to a battle where Venezuelan hero Zamora defeated "the Goths"). He also used the theme of "Florentino and the devil" (from a popular Venezuelan song) and anointed himself Florentino and the devil "Mr. Bush and his lackeys," i.e., the people who would vote in favor of the referendum (Espina and Rakowski 2007). His chosen heroes tend to be men engaged in armed, superhuman struggles.

The emphasis on struggle supports a key aspect of populism: the discursive construction of an "us" and a "them." "They" are the enemy blamed for people's problems, the rationale for mobilizing support for a class-based or nationalist project (Arenas 2005, 40). This discourse may seem empowering to many of Venezuela's marginalized groups, but it also bolsters Chávez's position as the leader of grassroots "movements." Thus, "bottom-up" organizing for change goes hand in hand with a parallel strategy of strengthening the executive (Ellner 2006). Virtuoso even argues that "Chávez sees himself in the role of a *caudillo* who guides the people to a new liberation." To fulfill his mission, he must have "absolute freedom of action, count on the maximum loyalty of his collaborators, and possess a high level of popular support" (2006, 301).

In addition to the construction of an enemy "other" and symbols linking contemporary and historical struggles, Chávez's discourse emphasizes the idea that genuine democracy and social justice never existed in Venezuela because the poor and dark skinned were always marginalized and exploited. Therefore, what is needed is a "starting over." He refers to his government as the "Fifth Republic" and as representing a complete break with the past.[8] Venezuelans, under his direction, are inventing the new socialism of the twenty-first century. These ideas unite and provide an identity for those who share them (Virtuoso 2006, 303). Since no one really knows what XXI Century Socialism will look like, Chávez's guidance is critical.

---

8. Chávez contrasts his "Fifth Republic" to the previous forty years of democracy (the Fourth Republic), to which he attributes responsibility for neoliberalism and all of Venezuela's social and economic problems, including class and racial inequality, crime, and discrimination against women (Arenas 2005, 46–49).

Charismatic Leadership

The preceding section reflects Laclau's assertion that populist discourse must be directed to "a people" and a populist leader must construct this people through a discursive identity and symbols (Laclau 1980, 1987, 2006b). Equally important to populist regimes is a charismatic leader who promises to resolve the people's problems and gives direction to the movement. Such leaders, including Chávez, claim to "own" the truth, and they communicate with the people constantly in order to "spread the word" (see Krauze 2005 and the discussion of Krauze in Margolies 2006, 170). Chávez accomplishes this through weekly radio programs and frequent televised national addresses carried, by law, on all stations. These addresses foment a sense of urgency, which Chávez reinforces with his demands for special powers that allow him to bypass institutionalized rules and procedures. This "sense of immediacy" reinforces the "direct relationship between the leader and society, at the expense of institutions and democracy" (Arenas 2005, 49).

In his speeches and in the pronouncements of his allies in ministerial offices, Inamujer, and the National Assembly, Chávez is consistently offered up as the only one capable of solving social problems. During a 2005 interview, for example, María León, president of Inamujer, proclaimed that "there is nothing above the leadership of our president, only God, and God is with Chávez" (León 2005). His leadership is reinforced by the attribution of all legal, economic, and social advances to him personally, described in more detail in the next section.

Charismatic leadership can fill a symbolic need in popular mobilizing and the construction of a more just social system. The marginalized identify with Chávez because they hope he can create real, radically different alternatives to the status quo (Raby 2006) and because he is "one of them" (he comes from humble origins and is of mixed race). The *misiones,* in theory, provide tangible examples of what a just social system would look like.

The *Misiones* as Populist Projects and Symbols

Social policy in the early years of Chávez's presidency was directed primarily at addressing social emergencies and assisting some of the poorest communities (D'Elia, Lacruz, and Maingon 2006). The resulting outreach programs, known as *misiones,* have been described as "programmatic, idealist notions of appropriate public policy" (Hawkins, Rosas, and Johnson forthcoming). They distribute the benefits of oil revenues directly to the needy (Penfold-Becerra 2007), and they are top-down initiatives designed and administered by central agencies. Thirty-one *misiones* had been established as of December 2009, though at least three were no longer functioning.[9] The names of many *misiones* evoke historical struggles and revolutionary heroes like Guaicaipuro (symbol of indigenous resistance) and Ezequial Zamora (military leader of an anti-*latifundio* movement).

The *misiones* represent an extraordinary array of services and programs that reach many people in many low-income neighborhoods and that are embraced and nurtured by local volunteers and community groups.[10] Although it is difficult to gain access to accurate, detailed, and up-to-date statistics, both the official statistics we reviewed from the larger *misiones* and estimates from research reports (see, e.g., D'Elia 2006; Mota Gutiérrez 2004) indicate significant numbers of "beneficiaries" (both numbers targeted and numbers actually enrolled) and that women are a majority in the largest *misiones* (especially in education and health care). Interviews conducted with some *misión* staff members and beneficiaries also confirm the importance to household finances of payments attached to participation in several *misiones* by multiple family members. In addition, with few exceptions (e.g., García V. 2005), interviews conducted by other researchers with government officials, *misión* volunteers, paid staff, and beneficiaries generally support the conclusion that the *misiones* have important and diverse social impacts (D'Elia 2006; Fender 2006; Hawkins, Rosas, and Johnson forthcoming; Maingon 2006; Simao Vieira 2007; Valencia Ramírez 2005; Welsch and Reyes 2006).

Several observations can be made about the success of the *misiones*. First, although there are many problems (staffing, logistics, supplies, funding, location,

9. The *misiones* are Barrio Adentro I, II, y III (medical services, including a dental program, Misión Sonrisa, and eye surgery—Misión Milagro); Robinson I y II (literacy and elementary education); Sucre (university scholarships); Ribas (high school); Guaicaipuro (support to indigenous communities); Miranda (militias and army reserves); Piar (mining); Alimentación (food distribution through subsidized markets and community kitchens); Identidad (identity card campaign); Vuelvan Caras (technical training, closed); Hábitat y Vivienda (housing and community development); Zamora (land "recovery"); Cultura (recovery of popular values and practices); Negra Hipólita (for the homeless); Ciencia (takes science to the people); Madres del Barrio (support to poor mothers); Árbol (environmental conservation); Alma Mater (new public universities); Revolución Energética (energy conservation); Villanueva (new cities); Ché Guevara (cooperatives, technical training); 13 de Abril (communes); Música (music training); Cristo (Millennium Development Goals); José Gregorio Hernández (health care for the handicapped), and Niños y Niñas del Barrio (street children's program). The Web pages for the *misiones* can be found at http://www.gobiernoenlinea.ve/misceláneas/misiones.html.

10. According to Inamujer staff members and data from the largest *misiones,* more than half the participants in *misiones* and voluntary community organizations are women.

etc.), the *misiones* have contributed material benefits to many individuals, house-holds, and communities. Access to basic health care, educational services, and subsidized foodstuffs improved for a significant percentage of the urban poor through 2008 (but declined in 2009 owing to declining budgets). Scholarships, cash incentives, and bonuses that come with some *misiones* have provided much-needed income to the tens of thousands of households they reach.[11] Second, "cross-fertilization" among *misiones* has created a "parallel economy" and a par-allel system of public services, although it contributes less to autonomous orga-nizing (Hawkins, Rosas, and Johnson forthcoming). Third, *misiones* contribute to the collective identity of the populist project and help consolidate the direct relationship between Chávez and "his people." That is, they not only are redis-tributive programs that can reduce extreme poverty, but they also play a role in identity construction.

In addition to their symbolic association with heroic figures of the past, most *misiones* give names to participants that reflect the discourse of confrontation and struggle. *Misión* names (and mottos like "Yes, I can") are intended to dis-rupt expectations based on a lifetime of failure and social and economic barri-ers; they connote armed struggle against injustice and the "other." They are intended to improve self-esteem and foster a self-image based on capability, sol-idarity, and entitlement. *Misión* names include "patriots," "comrades," "fighters," "victors," "battalions," "brigades," and "lancers," among others. Chávez is the *comandante* who leads and defends these troops. Despite their masculine ori-gin, these names are applied equally to women and men, sometimes with fem-inine versions—e.g., *venceros* and *venceras* (male and female "victors"). They reinforce the militaristic underpinnings of "the revolution."

Some *misiones* affirm the discourse of struggle through goal statements and the "official" history of their founding. For example, the Misión Alimentación (food distribution) Web site begins, "Forty years of hunger. During 40 years of a government submissive to the empire, Venezuelans from the most dispos-sessed classes could not count on a government program to guarantee the right to food. . . . By the end of the 1990s, 80 percent of Venezuelans were poor.[12] This situation was the result of a process induced by the world hegemonic bloc through their local representatives." Chávez's announcement of the creation of Misión Alma Mater (Bolivarian universities) read in part, "We need to modify systems

11. Some cash subsidies and incentives ended in 2007 and 2008 (i.e., for education and job training).

12. Actually, the proportion of the population below the poverty line, while it increased rapidly in the 1990s, never reached 80 percent. Government reports placed it at closer to 65 percent.

for admission to higher education. Let the universities take to the streets, because the university cannot remain cloistered . . . and manipulate results in secret in order to admit the privileged."

Each *misión*'s Web page identifies Chávez as personally responsible for its creation, citing the date of the decree that established the *misión*. In this way, regardless of which ministry or government office was put in charge of administering a *misión*, "the people" would retain the sense of personalism that associated the leader with its origin. This reinforces two aspects of the symbolism important to Chavista populism—the idea that he "cares about the people" and is the "only one" who can solve their problems. Since Chávez *is* the state, and since he says that the people dictate to the state, Chávez can claim that he doesn't just represent the people but that his voice is the people's voice. Conversely, when participants in the *misiones* become aware of corruption, or when they fail to receive promised benefits, or when programs operate poorly, they do not blame Chávez personally. In interviews with groups of women who participated in education and health *misiones*, D'Elia (2006) found that beneficiaries and volunteers declared that Chávez didn't know about the corruption or failures in the system; the people around him were the problem.

Women's Participation in the Misiones

The medical and educational *misiones*—particularly Robinson (literacy, primary education) and Ribas (secondary education)—and Misión Alimentación (especially the Mercal discount food centers) have had the greatest populist impact in terms of enrollment and number of people reached, particularly women and children. Barrio Adentro I (preventive health care), the educational *misiones*, and the *casas de alimentación* (community kitchens located in private homes) also have mobilized the greatest number of volunteers—primarily women. Many volunteers are long-term community activists, public schoolteachers, or graduates of *misiones* themselves. Some women's voluntarism suggests that their long-term commitment to their communities shifted easily to the ideals of the Bolivarian revolution; in other cases, women who had no prior experience as volunteers have been motivated to join in "the process" of revolutionary social change.[13]

Women's participation as beneficiaries of the educational *misiones* has been outstanding, far exceeding men's participation (D'Elia 2006 found that 75 percent of participants in Caracas, on average, were women, and that a greater proportion

---

13. Venezuelans refer to social change under Chávez as *el proceso*. This is shorthand for support for the goals and ideals of the Bolivarian revolution.

of women than men received scholarships and incentives). A study of Misión Ribas (secondary education) in the state of Mérida also found that women were more likely than men to complete the program, though no possible reasons were given (Marquina Rodríguez 2005).

Women make up the majority of both volunteers and paid staff in Barrio Adentro (health care), the educational *misiones,* and Mercal food-distribution centers. They also make up almost all of the volunteers who run the community kitchens (D'Elia 2006; Castro et al. 2006; Fernandes 2007a). In the case of Barrio Adentro, they also are a majority in the local health committees that are responsible for organizing the community, conducting needs assessments, submitting program requests, and providing logistical support, clinic labor, and social accounting (oversight of budgets and medicines) once a program is allocated. Most women volunteers are involved in several community activities, which some combine with paid employment and almost all combine with domestic responsibilities. Though many are overworked and stressed, they say that the work they do is important and contributes to the future of Venezuela (D'Elia 2006, 176).

Misión Madres de Barrio is the only *misión* that targets women exclusively. Although Chávez initially justified its founding on the basis of retired housewives' legal right to a pension at age fifty-five, it enrolled young mothers with several small children. The first hundred thousand women enrolled were selected from Vuelvan Caras (job training); community-level committees were formed later to select other women for the program. Stipends have been far more generous than in any other program—60 to 80 percent of the minimum wage, or three to four times greater than those of other programs. In exchange, women are required to participate in community programs as volunteers and to enroll in job-training or production cooperatives.

The Puntos de Encuentro and Red de Usuarias

The two main national organizations that target women for participation under Chavista populism are Inamujer, the state women's institute, and Banmujer, the women's bank. We have discussed these at length elsewhere (Rakowski and Espina forthcoming) and will limit the discussion here to their relevance to Chavista populism. Inamujer's 2004 annual report indicates that a main objective is to "guarantee the implementation of the Bolivarian revolution and women's roles as key actors." As recently as mid-2008, the Inamujer Web site placed the number of *puntos de encuentro* ("encounter points" are groups of three to ten women) at 17,761, and the number of women organized in *puntos* at 177,610.[14] *Puntos* were established to link women at the grass roots with the state. They have access to small-loan programs. And they participate in consultations for the National Plans for Women's Equality, in regional, national, and international encounters, in women's health campaigns, and in marches and electoral campaigns to support change. A national team and state and municipal coordinators manage the *puntos* network. Once registered, all groups can receive training through five workshops: fighting poverty, gender and rights, solidarity against violence, constitution and politics, and dealing with stress.

Through their involvement in the *puntos*, some women became involved in the *misiones* as beneficiaries and volunteers. Some also have participated in local groups that address domestic violence and sexual and reproductive health (Inamujer sponsors an antiviolence program). Some *punto* women are active in the urban land committees and the *consejos comunales*. Inamujer president María León has asked *punto* members to select delegates to serve on the *consejos comunales* in order to "mainstream a gender perspective."[15] *Punto* members have various kinds of activist experience but, as indicated above, many are older women who were activists under previous administrations. Some of these women also continue to be members of women's and neighborhood groups that predate Chávez.[16]

Inamujer is the primary proponent of a discourse that reflects the language of transnational campaigns promoted by feminists in international agencies—the discourse of a "gender perspective." In support of the gender perspective, Inamujer extends "gender" training to *consejos comunales* and *misiones* in order to bring this perspective to their projects and budgets. In 2005 León announced that each *misión* would develop a "plan for equality of women" to give it a gender perspective. Plans were to build on a model developed for gender-sensitive budget processes for all state organizations (Simao Vieira 2007; Llavaneras Blanco 2006). Training for a gender perspective is funded by international organizations such as Unifem, Unicef, and the UN Population Fund (Rakowski and Espina 2006).[17]

14. Inamujer no longer makes public the number of groups or members; reports on the *puntos* are not open to public or scholarly scrutiny.

15. Inamujer has the authority to provide training on gender perspectives to any public-sector office or organization and then to monitor implementation.

16. We want to thank Solana Simao (whom we interviewed on July 13, 2007, in Ciudad Guayana) and Masaya Llavaneras from Inamujer (whom we interviewed on July 23, 2007, in Caracas) for sharing information on *puntos* women they have studied and worked with.

17. As of December 2009 we could find no evidence that any *misión* had complied.

Although we could find no evidence that Chávez has ever used the term "gender," he has backed up such initiatives implicitly or explicitly—whether by signing international agreements,[18] making occasional references to women's rights laws during his weekly talk show *Aló, Presidente,* or in speeches directed at audiences of women supporters. Staff at Inamujer and Banmujer and members of the National Assembly who have sponsored women's rights legislation would never have done so without authorization to speak on his behalf. In turn, they attribute all women's rights advances to him.

The Women's Development Bank, Banmujer, was created on March 8, 2001, to "develop public policies with a gender perspective to make women's poverty visible and seek solutions," according to its Web site. Banmujer is widely written about because of its success in disbursing loans and for its educational and organizational work through its *red de usuarias,* or "user network."

Through the *red,* members can request training in job skills, cooperative organizing, accounting, marketing, and ideology (on gender and socialism). Some women also ask Banmujer to arrange for workshops on other topics, such as the domestic violence law, the constitution, how *consejos* function, leadership training, and so on. Banmujer reports that it prioritizes work with the most marginalized women—indigenous, rural, Afro-Venezuelan, and homeless women. It has worked with communal banks in low-income communities, with job-training *misiones,* and with several ministerial offices.

Discourse and Symbols *for* Women: Gender Justice and Revolutionary Motherhood

The Chavista discourse of confrontation and struggle is militaristic and masculinist. It resonates with many popular women because of experiences they share with men of their class and, for some, because of many cultural references to the importance of Venezuelan women in conflicts dating from the time of Simón Bolívar. But there also is a subset of discourse and symbols developed specifically for women. These reinforce an image of Chávez as the liberator of women, a leader who has a special place in his heart for popular women, who understands and appreciates their sacrifices and struggles to care for their families and communities. Although promoting "popular feminism" continues to

18. Chávez approved a *punto de cuenta* (agenda item) in May 2005, declaring his intention to achieve gender equality in Venezuela (Morillo 2007). He also signed an agreement with Unifem in 2006 promising to make public budgets gender-sensitive.

be a goal of Inamujer staff (Rakowski and Espina 2006), the concept of feminism almost never appears in official discourse or in Chávez's speeches or radio programs. Instead, the emphasis is on women's rights as a marginalized group, which are in turn tied to socialism and, more specifically, to Chávez.

It is clear from data on women's participation in the *misiones, puntos,* and Banmujer user networks that women are a significant source of political support for Chávez's presidency as well as the main source of volunteer labor for the Bolivarian revolution. This is reason enough to target women's issues and promote their interests. Other discourses also have legitimated targeting women. These include (a) the idea that "women are the poorest of the poor" (a theme developed by transnational feminists since 1970 and long an important component of women's rights discourse in Venezuela), and (b) the idea that socialist goals of equity and social justice are for everyone—regardless of race, ethnicity, age, ability, or gender (1999 constitution). The discourse on women as the poorest of the poor and the need for "righting the wrongs" of gender inequality are compatible with Chavista discourse on the class-based "battle" against "the enemy." In July 2008 the Inamujer Web site included the following statements: "A new social order cannot be constructed without gender equity," and "women are constructing XXI Century Socialism [with] gender consciousness, class consciousness, and country consciousness." However, the only *misión* that has included feminist language is the Misión Madres del Barrio (barrio mothers). Its Web site declared, "For years, it has been said that poverty has a woman's face and how could it not be so? Poor women have inherited for centuries a double exclusion: as poor and as women. In 40 years of representative democracy, Venezuelan women, especially those with the least resources, have suffered the humiliations of a *machista* and classist society that excluded them from the enjoyment of all their fundamental rights."[19]

One discourse that has garnered significant attention in the goals of Inamujer advances the notion of women's "economic rights," a concept guaranteed in the constitution. For example, Inamujer's Plan de Igualdad (plan for equality) gives its main goal as "to promote women's incorporation in paid employment" (Inamujer 2007, 27). Banmujer, of course, supports this goal through loans and training. But the constitution also recognizes the economic and social value of domestic work, something long sought by feminists and an issue that resonates with women for whom work as wives and mothers has been their main source of identity and their priority social role. Chávez tends to emphasize the latter

19. See http://www.gobiernoenlinea.ve/miscelaneas/misiones.html (accessed May 22, 2007).

when addressing women directly, especially popular women. This has become part of a discourse of revolutionary motherhood.

Revolutionary Motherhood: Chávez's Personal Appeal to Women

Chávez often says that the country needs revolutionary mothers to advance social change. This discourse honors and reinforces both women's traditional roles as self-sacrificing mothers and wives and their unpaid work as volunteers in their communities and the *misiones*.[20] One explanation for the president's popularity among popular women is that women feel recognized for their contributions and sacrifice; another is that they respond to his personal appeal. When speaking to women, Chávez often talks about his love for his mother, his grandmother, his young daughter. He uses terms of endearment such as "my love" when addressing women. He reaches out emotionally, verbally, and even physically (photos abound of him hugging women in crowds and shaking their hands from his car) to make personal contact with the women who come to see and hear him talk. He promises to relieve their suffering, tells them how beautiful and courageous they are, emphasizes the importance of their sacrifices.

Excerpts from Chávez's speeches to thousands of women assembled in Caracas on International Women's Day (March 8, 2002, and March 8, 2003) illustrate how he interacts with popular women and how he conceptualizes their roles in his revolutionary project.

> Long live woman! Long live Venezuela! . . . The country is woman, the nation is woman, the republic is woman, the revolution is woman. . . . Venezuelan women are the soul and essence of the revolutionary process . . . [of] this great and grand task of constructing, of making, of giving birth to a new country, of giving birth to a new path. . . . Being a housewife is dignifying work. . . . You women have a beautiful role . . . [you are] a vital part of the soul of the revolution. . . . *Just as a man and a woman make a child together, so shall we* make a daughter, the daughter Venezuela that we dream of . . . *we have given birth to her.* The Bolivarian Venezuela is two years old, she is just a baby. . . . We count on the fervent, ardent,

20. In parallel fashion, Chavez uses references to women's traditional roles when speaking about the *misiones:* "Mision Robinson [literacy] is the 'mision madre,' the firstborn. From her were born Robinson II, Ribas, Sucre, Vuelvan Caras, Barrio Adentro I, Barrio Adentro II . . ." (*Aló, Presidente,* October 28, 2005). Also interesting are the names given by several *misiones* to delivery services and "enterprise incubator" centers; they are called *nodrizas* (wet nurses).

passionate, beautiful and infinite participation of the women of Venezuela. (Speech given in 2002, emphasis added)

The country is beautiful, she is a woman, too. . . . The revolution gives birth to a new country, a better country. . . . *Every day I love you more, I adore you [women] more and I carry you in my heart.* . . . It is worth remembering that women's initiative, revolutionary women, helped to mold the constitutional process, with a role in designing new laws. . . . This has been fundamental. (Speech given in 2003, emphasis added)[21]

In the 2003 speech, Chávez also appealed to women's practical concerns as wives and mothers by telling them about policies he had introduced to provide better and cheaper food for the Venezuelan family. He also encouraged women to join in one large association, first called a Bolivarian *fuerza* (force) or *círculo* (circle) of women and later a union of women—both under the direction of Inamujer.

Part of the discourse on revolutionary motherhood includes references to Chávez as the child of women in the revolution. In a booklet published by Inamujer following a short-lived coup (four days in April 2002), Chávez is quoted as referring to himself in a speech as "the favored son of revolutionary women," because it was women who first left the barrios in the hills and filled the streets in support of the president. In a speech she gave at an event celebrating the fifth anniversary of Banmujer, in September 2006, María León repeated this phrase: "you are the favored son of all revolutionary mothers in Venezuela."

Other statements made by María León and by staff from both Inamujer and Banmujer in media interviews tend to exalt Chávez as patriarch (father and supreme authority): "Uniting women is the exclusive task of President Hugo Chávez. . . . He is the one who convokes . . . and if our president wants women's movements to unite, they must unite" (León 2005).

María del Mar Alvarez, former defender of women, has discussed women's participation in the revolution as a type of feminist empowerment: "in this revolution women have participated extraordinarily. We have achieved a constitution that is a model for the world for justice and equality. It has empowered them. Usually feminism caters to the upper and middle classes. However this revolution has woken women up and feminism is reaching the popular sectors. Now all women know they have the right to participate" (quoted in Wagner 2005b).

21. This, of course, selectively ignores the important role played by women of diverse political affiliations and the fact that educated women were instrumental.

León has also expressed a desire to promote "popular feminism" among the masses. But she acknowledges that there are problems: "We have achieved a lot—in quantity, but still not quality. . . . Women lack understanding of what gender consciousness is. . . . They have doubts because they see it as a feminist, academic concept. . . . We have gender experts, we plan with gender in mind, research with gender in mind . . . but the masses have not assumed it. . . . We have to deal with thousands of years of culture, customs, language. . . . Our consciousness of women's rights is advancing, but not as quickly as we want" (León 2005).

Our research has focused on the top-down process of implementing populist programs and discourses. We cannot speak to popular women's perspectives or empowerment. But research by others suggests that popular women reject discourse that sounds feminist, even a women's rights discourse, in favor of a class-based discourse. Other researchers also confirm the effectiveness of Chávez's style of direct appeal to the people and the importance of the *misiones* for mobilizing followers:[22]

> Commander Chávez was the one that gave me the incentive . . . that I could do it, that I should do it, and so I can. Why? Because of his words that filled me with hope. Truly. And it gave me satisfaction. This is when I became aware that someday I could be a fighter, I dreamt this even though I was awake, dreamt that I got up one day, took a microphone in my hands and called on people to come near. . . .
>
> This clinic where we are today, this achievement is ours [*de nosotras,* feminine version of "ours"]. (D'Elia 2006, 152–53)

Conclusions

Our analysis of Chavista populism leads to the following conclusions. First, women are important as beneficiaries of the *misiones,* and they also provide most of the volunteer labor. Second, despite the emphasis on the participation and political activism of "the people" in the discourse of the Bolivarian revolution, decisions are made primarily at the top. Third, several discursive frames are employed to garner popular support and mobilize followers, the primary one being struggle and confrontation and a secondary one, revolutionary motherhood. Fourth, many *misiones* target social problems that are important to women's

22. See Sujatha Fernandes's chapter in this volume for more information on community activists in La Vega, Caracas.

traditional roles as wives and mothers—food, health care, housing, income. Fifth, the work of Inamujer and Banmujer has guaranteed that women as a group are included in the discourse and goals of the revolution. There have been significant legal advances for women, including the passage of antiviolence initiatives, and the state has channeled some resources to women's programs and concerns. Sixth, achieving a "gender perspective" in all public organizations—from government ministries, to *misiones,* to citizen groups—remains an important goal, though serious questions have been raised regarding resistance to its implementation, both open and behind the scenes.

Important challenges face women in the near future nevertheless. The dependence of *misiones* on women's labor, for example, has added greatly to women's workload, and in some cases women's work with the *misiones* conflicts with their need to make money. In the name of "co-management" or "co-responsibility," women's volunteer labor has subsidized the state's responsibility for public services. Ironically, both *misiones* and the revolutionary discourse of motherhood reinforce women's traditional gender roles and their unpaid labor. The lack of attention to creating collective services such as child care and laundries, and the failure to target gender in men's ideological training, suggest that women are likely to continue to bear the burden of domestic work.

Additionally, the symbolism of women in Chavista discourse is both diverse and contradictory. On the one hand we have Chávez's image of the self-sacrificing mother who defends and nurtures her "children," who gives birth to a new Venezuela. On the other we have Inamujer's image of popular women as community leaders and political activists—even "popular feminists"—who are urged to organize to defend their rights. Women enroll in job-training programs, take out small-business loans, and organize in cooperatives.

There are structural challenges relating to Venezuela's dependence on oil and the clientelist nature of the *misiones.* The international price of oil dropped precipitously in 2008 and has not rebounded significantly as of December 2009. Inflation averaged about 35 percent in 2008 and was higher in 2009. Much of the infrastructure for water and electricity in large cities has collapsed from lack of maintenance and needs replacement, for which there is no budget allocation. This has left large numbers of angry people and businesses suffering from a chronic lack of public services.

These circumstances have affected the *misiones,* especially programs like Mercal's food-distribution centers. Long-term shortages of such staples as milk, eggs, chicken, and beans have generated widespread protests. *Misiones* that once offered generous incentives and payments for participation have reduced or eliminated them. Programs have been cut back or postponed, leading to growing frustration among the populace. Some health-care *misiones* have been abandoned; others lack personnel, equipment, and medicine.

Political crises continue to arise. Mass demonstrations led by university students demanding that democratic procedures be respected followed Chávez's announcement, in 2007, that he would reform the constitution without a national referendum. He finally gave in, and the referendum was held in December 2007; his proposals failed. Bolstered by his party's control of the National Assembly, Chávez then set about passing legislation by presidential decree to mandate some of the changes the voters had rejected. This action generated renewed protests. One such change—suspending term limits for Chávez and allowing him to be reelected indefinitely—was approved by the electorate in February 2009. Since then Chávez has stepped up the pace of recentralizing authority and bypassing locally elected officials, especially members of the opposition. As noted above, he has removed the oversight of services from the authority of these officials, transferring them to federal agencies, and denied municipal governments their funds from the *situado constitucional*—important revenues for municipal services. Public-sector workers frequently strike or publicly protest failure to pay them or shortages of work materials. In late 2009 students closed down universities to protest crime, and a small group of students staged a hunger strike to protest human rights abuses.

Seizures of public and private property and banks have increased, as Chávez has authorized the systematic expropriation of corporate and privately owned property for distribution to members of cooperatives. But salary increases for public workers have not materialized in a period of tight budgets, despite the increasing number and intensity of worker and union demands. Banks and private businesses are being nationalized to "serve the revolution."

It is difficult to predict the future directions in which these crises may lead. But, given the dependence of the Bolivarian revolution on oil revenues, serious questions arise as to the continued effectiveness of redistributive programs. Nonetheless, the class-based discourses of confrontation and struggle have intensified in Chávez's speeches. After eleven years as president, he still blames the Fourth Republic, the United States, and capitalism for Venezuela's problems. And he has renewed calls for men and women to take up arms to defend socialism, with "socialism or death" as the motto, thus ratifying the symbolism of a revolution and a struggle of good against evil.

References

Arenas, Nelly. 2005. "El gobierno de Hugo Chávez: Populismo de otrora y de ahora." *Nueva Sociedad* 200:38–50.

Cammack, Paul. 2000. "The Resurgence of Populism in Latin America." *Bulletin of Latin American Research* 19 (2): 149–61.

Castro, Arachu, Renato d'A. Gusmao, María Esperanza Martínez, and Sarai Viva, eds. 2006. *Barrio Adentro: Derecho a la salud e inclusión social en Venezuela.* Caracas: Organización Panamericana de la Salud.

Corrales, Javier, and Michael Penfold. 2007. "Venezuela: Crowding Out the Opposition." *Journal of Democracy* 18 (2): 99–113.

De la Torre, Carlos. 1994. "Los significados ambiguos de los populismos latinoamericanos." In *El populismo en España y América,* ed. J. Álvarez Junco and R. González Leandro, 39–60. Madrid: Editorial Catriel.

D'Elia, Yolanda, ed. 2006. *Las misiones sociales en Venezuela: Una aproximación a su comprensión y análisis.* Caracas: Instituto Latinoamericano de Investigaciones Sociales.

D'Elia, Yolanda, Tito Lacruz, and Thais Maingon. 2006. "Los modelos de política social en Venezuela: Universalidad vs. asistencialismo." In *Balance y perspectivas de la política social en Venezuela,* ed. Thais Maingon, 185–228. Caracas: Instituto Latinoamericano de Investigaciones Sociales.

Ellner, Steve. 2006. "Las estrategias 'desde arriba' y 'desde abajo' del movimiento de Hugo Chávez." *Cuadernos del Cendes* 23 (62): 73–94.

Espina, Gioconda. 1994. "Entre sacudones, golpes y amenazas: Las venezolanas organizadas y las otras." In *Mujeres y participación política: Avances y desafíos en América Latina,* ed. M. León, 167–81. Bogotá: Editores T/M.

———. 2001. "Cada una, cada uno: La masa y el comandante en jefe de Venezuela (1998–2000)." In *Estudios latinoamericanos sobre cultura y transformaciones sociales en tiempos de globalización,* vol. 2, ed. Daniel Mato, 55–78. Caracas: UNESCO and CLACSO.

Espina, Gioconda, and Cathy A. Rakowski. 2002. "'Movimiento de mujeres o mujeres en movimiento': El caso de Venezuela." *Cuadernos del Cendes* 19 (49): 31–48.

———. 2007. "Chávez, populismo y las venezolanas." Paper presented at LASA2007, Congress of the Latin American Studies Association, Montreal, September 5–8.

Fender, Jennifer. 2006. "Political Polarization in Venezuela: Urban Positions on Misión Zamora—Political Opportunities and Challenges." Master's thesis, University of Guelph.

Fernandes, Sujatha. 2007a. "Barrio Women and Popular Politics in Chávez's Venezuela." *Latin American Politics and Society* 49 (4): 97–127.

———. 2007b. "A View from the Barrios: Hugo Chávez as an Expression of Urban Popular Movements." *LASA Forum* 38:17–19.

Friedman, Elisabeth. 2000. *Unfinished Transitions: Women and the Gendered Development of Democracy in Venezuela, 1936–1996.* University Park: Pennsylvania State University Press.

García-Guadilla, María Pilar. 2007. "Consejos comunales: Competencias y conflictos con otras iniciativas bolivarianas." Paper presented at LASA2007, Congress of the Latin American Studies Association, Montreal, September 5–8.

García V., Haydée. 2005. "Mortalidad infantil y políticas públicas: Estudio de casos sobre factores de riesgo en un municipio venezolano." Working paper for the Venezuelan NGO Liderazgo y Visión, November.

Garretón, Manuel A. 1986. "Political Processes in an Authoritarian Regime: The Dynamics of Institutionalization and Opposition in Chile, 1973–1980." In *Military Rule in Chile: Dictatorship and Oppositions,* ed. J. S. Valenzuela and A. Valenzuela, 144–83. Baltimore: Johns Hopkins University Press.

Hawkins, Kirk A. 2003. "Populism in Venezuela: The Rise of Chavismo." *Third World Quarterly* 24 (6): 1137–60.

Hawkins, Kirk A., Guillermo Rosas, and Michael E. Johnson. Forthcoming. "The Misiones of the Chávez Government." In *Participation and Public Sphere in Venezuela's Bolivarian Democracy,* ed. D. Smilde and D. Hellinger. Durham: Duke University Press.

Inamujer. 2007. "Informe encuentro preparatorio para el I Congreso Nacional de Puntos de Encuentro con Inamujer, sábado 24 de febrero de 2007: Conclusiones mesas de trabajo." Caracas: Inamujer.

———. N.d. *Plan de Igualdad para las mujeres: Venezuela, 2004–2009.* Caracas: Inamujer.

Kornhauser, W. 1960. *The Politics of Mass Society.* London: Routledge and Kegan Paul.

Krauze, Enrique. 2005. "Decálogo del populismo Iberoamericano." *El País* (Madrid), October 14.

Laclau, Ernesto. 1977. *Politics and Ideology in Marxist Theory.* London: Verso.

———. 1980. "Hacia una teoría del populismo." In Laclau, *Política e ideología en la teoría Marxista,* 165–233. Mexico City: Siglo XXI.

———. 1987. "Populismo y transformación del imaginario político en América Latina." *Boletín de Estudios Latinoamericanos y del Caribe* 42:25–38.

———. 2006a. "Consideraciones sobre el populismo latinoamericano." *Cuadernos del Cendes* 23 (62): 115–20.

———. 2006b. "Por qué construir un pueblo es la tarea principal de la política radical." *Cuadernos del Cendes* 23 (62): 1–36.

León, María. 2005. "María León: 'El socialismo del siglo XXI es el comunismo.'" Interview by Lolita [Edith Franco], September 5. *Jóven Guardia,* http://www.jotaceve.org/ (accessed March 15, 2007).

Llavaneras Blanco, Masaya. 2006. *El ABC de los presupuestos sensibles al género en la República Bolivariana de Venezuela.* Caracas: Inamujer.

Maingon, Thais, ed. 2006. *Balance y perspectivas de la política social en Venezuela.* Caracas: Instituto Latinoamericano de Investigaciones Sociales.

Margolies, Luisa. 2006. "Notes from the Field: Missionaries, the Warao, and Populist Tendencies in Venezuela." *Journal of Latin American Anthropology* 11 (1): 154–72.

Marquina Rodríguez, Alicia. 2005. "Participación de la mujer merideña en la Misión Ribas." Mérida: Ministerio del Poder Popular para la Educación Superior.

Mota Gutiérrez, Gioconda. 2004. "Programas sociales nacionales (fichas descriptivas)." Serie Cuadernos Técnicos 19. Caracas: Fundación Escuela Gerencia Social, Ministerio de Planificación y Desarrollo.

Paramio, Ludolfo. 2006. "Giro a la izquierda y regreso del populismo." *Nueva Sociedad* 205:62–74.

Penfold-Becerra, Michael. 2005. "Social Funds, Clientelism, and Redistribution: Chávez's 'Misiones' Programs in Comparative Perspective." Working paper, Instituto de Estudios Superiores de Administración, Caracas.

———. 2007. "Clientelism and Social Funds: Empirical Evidence from Chávez's 'Misiones' Programs in Venezuela." *Latin American Politics and Society* 49 (4): 63–84.

Raby, Diane. 2006. "El liderazgo carismático en los movimientos populares y revolucionarios." *Cuadernos del Cendes* 23 (62): 59–72.

Rakowski, Cathy A., and Gioconda Espina. 2006. "Institucionalización de la lucha feminista/femenina en Venezuela: Solidaridad y fragmentación, oportunidades y desafíos." In *De lo privado a lo público: Treinta años de lucha ciudadana de las mujeres en América Latina,* ed. E. Meier and N. Lebon, 310–30. New York: Siglo XXI and Unifem.

———. Forthcoming. "Hugo Chávez, the Bolivarian Revolution, and the Women's Rights Agenda." In *The Bolivarian Revolution,* ed. J. Eastwood and T. Ponniah. Cambridge: Harvard University Press.

Rodríguez, Enrique. 2006. "Política social actual: Una visión desde el gobierno." In *Balance y perspectivas de la política social en Venezuela,* ed. Thais Maingon, 269–90. Caracas: Instituto Latinoamericano de Investigaciones Sociales.

Rodríguez Pons, Corina. 2006. "Falta de transparencia empaña el gasto de Bs 27,7 billones en misiones." *El Nacional* (Caracas), September 24.

Simao Vieira, Solana. 2007. *Estudio diagnóstico desde una perspectiva de género, con características participativas y propositivas, del gasto programado y ejecutado en el presupuesto de los organismos adscritos a la Coordinación de Desarrollo Social y de Promoción Económica de la Alcaldía del Municipio Caroní, durante los años 2004 y 2005.* Ciudad Guayana: UN Population Fund.

Traynor, Ian. 2007. "Bush Relaunches Campaign for Democracy But US Policy Provokes Backlash Across the World." *Guardian* (Manchester), June 6, http://www.guardian .co.uk (accessed June 8, 2007).

Valencia Ramírez, Cristóbal. 2005. "Venezuela's Bolivarian Revolution: Who Are the Chavistas?" *Latin American Perspectives* 32 (3): 79–97.

Virtuoso, José. 2006. "La política social desde los sectores populares de los barrios urbanos." In *Balance y perspectivas de la política social en Venezuela,* ed. Thais Maingon, 291–308. Caracas: Instituto Latinoamericano de Investigaciones Sociales.

Wagner, Sarah. 2005a. "The Bolivarian Response to the Feminization of Poverty in Venezuela." http://www.Venezuelanalysis.com/, posted February 5.

———. 2005b. "Women and Venezuela's Bolivarian Revolution." http://www.Venezuel analysis.com/, posted January 15.

Welsch, Friedrich, and Gabriel Reyes. 2006. "¿Quiénes son los revolucionarios? Perfil socio-demográfico e ideopolítico del Chavecismo." *Stockholm Review of Latin American Studies* 1 (November): 58–65.

10

GENDER, POPULAR PARTICIPATION,
AND THE STATE IN CHÁVEZ'S VENEZUELA

Sujatha Fernandes

Soon after he was reelected in December 2006, Hugo Chávez gave a speech at a swearing-in ceremony at the Teatro Teresa Carreño. I watched the televised speech with my friend Yajaira, a middle-aged black woman, at her home in the popular parish of El Valle, where she lives with her *compañero,* Johnny. Yajaira was carrying out her evening chores, scrubbing pots in the sink, preparing meat for Johnny's dinner, making juice, and struggling with the temperamental washing machine. She had turned up the volume on the small television set in the living room, and she would come in and out of the room, listening to the speech and offering her own comments to the screen. She talked with Chávez throughout his speech, discussing certain points with him, criticizing him, and laughing at his small diversions, jokes, and songs. At one point Chávez began to talk about corruption, saying that men who beat up their wives are also corrupt. "I want to come out and ask the men to respect women," said Chávez. Hearing this statement, Yajaira came in from the kitchen and paused in front of the screen, making emphatic sounds of agreement, nodding and repeating Chávez's words.

At one point toward the end of the three-hour speech, a few people began leaving the hall. Chávez reprimanded them. "Please, we haven't finished here. . . . Look, we haven't finished. Discipline, I ask for discipline, I ask for discipline." Coming out of the kitchen, Yajaira wiped her hands on her dishcloth and exclaimed affectionately, "Ay, Chávez, you're too much! These people come from so far to see you, and now they have to get buses and find transportation to get home," she chided. "They have to go to their families." She looked over at me. "Just because Chávez has no family responsibilities—he is divorced from his wife, his children are grown up—he can talk this way." While Chávez frames women's participation in terms of their family and maternal roles, Yajaira uses the same idea of the family to criticize his overzealous masculine concept of revolutionary "discipline." Because Chávez has freed himself from his own family responsibilities, Yajaira feels that there are limits to his ability to understand the necessary domestic responsibilities of people, particularly women.

Chávez went on in his speech to elaborate his notion of revolutionary discipline, likening it to a Christian ideal of sacrifice. "If we want to be leaders of popular power, we have to give the example, friend, of force, of dedication to study, to work; for you there shouldn't be Saturdays or Sundays, or Easter, or Carnival, or anything. . . . The leader should be capable of being like Christ going to the cross, that is, going to sacrifice—and not one day, but every day of their life." Yajaira continued to respond to the image on the screen. "Ay, Chávez!" she sighed. "Now you're saying we won't have our Sundays, our Christmas, our *parrandas* [Christmas celebrations], our vacations? No, no, this is too much!" For ordinary people like Yajaira, whose sense of community is rooted in shared Sunday meals, Christmas festivities, and vacations home to Barlovento or Aragua, the ideal of the disembodied militant is divorced from reality.

Yajaira's dialogue with the televised image of her president was an expression of the individual relationship many barrio women feel that they have with *el comandante.* He is someone who listens to their stories, and he is mindful of their concerns, but he is also a human being who makes mistakes and needs their guidance and protection. In this chapter I look at the relationship between populist leadership and women's agency in Chávez's Venezuela. I argue that poor women have been spurred to action as a result of Chávez's direct appeal to them as mothers and nurturers, but that they also continue to engage the state critically. The ability of barrio women in Caracas to build local spaces of participation partly outside state control has increased their power of negotiation within state-sponsored programs such as soup kitchens. Despite male leadership and authority, the growing presence of women in local committees, assemblies, and communal kitchens has created forms of democratic participation that challenge gender roles, collectivize private tasks, and create alternatives to male-centric politics. Women's experiences of shared struggle in previous decades, along with their use of democratic methods of popular control such as local assemblies, help to prevent the state's appropriation of women's labor for its own ends. But these spaces of popular participation exist in dynamic tension with more vertical populist notions of politics that are characteristic of official sectors of Chavismo.

Drawing on theoretical frameworks developed by scholars of popular women's activism and those who study gender politics in populist states, this chapter seeks to examine barrio women's activism in Chávez's Venezuela. It begins with an overview of the literature, provides background on the Chávez government, and traces the rise in barrio women's participation since Chávez came to power in 1998. It then looks at experiences of local organizing in a popular sector of Caracas known as the Carretera Negra of La Vega.

The analysis is based on nine months of field research in three parishes of Caracas: San Agustín, 23 de Enero, and La Vega, conducted between January 2004 and January 2007. I carried out individual and collective interviews with women activists, observed local committee meetings and assemblies, and collected documents produced by various community organizations. I also spent time getting to know the women while living in a popular barrio for nine months.

Women's Activism and Populism

This chapter seeks to provide the context for popular women's organizing in Caracas within the complexities of a revolutionary-populist system, in which women's local participation is both nationally valorized and initiated from above. Following Kenneth Roberts, I define populism as "a form of personalistic leadership that mobilize[s] diverse popular constituencies behind statist, nationalistic and redistributive development models" (2003, 35). I describe Chavismo as revolutionary-populist in order to distinguish it from the trend of neopopulism, whereby charismatic and personalistic leaders across Latin America such as Alberto Fujimori, Carlos Menem, and Chávez's predecessor, Carlos Andrés Pérez, mobilized their constituencies in favor of neoliberal economic reforms. The concept of revolutionary populism cannot describe all aspects of Venezuelan politics under Chávez, however; it is one privileged element of political discourse and culture among other elements (Burbano de Lara 1998, 24).

Gender politics in Chávez's Venezuela is distinct from the postrevolutionary contexts of Cuba and Nicaragua, where political leaders created state women's agencies in order to promote women's interests and rights within a broader project of state building (Molyneux 2000; Craske 1999). Nikki Craske suggests that rather than becoming subsumed into the state, women need to maintain an independent women's movement in order to "provide alternative agendas and strategies, which in turn maintain pressure on the regime" (1999, 140). The experiences of barrio women in Chávez's Venezuela, however, do not fit neatly into the categories of either mass women's organizations or independent women's movements as defined in this literature.

Barrio women in Venezuela are not organized within mass women's organizations. Women in the Chávez administration created a new National Institute

for Women, known as Inamujer, which was established by presidential decree in 2000. Inamujer's predecessors were the National Women's Council
(CONAMU), created in 1992, and the Presidential Women's Advisory Commission (COFEAPRE), established in 1974 (Friedman 2000). Inamujer works with
barrio women, but it does not have a mass membership like its counterparts in
Cuba and Nicaragua. Inamujer presides over such women's groups as the Fuerzas
Bolivarianas (Bolivarian Forces) and the *puntos de encuentro* (encounter points),
but to date neither of these organizations has succeeded in incorporating barrio women to a significant degree. Nor have barrio women formed autonomous women's movements like Mujeres por la Dignidad y la Vida (Women
for Dignity and Life) in the revolutionary context of El Salvador, or Mothers of
the Plaza de Mayo in Argentina. The Círculos Femeninos of the 1970s were not
an autonomous social movement; they were linked to a Christian nongovernmental organization known as the Centro al Servicio de Acción Popular (Popular Action Service Center, or CESAP).

Rather than form either mass organizations or independent movements, barrio women in Venezuela work in the context of local community organizations,
some of which have long histories. Yet, while these women tend to work in local
spaces and engage in struggles outside the government, they still strongly identify with government-directed programs and leaders such as Chávez. How can
we conceptualize this kind of political activism? As argued elsewhere, we need
alternatives to dichotomous classifications of state feminism and independent
movements. My earlier article (Fernandes 2006) draws on the distinctions made
by various scholars between "independent movements," which set their own
goals; "associational linkages," where autonomous groups choose to work with
other political organizations; and "directed mobilization," where authority and
initiative come from outside (Randall 1998; Molyneux 1998). Like the activists
of the Cuban feminist organization Magín (see Fernandes 2006), barrio women
in Venezuela also work in association with official institutions and programs,
while maintaining a degree of autonomy through their local organizing work
in domestic and community spaces. At the same time, barrio women are always
vulnerable to directed mobilization from above and the institutionalization of
their struggles, which Amy Lind (2005, 90) argues may lead to increased work
responsibilities without changes in women's conditions of life.

In addition to the practical consequences of women's involvement in state-
managed programs, this chapter explores the role of discourse, self-esteem, and
nurturance in women's mobilization under a revolutionary-populist system.
Lola Luna has described the impact of classical populist discourse on women's

movements in Latin America. On the one hand, she suggests that the populist regimes of Perón in Argentina, Cárdenas in Mexico, and Vargas in Brazil developed a maternalist ideology that sought to maintain reproductive control over women, to use their capacities as social agents of development, and to exploit their economic productivity (Luna 1995, 252). On the other hand, the contradictions of this maternalist ideology, and the new social order that it represented, opened possibilities for women to construct new subjectivities in response to their political exclusion (254). This schema needs to be retooled for an analysis of contemporary populism—whether revolutionary or neopopulist—in which maternalist ideology is no longer rooted in developmentalist concerns of labor discipline, particularly given changing regimes of labor and capital. Women's emerging activism needs to be understood in relation to what Magdalena Valdivieso (2004) has called "the foundational imaginary of heroism," latent in much of Chávez's political rhetoric, as well as ideological constructions of women as nurturers and caregivers. Like the Sandinista maternal ideal of Madres Sufridas that Lorraine Bayard de Volo (2001, 121) examines in Nicaragua, notions of revolutionary motherhood are also used in Venezuela to appeal to barrio women, a construction that both reinforces older roles and creates the groundwork for possible new roles and identities to emerge.

Histories of Gender and Politics

Barrio women's activism under Chávez must be located within the history of women's organizing in Venezuela, and also the history of grassroots community movements in the barrios. In the early phase of the women's movement in Venezuela, during the 1940s, it was mainly middle-class women who mobilized in support of civil and economic demands (Friedman 2000, 6). But during the struggle against the Marcos Pérez Jimenez dictatorship in the 1950s, women from a range of socioeconomic classes became engaged in politics. Cross-party and cross-class organizing was facilitated by the creation of a Women's Committee (Comité Femenino). Following the transition to democracy in 1958, however, women were demobilized. The Women's Committee was converted into the National Women's Union and was then disbanded in 1961 (ibid., 128).

Women were involved in the guerrilla struggles of the 1960s. But given the male-dominated structures of guerrilla organizations, they did not often play a primary role. It was not until the 1970s that women again engaged in grassroots activism. During this period, women began to organize autonomously in response to their exclusion from political life. As Friedman (2000, 163) shows, this new phase in women's organizing was often divided by issues of class, as middle-class women organized in the feminist movement and lower-class women in local community organizations.

Barrio women's organizing in the early 1970s emerged with the formation of the Círculos Femeninos, which sought to address the specific problems of poor women. They rejected interference by political parties and attempted to build a decentralized and nonhierarchical movement (ibid., 169–71). The aims of the Círculos Femeninos were closely linked to problems in the barrio in the areas of health, education, jobs, and facilities. At the same time, the Círculos were a part of CESAP, a large, male-dominated NGO. Being part of this institution prevented poor women from taking up more radical feminist demands, but as they started to participate in coalitions of feminist groups in the 1980s, they began to question the male leadership of CESAP and the organization's gendered division of labor (García Guadilla 1993, 76–77).

At the same time, barrio women had begun to engage in organic forms of community activism jointly with the men in the barrio. The 1970s saw the growth of community-based activism in many parishes and barrios across Caracas. Large numbers of barrio women mobilized during the protests and hunger strikes led by Jesuit worker priests (*curas obreros*) like Francisco Wuytack and José Antonio Angós. In 1976 there was a major landslide in the Los Canjilones sector of Caracas, and several barrio residents were trapped and died. Hermelinda Machado, a barrio resident from Callejon 19 de Abril, recalls that the women of the barrio launched large protests against the government for its failure to carry out rescue efforts. Barrio women played an important role in community organizations and struggles but, unlike the middle-class feminists, they had little access to the political arena (García Guadilla 1993, 84). As Machado puts it, "We had a voice, but we were not heard."[1]

During the 1980s and 1990s, Venezuelan women faced a new series of challenges, given the economic and political crisis the country faced. When Pérez returned to office in 1989, he announced the adoption of a "neoliberal package" of austerity measures that included dismantling government subsidies to local industries, deregulating prices, and reducing spending on social services. The initial price increases associated with these measures led to massive popular riots on February 27, 1989, known as the *caracazo*, which induced the government to

---

1. See *La vega resiste*, a film documentary produced by Consejo Nacional de la Cultura in 2004. All translations are my own unless otherwise indicated.

implement some social policies for an interim period. The neoliberal package was revived in April 1996 in consultation with the IMF, as a program of macro-economic stabilization known as Agenda Venezuela. While Agenda Venezuela did succeed in stabilizing the economy to some degree, it also contributed to an increase in poverty and unemployment. Major cuts were made in social spending; education was cut by more than 40 percent, housing by 70 percent, and health by 37 percent (Roberts 2004, 59). Unemployment, inflation, and spending cuts hit the poorest 40 percent of the population the hardest, leading to growing urban segregation.

In the context of growing urban poverty and declining services, women created their own alternative organizations and survival networks to confront the crisis. In 1992 the Círculos Femeninos split from their parent organization, CESAP, and began to organize more autonomously. At the same time, increased funding became available from international donors and women's NGOs. The Coordinadora de Organizaciones No-Gubernamentales de Mujeres (Coordinating Committee of Women's NGOs, or CONG), founded in the 1980s, received international financial support during the preparations for the UN World Conferences on Women in Nairobi and Beijing in 1985 and 1995, respectively (Friedman 1999).

Many theorists have noted the paradoxes of international donor funding for women's organizations (Alvarez 1999; Schild 1998; Lind 1997, 2005). In a context of privatization and cutbacks to social welfare, women in NGOs often find themselves providing the services that used to be the responsibility of the state. In Venezuela, international foundations such as UNICEF and the Fondo Nacional de Atención a la Infancia (National Fund for Infant Attention, or FONAIN) provided funding for day-care centers in 1987, with the aim of establishing forty-two thousand centers by 1993. This program, which involved large numbers of women as "carer mothers," was a continuation of programs established during Pérez's first administration (Delgado Arria 1995, 62). The Círculos Femeninos were also incorporated into the World Bank–funded Fondo Social (Social Fund), which was in charge of more than fourteen compensatory programs.[2] While providing some relief for women in a time of economic crisis, these programs also helped institutionalize women's struggle for survival (Lind 2005, 89). This often meant an increased workload for poorer women and a lower likelihood that the conditions brought about by neoliberal structural adjustment policies would be challenged.

2. Thanks to Cathy Rakowski for providing this information.

Chávez and the Resurgence of Women's Participation

While the events of the *Caracazo* occurred in the context of a growing crisis, they also helped to spark the reemergence of urban social movements in the barrios of Venezuela. Coinciding with growing activism in the barrios was the emergence of a clandestine radical group within the military known as the Movimiento Bolivariano Revolucionario 200 (MBR-200), which was led by Hugo Chávez (López Maya 2004). Following an unsuccessful coup in February 1992, Chávez was imprisoned in military jail, and in November of the same year his fellow officers launched a second coup attempt, also unsuccessful. The coup attempts and Chávez's attainment of office in 1998 catalyzed the politicization and growing participation of broader sectors of society, including women, in new spheres of popular action. Women organized to elect women-friendly candidates to the new Constituent Assembly that Chávez convened in 1999, and they lobbied to include articles pertaining to sexual and reproductive rights in the drafting of the new constitution, approved by referendum in 1999 (Rakowski 2003; Castillo and Salvatierra 2000; Muñoz 2000).

Longtime feminists have occupied important positions in the Chávez government and in the state women's agency, Inamujer. Some women have been involved in the Chavismo movement, which includes Chávez's party, the Movimiento Quinta Republica (Fifth Republic Movement, or MVR), mass organizations such as the Frente Francisco Miranda (Francisco Miranda Front), and the Unión Nacional de Trabajadores (National Union of Workers, or UNT). But Chavista organizations tend to be hierarchically organized and dominated by men, along the lines of traditional political parties and unions. For this reason, rather than join Chavista organizations, many barrio women have become involved in the parallel social revolution, known as the *proceso*. José Roberto Duque (2004) defines the *proceso* as an underground movement that defends the Chávez government and is parallel to the MVR but has its own trajectory, independent of central government directives. Many women who participate in the *proceso* do not identify themselves as Chavista. They may participate in Chávez's soup kitchens, land committees, and *misiones,* and they may even look to Chávez for leadership and direction. But their identity comes from their barrio or parish and forms the basis of alternative social and community networks.

New sectors of women have entered into community work through the social programs introduced by the Chávez government. One of these is a college-level work-study program known as Misión Ribas. Billboards for the program, placed strategically in Caracas subway stations and at the intersection of central roads and highways in the barrios, appeal specifically to women. One shows a young *mestiza* woman, Ana Guerrero, standing in front of her small house, or *rancho*. The caption says that while today she is a housewife, tomorrow she will be a business administrator. Other billboards show black and indigenous women who are moving out of their traditional roles as domestic workers and craftspersons to become social workers and doctors. The inclusion of black and *mestiza* women in billboard ads marks a radical departure from standard commercial advertisements, such as the beer ads that dot the city landscape featuring highly sexualized portraits of women in skimpy bikinis, with European features and long, flowing blond hair. The representation of barrio women as business administrators, social workers, and doctors also represents a dramatic change from conventional depictions and class expectations. In addition to the educational programs, Chávez has encouraged the formation of *comités de tierra* (urban land committees), popular clinics in the barrios, and a women's lending agency known as the Banco de la Mujer, or Women's Bank. The Chávez administration has also introduced *casas alimentarias* (soup kitchens), where needy children and single mothers from the barrios receive one free meal a day. In 2004, 4,052 soup kitchens were established in Venezuela.[3]

Not surprisingly, the participants in these programs and committees have been overwhelmingly female.[4] As many scholars have noted, the centrality of women to the life of the barrio (Martín-Barbero 1993, 198), gender roles that assign domestic and child-rearing tasks to women (Rodriguez 1994, 34), and women's exclusion from traditional male spheres of politics such as political parties and trade unions (Caldeira 1990) have bolstered their participation in such domestic, community-related concerns as health and education. Women themselves made this clear when asked about the reasons for their participation. In June 2004 a group of women from San Agustín went door to door conducting a census of the residents of the *ranchos* in the upper reaches of the barrio Hornos de Cal and other barrios of the parish, for the purposes of allocating funds for new social programs. One of the women, Clara Brinson, told me that women were mobilizing behind the social programs because "we women are the ones who almost always have to carry the burden of housework; we are the ones who most feel the weight of this work. Men, by nature, are used to coming

---

3. See http://www.infocentro.gov.ve/viewusuario/detalleNoticia.php?id'2288&cc'93 (accessed March 2006).

4. Although no data are available on the percentage of women who participate in these programs, from my own observations and conversations with others it is clear that most committees, especially health committees, are more than 90 percent female.

home on Fridays, having their beer." It is this awareness of domestic responsibility that encourages some women to become central actors in community and social work.

Other women, however, pointed to the importance of Chávez as a catalyst for the mass involvement of women in popular politics. Carmen Teresa Barrios, an activist from the Carretera Negra sector of La Vega, pointed to the April 2002 coup against Chávez and the role of women in bringing him back to power:

> For me, this comes since Chávez. I am forty-something years old, and never in my life have I cared about what was happening in my country, and I'm saying my country, but also my Carretera, where I live. . . . It's like I am fulfilled. This work fulfills me. I want to be involved in everything, I want to participate in everything, I really feel that someone needs me and I can do it. . . . That's why I say, it was Chávez who awoke the woman. He gave us importance, value. . . . I studied, but I never felt interested enough to participate or do other things, to care about people other than myself. . . . It was this voice that told us we could do it, that if we are united we can achieve something. I was one of those people who never thought about taking to the streets, like I did on April 11th, when they overthrew our president. I said, "My God, is this what you feel when you fight for what is yours?" I went all the way to Maracay in a car. I took a flag and I said to the others, "My God, what am I doing?" I didn't recognize myself. . . . This was all asleep within me and because of this man, his calling, his way of being, or I don't know what, I got involved in this thing. . . . And then I wanted to face the president himself, and tell him how things should be, [that] you may want to do it this way, but I don't agree, that we should do it in this other way in order to achieve what we aim to do. That's why I tell you, it was an awakening, a calling, and he made us women go out into the streets, he made us realize that as women we can also struggle, we can do it and be involved. (Carmen Teresa Barrios, interview by author)

Carmen Teresa's narrative contains several layers. On the one hand, she tells a story of an almost religious awakening, of a "calling" that women have heard and responded to. As Richard Gott (2000, 146) argues, Chávez often appeals to a highly religious population with his evangelical rhetoric, invoking love and redemption; his millenarian notion of a new start after the evils of the past; and his campaign posters, which feature portraits of himself that resemble evangelical pictures of Christ. Carmen Teresa's narrative reflects this kind of popular religious discourse that Chavismo has appropriated. On the other hand, Carmen Teresa is aware that she knows her "Carretera," as she calls her barrio, better than the president ever could, and when she disagrees with Chávez she is not shy about showing him his error. Carmen Teresa's assertiveness and independence of mind complicate our understanding of populism as a necessarily manipulative relationship, for she is clearly expressing her own initiative, her own judgment of what is best for her community, without waiting for orders from above. Carmen Teresa's narrative also demonstrates the self-worth that poor women activists feel as a result of Chávez's emphasis on the centrality of the poorer classes as a force for social change.

The other notable aspect of Carmen Teresa's narrative, one found in other narratives as well, is the quality of nurturance: "I really feel that someone needs me and I can do it." Many women's narratives emphasized these emotional aspects of community participation, which also go beyond the more economy-focused explanations of "practical needs" prevalent in the literature (Molyneux 1985; Massollo 1999; Safa 1990). This aspect of nurturance and maternal caring is not only common to the new activists who have been spurred into action through Chávez. Susana Rodríguez, a leftist militant for more than twenty years in the parish 23 de Enero, noted, "Women are always at the forefront, and I think this has to do with maternity, with this necessity to look after and protect. To look after the fatherland, to look after the barrio, to look after friends, to look after the husband, to look after the president. It is a feeling that is generated among us women." Veteran women activists, as well as newer ones, used tropes of motherhood as a way of describing their involvement in politics. Various scholars have also found that women use discourses of nurturance and their maternal role to frame their participation and construct a sense of collective identity (Morgen 1988; Bayard de Volo 2001; Lind 2005; James 2000). But as Lynn Stephen (1997) argues, rather than understanding women's participation in terms of uniform identities of motherhood, we need to look at the internal contradictions being negotiated among women. Veteran women activists tend to locate their political awakening in shared community struggles, while newer activists point to Chávez as their reason for becoming active in politics.

There are also differences between men and women, in that veteran male activists stress the importance of movements that predated Chávez and place more importance on building local and independent leadership. Freddy Mendoza, one of the community leaders in the Carretera Negra, came to Caracas as a child. From a young age he was involved in community activism with other young people, such as Edgar "El Gordo" Pérez, from Las Casitas. These leaders came of age during the struggles of the 1970s and 1980s, when residents from the Carretera Negra participated in hunger strikes for education, employment, and basic services. El Gordo told me, "Our process didn't begin with Chávez and it won't end with Chávez." Long-term male activists have sought to articulate this position of autonomy rather than dependency in relation to the Chávez government.

Daily Life and Popular Organizing

By looking at the intersection of everyday life and popular organizing, what Elizabeth Jelin (1987, 11) refers to as *lo cotidiano*, or "the everyday," this section attempts to give greater depth to the daily experience of popular organizing. I focus on the experiences of activists in the Carretera Negra, where I have carried out ongoing research with the women of the barrio. The barrio consists of a line of houses located along a stretch of highway from which its name, "Black Highway," comes, and along three smaller lanes, Oriente, 24 de Julio, and Justicia, situated in the parish of La Vega in the west of Caracas. The barrio is composed of about 140 families and is a close-knit community with a long history of organizing tied to the parish of La Vega.

Many women of the Carretera Negra were also involved in these struggles. Through these struggles and the history of democratic participation in the sector, including decision making by popular assembly, the activists have been able to retain a sense of their individual identity as they participate in the *proceso*. The women of the Carretera Negra first formed their health committee in July 2003, when a Cuban doctor was sent to the barrio. The women found a house that was to be used as the popular clinic; they looked for equipment, chairs, and beds, and they found the doctor a residence within the barrio. They organized meetings between the doctor and the community, took health censuses, and visited families to explain the idea of the popular clinics. In September 2003 the women started an urban land committee, which consisted of twenty-one people who took a census and began to distribute land titles, giving titles to ninety-eight families by June 2004. In September 2004 the activists set up a soup kitchen and had it functioning by October.

The soup kitchen is located in the house of barrio resident Osvaldo Mendoza, a police officer, who had never before participated in community work. Osvaldo told me, "I was never a neighbor who was very involved with the community because of my work . . . but seeing the necessities of our communities, what I've seen as a police officer, the necessities you see in the streets, I offered my house when this opportunity came." Osvaldo and his family worked with the women of the community to set up the kitchen, and he is actively involved in unloading materials from the trucks, serving the children, and carrying out surveys in the barrio. He is often the only man present in community assemblies, which tend to be dominated by women. According to Osvaldo, people even joke about his presence as a man. "In the meetings," he says, "we have a joke, a game that when they speak of *ellas* [the women] or *nosotras* [we women], I'm included. The women make fun of me: 'Well, the señora Osvalda.'" The jokes reveal the gendered nature of community work, which, like domestic chores, is still assumed to be women's work. But the participation of men is changing perspectives about domestic responsibility. As Osvaldo told me, "I don't feel bad because this is women's work; no, this is also men's work." The participation of men in the soup kitchen is a signal to other men that cooking and domestic work are not only women's work.

A popular assembly was held on June 22, 2005, at which the activists of the barrio came together to discuss the progress of the soup kitchen. Such assemblies illustrate the possibilities and the limitations of popular organizing for creating new forms of gender relations and popular politics. Following other work on soup kitchens in Lima, Peru, I have found that participation in such collective experiences, while not explicitly feminist, is important in challenging a gendered division of labor and perceptions of women's role in politics (Mujica 1992; Lind 1997).

The process of organizing the soup kitchen had been a positive experience for the women. As with the popular clinic, they had taken the initiative in repainting the rooms, stocking them with the necessary cookware, and carrying out a census to determine which needy families were eligible for meals. Every day a government truck arrives with supplies, and Osvaldo is usually on hand to help the women unload them, but all of the food preparation is done by women. While the participation of women activists in the soup kitchen is not overtly challenging traditional gender roles, it is bringing about other changes, as Helen Safa has argued in another context: "the collectivization of private tasks, such as food preparation and child care, is transforming women's roles, even though they are not undertaken as conscious challenges to gender subordination" (1990, 361). Food preparation is increasingly being seen as a job, performed for the most part by women, that should be assumed by the community and not by individual women. The basis of the soup kitchen is women's voluntary participation and the networks of mutual support that have existed for many years in the barrio.

The assembly was convened for 3:00 P.M., but since the *vecinas* [female neighbors] all live close by one another, they just called to one another and knocked on doors as they made their way to the kitchen. There, we sat around on wooden chairs, mostly borrowed from neighbors. Twenty-five people attended, twenty-two women and three men. The soup kitchen is run by five women who work full-time, five days a week, to provide lunch to more than 140 people daily. The women began the assembly by raising concerns about the amount of work involved in maintaining the kitchen. One of the cooks, Gladys, recounted that the women must begin the work the evening before, washing and soaking the beans, cleaning the rice, cutting the chicken, and generally preparing the food. At 1:30 P.M. the children come for lunch, and they must be served and attended to. Afterward, the women spend several hours cleaning up. Gladys said that since the women are not paid, they must simultaneously attend to the needs of their own families. The problem Gladys raised is akin to what Caroline Moser (1986) has referred to as a "triple burden," which includes productive work, reproductive work, and community work.

Some scholars have noted the ways in which women's labor has been appropriated under neopopulist governments, such as Alberto Fujimori's in Peru, or Sixto Durán-Ballén's in Ecuador, as a means of providing essential services to households as the neoliberal state retreats from this role (Barrig 1996; Lind 2005; Paley 2001). This devolution of responsibility for welfare services was characteristic of the day-care centers and World Bank–funded women's projects under the previous administrations of Herrera Campins and Pérez in Venezuela. Social policy under Chávez is guided by contradictory principles that retain some aspects of this neoliberal approach toward decentralization of service provision, shifting responsibility to poorer sectors. At the same time, state-sponsored programs under Chávez are part of a range of other social welfare strategies that aim to channel funds toward social development and away from a neoliberal market model. Moreover, in contrast to the "privatization of the struggle for daily survival" (Lind 1997, 1208), women's use of popular assemblies is a means of exercising democratic control over the soup kitchens and thinking through collective solutions to the problem of a double or triple workload. The assembly I attended had been called for precisely this reason. Various people proposed that they recruit more people to help with the work, so that it would not fall on the five women only, and others suggested taking up a collection in the community to pay the women a small wage.

A woman named Judy raised a problem related to the food delivered by the government. While the soup kitchen received fixed menus from the government, the ingredients delivered often do not match the menus. Just as mothers are accustomed to employing creative strategies to stretch the family income and resolve problems (Safa 1990, 357), so too in the soup kitchen they must invent new recipes in order to spread the scarce government food to feed more mouths. If the spaghetti does not arrive, they may need to make tuna croquettes for lunch instead.

Gladys suggested that the women reject the government-dictated menus and come up with their own weekly menus, as this would give them more leverage and make them feel more creative with their work. Since there are five cooks, each could determine the menu on one day of the week, she suggested. For instance, they had been receiving an oversupply of black beans for several weeks and needed to come up with creative ways of preparing the beans. The women discussed various options, including letting the diners decide the menu. But they concluded that this would promote the idea of the soup kitchen as a consumer service, when in fact it was intended as a survival strategy to ease the burden of poor barrio women. In the daily work of organizing a soup kitchen, the women were engaging in a range of debates that included their leverage and agency in a state-directed program, and the meaning of what they were doing in the context of the community.

At one point, Orlando mentioned that the previous day militants from the Chavista vanguard youth organization Frente Francisco de Miranda had stopped by the soup kitchen and demanded that a banner be hung outside the kitchen with the insignia of the Chavista mayor and the name of one of the founding heroes, such as Bolívar or Sucre. Orlando was angry that these Chavista militants were trying to dictate to the community, when the community was doing all the work of constructing and maintaining the kitchen. Freddy responded in disgust, "Why should we name our soup kitchen after Simón Bolívar or Sucre? It's always the same old heroes of the republic. We have to think with our heads. Until when will we be stuck in the same old schema? Why can't we name the soup kitchen after Benita Mendoza, a working woman here in the barrio, who has raised three kids, been left by three husbands, studied in spite of all the difficulties, and retired to work here as a volunteer?" Gladys agreed with Freddy, adding, "If the militants from the Frente come by here again, tell them to come to the next assembly and put it to the community, because that is who makes decisions in this barrio." The Frente Francisco de Miranda represents a *machista* conception of politics, or *oficialismo*. As Valdivieso (2004, 141) argues, the heroic Chavista conception of politics, marked by grand stories of liberation, is taken directly from republican discourse. By contrast, in their discussions and practice, community activists challenge the current political rhetoric and seek to place barrio women at the center of new liberatory narratives. Orlando's story echoed the experience of "family kitchens" under the populist government of Fernando Belaúnde in Peru, where, Maruja Barrig (1996, 60) notes, the provision of infrastructure and food was given in exchange for support of the governing political party.

The Carretera Negra activists rejected this kind of clientelism, as it ran counter to the politics of collective accountability and participation that they were trying to build. The meeting that afternoon demonstrated the shifting relationships of barrio women with the state: They are dependent on clientelist relationships as a means of securing food and other resources for their soup kitchen, but at the same time they are trying to build local autonomy and identity. Spaces of participatory democracy are built both together with and in defiance of clientelist logic.

At this point in the meeting, three of the cooks, Ana, Mercedes, and Judy, left the room and entered the adjoining kitchen to begin preparations for the next day's meal. Gladys stayed behind. The three men present began discussing questions of financing for the soup kitchen. Gladys noticed that the women were being left out of the conversation, and she called out to them, "Leave your *caraotas* [beans] and come and join in the discussion." Through her involvement in politics, Gladys was more alert to the gender differences that emerge in the process of popular organizing, and she was more ready than the men to point this out. The women returned, and the activists finished the meeting quickly. I was surprised to see all three men enter the kitchen and help with cleaning the rice, washing the beans, and cutting the meat. These people seemed to understand that rather than replicate gender divisions, men and women should have equal participation in all aspects of community organizing. Treating the soup kitchen as a collective responsibility, and not as the sole work of the women volunteers, had the effect of challenging the notion that cooking is the sole domain of women. Community activism is a space in which men and women are attempting to define new perspectives together, based on the realities of daily life. Although men continue to dominate as leaders, through the process of community activism both men and women are learning to challenge instances of gender domination, as women take on positions of leadership and responsibility.

Conclusion

This chapter has addressed the links among populism, gender, and democracy in Chávez's Venezuela. Many barrio women have become politicized under Chávez.

Chávez's appeals to women as mothers and nurturers, and his promotion of programs that alleviate women's domestic burden, have helped project women into the public sphere. It is precisely through their associational links with a revolutionary-populist president and state-managed programs that barrio women have been able to build new spaces of community participation. They have used a maternal notion of responsibility and nurturance as the basis of their political identity. At the same time, they are willing to criticize the state, and the clientelist methods of state agencies, when necessary. While most accounts of populism have presented barrio women as either reactive or manipulated by the state, I would argue that these women are active agents who are building new spaces of democratic community participation.

References

Alvarez, Sonia. 1999. "Advocating Feminism: The Latin American Feminist NGO 'Boom.'" *International Feminist Journal of Politics* 1 (2): 181–209.

Baptista, Felix, and Oswaldo Marchionda. 1992. "¿Para que afinques?" BA thesis, Escuela de Antropología, Universidad Central de Venezuela.

Barrig, Maruja. 1989. "The Difficult Equilibrium Between Bread and Roses: Women's Organizations and the Transition from Dictatorship to Democracy in Peru." In *The Women's Movement in Latin America: Feminism and the Transition to Democracy,* ed. Jane Jaquette, 151–76. Boston: Unwin Hyman.

———. 1996. "Women, Collective Kitchens, and the Crisis of the State in Peru." In *Emergences: Women's Struggles for Livelihood in Latin America,* ed. John Friedman, Rebecca Abers, and Lilian Autler, 59–77. Los Angeles: UCLA Latin American Center Publications.

Bayard de Volo, Lorraine. 2001. *Mothers of Heroes and Martyrs: Gender Identity Politics in Nicaragua, 1979–1999.* Baltimore: Johns Hopkins University Press.

Botía, Alejandro. 2005. "Círculos Bolivarianos parecen burbujas en el limbo." *Últimas Noticias* (Caracas), March 20.

Burbano de Lara, Felipe. 1998. "A modo de introducción: El impertinente populismo." In *El fantsma del populismo: Aproximación a un tema [siempre] actual,* ed. Felipe Burbano de Lara, 9–24. Caracas: Nueva Sociedad.

Caldeira, Teresa. 1990. "Women, Daily Life, and Politics." In *Women and Social Change in Latin America,* ed. Elizabeth Jelin, 47–78. London: Zed Books.

Castañeda, Nora. 2004. "Por una sociedad justa y amante de la paz." In *Bolivarianas: El protagonismo de las mujeres en la revolución venezolana,* ed. Mónica Saiz, 25–36. Caracas: Ediciones Emancipación.

Castillo, Adicea, and Isolda H. de Salvatierra. 2000. "Las mujeres y el proceso constituyente venezolano." *Revista Venezolana de Estudios de la Mujer* 5 (14): 37–88.

Chun, Lin. 2001. "Whither Feminism: A Note on China." *Signs: Journal of Women in Culture and Society* 26 (4): 1281–86.

Contreras, Juan. 2000. *La coordinadora cultural Simón Bolívar: Una experiencia de construcción del poder local en la parroquia "23 de enero."* BA thesis, Escuela del Trabajo Social, Universidad Central de Venezuela.

Craske, Nikki. 1999. *Women and Politics in Latin America*. Cambridge: Polity Press.

Delgado Arria, Carol. 1995. *Mujeres: Una fuerza social en movimiento*. Caracas: Comite Juntas por Venezuela Camino a Beijing.

Díaz-Barriga, Miguel. 1998. "Beyond the Domestic and the Public: *Colonas* Participation in Urban Movements in Mexico City." In *Cultures of Politics/Politics of Cultures: Revisioning Latin American Social Movements,* ed. Sonia Alvarez, Evelina Dagnino, and Arturo Escobar, 252–77. Boulder, Colo.: Westview Press.

Duque, José Roberto. 2004. "Un gobierno, un proceso." *Patriadentro,* May 21–27, 2.

Ellner, Steve. 2005. "The Revolutionary and Non-Revolutionary Paths of Radical Populism: Directions of the Chavista Movement in Venezuela." *Science and Society* 69 (2): 160–90.

Fernandes, Sujatha. 2006. "Transnationalism and Feminist Activism in Cuba: The Case of Magín." *Politics and Gender* 1 (3): 1–22.

Friedman, Elisabeth. 1998. "Paradoxes of Gendered Political Opportunity in the Venezuelan Transition to Democracy." *Latin American Research Review* 33 (3): 87–135.

———. 1999. "The Effects of 'Transnationalism Reversed' in Venezuela: Assessing the Impact of UN Global Conferences on the Women's Movement." *International Feminist Journal of Politics* 1 (3): 357–81.

———. 2000. *Unfinished Transitions: Women and the Gendered Development of Democracy in Venezuela, 1936–1996*. University Park: Pennsylvania State University Press.

García Guadilla, María-Pilar. 1993. "*Ecologia:* Women, Environment, and Politics in Venezuela." In *"Viva": Women and Popular Protest in Latin America,* ed. Sarah Radcliffe and Sallie Westwood, 65–87. London: Routledge.

Gott, Richard. 2000. *In the Shadow of the Liberator: Hugo Chávez and the Transformation of Venezuela*. London: Verso.

Grohmann, Peter. 1996. *Macarao y su gente: Movimiento popular y autogestion en los barrios de Caracas*. Caracas: Nueva Sociedad.

Herrera de Weishaar, Maria Luisa, Maria Ferreira, and Carlos Cabrera. 1977. *Parroquia La Vega: Estudio micro-historico*. Caracas: Consejo Municipal del Distrito Federal.

Howell, Jude. 1998. "Gender, Civil Society, and the State in China." In *Gender, Politics, and the State,* ed. Vicky Randall and Georgina Waylen, 166–84. London: Routledge.

James, Daniel. 2000. *Doña María's Story: Life History, Memory, and Political Identity*. Durham: Duke University Press.

Jelin, Elizabeth. 1987. *Movimientos sociales y democracia emergente*. Buenos Aires: Centro Editor de América Latina.

Karl, Terry. 1987. "Petroleum and Political Pacts: The Transition to Democracy in Venezuela." *Latin American Research Review* 22 (1): 63–94.

Levine, Daniel. 1998. "Beyond the Exhaustion of the Model: Survival and Transformation of Democracy in Venezuela." In *Reinventing Legitimacy: Democracy and Political Change in Venezuela,* ed. Damarys Canache and Michael R. Kulisheck, 187–214. Westport, Conn.: Greenwood Press.

Lind, Amy Conger. 1992. "Power, Gender, and Development: Popular Women's Organizations and the Politics of Needs in Ecuador." In *The Making of Social Movements in Latin America: Identity, Strategy, and Democracy,* ed. Arturo Escobar and Sonia Alvarez, 134–49. Boulder, Colo.: Westview Press.

———. 1997. "Gender, Development, and Urban Social Change: Women's Community Action in Global Cities." *World Development* 25 (8): 1205–23.

————. 2005. *Gendered Paradoxes: Women's Movements, State Restructuring, and Global Development in Ecuador.* University Park: Pennsylvania State University Press.

López Maya, Margarita. 2004. "Hugo Chávez Frías: His Movement and His Presidency." In *Venezuelan Politics in the Chávez Era: Class, Polarization, and Conflict,* ed. Steve Ellner and Daniel Hellinger, 73–92. Boulder, Colo.: Lynne Riener.

López Maya, Margarita, David Smilde, and Keta Stephany. 1999. *Protesta y cultura en Venezuela: Los marcos de acción colectiva en 1999.* Caracas: CENDES.

Luna, Lola. 1995. "Los movimientos de mujeres en América Latina o hacia una nueva interpretación de la participatión política." *Boletín Americanista* 35:249–56.

Martín-Barbero, Jesús. 1993. *Communication, Culture, and Hegemony: From the Media to Mediations.* London: Sage Publications.

Massollo, Alejandra. 1999. "Defender y cambiar la vida: Mujeres en movimientos populares urbanos." *Cuicuilco* 6 (17): 13–23.

Molyneux, Maxine. 1985. "Mobilization Without Emancipation? Women's Interest, the State, and Revolution in Nicaragua." In *Transition and Development: Problems of Third World Socialism,* ed. Richard R. Fagen, Carmen Diana Deere, and Jose Luis Goraggio. New York: Monthly Review Press and Center for the Study of the Americas.

————. 1998. "Analysing Women's Movements." *Development and Change* 29:219–45.

————. 2000. "State, Gender, and Institutional Change: The Federación de Mujeres Cubanas." In *Hidden Histories of Gender and the State in Latin America,* ed. Elizabeth Dore and Maxine Molyneux, 291–321. Durham: Duke University Press.

————. 2001. *Women's Movements in International Perspective: Latin America and Beyond.* New York: Palgrave.

Morgen, Sandra. 1988. "'It Is the Whole Power of the City Against Us': The Development of Political Consciousness in a Women's Health Care Coalition." In *Women and the Politics of Empowerment,* ed. Sandra Morgen and Ann Bookman, 97–115. Philadelphia: Temple University Press.

Moser, Caroline. 1986. "Women's Needs in the Urban System: Training Strategies in Gender Aware Planning." In *Learning About Women and Urban Services in Latin America and the Caribbean,* ed. J. Bruce, M. Kohn, and M. Schmink. New York: Population Council.

Mujica, Maria-Elena. 1992. "Nourishing Life and Justice: Communal Kitchens in Lima, Peru." *Latin American Anthropology Review* 4 (2): 99–101.

Muñoz, Mercedes. 2000. "Derechos sexuales y reproductivos y proceso constituyente." *Revista Venezolana de Estudios de la Mujer* 5 (14): 123–46.

Paley, Julia. 2001. *Marketing Democracy: Power and Social Movements in Post-Dictatorship Chile.* Berkeley and Los Angeles: University of California Press.

Petzoldt, Fania, and Jacinta Bevilacqua. 1979. *Nosotras también nos jugamos la vida: Testimonios de la mujer Venezolana en la lucha clandestina, 1948–1958.* Caracas: Editorial Ateneo de Caracas.

Rakowski, Cathy A. 2003. "Women's Coalitions as a Strategy at the Intersection of Economic and Political Change in Venezuela." *International Journal of Politics, Culture, and Society* 16 (3): 387–405.

Ramos, Nelly. 2004. "Trabajadora cultural a tiempo completo." In *San Agustin: Un santo pecador o un pueblo creador,* ed. Antonio Marrero, 173–82. Caracas: Fundarte.

Ramos Rollon, Maria Luisa. 1995. *De las protestas a las propuestas: Identidad, accion y relevancia politica del movimiento vecinal en Venezuela.* Caracas: Instituto de Estudios de Iberoamerica y Portugal.

Randall, Vicky. 1998. "Gender and Power: Women Engage the State." In *Gender, Politics, and the State,* ed. Vicky Randall and Georgina Waylen, 185–205. London: Routledge.

Roberts, Kenneth. 2003. "Social Correlates of Party System Demise and Populist Resurgence in Venezuela." *Latin American Politics and Society* 45 (3): 35–57.

———. 2004. "Social Polarization and the Populist Resurgence in Venezuela." In *Venezuelan Politics in the Chavez Era: Class, Polarization and Conflict,* ed. Steve Ellner and Daniel Hellinger, 55–72. Boulder, Colo.: Lynne Riener.

Rodriguez, Lilia. 1994. "Barrio Women: Between the Urban and the Feminist Movement." *Latin American Perspectives* 21 (3): 32–48.

Safa, Helen. 1990. "Women's Social Movements in Latin America." *Gender and Society* 4 (3): 354–69.

Schild, Veronica. 1998. "New Subjects of Rights? Women's Movements and the Construction of Citizenship in the 'New Democracies.'" In *Cultures of Politics/Politics of Cultures: Re-visioning Latin American Social Movements,* ed. Sonia Alvarez, Evelina Dagnino, and Arturo Escobar, 93–117. Boulder, Colo.: Westview Press.

Silva Michelena, Héctor. 1999. "La polítíca social en Venezuela durante los años ochenta y noventa." In *Política social: Exclusión y equidad en Venezuela durante los años noventa,* ed. Lourdes Alvares, Helia Isabel del Rosario, and Jesús Robles, 85–114. Caracas: Nueva Sociedad.

Stephen, Lynn. 1997. *Women and Social Movements in Latin America: Power from Below.* Austin: University of Texas Press.

Valdivieso, Magdalena. 2004. "Confrontación, machismo y democracia: Representaciones del 'heroismo' en la polarización política en Venezuela." *Revista Venezolana de Economía y Ciencias Sociales* 10 (2): 137–54.

Westwood, Sallie, and Sarah Radcliffe. 1993. "Gender, Racism, and the Politics of Identities in Latin America." In *"Viva": Women and Popular Protest in Latin America,* ed. Sarah Radcliffe and Sallie Westwood, 1–25. London: Routledge.

Karen Kampwirth

It emerges clearly from the chapters in this volume that Latin American populism is highly gendered, but in sometimes unpredictable ways. At the same time, these chapters open up a host of new questions. In concluding her comparison of Mexican politics under Cárdenas and Echeverría, Jocelyn Olcott notes, "Despite significant historical differences, in both administrations the populist tension between promoting modernization and honoring traditional cultural practices complicated efforts to shape gender ideologies and promote women's rights." The "populist tension," as Olcott named it, echoes throughout all of these chapters. Perhaps it is inevitable, in studying a political phenomenon that is defined by the politics of personality rather than the politics of ideology, to find that its gendered politics are defined by tension. Indeed, it is not easy to find consistent patterns of gender politics that unite the many populists analyzed in this book. The one quality that does unite these national leaders, with the exception of Eva Perón, is that they were men.

Is there something inherently masculine about populist leadership? Could it be rooted in the greater freedom men enjoy, their greater opportunity to be eccentric? Or perhaps it is so masculine because of the populist tendency to cast the world in terms of conflict between "us and them," which cuts against cultural expectations that females, even female politicians, will be conciliators? Would populist generosity and effusiveness be seen as a sort of promiscuity if carried out by a woman? Or is the masculine nature of populist leadership rooted in Christian culture, in which the role of the Savior, Jesus Christ, is one that male politicians (at least male politicians sufficiently lacking in modesty) may appropriate for themselves? In contrast, the religious role model available to female politicians, that of the Virgin Mary, is inherently a model of an intermediary, one who brings people together, rather than an individual who saves the world on her own. Yet these models are clearly not all constraining: Evita managed to forge a populist leadership style in which she railed against an oligarchical "them," at the same time as her followers painted her in the image of the Virgin Mary.

But it is possible that these questions lead us in the wrong direction. It may be that historically there have been almost no national female populist leaders simply because there have been so few female presidents.[1] In his contribution to this volume, Michael Conniff encourages us to explore this hypothesis. He notes that the cases he studies "indicate that populism is not necessarily masculine in Brazil, as it is in other countries, and that female populists are more likely to be found at lower echelons of government than at the top. Their scarcity in the upper ranks is most probably a symptom of the great difficulties women face in competitive politics in general." Furthermore, Conniff argues, if we look at politics at the regional and local levels, we may very well find female populists. Heloísa Helena, the senator from the Brazilian state of Alagoas, is one female populist from whom we may be hearing more in the future. Her "background fits the pattern of other populists, except for her gender," Conniff notes.

Of course, even if no female populist is ever elected president, populism will continue to involve women in important ways. All of the contributors to this volume explore the relationship between leader and followers, and they find that populism's potential for bringing about or deepening democracy depends on the nature of this relationship. In fact, of course, populist leaders never fully control their followers. As Joel Wolfe notes in his chapter on Brazil, "Kubitschek's developmentalism embraced the most conservative and seemingly traditional gender roles for Brazil's working class." And yet Kubitschek's policies had the unintended consequence of creating "a working class that pressured its employers and the state for the wages and benefits Kubitschek and others had so often promised. In pressing those demands, male and female workers brought about real change in Brazil." Jocelyn Olcott also points out that followers often wield important power in the leader-follower relationship, and that this is important because of what it tells us about followers as political actors, and also because it forces us to rethink the phenomenon of populism itself: "if we understand populism not only as a state-driven enterprise but also as an opening for popular organizing, we see a polity that is less tidy and predictable, but also less nefarious, than populism's detractors would have us believe."

1. Juan Perón's wife and vice president Isabel, became president upon his death in 1974 and served until she was overthrown in a military coup in 1976. Since 1990 five Latin American women have been elected president: Violeta Barrios de Chamorro (Nicaragua), Mireya Moscoso (Panama), Michelle Bachelet (Chile), Cristina Fernández de Kirchner (Argentina), and Laura Chinchilla (Costa Rica).

At the same time, sometimes populist leaders are dictatorial, and sometimes their followers must share the blame. As a number of the chapters in this volume have shown, there is nothing inherently democratic about women taking to the streets to support their leader. Certainly the followers of Nicaragua's Somoza family, who, according to Victoria González-Rivera, defended what they saw as a project of secular liberal values—which gave women both the vote and jobs— also defended a dictatorship. In fact, by the 1970s, it was a brutal dictatorship. The same could be said of the Argentine women who supported Juan and Eva Perón during their years in power, and who continued to organize their political lives around that legacy a generation later. Writing on Ecuador, Ximena Sosa-Buchholz finds that many working-class women came out to support both Velasco Ibarra and Bucaram, seemingly unconcerned with their sometimes dictatorial ways. But upper-class women did not participate in street demonstrations in notable numbers until the 1997 demonstrations that ousted Bucaram. While she only touches on the role of women who opposed Bucaram, Sosa-Buchholz points to the need to explore antipopulist politics. In recent years, Venezuela and Nicaragua have also seen massive antipopulist demonstrations in which women have played key roles. At the same time that we ask what attracts certain women to populist leaders, we also need to ask the far less explored question: What is it that repels other women?

One of the things that seem to have repelled some women is populists' attempts to ignore, co-opt, or attack feminists. Karin Grammático quotes Eva Perón's less than flattering description of feminists, who she said belonged "to another race of women. To say they are like men is to unfairly insult men. . . . We have seen the rise of a class of female leaders who are frivolous and of little use to the nation . . . [who spend their time] just waiting for death, without doing anything worthwhile." And yet the legacy of Evita is a complicated one, for feminist thought emerged from within Agrupación Evita, the Montonero group that paid homage to Perón's wife. Grammático's and González-Rivera's explorations of the legacy of populism a generation later, and of the ways in which women's roles in the original project are remembered—or forgotten— raise more questions. Is the wide range of interpretations of what it "truly" means to be a Peronist or Somocista typical of populism, which is distinguished by its ideological flexibility? Certainly a political movement that is based on the figure, or the memory, of a particular leader lends itself to multiple interpretations that cannot be resolved by returning to core texts. Or do memories of political movements always vary widely?

In their chapter on Venezuela, Gioconda Espina and Cathy Rakowski argue that "although promoting 'popular feminism' continues to be a goal of Inamujer staff," and although some National Assembly deputies consult with feminists on legal projects, "the concept of feminism never appears in official discourse or in Chávez's speeches or radio programs. Instead, the emphasis is on women's rights as a marginalized group, which are in turn tied to socialism and, more specifically, to Chávez." So is populism so personalistic that it is inherently incompatible with feminism? Across the region, feminist movements have typically sought autonomy or independence from political parties and politicians. Can such social movements coexist with often unpredictable populist leaders, with their tendency to concentrate power in their own hands? Kurt Weyland warns in his foreword that feminists who ally with populists may make "a pact with the devil." Even a populist who promotes gender equality today may reverse that position tomorrow, depending on his whim or on the political opportunities that present themselves.

But some broader notion of women's rights may be very compatible with populism. As most of the chapters in this volume demonstrate, populists have promoted women's rights in a variety of ways: giving women the right to vote, putting individual women into positions of power, creating or expanding state women's agencies, and providing resources for women, especially poor women, that ease the burdens of their daily lives. Moreover, feminists may have little choice. For reasons outlined in the introduction to this volume, it is unlikely that Latin American populism will go away anytime soon, although individual populists sometimes have short careers. If they can't work with—or at least coexist with—populist figures, feminists may find themselves facing disaster. As I found in chapter 8, on Nicaragua, one of the unintended consequences of feminist efforts to seek autonomy from Daniel Ortega's FSLN, over a period of fifteen years, was that they were unable to stop him when he decided that outlawing abortion, even to save the life of the pregnant woman, might win him some votes, or at least stop the Catholic Church from campaigning against him.

Finally, the latest round of radical populist movements, some of which claim to be revolutionary, open up many questions. Chapters 7, 8, 9, and 10 in this volume show that there is a very complicated relationship between populism, revolution, and gender politics. Populist elements within a revolutionary movement boded very badly for women's rights in Nicaragua but opened up a number of opportunities for women's rights in Venezuela, albeit sometimes lost opportunities. In fact, Sujatha Fernandes argues that while grassroots activism predated Chávez's Bolivarian revolution, it has changed qualitatively since Chávez's arrival on the scene. It is "precisely through their associational links with a revolutionary-populist president and state-managed programs that barrio women have been able to build new spaces of community participation. They have used a maternal notion of responsibility and nurturance as the basis of their political identity. At the same time, they are willing to criticize the state, and the clientelist methods of state agencies, when necessary." So what determines whether revolutionary populism represents an opportunity or a threat for those who would promote greater gender equality?

In her comparison of Peruvian neopopulist Alberto Fujimori and Bolivian radical populist Evo Morales, Stéphanie Rousseau notes that in terms of their political and economic policies, the two politicians were dramatically different. "Fujimori implemented one of the harshest structural adjustment and liberalization plans, while Morales assumed state power at the crest of a massive antineoliberal mobilization." And, indeed, there were differences in their gender agendas; they appealed to different sorts of women with different discourses. But Rousseau also finds common features in their gender politics. "Both of their populist projects clash with the feminist movement at some levels. In contrast to some cases of classic populism, however, each of these new populist leaders also insisted on promoting women's political leadership, even at the highest levels." Clearly the relationship between different waves of populism and gender politics is a complicated one. Do particular economic policies (ISI for the classic populists, neoliberalism for the neopopulists, anti-neoliberal fair trade for the current radical populists) require certain gender policies and discourses? Or are they more compatible with some sorts of gender politics over others? In other words, are there affinities between economic policy and gender policy?

One of the things that distinguish the latest round of populism, in addition to its obvious rejection of neoliberalism, is its international nature. Though earlier populists certainly spoke of the Americas and their place within it, they governed for the most part as nationalists drawing on national resources. By contrast, the new populists govern increasingly in alliance with other populists. Rousseau notes that Evo Morales's redistribution plans rely on the support of "Cuban and Venezuelan cooperation to provide direct social services, such as medical and literacy campaigns, to the poorest." The same can be said of Daniel Ortega's promises to provide services to the poor, and indeed to keep Nicaragua's economy—dependent on oil, as are all modern economies—from further collapse. Chávez's efforts to build the multinational Bolivarian Alternative for the Americas (Alternativa Bolivariana para las Américas, or ALBA) indicate that the days of populism in one country may be past. At the same time, each populist leader and each set of populist followers bring their own national idiosyncrasies to their movement, despite international links.

Books are always years in the making, and so many populists rose to national prominence after the chapters for this volume were written. Even if this were not the case, some interesting cases would have had to be left out for reasons of space. No doubt some readers will be unhappy that their favorite populist does not appear in these pages. Hopefully future researchers will fill in some of the inevitable gaps. It would be also be worth analyzing the latest wave of radical populism on its own. These are exciting times for Latin American populism, and there is a lot more to be done to understand this latest wave.

Contributors

Michael Conniff earned degrees at the University of California, Berkeley, and Stanford University and taught in Brazil, New Mexico, Alabama, and Florida before arriving at San José State University in 2002, where he directs the Global Studies Initiative. He has raised several million dollars in grants and contracts and has written nine books and numerous articles.

Gioconda Espina holds a BA in literature, a master's degree in Asian studies, and a PhD in development studies. A feminist activist since 1978, she is a co-founder of the Coordinating Committee of Women's Non-governmental Organizations, and of the Center for Women's Studies and the women's studies program at the Central University of Venezuela, where she currently teaches feminist theory in the master's program in women's studies.

Sujatha Fernandes is an assistant professor of sociology at Queens College and at the Graduate Center of the City University of New York. She received her PhD in political science from the University of Chicago in 2003. She is the author of *Cuba Represent! Cuban Arts, State Power, and the Making of New Revolutionary Cultures* (Duke University Press, 2006) and *Who Can Stop the Drums? Urban Social Movements in Chávez's Venezuela* (Duke University Press, 2010).

Victoria González-Rivera grew up in Nicaragua. She holds a PhD in Latin American history from Indiana University. She is co-editor, with Karen Kampwirth, of *Radical Women in Latin America: Left and Right* (Pennsylvania State University Press, 2001). Her book *Before the Revolution: Women's Rights and Right-Wing Politics in Nicaragua, 1821–1979* is under contract with Penn State University Press. She is currently an assistant professor in the Department of Chicana and Chicano Studies at San Diego State University.

Karin Grammático teaches history in the School of Philosophy and Literature at the University of Buenos Aires. She is a researcher and teacher at the Interdisciplinary Institute for Gender Studies and holds a master's degree in historical investigation from the University of San Andrés in Buenos Aires. She has published articles on the political activism of the 1960s and 1970s and on the feminist movement in recent Argentine history, and is co-editor of the journal *Historia, género y política en los '70* (Buenos Aires).

Karen Kampwirth (PhD, University of California, Berkeley) is a professor of political science and chair of the Latin American Studies Program at Knox College. She is co-editor, with Victoria González-Rivera, of *Radical Women in Latin America: Left and Right* (Pennsylvania State University Press, 2001), and the author of *Women and Guerrilla Movements: Nicaragua, El Salvador, Chiapas, Cuba* (Pennsylvania State University Press, 2002) and *Feminism and the Legacy of Revolution: Nicaragua, El Salvador, Chiapas* (Ohio University Press, 2004). In 2009 she taught at the University of Buenos Aires with the support of a Fulbright Fellowship.

Jocelyn Olcott, an associate professor of history at Duke University, is the author of *Revolutionary Women in Postrevolutionary Mexico* (Duke University Press, 2005) and co-editor of *Sex in Revolution: Gender, Politics, and Power in Modern Mexico* (Duke University Press, 2006). She is currently working on two books, *The Greatest Consciousness-Raising Event in History: International Women's Year and the Challenge of Transnational Feminism* (Oxford University Press) and *Sing What the People Sing: Concha Michel and the Cultural Politics of Mexican Maternalism.*

Cathy A. Rakowski is an associate professor of rural sociology and women's studies at Ohio State University. She received her PhD in sociology from the University of Texas at Austin and for many years has conducted research in Venezuela, where she has also worked as a policy consultant and social planner. Her research focuses on processes of social change, and she is working on a book on the gendering of public administration and social policy in Ciudad Guayana, Venezuela's planned industrial city. She has also been involved in research and curriculum development in Mexico, India, and Africa.

Stéphanie Rousseau is an assistant professor in the Department of Sociology at Laval University (Quebec, Canada). She has a PhD in political science from McGill University and was a postdoctoral fellow at the Institute of Latin American Studies, University of North Carolina at Chapel Hill. Her research focuses on women's movement dynamics, gender, and citizenship in Peru and Bolivia. She recently published *Women's Citizenship in Peru: The Paradoxes of Neopopulism in Latin America* (Palgrave Macmillan, 2009).

Ximena Sosa-Buchholz earned her PhD in history as a Fulbright scholar at the University of New Mexico. She is the academic coordinator of the Trent in Ecuador Program in the International Development Studies Department at Trent University, Canada. She was the assistant director of the Center for Latin American and Caribbean Studies at Indiana University and chaired the Ecuadorian section of the Latin American Studies Association. She has published articles on José María Velasco Ibarra, indigenous peoples, and women. She co-edited, with William Waters, *Estudios ecuatorianos: Un aporte a la discusión* (FLACSO, ABYA-YALA, and Ecuadorian Section/LASA, 2006).

Kurt Weyland is the Lozano Long Professor of Latin American Politics at the University of Texas at Austin. He is the author of *Democracy Without Equity: Failures of Reform in Brazil* (University of Pittsburgh Press, 1996), *The Politics of Market Reform in Fragile Democracies* (Princeton University Press, 2002), *Bounded Rationality and Policy Diffusion: Social Sector Reform in Latin America* (Princeton University Press, 2007), and many articles on democratization, neoliberalism, populism, and social policy in Latin America. His new project analyzes the wavelike diffusion of political regime changes across countries, starting with the explosive spread of the 1848 revolution in Europe and Latin America.

Joel Wolfe received his PhD at the University of Wisconsin–Madison and teaches Latin American history at the University of Massachusetts, Amherst. He is the author of *Working Women, Working Men: São Paulo and the Rise of Brazil's Industrial Working Class, 1900–1955* (Duke University Press, 1993) and *Autos and Progress: The Brazilian Search for Modernity* (Oxford University Press, 2010).

Index

abortion
  in Argentina, 128
  in Mexico, 41
  in Nicaragua, 87, 165–66, 173–75, 177, 177
    n. 7, 225
  in Peru, 148
accountability problems, ix–x
activists
  Bolivian women as, 154, 157–58
  classical populism opposed by, 4–5
  Venezuelan (see Venezuelan women activists)
Adum, Alfredo, 61, 61 n. 17
advertising, for Venezuelan educational
  programs, 209–10
Afro-Brazilians, citizenship rights for, 96
Agenda Venezuela, 208
Agrarian Department (Mexico), 35
agrarian reform, Mexican, 35–37
Agrupación Evita, 123–39
  establishment of, 124–25, 134
  Feminine Peronist Party's relationship to,
    124–25, 134, 135–36
  feminists and, 131–32, 224
  goals of, 125, 134, 135–37
  need for, 136
  political identity of women in, 129–30, 137–39
Ala Femenina del Partido Liberal Nacionalista
  (Nicaragua), 69–70, 74–77, 83–85
Alemán, Arnoldo
  conviction of, 74, 169
  election to presidency, 73–74, 168–69
  feminists' relationship with, 6, 14, 88
  imprisonment of, 169, 171
  market women on, 81, 82
  masculinization of Liberalism under, 73,
    87–88
  Ortega's pact with, 74, 87, 168–71
  Somocista women's views on, 78–79, 81, 82,
    86
Alianza Anticomunista Argentina, 127 n. 4
Alianza Democrática Ecuatoriana, 50 n. 5
Alimentación, Misión, 188, 189
Alma Mater, Misión, 188–89
Aló, Presidente (talk show), 192
Alternativa Bolivariana para los Pueblos de
  Nuestra América, 117
Alvarez, Rosa, 73, 77–79, 80, 81, 83, 85
Amaral Peixoto, Ernani do, 111, 112

AMNLAE. See Asociación de Mujeres
  Nicaragüenses Luisa Amanda Espinosa
AMPRONIC. See Asociación de Mujeres Ante
  INIES
AMUPEI. See Articulación de Mujeres por la
  Equidad e Igualdad
Angós, José Antonio, 207
antielitism
  in attitudes toward feminists, 14
  in definition of populism, 2
antifeminism, Nicaraguan, 175
antipopulist politics, 224
APRA movement, 11
Arafat, Yasser, 26
Aramburu, Pedro E., 123, 124
Argentina, 20, 122–39. See also specific leaders
  abortion in, 128
  classical populism in, rise of, 3
  family in, 127–28, 133–34
  feminists of, 130–33, 224
  housewives in, 127–29
  independent women's movement in, 205
  myths about Eva Perón in, 9
  neopopulism in, 117
  presidential election of 1973 in, 126, 126 n. 3
  Velasco Ibarra in exile in, 51
  women politicians in, viii, xi, 223 n. 1
  women's role in populist movements in, xii
  women's suffrage in, xi, 4, 13–14, 127, 131
Argentine Feminist Union, 132
Arias, Arnulfo, 3, 4
Arraes, Miguel, 111
Arrostito, Norma, 124
Arroyo del Rio, Carlos, 50, 56
Arteaga, Rosalia
  in Bucaram's appeal to women, 49, 60–61
  political career of, 60, 62
  social class of, 60, 61
  in succession to presidency, 61, 62 n. 19
Articulación de Mujeres por la Equidad e
  Igualdad (AMUPEI), 156–57
Asociación de Mujeres Ante INIES
  (AMPRONIC), 165
Asociación de Mujeres Nicaragüenses Luisa
  Amanda Espinosa (AMNLAE), 164, 165
athleticism
  of Bucaram, 53
  in masculine images of leaders, 10

Aurora de Nicaragua (newspaper), 68
authoritarianism
    of Bucaram, 49
    in Chavista populism, 184
    democratic process in context of, 13
    as threat to democracy, 120–21
automobile industry, Brazilian, 92, 101–6
Auyero, Javier, 15–16, 72, 85
Aymara, 150, 154–55
Ayora, Isidro, 48

Bachelet, Michelle, 223 n. 1
ballots, in Brazil, 121
banana boom, in Ecuador, 50
Banmujer
    and Chávez's appeal to women, 195
    establishment of, 192, 210
    ideological training in, 180, 181
    mobilization of women in, 180, 190, 192
    women's rights in, 193
Barcelona soccer club, 53
Barreto, Juan, 10
Barrig, Maruja, 217
Barrio Adentro, 189, 190
Barrios, Carmen Teresa, 211–12
Barrios de Chamorro, Violeta, 67, 167, 168, 223
    n. 1
barrio women. *See* Venezuelan women
    activists
Barros, Adhemar de, 112, 114, 115, 119
base, in Mexican populism, 28
Basurto, Jorge, 39
Batalla de Bassols, Clementina, 37, 38
Bauer, Arnold, 34
Bayard de Volo, Lorraine, 206
Belli, Gioconda, 174
Belo Horizonte (Brazil), 101
benefits, employee, in Brazilian auto industry,
    103, 104
Bhutto, Benazir, xii
Bianchi, Susana, 128–29
birth control. *See* family planning
Blanco, Bertha, 158
Bobbitt, Lorena, 10, 60, 60 n. 15, 61
Bolaños, Enrique, 73
Bolívar, Simón, 53, 117 n. 3, 185
Bolivarian revolution
    constitutional reform in, 181
    ideological training in, 180, 181
    named after Bolívar, 117 n. 3, 185
    socialism as aim of, 180
    women's role in, 193
Bolivia, 20, 150–59. *See also specific leaders*

Aymara culture in, 154–55
    coca farming in, 150, 151, 158
    Congress of, 151, 158
    Constituent Assembly of, 151, 155, 156, 158
    constitution of, 151–52, 156–57
    equal rights for women in, 156–57
    ethnopopulism in, 140
    feminists of, 157–58, 159
    "gas war" of 2003 in, 154
    gender complementarity in, 154–55, 158, 159
    indigenous population of, 150–59
    poverty in, rise of, 151
    presidential election of 2005 in, 151
    universal suffrage in, 151
    women activists in, 154, 157–58
    women politicians in, xi, 141, 155, 156, 158
Borges de Medeiros, Antônio Augusto, 93
Borghi, Hugo, 114, 115
Bowen, Sally, 142
Brasília
    Kubitschek's role in building, 19, 92, 100, 105
    problems with, 105, 105 n. 5
    residential design of, 100, 105
Brazil, 19–20, 91–106, 110–21. *See also specific
    leaders*
    classical populism in, rise of, 3
    Congress of, 114–16
    constitutional revolution of 1932 in, 95
    constitution of, 93, 98
    feminists of, 98, 113–14, 121
    housewives in, 93, 97, 104, 105, 106
    middle class in, creation of, 92, 100–106
    nationalism in, 99
    neopopulism in, 117, 120
    presidential elections in: 1930, 91, 93; 1950,
        98–99, 101, 110–11, 113; 1955, 100, 118; 2002,
        106, 117; 2006, 106, 117; 2010, 117
    radical populism in, 116–17
    1930 revolution in, 91, 95
    Senate of, 98 n. 2, 112, 116–17
    slavery in, end of, 91
    universal suffrage in, 91, 98
    women campaign managers in, 110–11, 112–
        14
    women followers/voters in, 110, 111, 118–21
    women politicians in: at lower *vs.* higher
        levels, 110, 223; profiles of, 111, 114–17, 120–
        21
    women's suffrage in, xi, 93, 96, 98, 111, 113
Brazilian Democratic Movement (MDB), 115
Brazilian Federation for Feminine Progress,
    113–14
Brinson, Clara, 210–11

Britain, Mexican relations with, 26
Brizola, Leonel, 111, 115, 116
Bucaram, Assad (Don Buca), 51
Bucaram, Martha, 52
Bucaram Ortiz, Abdalá, 19, 47–63
  authoritarian behavior of, 49
  career overview, 51–52
  characteristics of leadership of, 47
  corruption accusations against, 52
  education of, 51
  election to presidency, 49, 52
  family of, 53
  feminists' relationship with, 61, 63
  illiterate voters supporting, 49, 54, 63
  on love for the people, 9
  masculine image of, viii, 10, 11, 48–49, 52–56,
    61, 62
  as member of the people, 53
  neoliberal economic policies of, 52, 55 n. 10
  as neopopulist, 47, 48
  overthrow of, 6, 49, 52, 55, 62, 63
  party founded by, 51–52
  physical appearance of, 56
  on the poor, 55
  understanding of the people, 48–49
  vulgarity of, 10, 62
  women voters supporting, 60–62
Burns, James MacGregor, x
Bush, George W., 29, 180

Calderón, Felipe, 28
Cammack, Paul, 182
Cámpora, Héctor, 126, 126 n. 3
car(s). See automobile industry
Caracas (Venezuela), Carretera Negra sector of
  La Vega in, 211–17
caracazo, 183, 207–8, 209
Carbo, Gloria de, 59
Cárdenas, Cuauhtémoc, 28
Cárdenas, Lázaro, 18–19, 31–38
  on citizenship rights for women, 32, 33
  in classical populism, rise of, 3, 28
  constitutional amendments proposed by, 26
  course of populism after, vii
  demands of the people and, 31, 34–38
  vs. Echeverría, 25–26, 39
  and exceptionalism of Mexican populism,
    28
  impact on women's status, 26, 31–32, 38, 43–
    44
  masculine image of, 11–12, 30 n. 6
  motivations of, 32, 37, 38, 39
  names for, 12

nationalism of, 25–26
paternalism of, 12
political successors to, vii
repression under, 28
rural mobilization by, 3 n. 4
UNMM's praise of, 25
vs. Vargas, legacies of, 100 n. 3
women followers of, 16–17
and women's suffrage, xi, 4, 26, 38
Cárdenas, Nancy, 42
Cardoso, Fernando Enrique, 29, 38
Carretera Negra sector of La Vega, Caracas,
  211–17
Carrillo Puerto, Elvia, 33
Carta Echeverría, 26, 39
Castañeda, Nora, 180–81
Castillo, Ramón, 122
Catholicism
  in Bolivian constitution, 156
  and Fujimori's family-planning policies,
    146, 148
  and land reform, 17
  vs. Liberalism, 49, 49 n. 3, 58
  in masculine images of leaders, 10–11
  of Ortega, 171–75
  of Velasco Ibarra, 49, 49 n. 3, 57, 58
  and women's leagues, 38
  and women's suffrage, 32, 38
caudillo (strongman) rule
  in Nicaragua, 162, 163
  in Venezuela, 184, 185
Cavallo, Domingo, 52
Cavarozzi, Marcelo, 123
Central Intelligence Agency (CIA), 170
Centro al Servicio de Acción Popular
  (CESAP), 205, 207, 208
Centro de Pesquisa e Documentação de
  História Contemporánea (CPDOC), 112
CESAP. See Centro al Servicio de Acción
  Popular
CFP. See Concentración de Fuerzas Populares
chachawarmi, 154–55
Chamorro, Violeta, 73
charismatic leadership, of Chávez, 186
Charter on the Economic Rights and Duties of
  States, UN (1974), 26
Chávez, Hugo, 21, 180–98, 202–18. See also
  Chavista populism
  Bolivarian revolution of, 117 n. 3, 180, 181,
    185, 193
  charismatic leadership of, 186
  coup attempts by (1992), 209
  crises under, 198

Chávez, Hugo (*continued*)
  defensive posture of, 182
  on discipline, 202–3
  discourse of, 184–85, 192–96
  election to presidency, 181 n. 2
  on feminism, 1, 193, 225
  feminists' relationship with, 14
  on Fifth Republic, 185, 185 n. 8
  financial resources of, 7
  Left's relationship with, 183 n. 6
  masculine image of, 10
  misiones under, 186–92
  on motherhood, 193–96, 197
  motivations of, 29
  neoliberalism rejected by, 6
  and Ortega, 176–77
  on the other, 185
  the people's relationship with, 186, 188, 189
  as radical populist, 7, 117 n. 3, 180
  recentralization under, 184, 184 n. 7, 198
  redistributive programs of, 183, 188, 198
  religious images of, 203, 211–12
  in revival of populism, vii
  on Rice (Condoleezza), 10, 10 n. 6
  rise to power, 182–83
  romantic images of, 18, 18 n. 7
  women activists under, 203, 209–13, 218
  women followers of, 17–18, 193, 194–96
  on women's rights, 181, 192, 192 n. 18, 193
  women voting for recall of, 15
Chávez, Margarita, 79–80
Chavista populism (Chavismo), 180–98. *See also* Chávez, Hugo
  vs. classical populism, 182
  collective identity in, 185, 188
  definition of, 180
  discourse of, 184–85, 192–96
  goal of, 182
  key features of, 180, 181, 183–84
  vs. neopopulism, 182, 182 n. 5, 204
  origins of, 182–83
  as revolutionary-populist, 204
  symbolism in, 185, 189, 192
child support, in Nicaragua, 71
Chile, women presidents of, 223 n. 1
Christianity. *See* Catholicism; Protestantism; religion
chusma, 48
CIA. *See* Central Intelligence Agency
Círculos Femeninos, 205, 207, 208
citizens, as children, in father metaphor, 12–13, 120
citizenship, redefinition of, in Argentina, 122

citizenship rights
  in Argentina, 123
  in Bolivia, 153
  in Brazil, 91, 92, 96
  in Mexico, 32–34
Ciudad del Niño, 59 n. 14
classical populism. *See also specific countries and leaders*
  activists' opposition to, 4–5
  vs. Chavista populism, 182
  decline of, 4–5
  economic policies in, vii, 5, 47
  financial resources of, 5, 6
  as first wave of populism, 3–4
  gender policies of, 4
  masculine images of leaders in, viii
  vs. neoliberal populism, vii, 5, 47
  political mobilization in, 3
  rise of, 3, 27
  women's roles in, 4
  and women's suffrage, xi, 4
clientelism
  vs. client-ship, 48
  definition of, 70
  in definition of populism, 2
  in Nicaragua, 70–73
clientelistic populism, 13
client-ship, *vs.* clientelism, 48
CLT. *See* consolidated labor laws
coalitions, in definition of populism, 2
coca farming, Bolivian, 150, 151, 158
Cockcroft, James, 166 n. 2
COFEAPRE. *See* Presidential Women's Advisory Commission
collaboration, among populists, difficulty of, 115
Collor de Mello, Fernando
  masculine image of, xi, 120
  as neopopulist, 117, 120
  in revival of populism, vii
  women in power under, viii, xi
Colombia. *See also specific leaders*
  classical populism in, rise of, 3
  women politicians in, xi
colonialism, Morales on, 154
combatants, women, in FSLN, 164–65
Comercio, El (newspaper), 50
communications technology, 28, 39
community organizations, Venezuelan. *See* Venezuelan women activists
Companhia Siderúrgica Nacional (CSN), 99
CONALCAM. *See* Cordinadora Nacional por el Cambio

CONAMU. *See* Consejo Nacional de la Mujer; National Women's Council
CONAPRO, 165
Concentración de Fuerzas Populares (CFP, Ecuador), 51
CONG. *See* Coordinadora de Organizaciones No-Gubernamentales de Mujeres
Congress, Bolivian
    Morales as member of, 151
    women members of, 158
Congress, Brazilian, women members of, 114–16
Congress, Ecuadorian, Velasco Ibarra as member of, 50
Congress, Peruvian
    Fujimori's suspension of, 143, 144
    women members of, 147, 150
Conniff, Michael, 12
Consejo Nacional de la Mujer (CONAMU), 60
consejos comunales, 181, 181 n. 4, 191
Conservative Party (Ecuador), 48, 50, 50 n. 4
Conservative Party (Nicaragua), 68
consolidated labor laws (CLT), of Brazil, 97
Constituent Assembly, Bolivian
    chachawarmi in, 155
    establishment of, 151
    women members of, 155, 156, 158
Constituent Assembly, Venezuelan, 181, 209
constitutional revolution of 1932 (Brazil), 95
constitutions, in democracy, 63. *See also specific countries*
consumers, Brazilian, in Kubitschek's developmentalism, 100, 102–5
contraceptives
    in Nicaragua, 166
    in Peru, 146, 148
Contras
    market women in, 82
    in 2006 presidential election, 171, 171 n. 3
Contra war, 164, 166, 167
Coordinadora de Organizaciones No-Gubernamentales de Mujeres (CONG), 208
Coordinadora Política de Mujeres Ecuatorianas (CPME), 61, 61 n. 16
Cordinadora Nacional por el Cambio (CONALCAM), 154
Cordovez Chiriboga, Fausto, 55
corn mills, motorized, 34–38
corporatism
    in Brazil, 94, 101
    in Peru, 144
Correa, Rafael, 6, 47

Correa, Sandra, 63 n. 20
corruption. *See also* fraud
    Bucaram accused of, 52
    Bucaram's toleration of, 63, 63 n. 20
    of Somozas, 69, 78
    Vargas accused of, 99–100
Cortez, Elena, 58
Costa Rica, classical populism in, 3
Council of State, Nicaraguan, 163
Couto, Golbery e, 115
CPDOC. *See* Centro de Pesquisa e Documentação de História Contemporánea
CPME. *See* Coordinadora Política de Mujeres Ecuatorianas
Craske, Nikki, 204
Crespo de Ortiz, Lola, 59
Cristero Rebellion, 17
Cruz, Rocío, 81
CSN. *See* Companhia Siderúrgica Nacional
Cuba
    Family Code in, 43
    mass women's organizations in, 204, 205
    Morales supported by, 153
    Venezuelan socialism modeled on, 181
Cuban Revolution (1959), 4, 123

daily life, and popular organizing, in Venezuela, 213–17
dance, in Bucaram's presidential campaign, 61
day-care centers, Venezuelan, 208
debt crisis of 1982, 5
de la Torre, Augusto, 52
de la Torre, Carlos, 13, 14, 53 n. 9, 63
del Campo, Ester, 62 n. 18
D'Elia, Yolanda, 189–90
del Mar Alvarez, María, 195
Deloya Cobián, Guillermo, 29
del Villar, Rosalia, 158
demands of the people
    in Ecuador, 47, 48
    in Mexico: Cárdenas's response to, 31, 34–38; Echeverría's response to, 31, 41–44
    transition into entitlements, 34–38, 44
democracy, 12–13
    authoritarianism as threat to, 120–21
    in Chávez's discourse, 185
    constitutional safeguards in, 63
    paternalism as threat to, 12–13
    populism as threat to, 49, 63
    relationship of populism to, 12–13, 49, 62–63
    relationships between leaders and followers in, 223–24
Descamisado, El (newspaper), 129

descamisados, 8, 8 n. 5, 9
developmentalism
  of Kubitschek, 92, 100–105
  of Vargas, 99
dictatorships
  followers' role in, 224
  as response to classical populism, 5
  of Vargas, 93, 95, 96, 98, 114
  of Velasco Ibarra, 49, 50–51, 63
discipline, Chávez on, 202–3
discourse, of Chávez, 184–85, 192–96
discrimination against women. *See* sexism
distributional memories
  definition of, 72
  of Somocista women, 72–73, 83–87
División de Trabajo y Asistencia de la Mujer
  (Argentina), 127
divorces, viii
  conservative views of, 50 n. 4
  of Fujimori, viii, 146
  of Menem, viii
  of Velasco Ibarra, 50, 50 n. 4
domestic labor, female
  in Mexico: motorized corn mills and, 34–36;
    women in labor market and, 41, 43
  in Venezuela, recognition of value of, 193–
    94, 197
Drake, Paul, vii, viii
Duque, José Roberto, 209
Duran Ballen, Sixto, 60
Dutra, Eurico, 113

earthquakes, in Nicaragua, 69
Echeverría, Luis, 18–19, 39–44
  vs. Cárdenas, 25–26, 39
  as classical populist, 28
  constitutional amendments proposed by, 26
  demands of the people and, 31, 41–44
  equal rights for women under, 26, 26 n. 3, 40
  and exceptionalism of Mexican populism, 28
  impact on women's status, 26, 40, 43–44
  in International Women's Year conference,
    27, 39–43
  masculine image of, 30 n. 6
  motivations of, 39
  nationalism of, 25–26
  before neopopulism's rise, 27–28
  on population control, 40
  repression under, 28, 39 n. 25
  UNMM's critique of, 25
economic development
  population control in, 40 n. 28, 41
  women in labor market and, 41, 43

economic freedom, for market women, 82
economic policies. *See also specific leaders and
  policies*
  in definition of populism, 2
  gender politics associated with types of, 226
  of neoliberal *vs.* classical populism, vii, 5, 47
economic rights of women, in Venezuela,
  193–94
Ecuador, 19, 47–63. *See also specific leaders*
  classical populism in, 3, 47
  Congress of, 50
  constitution of, 48
  demands of the people in, 47
  democracy's expression in, 63
  feminists of, 56–63
  La Gloriosa in, 50, 54
  masculine ideal in, 52–56
  mass politics in, origins of, 54
  National Assembly of, 49
  neopopulism in, 47
  overview of political history of, 49–52
  presidential elections in: 1934, 48; 1940, 50;
    1996, 52, 60–61; democratic, 49; fraud in,
    50, 51, 54, 63; Velasco Ibarra in, 48, 49, 50
  universal suffrage in, 48, 54
  women politicians in, 59–60, 62, 62 n. 18
  women's suffrage in, xi, 48, 56, 57
  women voters in: for Bucaram, 60–62; for
    Velasco Ibarra, 48, 49, 56–60, 61–62
education
  in Argentina, 136
  in Brazil, 98, 102
  in Ecuador, 49, 56–58
  in Venezuela, 188–90, 209–10
Education and Public Health, Ministry of
  (Brazil), 98
el-Dahdah, Farès, 105 n. 5
elections. *See specific countries*
electoral fraud, in Ecuador, 50, 51, 54, 63
elites
  Brazilian: in auto industry, 104–5; Vargas's
    relationship with, 94, 95, 101, 113
  feminists as, 14
  non-white, 140
  opposition to, in definition of populism, 2
El Salvador, independent women's movement
  in, 205
emotion in populism, 1, 1 n. 1, 2 n. 1, 9, 18
employment. *See* working women
enemy, the. *See also* other, the
  in Chávez's discourse, 185
  feminists as, 130–31, 170, 177
  Fujimori's creation of, 143–44

Morales's creation of, 152–53
vs. the people, 141, 159
of Peronism, 130–31
entitlements, transition of demands into, 34–38, 44
equal rights for women
in Bolivia, 156–57
in Ecuador, 57, 59–60
in Mexico, 26–27, 26 n. 3, 40
in United States, 26 n. 3, 40
in Venezuela, 191–92, 192 n. 18, 193–94
Espina, Gioconda, 7
Estado Novo (Brazil)
democracy threatened by, 121
establishment of, 93, 96
families in, 96–97
ethnopopulism
in Bolivia, 140
rise of, vii
eugenics, Lamarckian, 101
Eva Perón Foundation, 8
Evita Group. *See* Agrupación Evita
Excélsior (daily), 32
exceptionalism, Mexican, 27–31
exchange rate, in Ecuador, 52

family
Argentine, Perón on, 127–28, 133–34
Brazilian: in Kubitschek's populism, 92, 100; in Vargas's populism, 92, 96–97
Nicaraguan, policies on, 87
Venezuelan, Chávez's understanding of, 202–3
Family Code (Cuba), 43
family planning
in Nicaragua, 166
in Peru, 146, 148
family values, in Nicaragua, 87
father figures, 11, 120
democracy threatened by, 12–13
Vargas as, 92, 96, 100, 120
Velasco Ibarra as, 52, 55
fathers, Nicaraguan, child support from, 71
Febres Cordero, León, 52
Federación de Mujeres Campesinas Bartolina Sisa, 156
Federation for Feminine Progress, Brazilian, 113–14
Federation of Collective Kitchens, 149
Federation of Domestic Workers, 158
fem (magazine), 41
Feminine Branch. *See* Feminine Peronist Party
feminine interests, *vs.* feminist interests, xi, 164

Feminine Peronist Party (PPF, Feminine Branch)
Agrupación Evita's relationship to, 124–25, 134, 135–36
establishment of, 127, 133–35
Eva Perón in, 8, 125, 134–36
vs. feminism, 133
goals of, 134–35
after Perón's return from exile, 133–35
femininity, Mexican conceptions of, 27, 32–33, 35–36, 40–44
feminist(s), 13–14, 224–25
Argentine, 130–33, 224
Bolivian, 157–58, 159
Brazilian, 98, 113–14, 121
Chávez on, 1, 193, 225
Ecuadorian, 56–63
as elites, 14
as the enemy, 130–31, 170, 177
first wave of, 5, 56
interests of, *vs.* feminine interests, xi, 164
leaders' relationships with, 6, 13–14, 225
neopopulism's response to, 5–6
Nicaraguan (*See* Nicaraguan feminists)
Perón (Eva) on, 1, 130–31, 224
Peruvian, 6, 14, 147–48
second wave of, 5–6, 39–40, 43, 60, 177
Venezuelan, 192–93, 195–96, 207, 225
Feminist Assembly (Bolivia), 157
Fernandes, Sujatha, 7
Fernández de Kirchner, Cristina, xii, 223 n. 1
Fifth Republic, 185, 185 n. 8, 209
Figueiredo, João, 116
Figueres, José, 3, 4
Finance, Ministry of (Argentina), 127
followers, women, 14–18, 223–24. *See also specific leaders*
Argentine, 15–16, 127–30, 137
Brazilian, 110, 111, 118–21
in democracies *vs.* dictatorships, 223–24
leaders' outreach to, 14–16
leaders' relationships with, 223–24
mobilization of, 15–18
motivations of, 14, 16
as out of place, 17–18
role in movements, xii
Fondo Nacional de Atención a la Infancia (FONAIN), 208
Fondo Social, 208
Fonseca, Hazel, 164–65
food aid
in Peru, 144, 149–50
in Venezuela, 188, 189, 197, 210, 213–17

Food and Agriculture Organization, UN, 43
food consumption, in Brazil, 97
Ford do Brasil, 102, 103
Fox, Vicente, 32 n. 9
Francisco Miranda Front, 209, 216
fraud, electoral. *See also* corruption
　in Ecuador, 50, 51, 54, 63
freedom, economic, for market women, 82
FREJULI. *See* Frente Justicialista de Liberación
Frente Francisco Miranda, 209, 216
Frente Justicialista de Liberación (FREJULI),
　125
Friedman, Elisabeth, 207
FSLN. *See* Sandinista National Liberation
　Front
Fuerzas Bolivarianas, 205
Fujimori, Alberto, 20, 140–50
　career of, 142
　counterinsurgency under, 143, 146
　divorce of, viii, 146
　economic policies of, 140–45
　election to presidency, 142, 147
　on family planning, 146, 148
　feminists' relationship with, 6, 14, 147–48,
　　159
　food aid under, 144, 149–50
　gender politics of, 141, 144–50, 159
　leadership style of, 140, 142–44, 159
　masculine image of, viii, 142–43
　vs. Morales, 140–41, 159, 226
　as neopopulist, 117, 140
　popularity of, 144
　in revival of populism, vii
　rise to power, 141, 142
　self-coup by, 143, 144, 146
　structural adjustment plan of, 141, 142, 144,
　　146
　trial of, 150
　women politicians under, viii, xi, 141, 147,
　　150
　women voting for, 15, 147
　at World Conference on Women (1995),
　　145–46, 148
Fujimori, Keiko, 150
fundraising, for Velasco Ibarra, by women, 59

Gaitán, Jorge, 3, 4, 12, 13
Galimberti, Rodolfo, 126 n. 4
Galindo, Maria, 157
Gandhi, Indira, xii
García, Alan, vii
García, María del Rufugio, 34
García, Marta, 83, 85, 86–87

Garcia-Linera, Alvaro, 157
Garré, Nilda, 132, 133
Garretón, Manuel A., 182
gas. *See* natural gas
Gender, Generations, and Family, Subministry
　of (Bolivia), 155
gender complementarity, Bolivian beliefs
　about, 154–55, 158, 159
gendered nature of populism, viii–ix
　attention in scholarship to, viii–ix, 2
　contradictions in, viii–xi
gender perspectives, deployed in Venezuela,
　191, 191 n. 15, 197
gender roles
　in classical populism, 4
　in Mexican domestic labor, 35
　in Venezuelan community organizing,
　　213–14, 217
gender studies, in populism, viii–ix
General Motors do Brasil, 103
Gimnasio Educacional Femenino, 57
Gloriosa, La (1944), 50, 54
Gomes, Eduardo, 118, 120
Gott, Richard, 211
GOU. *See* Grupo de Oficiales Unidos
Goulart, João "Jango," 105, 110, 114, 115, 119
Gould, Jeffrey L., 69
government services. *See* social services
governors, Brazilian, 94
Gran Unidad Nicaragua Triunfa coalition, 171,
　172, 173–74
Great Britain. *See* Britain
Green Party (Brazil), 117
Grupo de Oficiales Unidos (GOU, Argentina),
　122
Guaicaipuro, 187
Guardia de Hierro (Argentina), 132
Guayaquil (Ecuador), 52
Guerrero, Ana, 210
guerrilla movements. *See also specific movements*
　defeat of, 5
　in response to classical populism, 4
Guevara Moreno, Carlos, 51, 51 n. 7
Gutierrez, Lucio, 47

Haya de la Torre, Victor Raúl
　in classical populism, rise of, 3
　masculine image of, 11, 12, 30 n. 6
　paternalism of, 12
health care
　by Brazilian auto industry, 103
　by Venezuelan *misiones,* 190, 198
　women's, in Peru, 146

Helena, Heloísa, 20
  career of, 111, 116–17, 223
  feminist goals of, 121
  as radical populist, 116–17
  women followers of, 120
heretical memories
  definition of, 72
  of Somocista women, 72–73, 83–87
Herrera Campins, Luis, 215
Higuchi, Susana, 146
Hilario, Emma, 150 n. 8
Hinojosa, Claudia, 42
Holston, James, 105 n. 5
home ownership, Brazilian, 104
hope, in Ecuadorian politics, 54
households, female-headed, in Nicaragua,
  70–71
housewives
  Argentine, 127–29
  Brazilian, 93, 97, 104, 105, 106
hunger strikes
  in Bolivia, 154
  in Venezuela, 198

Ibarra, Delia, 53
IBOPE. See Instituto Brasileiro de Opinião
  Pública e Estadística
ideological drift, 116
ideological training, in Bolivarian revolution,
  180, 181
illiteracy, in Ecuador, 48, 49, 54, 63
IMF. See International Monetary Fund
import-substitution industrialization (ISI), 5, 6
Inamujer, 190–92
  and Chávez's appeal to women, 195
  establishment of, 204–5
  feminism in, 193, 225
  gender perspectives in, 191, 191 n. 15
  goals of, 190, 193
  ideological training in, 180, 181
  mass membership in, lack of, 205
  mobilization of women in, 180, 190–92
  number of groups and members in, 190–91
Independent Movement for an Authentic
  Republic (MIRA), 60
independent women's movements
  Nicaraguan, 168, 175
  Venezuelan, 204–5
Indigenous Affairs, Ministry of (Bolivia), 155
indigenous nationalism, 157
indigenous population
  Bolivian, 150–59
  Ecuadorian, 48

industrial education, in Brazil, 102
industrialization
  in classical populism, 3
  in neopopulism, 5
industrial sector, Brazilian
  under Kubitschek, 101–5
  under Vargas, 93–97
inequality, clientelism as response to, 13
INNFA. See Instituto Nacional del Niño y la
  Familia
Instituto Brasileiro de Opinião Pública e
  Estadística (IBOPE), 111, 112, 118, 118 n. 4,
  120
Instituto Nacional del Niño y la Familia
  (INNFA), 59, 59 n. 14
interest representation, programmatic vs. populist, ix–xi
International Monetary Fund (IMF), 183, 208
International Women's Day
  2006 Bolivian celebration of, 154, 155
  1973 Mexican celebration of, 25
  Venezuelan celebrations of, 194–95
International Women's Year (IWY) conference
  (1975), 27, 39–43
Iron Guard (Argentina), 132
ISI. See import-substitution industrialization
IWY. See International Women's Year

James, Daniel, 100 n. 3
Jelin, Elizabeth, 213
Jesus Christ
  Chávez's use of imagery of, 203, 211
  in masculine images of leaders, 10–11, 222
Jews, 26
Jiménez, Crisóbal, 10
Joint United States–Brazil Technical Commis-
  sion, 99
jokes, vulgar, 10
Joseph, Gilbert, 30 n. 4
JPN. See Juventud Patriótico Nicaragüense
JTP. See Juventud Trabajadora Peronista
Juárez, Benito, 26
Júarez, Marta, 165
judiciary
  Nicaraguan, 170
  Peruvian, 143
Junta de Gobierno de Reconstrucción
  Nacional (Nicaragua), 162–63
JUP. See Juventud Universitaria Peronista
Justice Liberation Front (FREJULI), 125
Justice Ministry (Bolivia), 155, 156
Justicialista movement, 124, 124 n. 2
Juventud Patriótico Nicaragüense (JPN), 162

Juventud Peronista (JP), 124
Juventud Trabajadora Peronista (JTP), 124
Juventud Universitaria Peronista (JUP), 124

Kaiser Industries, 102
Kampwirth, Karen, 81–82
Kennedy, Duncan, 166 n. 2
Kirchner, Néstor, xii
Knight, Alan, 29
Kubitschek, Juscelino (JK), 19–20, 91–106
  auto industry under, 92, 101–6
  career of, 100–101
  characteristics of populism of, 100–106
  on citizenship rights, 91, 92
  developmentalist program of, 92, 100–105
  election to presidency, 100
  expansion of popular participation under, 92
  failure of program of, 93
  followers' relationship with, 223
  and housewives, 93, 104, 105, 106
  labor policies of, 101–6
  legacy of, 105–6
  on limitations of populism, 101, 105
  on the poor, 100, 101
  vs. Vargas, 92, 100–101, 103, 106, 106 n. 7
  after Vargas's suicide, 115

labor
  domestic (See domestic labor)
  sexual division of: in Argentina, 137; in
    Brazilian auto industry, 102–3
Labor, Industry, and Commerce, Ministry of
  (Brazil), 93, 94, 97
labor market
  Mexican, incorporation of women into,
    41, 43
  reforms of 1990s in, vii
Labor Party (PTB, Brazil), 99, 100, 113, 114–15,
  121
labor policies, Brazilian
  of Kubitschek, 101–6
  of Vargas, 93–100, 101
labor strikes, Brazilian, 94, 95, 101
labor unions
  Brazilian, 94, 97, 101
  in neoliberalism, 5
Lacayo, Antonio, 73
Lacerda, Carlos
  career of, 111
  ideological drift by, 116
  papers of, 112
  women followers of, 111, 119, 120
Laclau, Ernesto, 31, 34, 140–41, 184, 186

Lamarckian eugenics, 101
land reform, women followers in, 16–17
landslides, in Venezuela, 207
Lastiri, Raúl, 126 n. 3
Latin American Studies Association, ix
Lazarte, Silvia, 156
leaders, populist. See also specific leaders
  accountability problems with, ix–x
  in definition of populism, 2
  emotions of, 2 n. 1, 9, 18
  on feminine vs. feminist issues, xi
  feminists' relationships with, 6, 13–14, 225
  followers' relationships with, 223–24
  issues linked with, ix
  manipulation by, 16, 18, 29–30
  masculinity of (See masculine images of
    leaders)
  motivations of, 29–30
  in neoliberalism crisis, 5
  the people's relationship with, 2, 29, 47
  personalistic nature of, ix–x, 2, 6
  physical appearance of, 119, 120
  women as, lack of, xii, 222–23
Leaman, David, 29
Lebanese Ecuadorians, 53
left-wing activists, classical populism opposed
  by, 4–5
León (Nicaragua), 76
León, Guadalupe, 60, 61
León, María, 180–81, 186, 191, 195, 196
lesbian rights, in Mexico, 41–42
Lesbos, 41
Liberal Constitutionalist Party (PLC,
  Nicaragua), 74, 77, 169
liberalism
  in Ecuador, Catholicism and, 49, 49 n. 3, 58
  in Nicaragua, masculinization of, 73, 87–88
Liberal Party (Ecuador), 48, 50
Liberal Party (Nicaragua). See also Nationalist
  Liberal Party; Somocista women
  grassroots women leaders in, 77–79
  market women in, 81–83
  masculinization of, 73, 87–88
  new vs. old women's movement in, 82–83, 87
  non-Somocistas in, 73, 82
  periods of domination by, 68
  return to power in 1996, 73–74, 81
  rise of, 68
  versions of Somocismo history in, 72, 83–87
  on women's roles, 68
life expectancies, for Nicaraguan women, 81
Ligas Femeniles de Lucha Social, 34. See also
  women's leagues

Lind, Amy, 205
Lins de Barros, João Alberto, 94–95, 96
literacy
  in Brazil, 102
  in Ecuador, 48, 49, 54, 63
López, Juana, 150 n. 8
López, Maribel, 79–81, 83
López Obrador, Andrés Manuel, 28
López Portillo, José, 28
love, leaders' expression of, 2 n. 1, 9
lower classes, Ecuadorian, in concepts of the
  people, 48–49
Loyalty Day, 11
Lugo, Fernando, 6
Luisa Amanda Espinosa Association of
  Nicaraguan Women (AMNLAE), 164
Lula da Silva, Luís Inácio
  on auto industry, 104–5
  election to presidency, 106, 117
  political party of, 116
Luna, Lola, 4, 13, 205–6
Lutz, Bertha, 113–14

Machado, Hermelinda, 207
machismo, Morales on, 154
Madero, Francisco, 28
Madres de Barrio, Misión, 190, 193
Madrid, Raul, 153
Magín, 205
majoritarian nature of populism, x, xi
Mal-Amadas, 111, 119, 119 n. 5
malnutrition, in Brazil, 97
Maltez de Callejas, Mary Coco, 67
Managua (Nicaragua), 1972 earthquake in, 69
Manichean discourse, 13, 47, 50, 54
Marines, U.S., Nicaragua occupied by, 68
market reforms of 1990s, vii
market women, 73, 81–83
marriage, in Aymara worldview, 154–55
MAS. See Movimiento al Socialismo
masculine images of leaders, viii, xi, 9–12. See
  also specific leaders
  exceptions to, 30 n. 6
  popular vs. traditional, 53, 55, 62
  religion in, 10–11, 222–23
  types of, 10–12, 52–53
  vulgarity in, 10, 62
masculinity
  Ecuadorian ideal of, 52–56
  Mexican conceptions of, 27, 32–33, 40–44
masculinization, of Nicaraguan Liberalism, 73,
  87–88
masses, the. See people, the

mass organizations
  of Montoneros, 124–25, 126
  women's movements as, 204–5
mass politics, Ecuadorian, 54
maternalist ideology
  in classical vs. contemporary populism, 206
  and women's suffrage, 4
May revolution (1944). See Gloriosa, La
MBR-200. See Movimiento Bolivariano
  Revolucionario 200
MDB. See Brazilian Democratic Movement
media coverage
  of Brazilian auto industry, 104
  of Nicaraguan 2006 presidential election,
    172, 173–74
memories
  heretical vs. distributional: of Peronism, 72;
    of Somocista women, 72–73, 83–87
  public vs. private, 86
Méndez, Juana, 170
Mendoza, Freddy, 212, 216
Mendoza, Osvaldo, 213–14
Menem, Carlos
  accountability problems with, x
  divorce of, viii
  masculine image of, viii, xi
  as neopopulist, 117
  in revival of populism, vii
  women politicians promoted by, viii, xi
men's associations, Velasco Ibarra's lack of
  membership in, 53
Mény, Yves, 63
Mercado Oriental, 81
mestiza classes, Ecuadorian, Velasco Ibarra on,
  48
mestiza women, Venezuelan, educational programs for, 210
Mexican Communist Party, 26, 37, 37 n. 18
Mexican Revolution (1910), 28
Mexico, 18–19, 25–44. See also specific leaders
  citizenship rights for women in, 32–34
  classical populism in, rise of, 3, 27–28
  constitution of, 26–27, 40
  diversity of populism in, 28
  equal rights for women in, 26–27, 26 n. 3, 40
  exceptionalism of, 27–31
  femininity in, conceptions of, 27, 32–33, 35–
    36, 40–44
  feminists of, 39–40, 41
  International Women's Year conference in,
    27, 39–43
  land reform in, 16–17
  lesbian rights in, 41–42

Mexico (*continued*)
  nationalism in, 25–26
  nationalization of petroleum in, 26
  neopopulism in, rise of, 27–28
  political parties of, 32 n. 9, 33–34
  presidential election of 1946 in, 38
  repression in, postrevolutionary, 28, 39–40,
    39 n. 25
  U.S. relations with, 26
  waves of populism in, 25 n. 2, 27–28
  women's suffrage in, xi, 4, 26, 32, 38
middle class
  Argentine, and Peronism, 123
  Brazilian, creation of, 92, 100–106
  Nicaraguan, Somocista women in, 70–71,
    83
  Peruvian, feminists in, 147
  Venezuelan, women activists in, 206–7
migration, of Brazilian workers, 102, 104
military, in masculine images of leaders, 10
military dictatorships, as response to classical
  populism, 5
Minas Gerais (Brazil), 100, 101
MIP. *See* Movimiento de Inquilinos
  Peronistas
MIRA. *See* Movimiento Independiente para
  una República Auténtica
misiones, Venezuelan, 180, 186–92
  in Bolivarian revolution, 180, 181
  Chávez's role in, 189
  educational, 188–90, 209–10
  feminism in, 193
  impact of, 187–88, 197–98
  language of motherhood in, 194 n. 20
  list of, 187 n. 9
  mobilization through, 187, 189–90, 196
  number of, 187
  origins of names of, 187
  services of, 186–87
  women participants in, 187, 187 n. 10, 189–90,
    197
mobilization, political
  in Argentina, of Peronist women, 127–30
  in classical populism, rise of, 3
  in definition of populism, 2
  in Ecuador, by women's committees, 49,
    58–59, 62
  in Mexico, through women's leagues, 37–38,
    44
  in Nicaragua, through women's leagues,
    69–70
  state-led *vs.* independent, 205
  urban *vs.* rural, 3, 3 n. 4, 28

  in Venezuela: through Inamujer and
    Banmujer, 180, 190–92; through *misiones,*
    187, 189–90, 196
  of women voters, 15–18
modernism, in Brasília, 105, 105 n. 5
modernity, women's rights as marker of,
  33, 43
Molina, Violeta, 56
Molyneux, Maxine, 31–32, 164
Monasterios, Karin, 157
Montesinos, Vladimiro, 143
Montoneros, 20, 122–39
  feminists and, 131–32
  goals of, 123
  identity of, as Peronists, 123
  ideology of, 123–24
  images of women promoted by, 123
  mass organizations associated with, 124–25,
    126
  origins of, 123
  on Perón (Eva), 9, 125
  on political identity of women, 130
  political participation by, 125, 126
  underground status, 126, 127 n. 4
  women's branch of (*See* Agrupación Evita)
Morales, Evo, 20, 150–59
  children of, 155
  clothing of, 152
  in Congress, 151
  diversity of followers of, 151
  election to presidency, 151
  as ethnopopulist, 140
  feminists' relationship with, 157–58, 159
  vs. Fujimori, 140–41, 159, 226
  gender politics of, 141, 154–58, 159
  leadership style of, 140, 152–54, 159
  masculine image of, 152, 155
  neoliberalism rejected by, 6
  redistribution plans of, 153
  in revival of populism, vii
  rise to power, 141, 150–51, 152–53
  women politicians under, xi, 141, 156, 158
Morales Carazo, Jaime, 171, 171 n. 3
moral guardians, Velasco Ibarra on women as,
  56, 57–58, 62
Moscoso, Mireya, 223 n. 1
Moser, Caroline, 215
mothers
  Argentine, 128–29, 131, 136–37
  Brazilian, 97, 104
  Nicaraguan, 70, 70 n. 5, 166
  Venezuelan, 193–96, 197
Mothers of the Plaza de Mayo, 205

Movimiento al Socialismo (MAS, Bolivia)
  chachawarmi in, 155
  on constitution, 151–52
  diversity of followers of, 151
  establishment of, 151
  feminists' relationship with, 157–58
  indigenous identity of, 151, 152
  social movements within, 153, 154, 157–58
  women elected from, 156, 158
Movimiento Bolivariano Revolucionario 200
  (MBR-200), 209
Movimiento de Inquilinos Peronistas (MIP),
  124
Movimiento de Liberación Femenina, 132
Movimiento de Renovación Sandinista (MRS),
  166, 168, 174
Movimiento de Villeros Peronistas (MVP), 124
Movimiento Independiente para una
  República Auténtica (MIRA), 60
Movimiento Quinta Republica (MVR), 209
Moyano, Maria-Elena, 150, 150 n. 8
Moyano, Marta, 150
MRS. See Movimiento de Renovación
  Sandinista
MRTA. See Tupac Amaru Revolutionary
  Movement
Múgica, Francisco, 37
Mujeres Creadno, 157
Mujeres por la Dignidad y la Vida, 205
Mundo Peronista (magazine), 128
Murillo, Rosario
  on abortion, 173–74
  children of, 166, 166 n. 2, 167
  feminine image of, 163, 176
  political role of, 166, 173, 176
  popular response to, 176 n. 6
  on sexual abuse accusations, 169
MVP. See Movimiento de Villeros Peronistas
MVR. See Movimiento Quinta Republica

narratives, heretical vs. distributional, 72
Narváez, Zoilamérica, 169–70
National Assembly, Ecuadorian, 49
National Assembly, Nicaraguan, 169
National Assembly, Venezuelan, 192, 198
National Council of Women, 60
National Federation of Peasant Women "Bar-
  tolina Sisa," 158
National Fund for Infant Attention
  (FONAIN), 208
National Guard, Nicaraguan, 68
National Institute of Children and the Family
  (INNFA), 59, 59 n. 14

National Institute of Women. See Inamujer
nationalism
  Brazilian, 99
  indigenous, 157
  Mexican, 25–26
Nationalist Liberal Party (PLN, Nicaragua), 67.
  See also Ala Femenina del Partido Liberal
  Nacionalista
nationalization
  of Bolivian gas and petroleum, 153
  of Mexican petroleum, 26
  in Venezuela, 198
national liberation movement, Argentine, 123,
  132, 133, 135
National Reconstruction Governing Council.
  See Junta de Gobierno de Reconstrucción
  Nacional
National Revolutionary Party (Mexico). See
  Partido Nacional Revolucionario
National Steel Company (CSN, Brazil), 99
National Union of Workers (UNT, Venezuela),
  209
National Women's Council (CONAMU,
  Venezuela), 205
National Women's Union (Venezuela), 206
natural gas, in Bolivia, 151, 153, 154
Navarro, Marysa, 8
neoliberalism
  of Bucaram, 52, 55 n. 10
  leaders rejecting, 6
  in neopopulism, 5, 6, 47, 117–18
neoliberal populism
  characteristics of, vii
  vs. classical populism, vii, 5, 47
  economic policies of, vii, 5, 47
  masculine images of leaders in, viii
  rise of, vii
  women in power in, viii, xi
neo-neopopulism, 7
neopopulism. See also specific countries and
  leaders
  vs. Chavista populism, 182, 182 n. 5, 204
  decline of, 6
  definition of, 116–17
  economic policies of, 5, 6, 47, 117–18
  financial resources of, 5, 6
  gender policies of, 5–6
  rise of, 5, 27
  on second-wave feminism, 5–6
  as second wave of populism, 3, 4–6
  third wave of populism after, 7
  variants of (See neoliberal populism; radical
  populism)

neopopulism (*continued*)
  women's labor appropriated under, 206, 215
  women's rights extended in, xi
neo-Somocista women
  definition of, 68
  experiences of, 73, 79–83
  gaps in historical knowledge of, 73, 80–81,
    86, 88
  social class of, 68, 68 n. 2
New Left, sexism in, 39
New Right, in Nicaragua, 87
NGOs
  in Bolivia, feminists and, 157, 158
  in Peru, Fujimori's relationship with, 147,
    148, 149
  in Venezuela, and women's organizations, 208
Nicaragua, 19–21, 67–89, 162–77. *See also*
    specific leaders
  abortion in, 87, 165–66, 173–75, 177, 177 n. 7,
    225
  classical populism in, rise of, 3
  clientelism in, 70–73
  constitution of, 74, 165
  corruption in, 69
  feminists of (*See* Nicaraguan feminists)
  Liberal *vs.* Conservative parties in, 68
  life expectancies in, 81
  masculinization of Liberalism in, 73, 87–88
  mass women's organizations in, 204, 205
  middle class in, 70–71, 83
  National Assembly of, 169
  overview of political history of, 68–72
  presidential elections in: 1984, 163, 167; 1990,
    67, 163, 167, 168, 174; 1996, 73–74, 163, 168;
    2001, 163; 2006, 68, 74, 167, 170–75, 175 n. 4
  social services expanded in, 70
  U.S. involvement in politics of, 68, 87–88
  U.S. occupation of, 68
  women presidents of, 223 n. 1
  women's suffrage in, 70
Nicaraguan feminists, 163–77
  abortion and, 174–75, 225
  antifeminist movement against, 175
  autonomous, rise of, 168, 175
  on emancipation of women, 166
  in FSLN, 168, 174
  in MRS, 168, 174
  Ortega's relationship with, 14, 163, 164, 170, 177
  after 1990 presidential election, 168, 174
  second wave of, 6, 177
  on sexual abuse accusations against Ortega,
    169–70, 174
  in Somocismo, 70, 88

Nicaraguan Patriotic Youth (JPN), 162
Noguera Carazo, Lucrecia, 83–84
nonelites. *See* people, the
nongovernmental agencies. *See* NGOs
Novedades (newspaper), 83–84
Nugent, Daniel, 30 n. 4
Núñez de Saballos, Olga, 67
nurturance, in Venezuelan women activists,
    212

Obando y Bravo, Miguel, 173
Oikabeth, 41
oil industry. *See* petroleum industry
Ojala, Eric, 43
Ojeda Paullada, Pedro, 40–41
opinion polls, in Brazil, 111, 118, 120
Ortega, Daniel, 20–21, 162–77
  on abortion, 165, 166, 175 n. 4, 177
  Alemán's pact with, 74, 87, 168–71
  Catholicism of, 171–75
  as *caudillo*, 163
  children of, 166, 166 n. 2, 167
  1984 election to presidency, 163, 167
  2006 election to presidency, 74, 167, 170–75,
    175 n. 4
  electoral defeat of, 73, 163, 167, 168
  on emancipation of women, 164, 174
  feminists' relationship with, 14, 163, 164, 170,
    177, 225
  on governing from below, 168
  immunity for, 169, 170
  imprisonment of, 162
  masculine image of, 163, 167, 176
  neoliberalism rejected by, 6
  in opposition to Somocismo, 162
  on the other, 163
  between presidential terms, 168–71
  as radical populist, 176
  rise to power, 7, 162–63
  sexual abuse accusations against, 169–70,
    174
  and Somocista women, 82
  in third wave of populism, 7
  transition from revolutionary *vs.* populist,
    163–64, 167–68, 171–73, 176
  wife of, 163, 166–67, 169, 173–74, 176
  on women combatants, 164–65
Ortiz Bilbao, Luis Alfonso, 59
Ostiguy, Pierre, viii
other, the. *See also* enemy, the
  in Chávez's discourse, 185
  in Ecuadorian politics, 47, 54
  in Nicaraguan politics, 163

Palermo, Silvana, 131
Panama
    classical populism in, rise of, 3
    women presidents of, 223 n. 1
Panizza, Francisco, 30, 63
Parral, Corina, 51, 53, 59–60
Partido de la Revolución Mexicana (PRM), 32
    n. 9, 37
Partido dos Trabalhadores (PT, Brazil), 116, 117,
    121
Partido Liberal Constitucionalista (PLC,
    Nicaragua), 74, 77, 169
Partido Liberal Nacionalista (PLN). See
    Nationalist Liberal Party
Partido Nacional Revolucionario (PNR,
    Mexico), 32, 32 n. 9, 33–34
Partido Peronista Femenino. See Feminine
    Peronist Party
Partido Revolucionario Institucionalizado
    (PRI, Mexico), 32 n. 9
Partido Roldosista Ecuatoriano (PRE), 51–52, 56
Partido Social Democrático (PSD, Brazil), 99,
    115, 121
Partido Socialismo e Libertade (PSOL, Brazil),
    117
Partido Traballhista Brasileiro (PTB), 99, 100,
    113, 114–15, 121
passion in populism, 1, 1 n. 1, 9, 18
paternalism. See also father figures
    in definition of populism, 2
    democracy threatened by, 12–13
    in masculine images of leaders, 12
    toward Mexican women's leagues, 36–37
patriarchy, in Mexico, 36
patronage politics, in classical populism vs.
    neopopulism, 6
Patronato del Niño, 59 n. 14
Pazos, Julio, 53
people, the
    Chávez's relationship with, 186, 188, 189
    in definitions of populism, 2, 29, 141
    demands of (See demands)
    vs. the enemy, 141, 159
    leaders' emotions regarding, 2 n. 1, 9
    leaders' relationship with, 2, 29, 47
    in majoritarian movements, x
    manipulation of, 29–30
    vs. the other, 47, 54, 163
    Peronist women as part of, 128
    Vargas's vs. Kubitschek's understanding of,
        100
    Velasco Ibarra's vs. Bucaram's understand-
        ing of, 48–49

Pérez, Carlos Andrés, 183
Pérez, Edgar "El Gordo," 212–13
Pérez Jimenez, Marcos, 206, 207–8, 215
Perón, Eva
    in Feminine Peronist Party, 8, 125, 134–36
    on feminists, 1, 130–31, 224
    on Juan Perón, 1, 9
    in Juan Perón's career, 1, 8–9
    mobilization of women by, 127
    Montoneros on, 9, 125
    political power of, xii, 8–9, 141 n. 3
    religious imagery and, 9, 222–23
    in rise of classical populism, 3
    women followers of, 15–16
    and women's suffrage, xi, 4, 14, 127
    on working women, 128–29
Perón, Isabel, 223 n. 1
Perón, Juan, 20, 122–39. See also Peronism
    vs. Cárdenas, 28
    1955 coup against, 123
    course of populism after, vii
    death of, 126
    Economic Emergency Plan of, 127
    election to presidency, 126 n. 3
    emergence of, 122
    Eva Perón's role in career of, 1, 8–9
    in exile, 123, 133
    factions competing for endorsement of, 126,
        126 n. 4
    feminists' relationship with, 13–14
    Five-Year Plans of, 127
    ideological drift by, 116
    masculine image of, 11, 12
    mobilization of women by, 127
    paternalism of, 12
    political successors to, vii
    release from prison, 11, 17
    return to Argentina (1973), 133
    in rise of classical populism, 3
    and women's suffrage, xi, 4, 13–14, 127
    women voting for, 15
Peronism, 122–39
    of Agrupación Evita, 123–26
    citizenship redefined in, 122
    current power of, 15
    Eva Perón's role in, 8–9
    Feminine Branch of (See Feminine Peronist
        Party)
    feminists opposed by, 130–33
    government ban on, 123
    images of women promoted by, 123
    influence on Argentine history, 122
    memories of, 72

Peronism (*continued*)
  mobilization of women in, 127, 129–30
  multiple meanings of, 72
  political identity of women in, 127–30, 137
  religious imagery in, 11
  Right *vs.* Left in struggle for control of, 125,
    126, 126 n. 4
  vs. Somocismo, 72
  women as missionaries of, 15–16
  women's rights in, expansion of, 4
  young people in, 123
Peronist Shantytown Dwellers' Movement
  (MVP), 124
Peronist Tenants' Movement (MIP), 124
Peronist University Youth (JUP), 124
Peronist Worker Youth (JTP), 124
Peronist Youth (JP), 124
personalistic nature of populist leadership, ix–x
  in definition of populism, 2
  vs. patronage politics, 6
Peru, 20, 140–50. *See also specific leaders*
  classical populism, rise of, 3
  Congress of, 143, 144, 147, 150
  constitution of, 143, 144, 147
  crisis caused by García in, vii
  family planning in, 146, 148
  food aid in, 144, 149–50
  neopopulism in, 117, 140
  presidential elections in: 1990, 142; 1995, 147
  structural adjustment plan in, 141, 142, 144,
    146
  women politicians in, viii, xi, 141, 147, 150
Petrobras, 99
petroleum industry
  Bolivian, 151, 153
  Mexican, 26
  Venezuelan, 183–84, 197
physical appearance of leaders, 119, 120
pink populism, 7
plagiarism, 49, 63 n. 20
PLC. *See* Partido Liberal Constitucionalista
PLN. *See* Nationalist Liberal Party
Plotkin, Mariano Ben, 15
PNR. *See* Partido Nacional Revolucionario
PODEMOS, 156
Political Directorate of Ecuadorian Women
  (CPME), 61, 61 n. 16
political mobilization. *See* mobilization
political participation. *See* voter(s)
political parties, guerrilla movements turned
  into, 5. *See also specific parties*
political rights. *See* citizenship rights; equal
  rights; suffrage; women's rights

politicians, women. *See also specific politicians*
  Argentine, viii, xi, 223 n. 1
  Bolivian, xi, 141, 155, 156, 158
  Brazilian, 110, 111, 114–17, 120–21, 223
  Colombian, xi
  Ecuadorian, 59–60, 62, 62 n. 18
  limited role of, xii
  at lower *vs.* higher levels of government, 110,
    223
  in neoliberal populism, viii, xi
  Peruvian, viii, xi, 141, 147, 150
  religious imagery and, 222–23
  scarcity of, xii, 110, 141, 141 n. 3, 222–23
polls, in Brazil, 111, 118, 120
poor, the
  Bolivian: political participation by, 153; rise
    in number of, 151
  Brazilian: Kubitschek's plans for, 100, 101;
    Vargas's appeal to, 92, 96
  in democracy, 13
  Ecuadorian, Bucaram's concern for, 55
  leaders' manipulation of, 29
  Venezuelan: *misiones'* programs for, 187–88;
    rise in number of, 182, 188, 188 n. 12, 208;
    uprisings by, 183; women among, 193
Popular Action Service Center (CESAP), 205
Popular Front (Mexico), 26, 34
Popular Memory Group, 86
Population Conference, UN (1974), 40 n. 28
Population Fund, UN, 191
population policies
  in Argentina, 128
  at International Women's Year conference, 41
  in Mexico, 40, 41
  UN conference on, 40 n. 28
populism. *See also specific types*
  definitions of, 2, 140–41, 204
  difficulty with definitions of, viii, 28–31
  interest representation in, ix–xi
  international nature of, 226–27
  issues in, role of, ix, xi
  majoritarian nature of, x, xi
  masculinity in, viii, xi
  Mexican exceptionalism in history of, 27–31
  personalistic nature of, ix–x, 2, 6
  as political style *vs.* strategy, 29, 30–31
  predictions of end of, vii, viii, 4
  revival of (1990s), vii–viii
  scholarship on: attention to gender aspects
    in, viii–ix, 2; conceptual controversies in,
    viii; interdisciplinary, ix, xii; proliferation
    of, viii
  waves of, 3–8, 226

populist tension, 43–44, 222
Portes Gil, Emilio, 33
Portillo de Tamayo, Martha, 25
poverty. *See* poor, the
PPF. *See* Feminine Peronist Party
PRE. *See* Partido Roldosista Ecuatoriano
president(s), women, scarcity of, 223, 223 n. 1.
   See also leaders
presidential elections. *See specific countries*
Presidential Women's Advisory Commission
   (COFEAPRE), 205
press coverage. *See* media coverage
Prestes, Luis Carlos, 111
PRI. *See* Partido Revolucionario
   Institucionalizado
privatization, in Ecuador, 52
PRM. *See* Partido de la Revolución Mexicana
proceso movement, 209
Programa Nacional de Ayuda Alimentaria
   (PRONAA), 149–50
programmatic interest representation, ix–xi
PROMUDEH (Peru), 146, 148
PRONAA. *See* Programa Nacional de Ayuda
   Alimentaria
prostitution, in Nicaragua, 88
protectionism, in revival of populism, vii
Protestantism
   in masculine images of leaders, 10
   rise of, 11
PSD. *See* Partido Social Democrático
PSOL. *See* Partido Socialismo e Libertade
PSUV. *See* United Socialist Party of Venezuela
PT. *See* Workers' Party
PTB. *See* Partido Traballhista Brasileiro
public-private divide, 30, 129
public schools, Ecuadorian, 57, 57 n. 12
puntos de encuentro, 181, 190–91, 205

Quadros, Jânio, 105, 114–15, 119
quebra-quebras, 101

radical populism, 225–26
   of Chávez, 7, 117 n. 3, 180
   financial resources of, 7
   of Helena, 116–17
   of Ortega, 176
   revival of, vii
   as third wave of populism, 7–8
   use of term, 7
Rakowski, Cathy, 7
Ramírez, Sergio, 167
rationing, by FSLN, 82
red de usuarias, 192

redemption, in masculine images of leaders,
   11–12
redistribution
   Chávez's programs for, 183, 188, 198
   in definition of populism, 2
   Morales' plans for, 153
   Vargas' programs for, 93
Reed, Jean-Pierre, 2 n. 1
religion. *See also* Catholicism; Protestantism
   Chávez's use of imagery of, 203, 211–12
   in masculine images of leaders, 10–11, 222–23
repression, in postrevolutionary Mexico, 28,
   39–40, 39 n. 25
reproductive health, in Peru, Fujimori's policies on, 146
reproductive rights, in Bolivia, 156
Republican Party of Rio Grande do Sul, 93
residential design, in Brasília, 100, 105
revolution, and populism, compatibility of
   concepts, 7, 225
revolutionary motherhood, in Venezuela,
   194–96, 197, 206
revolutionary populism, 225–26. *See also*
   radical populism
   Chavista populism as, 204
   problems with term, 7
   as third wave of populism, 7
Revolutionary Tendency (Argentina), 125, 126,
   132
Revuelta (magazine), 41
Ribas, Misión, 189, 190, 209–10
Rice, Condoleezza, 10, 10 n. 6
right-wing activists, classical populism
   opposed by, 4–5
riots, of 1989 in Venezuela, 207–8
road building, in Brazil, 102
Roberts, Kenneth M., 2, 153, 204
Robinson, Misión, 189
Robleto, Eugenia, 83, 85
Rodríguez, Alí, 10
Rodríguez, Antonia, 73, 74–77
Rodríguez, Casimira, 156
Rodríguez, Susana, 212
Roldós, Jaime, 47, 52, 60
Rouquie, Alan, 126
rural areas, political mobilization in, 3, 3 n. 4, 28

Saad, Pedro, 50
Safa, Helen, 214
Salazar, Augusto, 59
Salinas de Gortari, Carlos, vii, 28
Samaniego Alvarez, Carlos, 59
Samaniego de Salazar, Victoria, 59

Sánchez, Homero, 118 n. 4
Sánchez Cerro, Luis, 3, 9, 11
Sanchez de Lozada, Gonzalo, 154
Sanchís, Norma, 128–29
Sandinista National Directorate
  Ortega in, 162–63
  women members of, 168
Sandinista National Liberation Front (FSLN)
  abortion ban under, 87, 174–75, 175 n. 4, 177
  electoral defeat of, 67, 168, 174
  on emancipation of women, 164, 165–66,
    174, 175
  establishment of, 162
  feminists in, 168, 174
  on governing from below, 168
  MRS split from, 168, 174
  Ortega recruited by, 162
  in pact with PLC, 74, 87, 169
  in presidential election of 2006, 68, 171–75
  rationing by, 82
  as response to classical populism, 4
  1979 revolution by, 69, 162
  rise to power, 67
  Somocista women on, 80, 81–82
  women combatants in, 164–65
Sandinista Renewal Movement. See
  Movimiento de Renovación Sandinista
Sandino, Augusto C., 75
Sanguinetti, Virginia, 132–33
Sanz, Susana, 137
São Paulo (Brazil)
  auto industry in, 102–5
  1932 civil war in, 95
  under Kubitschek, 102–4
  under Vargas, 94–97, 101
saviors, leaders as, 10–11, 54, 58
schools. See education; public schools
Scott, James, 105, 105 n. 5
Seligmann, Linda J., 70 n. 5
Senate, Brazilian
  Vargas in, 98 n. 2, 112
  women members of, 116–17
serial populism, 6
sexism
  in Bolivia, elimination of, 156–57
  in Ecuador, under Bucaram, 60
  in New Left movements, 39
sexual rights
  in Bolivia, 156
  at International Women's Year conference,
    41–42
  in Mexico, 41–42, 44
Shinawatra, Thaksin, 29

Shining Path
  deaths caused by, 142 n. 4, 150, 150 n. 8
  Fujimori's work against, 142, 144, 146, 150
  women attacked by, 149–50
Silva, Esther, 50
Silva, Marina, 117
SIN (Peruvian intelligence agency), 143
slavery, end of, in Brazil, 91
Soares de Oliveira Irmão, José, 104
social class. See also elites; middle class; work-
    ing class
  of neo-Somocista women, 68, 68 n. 2
  of Somocista women, 70–71, 83, 85
  Somoza Debayle (Anastasio) on, 84
Social Democratic Party (PSD, Brazil), 99, 115
socialism
  revival of populist version of, vii
  in Venezuela, 180, 181, 185, 198
Socialist Party (Argentina), 134–35
social justice
  in Brazil, Vargas on, 92
  in classical populism, activists' critique of,
    4–5
  in Nicaragua, Somocismo narratives of, 72,
    83–84
social mobility, in Brazil, 104–5, 106
social services
  in classical populism, expansion of, 3–4
  in Nicaragua, expansion of, 70
  women in provision of, 3–4, 70
Sola Lima, Vicente, 126 n. 3
Somocismo
  clientelism in, 70–71
  corruption in, 69
  decline of, 69
  feminists incorporated into, 70, 88
  multiple versions of history of, 72, 73, 83–87
  neo-Somocista interpretations of, 80–81, 88
  Ortega in opposition to, 162
  1979 overthrow of, 162
  populist characteristics of, 69
  rise of, 68
  U.S. influence on, 87–88
  violence in, 69
  women voters supporting, 70–71
Somocista women, 19, 67–89
  Ala leaders, 74–77, 83–85
  on Alemán, 78–79, 81, 82, 86
  as client-citizens, 70–71
  current status of, 87–88
  employment of, 70–72
  feminist, 70, 88
  on FSLN, 80, 81–82

grassroots leaders, 77–79
heretical *vs.* distributional memories of, 72–
    73, 83–87
market women, 73, 81–83
neo-Somocistas, 68, 73, 79–83, 86, 88
overview of history of, 68–72
social class of, 68, 68 n. 2, 70–71, 83, 85
Somoza Debayle, Anastasio
    on jobs for women, 71
    overthrow of, 7
    presidency of, 68
    on social justice, 84
    themes of campaign speeches by, 76
    on women's political participation, 86
Somoza Debayle, Luis, 68, 86
Somoza García, Anastasio
    assassination of, 68
    in classical populism, rise of, 3
    National Guard under, 68
    presidency of, 68
    rural mobilization by, 3 n. 4
    Sandino assassinated by, 75
    seizure of power, 68
    U.S. support for, 68
    and women's suffrage, 4
Sosa, Relinda, 149
soup kitchens. *See* food aid
South Asia, women populists in, xii
sports. *See* athleticism
state governors, Brazilian, 94
state interventionism, in revival of populism, vii
statism, in Chavista populism, 184
Stein, Steve, 12
Stephen, Lynn, 212
sterilization, surgical, in Peru, 146, 148
Street, Jorge, 95
strikes. *See* labor strikes
structural adjustment plans, Peruvian, 141, 142,
    144, 146
student movements
    Mexican, 39–40
    Venezuelan, 198
suffering, in masculine images of leaders, 11
suffrage, universal
    in Brazil, 91
    in Ecuador, 48, 54
suffrage, women's. *See also specific countries*
    Catholicism and, 32
    in classical populism, xi, 4
    leaders' advancement of, xi, 13–14
    social services expansion and, 4
sugar rationing, 82
Surel, Yves, 63

Tapia, Teodora, 158
Távora, Juarez, 120
taxes
    on Bolivian natural resources, 151, 153
    of Brazilian unions, 97
teachers
    Ecuadorian, 58
    Mexican, 35
Téllez, Dora María, 165–66
Tendencia Revolutionaria (Argentina), 125, 126,
    132
tension, populist, 43–44, 222
Terán de Terán Varea, Judith de, 58, 59
textile industry, Brazilian, 97, 101
Toto Gutiérrez, Mireya, 26 n. 3
trabalhismo, 115
"triple burden," 215
Tupac Amaru Revolutionary Movement
    (MRTA), 142, 143, 143 n. 4
24 de Mayo, 57, 57 n. 12, 58

UDN. *See* União Democrática Brasileira
UES. *See* Unión de Estudiantes Secundarios
UN. *See* United Nations
União Democrática Brasileira (UDN), 100
UNICEF, 208
Unicef, 191
Unifem, 191, 192 n. 18
union(s). *See* labor unions
Unión de Estudiantes Secundarios (UES), 124
Unión de Mujeres Revolucionarias, 38
Unión Feminista Argentina, 132
Unión Nacional de Mujeres Mexicanas
    (UNMM), 25, 26
Unión Nacional de Trabajadores (UNT,
    Venezuela), 209
Union of High School Students (UES), 124
United Nations (UN)
    Charter on the Economic Rights and Duties
        of States (1974), 26
    Echeverría's desire to serve as secretary-
        general of, 39
    International Women's Year conference
        (1975), 27, 39–43
    Population Conference (1974), 40 n. 28
    Population Fund of, 191
United Socialist Party of Venezuela (PSUV),
    183 n. 6
United States
    Bolivian coca farming opposed by, 150
    constitution of, 26 n. 3, 40
    Contra war funded by, 166, 167
    equal rights for women in, 26 n. 3, 40

United States (*continued*)
    Mexican relations with, 26
    in Nicaraguan politics, 68, 87–88
    Nicaragua occupied by, 68
    Peruvian food aid from, 149
UNMM. *See* Unión Nacional de Mujeres
    Mexicanas
UNO coalition, 168
UNT. *See* Unión Nacional de Trabajadores
urban areas
    female-headed households in, 70
    political mobilization in, 3, 3 n. 4
urbanization, in rise of classical populism, 3
urban land committees, Venezuelan, 181, 181 n.
    4, 210
Uribe, Alvaro, xi

Valdivieso, Magdalena, 206, 216
Vargas, Alzira, 112–14
    as campaign manager, 110–11, 113–14, 120
    as political secretary, 112–13
Vargas, Darcy, 112
Vargas, Getúlio, 19–20, 91–106
    vs. Cárdenas, 28
    characteristics of populism of, 92–100
    on citizenship rights, 91, 92, 96
    as classical populist, 3, 114
    1945 coup against, 93, 101, 105, 110
    course of populism after, vii
    developmentalist program of, 99
    as dictator, 93, 95, 96, 98, 114
    education of women under, 98
    1950 election to presidency, 98–99, 101, 110–
      11, 113–14
    expansion of popular participation under,
      91–92, 96, 106
    failure of program of, 93, 101, 105–6
    family of, 110–16
    as father figure, 92, 96, 100, 120
    and feminists, 98, 113–14
    vs. Kubitschek, 92, 100–101, 103, 106, 106
      n. 7
    labor policies of, 93–100, 101
    legacy of, 100, 100 n. 3
    masculine image of, viii, 12, 92
    motivations of followers of, 16
    papers of, 112
    party alliances of, 99
    paternalism of, 12
    and the poor, 92, 96
    as senator, 98 n. 2, 112
    on social justice, 92
    start of presidency (1930), 91, 93, 110

    suicide of, 93, 100, 105, 115
    and women's suffrage, xi, 4, 93, 96, 111,
      113
    women voting for, 15, 113–14, 118–19
    on working women, 92, 97–98, 106
Vargas, Ivete, 114–16
    career of, 111, 114–16
    in Congress, 114–16
    death of, 116
    feminist goals of, 121
    women followers of, 120
Vargas, Viriato, 114
Vargas Llosa, Mario, 142
Vázquez, Gabino, 35
Velasco, Alejandrino, 53, 59
Velasco Ibarra, José María, 19, 47–63
    appointment to presidency, 49, 50
    career overview, 49–51
    Catholicism of, 49, 49 n. 3, 57, 58
    in classical populism, 3, 47
    coalitions supporting, 51
    in Congress, 50
    coups against, 50, 55
    death of, 51
    as dictator, 49, 50–51, 63
    education of, 50
    on education of women, 56–58
    election to presidency, 48, 49, 50
    against electoral fraud, 50, 51, 54, 63
    on equal rights for women, 57, 59–60
    in exile, 51, 59
    family of, 53
    as father figure, 52
    fundraising for, 59
    legacy and reputation of, 55
    as liberal, 49, 49 n. 3, 58
    masculine image of, 11, 48, 52–56
    on moral role of women, 56, 57–58, 62
    party affiliation of, 49, 50, 51
    presidential terms of, 47 n. 1, 49
    understanding of the people, 48–49
    wives of, 50, 51, 53, 59–60
    women campaigning for, 58–59
    and women's suffrage, xi, 48, 56, 57
    women voters supporting, 48, 49, 56–60,
      61–62
    writing and speaking skills of, 55–56
Velasquismo
    consolidation of, 50
    end of, 51
    women followers of, 56, 58–59, 62
Venezuela, 21, 180–98, 202–18. *See also specific
    leaders*

activists in (*See* Venezuelan women activists)
Bolivarian revolution in, 117 n. 3, 180, 181, 185, 193
caracazo uprising in, 183, 207–8, 209
Constituent Assembly of, 181, 209
constitution of, 181, 181 n. 2, 193, 198, 209
coups of 1992 in, 183
education in, 188–90
feminism in, 192–93, 195–96, 207, 225
food aid in, 188, 189, 197, 210, 213–17
misiones in, 180, 181, 186–92
Morales supported by, 153
National Assembly of, 192, 198
neoliberalism in, 207–8
Ortega supported by, 176–77
political crises in, 198
poverty in, rise of, 182, 188, 188 n. 12, 208
presidential elections in, 181, 181 n. 2
presidential term limits in, 181 n. 2, 198
recentralization in, 184, 184 n. 7, 198
redistributive programs in, 183, 188, 198
revolutionary motherhood in, 194–96, 197, 206
revolutionary populism in, 204
socialism in, 180, 181, 185, 198
women's rights in, expansion of, 181, 191–94, 192 n. 18, 197, 209
Venezuelan women activists, 202–18
in Carretera Negra sector of La Vega, Caracas, 211–17
Chávez's influence on, 203, 209–13, 218
food aid programs of, 210, 213–17
history of, 206–8
international funding for, 208
as mass *vs.* independent movement, 204–5
vs. men activists, 212–13
rise of participation by, 203, 209–13
social class of, 206–7
veteran *vs.* new, 212
Virgin Mary, 9, 154, 222–23
Virtuoso, José, 185
Volkswagen, 102, 104
Volta Redonda (Brazil), 99
voluntarism, Venezuelan, 187, 189–90, 197
voter(s), women
Brazilian: populist, 110, 111, 118–21; for Vargas, 15, 113–14, 118–19
Ecuadorian: for Bucaram, 60–62; turnout of, 49; for Velasco Ibarra, 48, 56–60, 61–62
vs. men, 15, 118
Nicaraguan, for Somozos, 70–71
Peruvian, for Fujimori, 15, 147

physical appearance of candidates and, 119, 120
voting rights. *See* suffrage
vulgarity, in masculine images of leaders, 10, 62

wages, in Brazil, 97, 103, 104–5
Waldheim, Kurt, 39
wealth redistribution, in Brazil, under Vargas, 93
Weyland, Kurt, 7, 29
Willys-Overland do Brasil (WOB), 102, 103, 104, 104 n. 4
Wolfe, Joel, 16
women activists. *See* activists
women followers. *See* followers
women politicians. *See* politicians
Women's Committee (Venezuela), 206
Women's Development Bank. *See* Banmujer
Women's Labor and Welfare Division (Argentina), 127
women's leagues
on Mexican motorized corn mills, 34–38
mobilization by: in Ecuador, 49, 58–59, 62; in Mexico, 37–38, 44; in Nicaragua, 69–70
women's liberation. *See* feminist(s)
Women's Liberation Movement (Argentina), 132
women's movements. *See also* feminist(s)
Nicaraguan: new *vs.* old Liberal, 82–83, 87; rise of autonomous, 168, 175
Venezuelan, mass *vs.* independent, 204–5
women's rights. *See also* citizenship rights; suffrage
compatibility with populism, 14, 225
expansion of, 225; in classical populism, 4; leaders' selective advancement of, xi; in neopopulism, xi
as marker of modernity, 33, 43
women voters. *See* voter(s)
women workers. *See* working women
Workers' Party (PT, Brazil), 116, 117, 121
working class
Argentine, in Peronism, 122
Brazilian: Kubitschek's policies on, 101–6; Vargas's policies on, 92, 93–100
Nicaraguan, Somocista women in, 70–71
working women
Argentine: Agrupación Evita on, 130; Peronism on, 128–29
Brazilian: in auto industry, 102–3; Kubitschek's approach to, 92–93, 104; in labor strikes, 101; Vargas's approach to, 92–93, 97–98, 106

working women (*continued*)
  Nicaraguan, 70–72, 70 n. 5
  in social services, 3–4
World Bank, 208
World Conference on Women (1985), 208
World Conference on Women (1995), 145–46, 148, 208
Worsley, Peter, 63
Wuytack, Francisco, 207

Yánez Cossio, Consuelo, 55–56
Yánez de Carrillo, Zoila, 58
young people, in Peronism, 123

Zamora, Ezequiel, 185, 187
Zeledón, Maritza, 71
Zionism, 26
Žižek, Slavoj, 29
Zuno de Echeverría, María Esther, 30 n. 6, 43

CPSIA information can be obtained at www.ICGtesting.com
Printed in the USA
BVOW05s1438220714

360014BV00003B/181/P